CUBA
and the
UNITED
STATES

CUBA
and the
UNITED
STATES

A Chronological History

Jane Franklin

OCEAN PRESS

Melbourne • New York

For Bruce Franklin

Sections of this book were previously published as *The Cuban Revolution and the United States: A Chronological History* by Ocean Press, 1992. The publisher acknowledges the support given by the Center for Cuban Studies, New York, and its director, Sandra Levinson.

Cover design by David Spratt

ISBN 1-875284-92-3

First printed 1997

Printed in Australia

Published by Ocean Press
GPO Box 3279, Melbourne, Victoria 3001, Australia
PO Box 020692, Brooklyn, NY 11202, USA
E-mail: ocean_press@msn.com

FOR A LIST OF DISTRIBUTORS OF OCEAN PRESS TITLES
See inside back cover

Contents

About the author
Acknowledgments
Author's note on method and sources

— • —

Jane Franklin

Jane Franklin has been a contributing editor to *CUBA Update*, the journal of the Center for Cuban Studies, since 1979 and co-editor from 1984 to 1990. She is the author of *Cuban Foreign Relations: A Chronology 1959-1982* (Center for Cuban Studies: New York, 1984) and co-author of *Vietnam and America: A Documented History* (Grove Press: New York, 1985; revised and expanded edition 1995). Her chronology of the history of Panama was excerpted in *The U.S. Invasion of Panama* (South End Press: Boston, 1991). She has published numerous articles, poems, and film reviews and has lectured extensively about Cuba, Vietnam, Nicaragua, El Salvador and Panama. She is a frequent commentator about Cuba on radio and television.

Acknowledgments

I am grateful to Sandra Levinson, executive director of the Center for Cuban Studies, for initiating the idea of this book. Jerry Nickel, the Center's librarian, has been an extraordinary resource. Irving Kessler has provided reams of information along with his astute observations and encouraging friendship. I am indebted to Frank Scofi for constantly sending me materials from varied sources and for being a special friend. Bob Guild and Michael Krinsky have been generous in providing information about travel regulations and legal cases.

Members of the U.S. State Department, Congress, and the Cuban Mission to the United Nations have furnished a variety of materials and specific information.

Karen Franklin and Robert Franklin read most of the manuscript and made numerous perceptive suggestions. Gretchen Franklin furnished information about several legal cases. As this book has developed, they have developed families who are intertwined with everything I do.

My deepest appreciation is for my life companion, Bruce Franklin. He read the manuscript, of course, and offered his inimitably perceptive ideas. But, more than that, he provides constant care and understanding as part of my daily life.

∞

Author's note on method and sources

This book presents the Cuban revolution in its relations with the United States. The first section, on the background that led to revolution, traces relations from the time when both countries were colonies of European powers. Then comes the detailed, year-by-year chronology beginning on January 1, 1959. The connections between these two nations are placed in the context of global events and politics.

Designed to be used in many ways, this book may be read in whole or in part as narrative history or consulted as a reference guide to a wide range of topics. I have employed a chronological method to establish historical context, to organize a maximum amount of information and data, and to convey the inter-connectedness of lesser-known occurrences with major developments. Widely discussed episodes such as the Bay of Pigs invasion or the Missile Crisis of 1962 are too often seen in isolation rather than as part of a continuum of events, most of which are less dramatic and more obscure.

The index, an integral part of the book, may be used to reveal historical context. For example, if a reader wants to find out about the exodus from Mariel in 1980, the index will of course list direct references but it can do much more, for Mariel is just one episode in a long complex story indexed under "migration."

The index may also be used to trace the course of various people and issues — e.g., the U.S. trade embargo, the travel ban, national-ization and compensation, Félix Rodríguez, Jorge Mas Canosa and the Cuban American National Foundation, elections, hijackings, human rights, Radio and TV Martí. In many cases, additional cross references of related items are indicated in the text by dates within parentheses.

The principal sources are: official publications of the govern-ments of Cuba and the United States, including once-secret documents now declassified; contemporaneous journalistic accounts, especially in the *New York Times* and *Granma* (the official newspaper of the Cuban Communist Party), as well as the *Wall Street Journal, Washington Post, Los Angeles Times, San Francisco Chronicle, Miami Herald,* and *Star-Ledger* (Newark, New Jersey); Congressional hearings, most notably investigations of the assassination of President Kennedy and the CIA's covert activities. A broad spectrum of secondary sources has also been consulted. When relying on secondary sources, I have generally indicated this, usually by identifying the source. Whenever an item involves allegations or disputed facts, I have tried to so indicate. Except for matter-of-fact entries, and especially for those regarding complex or controversial issues and events, I have cross-checked multiple sources for accuracy. Two U.S. publications about Cuba, *CUBA Update* and, in recent years, *CubaINFO,* along with the legislative updates of the Cuba Information Project, have been especially useful.

Cuba's relations with countries other than the United States have of course had a profound influence on U.S.-Cuban relations. To maintain focus and to stay within a reasonable length, I have tried to include only the most telling events. The establishment or severance of diplomatic relations with certain countries, especially in the Western Hemisphere, is reported for the purpose of showing the kind of relations Cuba has maintained or established even when these relations were opposed by the United States. A fraction of the numerous state visits are included for the same reason. Some events are described solely to convey historical context. A few specifically domestic events in Cuba are described to show the direction of the revolutionary government or special developments that have affected U.S.-Cuban relations.

Since the Soviet Union disbanded, the U.S. Congress has intensified efforts to codify not only U.S. foreign policy toward Cuba but also Cuban domestic policy. Because a chronology of Congressional actions regarding Cuba would constitute a book longer than this one, I have limited those entries. For instance, I have tried not to include non-binding resolutions because they do not have the force of law; yet some are important because they show Congressional intent.

Background to revolution

1492-1958

1492   On his first voyage to the "New World," Christopher Columbus arrives in Cuba October 27 and claims the island for Spain.

1511   Diego Velázquez, appointed governor of Cuba by Spain, begins systematic subjugation of the island's indigenous peoples. In 1512, his invaders capture and kill Hatuey, a native leader who had come to Cuba to try to defend it against the Spanish after being driven from the island of Hispaniola. Within six years, Velázquez organizes the island into seven municipal departments. He grants *encomiendas*, whereby a Spanish colonist is allowed to force a large number of native people to work and to pay tribute in exchange for Christianization. Blacks are imported from Africa as slaves.

1533   The first recorded Black slave revolt in Cuba takes place at Jobabo mines. The slaves' heads are cut off and displayed, soon a common practice. Slave rebellions, however, continue with frequency.

1570s   By this time, the peoples who inhabited Cuba before the arrival of the Spanish — primarily Ciboney, Guanahuatabey and Taíno Arawak — have almost entirely disappeared. Some have emigrated. Most have either been killed outright or by the conditions of conquest, including malnutrition, diseases and suicide. The African slave trade increases as the Spanish colonists profit from cattle, timber, tobacco and especially sugar, a labor intensive industry introduced into the West Indies by Columbus in 1493.

1762-1763 During the Seven Years' War, the British occupy Havana for eleven months, increasing the slave trade and mercantilism. Breaking the Spanish economic monopoly, the British expand Cuban commerce to their colonies north of the island. Although Spain attempts to halt commercial ties between the British colonies and Cuba, the trade continues sporadically, becoming increasingly important to both parties.

1775-1783 Thirteen British colonies rebel, declare independence and establish the United States of America. This revolution with its promising Declaration of Independence encourages independence movements in colonies around the world.

1791-1804 François Dominique Toussaint L'Ouverture organizes a slave revolt in Hispaniola, forms a guerrilla group and gains control over the entire island. Though Toussaint dies in prison in 1803, this Black-led rebellion leads to independence from France and inspires many other movements against slavery and for independence. Some of the French landowners flee to Cuba, creating more plantations with subsequent increased demand for slaves. To meet this demand, Spain allows foreign vessels to transport slaves. U.S. shipowners play a major part in this lucrative business.

U.S. POLICY TAKES SHAPE

1801-1808 In his first presidential inaugural address March 4, 1801, Thomas Jefferson declares that the people of the United States are blessed by "possessing a chosen country, with room enough for our descendants to the thousandth and thousandth generation." Two years later the Jefferson Administration approximately doubles the size of the original states with the Louisiana Purchase from France. In 1808, Jefferson sends General James Wilkinson to Cuba to find out if the Spanish would consider ceding Cuba to the United States. Spain is not interested.

1809 Joaquín Infante organizes a plan for overthrowing the Spanish government in Cuba. Over the next decades the Spanish authorities use prison, exile, torture and death to quell insurrections.

1809-1810 Former President Jefferson writes to his successor, James Madison, in 1809, "I candidly confess that I have ever looked upon Cuba as the most interesting addition that can be made to our system of States." With Cuba and Canada, he says, "we should have such an empire for liberty as she has never surveyed since the creation." But Madison settles on a policy of leaving Cuba to the domination of Spain, a relatively weak country, while guarding against its seizure by any mightier power. In 1810, Madison instructs his minister to Great Britain to tell the British that the United States will not sit idly by if Britain were to try to gain possession of Cuba.

1818 Spain allows Cuban ports to open for international trade. Within two years, over half of Cuba's trade is with the United States.

1821-1823 With Simón Bolívar emerging as the Great Liberator in the battles for independence raging in Latin America, Cubans organize an underground. For example, in 1821 José Francisco Lemus and others form the *Soles y Rayos* [Suns and Rays] *de Bolívar* aimed at establishing an independent republic. Within two years, the Spanish arrest its leaders.

April 28, 1823 Having acquired East and West Florida from Spain a few years earlier, the United States has expanded to within 90 miles of Cuba. In a letter to Minister to Spain Hugh Nelson, Secretary of State John Quincy Adams describes the likelihood of U.S. "annexation of Cuba" within half a century despite obstacles: "But there are laws of political as well as of physical gravitation; and if an apple severed by the tempest from its native tree cannot choose but fall to the ground, Cuba, forcibly disjoined from its own unnatural connection with Spain, and incapable of self support, can gravitate only towards the North American Union, which by the same law of nature cannot cast her off from its bosom." Cubans calls this policy *la fruta madura* (ripe fruit); Washington would wait until the fruit is considered ripe for the picking.

December 2, 1823 In what becomes known as the Monroe Doctrine, President James Monroe stakes out the Western Hemisphere as a U.S. sphere of influence by warning Europe not to interfere in the affairs of any of the American nations that have recently become independent while stating concomitantly that the United States will not interfere in European affairs.

December 9, 1824 At the battle of Ayacucho in Peru, Simón Bolívar leads the defeat of the last Spanish forces on the mainland. Spain increases repression in its remaining possessions, Cuba and Puerto Rico. Some Cuban landowners, fearful that independence would mean the end of slavery as in Haiti, have become annexationists in alliance with slaveowners in the United States who want Cuba as a slave state. During the next decades, especially in the 1840s and 1850s, there are frequent "filibuster" or pirate expeditions from the United States aimed at seizing the island.

1830s-1870s Cuba's sugar industry becomes the most mechanized in the world. By 1850, sugar provides 83 percent of exports, with 40 percent of that going to the United States, part of the Triangular Trade: sugar to the United States, rum to Africa, slaves to Cuba.

1841 Cuba's slave population has increased from about 39,000 in 1774 to about 436,000, over 50 percent of the population. In the 19th century, more than 600,000 Africans are brought to the island as slaves. When Cubans in the 20th century say they are part of Africa, they are acknowledging the high percentage of Cubans descended from Africans.

November 5, 1843 A slave called Black Carlota leads a rebellion in which she loses her life. In her honor, on November 5, 1975, Cuba names its campaign in Angola "Operation Carlota."

1844 Spain discovers a major conspiracy for a slave uprising in Matanzas province and uses this to arrest more than 4,000 people, free Blacks as well as slaves. It is known as *La Escalera* [ladder] because suspects are tied to ladders and whipped to try to make them confess; some 300 are killed by this torture.

1847 As the Mexican War moves closer toward victory for the United States, proponents of Manifest Destiny step up efforts to annex Cuba. Some U.S. citizens conspire with a new secret organization of pro-annexation Cubans, the *Club de La Havana*.

1848 In May, Democrats in the United States nominate Senator Lewis Cass, who has publicly advocated the purchase of Cuba, for president. Later in the month, ignoring the counsel of northern Democrats opposed to extending slavery, Democratic President James Polk secretly decides to try to buy Cuba, in accordance with official policy of annexation only with the consent of Spain. In July, Secretary of State James Buchanan instructs U.S. Minister to Cuba Romulus Saunders to negotiate the deal, but negotiations fall apart amidst conspiracy and betrayal. General Zachary Taylor, a Whig, wins the November election.

1854 President Franklin Pierce, who won the 1852 election by a landslide as pro-expansionist and anti-abolitionist, signs in May the Kansas-Nebraska Act that repeals the Missouri Compromise of 1820, rendering Congress powerless to prevent slavery in the territories and newly admitted states. In October, Pierce's ministers to Spain (Pierre Soulé), France (J.Y. Mason) and England (James Buchanan) draw up the Ostend Manifesto recommending that the United States purchase Cuba. This Manifesto warns against permitting "Cuba to be Africanized and become a second St. Domingo [referring to the Black republic created by the slave insurrection led by Toussaint], with all its attendant horrors to the white race." If Spain refuses to sell, the ministers claim that "we shall be justified in wresting it from Spain... upon the very same principle that would justify an individual in tearing down the burning house of his neighbor if there were no other means of preventing the flames from destroying his own home." Although the Ostend Manifesto is rejected, it helps James Buchanan get the Democratic presidential nomination.

1857-1861 President James Buchanan tries repeatedly to interest Congress in buying Cuba, but Congress is too bitterly divided over slavery.

1861-1865 The Civil War decisively ends efforts to annex Cuba for slavery. In 1865, when the Civil War ends, the African slave trade ends in Cuba, but slavery itself continues.

THE FIRST WAR OF INDEPENDENCE

October 10, 1868 The Ten Years' War or Cuba's First War of Independence begins when plantation owner Carlos Manuel de Céspedes, accompanied by 37 other planters, proclaims the independence of Cuba in the *Grito de Yara* issued from his plantation. Céspedes frees and arms his slaves. Two days later the brothers Antonio and José Maceo — free blacks — join the rebel ranks. Some Dominican exiles, including Máximo Gómez, help to train the rebels, using their experience from fighting against Spain on nearby Hispaniola. Ignacio Agramonte leads the revolt in Camagüey until he is killed in battle in 1873.

January 1869 At age sixteen, José Martí founds a newspaper, *Patria Libre*, in which he writes in support of independence. Sentenced in 1870 to six years in prison on a minor charge, he is sent to Spain in 1871 and released on the condition that he not return to Cuba.

April 10, 1869 A Constituent Assembly in Guáimaro prepares the first Constitution of the Republic of Cuba and elects Carlos Manuel de Céspedes as the first president.

September 26, 1872 Colombian Foreign Minister Don Gil Colunje proposes a joint action to all Latin American republics and the United States to achieve Cuban independence and abolition of slavery. The plan, which would be carried out under the leadership of the United States, would offer to reimburse Spain for the loss of the colony with money raised from all the republics. The Latin American governments agree, but U.S. President Ulysses S. Grant rejects the idea.

March 22, 1873 Carlos Manuel de Céspedes, president of the Republic of Cuba in rebellion against Spain, asks the United States to support Colombia's plan. The U.S. government does nothing and continues to refuse cooperation when the plan is revitalized the following year.

November 1875 To quell continuing domestic demand for recognition of belligerency in Cuba, U.S. Secretary of State Hamilton Fish proposes that European countries pressure Spain to end the fighting in Cuba. He mentions neither independence nor abolition.

February 8, 1878 The majority of the House of Representatives, the official body of the Republic of Cuba in Arms, accepts a peace agreement offered by Spanish General Arsenio Martínez Campos.

February 10, 1878 The Zanjón Treaty is signed with Spain. General Antonio Maceo and many other leaders oppose the agreement because it provides neither independence nor total abolition of slavery. Maceo asks for a meeting with General Martínez.

March 15, 1878 Generals Maceo and Martínez meet at Mangos de Baraguá. Maceo presents what comes to be known as the Protest of Baraguá, explaining opposition to the Zanjón Treaty.

March 23, 1878 When the eight-day truce between Maceo and Martínez ends, fighting resumes.

May 1878 The remaining Cuban forces surrender and the Ten Years' War officially ends.

December 1878 José Martí returns to Cuba but is expelled to Spain again in 1879.

1879-1880 *La Guerra Chiquita* or the Little War, led by Major General Calixto García, attempts to carry forward the battle for independence.

1880s The U.S. government prepares for overseas expansion, wiping out Native American resistance in the West and building an offensive Navy. Investment by the United States in Cuba increases rapidly. Of Cuban exports, 83 percent go to the United States, only 6 percent to Spain.

1881-1895 José Martí, having moved to New York City, reports on life in the United States for Latin American newspapers and analyzes the methods of U.S. imperialism.

1886 Economic conditions have made it more profitable for most slaveowners to free their slaves and hire them for work by the day, avoiding the expense of year-round support. On October 7, with only about 26,000 slaves remaining, slavery is abolished in Cuba by royal decree.

1892 After two years of organizing Cubans both inside and outside the island, José Martí founds the Cuban Revolutionary Party.

January 31, 1895 José Martí leaves New York to join Máximo Gómez in Santo Domingo.

February 24, 1895 Fighting breaks out in Cuba. With the leadership of the Cuban Revolutionary Party, the Second War of Cuban Independence begins.

March 31, 1895 Antonio and José Maceo land in eastern Cuba from Costa Rica.

April 11, 1895 José Martí and Máximo Gómez land in eastern Cuba from Santo Domingo.

May 18, 1895 In his last letter, José Martí writes that it is his duty "to prevent, by the independence of Cuba, the United States from spreading over the West Indies and falling, with that added weight, upon other lands of our America. All I have done up to now, and shall do hereafter, is to that end.... I have lived inside the monster and know its insides."

May 19, 1895 José Martí is killed in battle at Dos Ríos in eastern Cuba.

July 5, 1896 José Maceo is killed in battle at Loma del Gato.

December 7, 1896 Antonio Maceo is killed in the battle of Punta Brava in western Cuba.

November 1897 Spain's queen regent offers autonomy to Cuba, but both the rebels and Cuban loyalists reject the offer. Meanwhile, in Washington, Navy Assistant Secretary Theodore Roosevelt is urging President William McKinley to intervene.

January 1898 The United States uses rumors of danger to U.S. citizens in Cuba as reason for dispatching the *USS Maine* to Havana.

February 15, 1898 The battleship *Maine* blows up in Havana's harbor, killing 260 officers and crew. The United States blames Spain. "Remember the *Maine*" becomes a battle cry as the U.S. "yellow press," spearheaded by William Randolph Hearst's chain, shapes public opinion.

April 10, 1898 Spain, having ordered a unilateral suspension of hostilities, sends a message to Washington offering a peaceful way out: the United States would indicate terms of an armistice; Cuba would be granted autonomy; the matter of the *Maine* would be submitted to arbitration.

U.S. INTERVENTION

April 11, 1898 President McKinley sends a message to Congress asking for authority to intervene militarily in Cuba. The message says, "The only hope of relief and repose from a condition which can no longer be endured is the enforced pacification of Cuba."

April 20, 1898 The U.S. Congress declares that Cuba has the right to be free and independent and authorizes the President to use military force to oust Spain. The Teller Amendment adds that the United States has no "intention to exercise sovereignty, jurisdiction, or control over said Island except for the pacification thereof." McKinley signs this declaration and sends it to Spain with the message that he will carry it out unless Spain responds satisfactorily by April 23.

April 22, 1898 President McKinley declares a blockade of the northern coast of Cuba and its port at Santiago, an act of war according to international law.

April 24, 1898 Responding to the U.S. act of war, Spain declares war.

April 25, 1898 The U.S. Congress formally declares war, saying that the state of war between the United States and Spain began April 21. In the United States, this is known as the Spanish-American War. In Cuba, it is known as the U.S. intervention in Cuba's War of Independence.

August 12, 1898 Spain and the United States sign a bilateral armistice. Cuba is not represented at the negotiations.

December 10, 1898 Spain and the United States sign the Treaty of Paris. The United States emerges with control of four new territories: Cuba, Puerto Rico, the Philippines and Guam. Although the treaty officially grants Cuba independence, the U.S. flag — not the Cuban flag — is raised over Havana. The United States installs a military government to pacify Cuba.

January 1, 1899 Spain formally surrenders its jurisdiction in Cuba to U.S. military forces commanded by General John R. Brooke, the first U.S. military governor.

December 23, 1899 General Leonard Wood, veteran of U.S. campaigns against Native Americans, replaces Brooke as military governor.

1900 General Wood calls an election for a Cuban constitutional convention, which meets in November and draws up a Constitution modeled upon the U.S. Constitution without specifying the nature of future relations with the United States.

1901 To codify control of Cuba, the U.S. Congress on March 2 adds the Platt Amendment to an Army Appropriations bill. The amendment provides that Cuba has only a limited right to conduct its own foreign policy and debt policy; the United States may intervene militarily at any time; the Isle of Pines shall be omitted from the boundaries of Cuba until the title to it is adjusted by future treaty; Cuba will sell or lease to the United States "lands necessary for coaling or naval stations at certain specified points to be agreed upon." Since the U.S. government makes it clear that its military occupation will not end until this amendment becomes part of Cuban law, Cuba incorporates the Platt Amendment into its 1901 Constitution.

1901 General Wood supervises what the United States calls a democratic election for national offices, but the franchise excludes AfroCubans, women and those with less than $250. Tomás Estrada Palma is elected president.

May 20, 1902   The U.S. military occupation ends as Estrada becomes president.

March 1903   Cuba and the United States ratify a treaty on commercial reciprocity, ensuring U.S. control of Cuban markets.

May 22, 1903   Cuba and the United States sign the "Permanent Treaty" which incorporates the Platt Amendment.

July 2, 1903   To follow up the Platt Amendment provision for selling or leasing coaling and naval bases to the United States, Cuba signs a treaty with the United States agreeing to lease Bahía Honda and Guantánamo. This prepares the way for construction of a U.S. naval base at Guantánamo, a deep-water port in eastern Cuba. The price of the lease for Guantánamo is set at $2,000 a year in gold. The same year, the administration of President Theodore Roosevelt engineers the separation of Panama from Colombia and arranges to build the Panama Canal.

July 2, 1903   On the same day that the treaty is signed about coaling and naval bases, the United States signs a treaty with Cuba agreeing to relinquish all claim to the Isle of Pines, but the U.S. Senate refuses to ratify within the stipulated seven months.

March 2, 1904   Cuba and the United States sign a new treaty about the Isle of Pines, this time with no deadline for ratification.

1904-1905   President Roosevelt formulates his corollary to the Monroe Doctrine: since the United States does not allow European nations to intervene in Latin America, then the United States has responsibility for preserving order and protecting life and property in those countries.

August 1906   President Estrada requests U.S. intervention to put down an insurrection. President Roosevelt sends Secretary of War William Howard Taft as mediator. Estrada objects to Taft's proposals and resigns in September. The United States exercises its Platt Amendment authorization to intervene and sends in U.S. Marines for a second military occupation.

September 29, 1906   The U.S. Secretary of War heads a provisional government of Cuba.

October 13, 1906 U.S. citizen Charles Magoon replaces Secretary of War Taft as head of the provisional government of Cuba. The United States openly rules "independent" Cuba for more than two years.

January 28, 1909 U.S. Military Governor Magoon turns the Cuban government over to President José Miguel Gómez, an Army general elected in November 1908.

1912 The *Agrupación Independiente de Color* [Independent Colored Party], led by Evaristo Estenoz who fought in the War of Independence, rebels against the Gómez government, which crushes the uprising with the slaughter of some 3,000 rebels. During the uprising, U.S. Marines land and two U.S. battleships anchor in Havana harbor but the administration of President William Howard Taft maintains this does not constitute intervention.

February-March 1917 President Woodrow Wilson lands U.S. Marines to shore up the government of President Mario García Menocal against an uprising led by Liberal Party forces because of what they consider the fraudulent victory of the Conservative Party in the 1916 election.

April 7, 1917 President Mario García Menocal enters World War I the day after the United States declares war and soon opens up the island as a training base for U.S. Marines, some of whom remain until 1922.

1919-1933 During this Age of Prohibition in the United States, Cuba becomes the playground of the Caribbean. In 1920, sugar prices plunge and U.S. investors buy up property at bargain rates.

1921 Woodrow Wilson, in the last weeks of his presidency, sends General Enoch Crowder to Cuba in January to supervise by-elections. Alfredo Zayas is inaugurated as president in May. Crowder stays on as the personal representative of the new U.S. president, Warren Harding, to President Zayas until 1922. In this role, Crowder uses the financial crisis in Cuba to engineer changes in Cuban domestic affairs favorable to U.S. business interests. Crowder presages the methods of the International Monetary Fund, exerting control in exchange for loans.

January 1923 J.P. Morgan and Company agrees to loan $50 million to the Zayas Administration in Cuba, cementing debt dependency. Congress in the same month takes up the matter of establishing an embassy in Havana.

February 1923 The U.S. government rewards General Crowder for his success in Cuba by naming him the first ambassador to Cuba.

June 1923   Cuba elevates its legation in Washington to the status of embassy.

1924   In response to the corruption of the Zayas government, the Veterans' and Patriots' Association leads a rebellion in April. At the request of President Zayas, President Calvin Coolidge declares an embargo on shipments of arms and munitions to Cuban buyers on May 2 while approving sales of war matériel to the Cuban government. Zayas quells the rebellion and Coolidge lifts the embargo in August.

March 13, 1925   After a delay of more than two decades, the U.S. Senate ratifies the 1904 treaty relinquishing U.S. claims to the Isle of Pines.

THE ERA OF MACHADO AND BATISTA

May 1925   General Gerardo Machado Morales, espousing nationalism but known to the U.S. business community as a friend, becomes president.

August 16, 1925   The first Communist Party of Cuba is formed. One of the founding members is Julio Antonio Mella, a leader of the student movement against the Machado dictatorship.

1928   President Machado controls the election process, gets himself reelected, and declares that this will be a six-year presidential term. Insurrections increase. Machado's police become notorious for torture and killing.

1929   At the University of Havana, the University Student Directorate is formed to oppose the Machado dictatorship. On September 30, 1930, when Machado's police kill Rafael Trejo, a leader of the Directorate, resistance increases.

1933   With Cuba in a state of revolution, President Franklin Delano Roosevelt dispatches Assistant Secretary of State Sumner Welles as Ambassador Extraordinary and Plenipotentiary. Welles is unable to salvage Machado and instead seeks an alternative.

August 12, 1933   Faced with a general strike and the defection of his own military, Machado resigns and flees the country (he ends up living in the United States). With Ambassador Welles's approval, Carlos Manuel de Céspedes becomes provisional president. The military along with militant students and revolutionary groups oppose this U.S. choice.

September 5, 1933 The "Sergeants' Revolt," supported by students and led by Sergeant Fulgencio Batista y Zaldívar, overthrows President Céspedes.

September 5-10, 1933 A junta (the *Pentarquía* — Ramón Grau San Martín, Sergio Carbó, Porfirio Franco, José Miguel Irisarri, and Guillermo Portela) runs the country. Ambassador Welles describes the rebels as having "communistic" ideas and on September 7 he asks for U.S. military intervention. President Roosevelt, despite his promotion of the Good Neighbor Policy toward Latin America, orders at least 29 warships to Cuba and to Key West, alerts the U.S. Marines and prepares bombers for use if necessary.

September 10, 1933 The rebels appoint Ramón Grau San Martín as president. The United States refuses to recognize his government and begins to pressure an ambitious Batista to desert the radicals.

January 15, 1934 Batista, now a colonel, overthrows President Grau San Martín.

January 15-18, 1934 Colonel Batista installs Carlos Hevia in a brief presidency.

January 18, 1934 Manuel Márquez Sterling y Guiral becomes president for less than a day until Colonel Batista replaces him with Colonel Carlos Mendieta Montefur. The United States recognizes the Mendieta government. Resistance persists. Batista continues to run the government as the "strongman" behind the scenes with U.S. approval.

May 29, 1934 Cuba and the United States sign the "Treaty on Relations between Cuba and the United States" abrogating the "Permanent Treaty" of 1903 and the Platt Amendment with the exception that the United States continues to occupy the naval base at Guantánamo.

December 11, 1935 Colonel Batista replaces President Mendieta, who resigns suddenly, with José A. Barnet y Vinageras as provisional president.

May 20-December 24, 1936 Miguel Mariano Gómez Arias, elected in January, is president until he is impeached after vetoing a bill that would have increased General Batista's power.

1936-1939 More than 1,000 Cuban volunteers join the internationalist brigades in Spain to defend the Republic against the fascists in the Spanish Civil War.

December 24, 1936-October 10, 1940 President Federico Laredo Brú cooperates fully with General Batista, clearing the way for Batista to be a presidential candidate in 1940.

1939 Cuban resistance to one corrupt government after another forces the convening of a constituent assembly to write a new Constitution, which takes effect in 1940.

1940 General Batista is elected and becomes president.

December 9, 1941 Cuba enters World War II, furnishing air and naval bases to the United States.

1943 General Batista legalizes the Communist Party of Cuba and establishes diplomatic relations with the Soviet Union, which is allied with the United States.

1944 General Batista's choice for president, Carlos Saladrigas Zayas, loses to Ramón Grau San Martín of the *Auténtico* party. After turning over the reins of power, Batista goes into self-imposed exile in Florida. Grau San Martín's term coincides with the end of World War II and a subsequent increase in the impact of organized crime in Cuba.

October 24, 1945 Cuba joins the United Nations on the day the UN Charter takes effect.

1947 Mafia chieftain "Lucky" Luciano arrives from Italy in January for a visit in Havana, meeting with U.S. organized crime bosses, including Meyer Lansky, who has spent considerable time in Havana and owns such profitable sites as the Hotel Nacional's casino. The Trafficante family (*see* April 1959) is allied with Luciano and Lansky. This meeting leads to the use of Havana as a key link in the chain of drug trafficking as some of Luciano's heroin travels from Europe to New York by way of Cuba and then Florida.

1947 At a special Pan American Conference near Río de Janeiro, the Truman Administration backs the Inter-American Treaty of Reciprocal Assistance (the Río Treaty), which is ratified in 1948 and requires signatory states to unite against armed attack on any American state.

1948 Carlos Prío Socarrás of the *Auténtico* party is elected president of Cuba. General Batista is elected senator from Las Villas province after running his campaign from Florida.

March 30-May 2, 1948 Meeting in Bogotá, Colombia, the Ninth International Conference of American States approves the Charter of the Organization of American States (OAS).

December 9, 1948 Cuba signs the Río Treaty.

1950 Cuba's ambassador to the United Nations provides critical support for the administration of President Harry Truman in the Security Council vote on taking action in Korea. But when President Prío offers to send troops to the war, Cubans organize a successful campaign around the slogan, "No cannon fodder for Yankee imperialists."

December 13, 1951 The OAS Charter goes into effect.

BATISTA'S DICTATORSHIP

1952 Fidel Castro, who graduated from law school in 1950, is running for Congress as a member of the Orthodox Party (*Partido del Pueblo Cubano — Ortodoxo*). General Batista runs for president but has little chance of winning. On March 10, Batista stages a coup, suspends the Constitution, cancels the elections and becomes dictator. The Truman Administration quickly recognizes his government and sends military and economic aid. Organized resistance begins.

July 16, 1952 Cuba ratifies its membership of the OAS.

July 26, 1953 Fidel Castro and other revolutionaries attack the Moncada Army Barracks in Santiago de Cuba. Despite the deaths of at least 70 participants and the imprisonment of the rest, including both Fidel and Raúl Castro, the July 26 Movement is born from this battle. *History Will Absolve Me*, Castro's defense at his secret trial on October 16, describes the society these revolutionaries would like to create and later becomes the basic program, the Moncada Program, of the Cuban revolution.

June 1954 In late June, when the CIA-supported "rebel army" aims at overthrowing the elected government of Jacobo Arbenz Guzmán in Guatemala, hundreds of young Cubans rush to the Guatemalan Embassy in Havana to enlist in the Guatemalan Army. The CIA succeeds in ousting Arbenz.

May 15, 1955 Responding to public demand, General Batista releases Fidel Castro and the other revolutionaries captured in 1953. Castro goes into exile in Mexico and begins to organize an expedition to return to Cuba to launch a revolution.

December 2, 1956   Fidel Castro, his brother Raúl Castro, Ernesto "Che" Guevara and 79 other revolutionaries aboard the cabin cruiser *Granma* land in Oriente province. Most of these guerrillas are soon killed. The survivors establish a base in the Sierra Maestra mountains, working with revolutionaries who have been organizing insurrection inside Cuba.

1957   In February, journalist Herbert Matthews, after meeting with Fidel Castro in the Sierra Maestra, introduces him to the United States in the pages of the *New York Times* with fairly sympathetic articles. Meanwhile, Arthur Gardner, the ambassador of the administration of President Dwight D. Eisenhower, suggests that the CIA assassinate Castro.

March 13, 1957   Cuban students attack the Presidential Palace for the purpose of assassinating General Batista. Other students, including José Antonio Echeverría, seize Radio Reloj, a major station in Havana, and announce Batista's death, unaware that the assassination attempt has failed. Moments later, Batista's police shoot and kill Echeverría, who was president of the Federation of University Students and a founder of the Revolutionary Directorate, an underground organization devoted to overthrowing Batista.

May 1957   In a trial of supporters of Fidel Castro in Santiago de Cuba, the judge, Manuel Urrutia Lléo, decides on acquittal, leading to judicial reprimand from Batista's government. Urrutia goes into exile in December 1957.

July 15, 1957   Earl E. T. Smith arrives in Cuba as the new U.S. ambassador.

July 30, 1957   In Santiago de Cuba, Batista's police shoot and kill Frank País, a July 26 Movement leader. Tens of thousands of people march to his funeral, sparking strikes in Cuba's three eastern provinces. U.S. Ambassador Smith offends General Batista by calling police violence excessive when he sees them beating up women at one of the demonstrations in Santiago after the funeral. Yet Smith maintains that a victory by Fidel Castro would be contrary to U.S. interests.

November 1957   General Batista has become a liability for the Eisenhower Administration, which is under considerable pressure to stop sending arms to a government that is bombing and strafing its own people in addition to torturing and killing suspected rebels and their sympathizers. The U.S. government is officially neutral, but it is still supplying arms and training to Batista's forces and maintains military missions in Cuba until 1959.

February 13, 1958 The United States indicts former Cuban President Carlos Prío Socarrás, who was overthrown by General Batista, and eight other Cubans on charges of conspiring to violate U.S. neutrality laws by financing and taking part in military expeditions to be carried out from U.S. territory against Batista. He is jailed for a brief time.

March 14, 1958 With the fall of General Batista's regime only a matter of time, the Eisenhower Administration announces an arms embargo. Ambassador Smith complains about this to the State Department.

June 16, 1958 In a decision that later becomes important in U.S.-Cuban relations, the U.S. Supreme Court for the first time declares that U.S. citizens have a constitutional right to travel abroad. The opinion in *Rockwell Kent and Walter Briehl* v. *John Foster Dulles* holds that "the right to travel is a part of the 'liberty' of which the citizen cannot be deprived without due process of law under the Fifth Amendment."

November 1958 As the revolutionaries move closer to victory, U.S. Ambassador Smith hopes that a free election in Cuba will produce an alternative to both Batista and Castro: but Batista's candidate for president, Andrés Rivero Agüero, wins an election that even Smith concedes is rigged.

December 9, 1958 A secret emissary from the Eisenhower Administration, William D. Pawley, meets with General Batista to try to persuade him to accept exile at Daytona Beach, Florida, leaving the government in charge of a U.S.-approved junta. Batista refuses.

December 27, 1958 A Cuban Air Force pilot flies a B-26 bomber to Miami and requests asylum because, in his words, "I don't like to bomb cities and kill innocent women and children."

Revolution

1959

January 1 Troops under the command of Che Guevara take Santa Clara, and General Fulgencio Batista flees to the Dominican Republic in the early morning hours. Revolutionary forces assume control in Havana. Fidel Castro and his troops enter Santiago de Cuba and seize the Moncada Army Barracks without firing a shot as 5,000 soldiers surrender to the July 26 Movement. Castro calls a general strike to prevent a counterrevolutionary coup. Cubans whose sympathies are with Batista start leaving Cuba while many Cubans in exile begin returning. In Washington, supporters of the revolution take over the Cuban Embassy.

January 2 The revolutionaries form a new government with Manuel Urrutia as president and José Miró Cardona as prime minister.

January 7 The United States recognizes the new Cuban government, already recognized by several countries in the Western Hemisphere. Yet, as officially acknowledged many years later, the CIA begins a campaign early in 1959 aimed at overthrowing the government.

January 8 After marching across the country from Oriente province, Fidel Castro and the main body of the revolutionary army enter Havana.

January 10 Earl E. T. Smith resigns as U.S. ambassador to Cuba. Philip W. Bonsal will replace him.

January 16 Cuba asks the United States to return "war criminals" of the Batista regime for trial along with the money taken from the treasury by General Batista and his followers.

January 21 Speaking to some 800,000 people, the largest assembly ever gathered in Cuba, Fidel Castro says that Cubans want not only political but economic freedom. He condemns U.S. interference in Cuba's internal affairs.

January 23 Fidel Castro heads a Cuban delegation on a state visit to Venezuela, his first of several trips to other countries in the Western Hemisphere during the first year of the revolution.

February 2 A U.S. citizen, Allen Mayer, is arrested after flying a small plane into Cuba with the aim of assassinating Fidel Castro.

February 7 The Fundamental Law of the Republic modifies and reinstates the 1940 Constitution, suspended by General Batista's coup in 1952.

February 7 Cuba declares Argentine-born physician, Che Guevara, a Cuban citizen in gratitude for his part in the revolution and as a legal step to allow him to hold office.

February 10 Cuba asks the Dominican Republic to "provisionally arrest" General Batista, pending a formal extradition request.

February 11 The *New York Times* reports that the Cuban Ministry of State has announced that the U.S. Army, Navy and Air Force military missions, which trained General Batista's armed forces, will be withdrawn from Cuba immediately.

February 13 Fidel Castro becomes prime minister after José Miró Cardona resigns because he decided that he wielded no real power as prime minister. Miró goes into exile in June 1960.

March 3 The Cuban government takes over control and management of the Cuban Telephone Company, an affiliate of the International Telephone and Telegraph Corporation (ITT). Rates are reduced and the government cancels a 1957 agreement by General Batista which extended the company's franchise and permitted a rate increase.

March 5 Former President Ramón Grau San Martín demands that the U.S. government give up its naval base at Guantánamo. This occupation of Cuban territory continues as a source of tension between the two countries. Cuba adopts a policy of not cashing the yearly checks for lease of the territory. The original annual rent of 2,000 dollars in gold later becomes 4,085 dollars (not in gold).

March 7 At a meeting with telephone workers, Prime Minister Castro denounces as counterrevolutionaries those who are arming themselves and conspiring in the United States against the Cuban revolution.

March 10-24 Examples of rapid reforms and innovations taking place in Cuba include reducing prices for medicines, enacting an Urban Reform Law that lowers rents by 30 to 50 percent, and creating the Cuban Film Institute (ICAIC).

March 26 Cuban police discover a plan, reportedly masterminded by Rolando Masferrer and Ernesto de la Fe, to assassinate Prime Minister Castro. De la Fe was Batista's Information Minister. Masferrer became a Senator for the *Auténtico* party during the Prío presidency and then supported General Batista after the 1952 coup, retaining his Senate post as well as his private army, "los tigres" [the tigers], with which he tried to defeat Fidel Castro's forces in the mountains of Oriente province in 1958. He fled Cuba for Florida by yacht on December 31, 1958.

April During the seizure of gambling casinos by the new government in Havana, crime boss Santo Trafficante Jr. is jailed until his deportation in July. (*See* September 1960)

April 15-26 At the invitation of the Association of Newspaper Editors, Prime Minister Castro makes an unofficial visit to the United States. Greeted wherever he goes by enthusiastic crowds, Castro tells the Senate Foreign Relations Committee that good relations can exist only on the basis of full equality. At a luncheon of newspaper editors broadcast on radio and television, he explains with examples the disadvantages to Cuba of current U.S. regulations that affect the U.S.-Cuban sugar trade. He meets with Vice-President Richard Nixon, who asks for his opinion of dictatorship and democracy. Castro responds, "Dictatorships are a shameful blot on America, and democracy is more than just a word," adding that there is no democracy while there is hunger, unemployment and injustice. He is a guest on "Meet the Press" and speaks at Columbia, Harvard and Princeton. He tells UN correspondents that the Cuban revolution is "not for export," that revolutions occur because of internal conditions, but that Cuba's example may prove helpful. He says Cuba will take an independent position at the United Nations. At a mass rally in his honor at Central Park in New York, he speaks for two hours. Before heading for Latin America, Castro visits Montreal, Canada, and Houston.

April 21 Cuba opens previously private beaches to the public.

May 2 Prime Minister Castro attends a meeting of the Committee of 21, the economic unit of the OAS, in Buenos Aires, Argentina. He proposes that the United States give $30 billion in public capital to Latin America over the next 10 years. After this meeting, Castro travels to Uruguay and Brazil.

May 2 Cuba signs a Point Four agreement with the United States for technical cooperation in the development of agrarian reform.

May 17 The Cuban government enacts the first Agrarian Reform Law, putting a limit on land holdings and expropriating the remainder with compensation offered in 20-year fixed-term government bonds paying an annual interest rate of 4.5 percent. (U.S. investment-grade corporate bonds paid an average of 3.8 percent in 1958.) The basis for compensation is the value of the land as assessed for taxes. Foreigners own 75 percent of Cuba's arable land. Five U.S. sugar companies own or control more than two million acres. The new law limits land ownership to 1,000 acres with the exception of a limit of 3,333 acres for land used for livestock, sugar, or rice production. The expropriated land along with land already owned by the state will be transferred to cooperatives or distributed free of charge in "Vital Minimum" (VM) tracts. Any agricultural worker with less than a VM tract (66 acres of unirrigated fertile land for a family of five) may apply for the VM acreage. (*See* June 11)

June Che Guevara undertakes a three-month trip to Africa, Asia and Europe to organize new economic and cultural agreements for Cuba.

June 3 The Agrarian Reform Law goes into effect.

June 5 Senator George Smathers (D-Florida) proposes an amendment to reduce the Cuban sugar quota.

June 11 The U.S. government protests the Agrarian Reform Law, in particular the terms of compensation. U.S. landowners object to Cuba's basis for compensation because it is based on tax assessment rates, which have not been adjusted to current land value for 30 or 40 years (thus allowing the owners to pay very low taxes). During the following years, Cuba negotiates compensation to property owners and to the governments of Britain, Canada, France, Italy, Mexico, Spain and Sweden, but the issue of U.S. compensation goes unresolved.

June 26 Cuba breaks diplomatic relations with the Dominican Republic for plotting to overthrow the Cuban government.

July 16 In a confrontation between Prime Minister Castro and President Urrutia, Castro resigns as prime minister and makes a speech on the following day in which he says Urrutia is impeding the progress of the revolution. Urrutia immediately resigns. The Council of Ministers appoints Osvaldo Dorticós Torrado as president. Castro resumes the office of prime minister on July 26. Urrutia obtains asylum in the Venezuelan Embassy and goes into exile.

August 10 Dominican Republic radio broadcasts an appeal to Cubans to revolt by setting fires and killing, and Cuba confirms that a counterrevolutionary plot, directed by Dominican dictator Rafael Trujillo and General Batista, has been exposed.

August 12 The OAS Foreign Ministers Conference convenes in Santiago de Chile to consider "tensions in the Caribbean" and "effective exercise of representative democracy." Cuba charges that this is an obvious attempt, instigated by the United States, to maneuver the OAS against the Cuban government. Cuba and Venezuela sponsor a resolution, approved by the conference, that all sessions be open to reporters. Usually there are closed working sessions.

August 13 A Dominican C-47, piloted by the pilot who flew General Batista out of the country to the Dominican Republic, lands in Trinidad in central Cuba. Cuban militia are waiting and capture the ten occupants and seize the arms and ammunition they are bringing into Cuba, ending the Dominican conspiracy.

August 20 The Cuban government reduces by 30 percent the rates for electricity paid to the Cuban Electric Company, which is owned by a U.S. corporation, the American Foreign Power Company.

October Showing its desire to keep tourism alive, Havana hosts the American Society of Travel Agents.

October 11-21 Three raids by planes flying from the United States bomb sugar mills in Pinar del Río and Camagüey provinces. Cuba is making efforts to purchase planes for its defense.

October 16 The United States tells Britain that it opposes a British plan to sell jet fighters to Cuba. Britain later cancels the sale, saying U.S. pressure has nothing to do with the decision.

October 17 Prime Minister Castro appoints his brother Raúl Castro Minister of the Armed Forces.

October 21 A plane raid on Havana results in two people killed in the streets and 45 wounded. Pedro Luis Díaz Lanz, former Cuban Air Force chief who fled to Miami, later admits to the U.S. Federal Bureau of Investigation (FBI) that he flew a plane over Havana on that date but claims that it dropped only leaflets. Cuba requests his extradition but a U.S. federal judge refuses to issue an arrest warrant. In July, Díaz Lanz testified to the Senate Internal Security Subcommittee that Communists occupy high places in the Cuban government. Díaz Lanz heads the *Cruzada Cubana Constitucional* in which Félix Rodríguez and Frank Sturgis are members.

October 22 In Las Villas province, an airplane strafes a train full of passengers. Responding to such attacks, Cubans form popular militia.

November 13 In a note to the U.S. government, the Cuban government says Cuba cannot be frightened, that Cuba "knows where it comes from, what it wants and where it is going." Moreover, continues the note, since the United States refuses to sell arms to Cuba and tries to prevent any such sales, Cuba will acquire planes and weapons for its defense from any available market.

November 25 Che Guevara is appointed director of the National Bank of Cuba. He sells Cuban gold reserves held at Fort Knox, Kentucky, transferring the money to Swiss and Canadian banks to prevent U.S. confiscation.

1960

January Cuba expropriates 70,000 acres of property owned by U.S. sugar companies, including 35,000 acres of pasture and forests owned by United Fruit Company in Oriente province. United Fruit owns approximately 235,000 acres in addition to this. By confronting United Fruit (later United Brands and Chiquita Brands), Cuba is antagonizing a powerful organization that played a major role in the 1954 overthrow of the elected Arbenz government in Guatemala. Secretary of State John Foster Dulles has been both a stockholder and a longtime legal adviser for the company, including preparation of contracts in 1930 and 1936 with the Ubico dictatorship in Guatemala; his brother Allen W. Dulles, director of the CIA, was once president of the company; UN Ambassador Henry Cabot Lodge has been a member of its board of directors; Walter Bedell Smith, head of the CIA before Dulles, became president of United Fruit after the overthrow of Arbenz.

January 11 The U.S. government protests the seizure of the land. Cuba rejects the protest. Agitation increases for cutting Cuba's sugar quota.

January 12 Incendiary bombs dropped from a plane burn 10 tons of sugarcane in Havana province.

January 21 Four 100-pound bombs from a plane damage Havana.

January 28-29 Planes bomb five sugarcane fields in Camagüey province and three in Oriente province.

January 29 President Eisenhower is seeking authority to cut off Cuba's sugar quota.

February 4 The U.S. government turns down Brazil's offer to mediate the sugar dispute between Cuba and the United States.

February 7 An air attack burns 30 tons of cane at several sugar mills in Camagüey as sabotage of sugar production and terrorism in urban areas continue.

February 13 In Havana, Soviet Deputy Prime Minister Anastas Mikoyan and Prime Minister Castro sign the first major trade agreement between Cuba and the Soviet Union, which will supply Cuba with crude oil and petroleum products as well as wheat, fertilizer, iron, and some machinery; purchase five million tons of sugar over a five-year period; and provide $100 million credit at 2.5 percent interest.

February 18 Robert Ellis Frost, a U.S. pilot, is killed when his plane blows up as he attacks a sugar mill in Matanzas province. Documents found in the wreckage reveal that he invaded Cuban territory on three previous occasions. Cuba charges that the plane came from the United States. The U.S. State Department later acknowledges that the flight did originate in the United States and expresses regrets.

February 23 More air attacks target sugar mills in Las Villas and Matanzas provinces.

February 29 Secretary of State John Foster Dulles rejects a Cuban offer to negotiate with the condition that the United States would take no unilateral action harmful to the Cuban economy during negotiations.

March Yielding to U.S. pressure, a consortium of Western European banks cancels plans for loaning $100 million to Cuba.

March 4 The *Coubre*, a French freighter loaded with Belgian arms and ammunition, explodes in Havana harbor, killing and injuring many people. Belgium has ignored the U.S. request to refuse to sell arms to Cuba.

March 8 An air attack burns more cane in Pinar del Río province.

March 17 President Eisenhower secretly orders CIA Director Allen Dulles to organize and train Cuban exiles for an invasion of Cuba. Training will take place mainly in Guatemala.

April Foreign Minister Raúl Roa García states that Guatemala is conspiring with United Fruit to invade Cuba. The Guatemalan government denies any involvement and severs diplomatic relations with Cuba. In March 1961, only a month before the invasion, Guatemalan UN Ambassador Carlos Alejos calls Cuba's continuing charges "Goebbels-like" propaganda.

April 4 Cuba sets in motion plans to expropriate the remainder of the land owned by United Fruit.

April 4 A plane flying out of the U.S. naval base at Guantánamo drops incendiary material in Oriente province.

April 25 Cuba establishes the Cuban Bank of Foreign Trade.

May 7 Cuba and the Soviet Union reestablish diplomatic relations, severed in April 1952 after General Batista's coup.

May 9 Indonesia's President Sukarno makes a state visit to Cuba.

May 17 Radio Swan, a CIA station, begins broadcasting to Cuba from Swan Island.

May 24 Cuba requires that foreign-owned oil refineries in Cuba — Cuba's only refineries — process the crude oil imported at favorable rates from the Soviet Union.

June 7 When the first shipment of crude oil arrives, the refineries — Shell (British), Esso and Texaco (both U.S.) — refuse to refine it because it would interfere with the principle of their managerial control.

June 27 The U.S. Congress begins to push through a newly amended Sugar Act which includes a clause authorizing the president to eliminate Cuba's sugar quota.

June 28 Cuba orders nationalization of the oil refineries, which have continued to refuse to refine Soviet-supplied crude.

June 29 Cuba nationalizes Texaco's refinery.

July 1 Cuba nationalizes Esso and Shell refineries.

July 3 Congress enacts the measure that allows termination of Cuba's sugar quota.

July 5 Cuba authorizes nationalization of all U.S. business and commercial property in Cuba.

July 6 President Eisenhower cancels Cuba's sugar quota, saying, "This action amounts to economic sanctions against Cuba. Now we must look ahead to other moves — economic, diplomatic and strategic." This means the United States will not purchase the 700,000 tons of sugar remaining in the 1960 quota.

July 9-10 Soviet Premier Nikita Khrushchev says, "If necessary, Soviet artillerymen can support the Cuban people with their rocket fire if aggressive forces dare to start an intervention against Cuba." At the UN General Assembly, Cuba responds that in the event of such an invasion, Cuba "could have no other course than to accept this assistance with gratitude." The Soviet Union agrees to buy the 700,000 tons of sugar that the United States has refused to purchase.

July 15 The Cuban Bank for Foreign Trade becomes the sole foreign trade agency in Cuba.

July 23 In its first commercial treaty with Cuba, China agrees to buy 500,000 tons of sugar annually for five years at the world market price.

August The CIA takes steps to recruit members of organized crime for help in assassinating Prime Minister Castro. According to testimony by Colonel Sheffield Edwards on May 30, 1975, to the Senate Select Intelligence Committee on Assassinations, Richard Mervin Bissell Jr., former Yale professor turned CIA chief of covert operations, asks Edwards, director of the CIA's Office of Security, to locate someone who could assassinate Castro. Bissell confirms this in his own 1975 testimony. Edwards decides to rely on Robert A. Maheu, a top aide to Howard Hughes and a former FBI agent.

August 6 Cuba nationalizes all U.S.-owned industrial and agrarian enterprises.

August 28 Meeting in San José, Costa Rica, the OAS votes to adopt the U.S.-sponsored "Declaration of San José," which condemns the "attempt of the Sino-Soviet powers to make use of the political, economic or social situation of any American state." However, Secretary of State Christian Herter fails to persuade the OAS to take the next step of condemning Prime Minister Castro or the Cuban government.

September Robert Maheu recruits underworld figure John Roselli who then meets at the Plaza Hotel in New York with both Maheu and Colonel Sheffield Edwards to discuss the plan to assassinate Prime Minister Castro. Roselli recruits Chicago crime boss Momo Salvatore (Sam) Giancana, who joins Roselli at their new headquarters in Miami's Kenilworth Hotel. Roselli also recruits Santo Trafficante Jr., who, according to his own testimony to the House Select Committee on Assassinations on September 28, 1978, introduces Maheu, Giancana and Roselli to some "very active" Cubans in Florida and acts as translator. As Richard Bissell later testifies (Senate Select Intelligence Committee, 1975), these crime chiefs are eager to return to the days of their lucrative business in Cuba. Trafficante ran gambling and drug operations in Havana until 1959. Old contacts are employed as their operatives inside and outside Cuba.

September 2 Cuba issues the "First Declaration of Havana," which condemns the "Declaration of San José" by the OAS, rejects the Monroe Doctrine, asserts Cuba's intention of establishing diplomatic relations with China and of trading with both China and the Soviet Union, and proclaims the rights of the poor and oppressed to certain basic needs such as health care, education, jobs and dignity.

September 8 Cuban civilian militia mobilize for "cleanup" operations in the Escambray region of Las Villas province against counterrevolutionary groups secretly supported by the CIA. These groups never gain much of a foothold in Cuba before being defeated by soldiers or civilian militia.

September 13 Following the OAS Declaration of August 28, the Eisenhower Administration agrees to the Act of Bogotá, promising more money and "attention" to Latin American development.

September 14 The U.S. State Department informs Cuba that when Prime Minister Castro attends the opening session of the UN General Assembly he will be restricted to the island of Manhattan and will be expected to live as close as possible to UN headquarters. Three other foreign leaders will be subject to these limits: Nikita Khrushchev (Soviet Union), Janos Kadar (Hungary) and Mehmet Shehu (Albania). This marks the first time that such limits have been imposed on persons of this rank attending the General Assembly.

September 17 Cuba announces that U.S. Ambassador Philip Bonsal will be restricted to the Vedado residential district of Havana while Prime Minister Castro is confined to Manhattan.

September 17 Cuba nationalizes all U.S. banks: First National Bank of Boston, First National City Bank of New York and Chase Manhattan.

September 18 Prime Minister Castro flies to New York for the UN General Assembly. While great numbers of police are assigned for his protection, he is greeted at the airport by thousands of well-wishers who follow him to his hotel.

September 18 Che Guevara, president of Cuba's National Bank, says Britain has refused to allow British Guiana to accept a Cuban offer of $5 million to develop its timber industry. The offer was announced in Havana August 24 by Cheddi Jagan, the colony's Minister of Trade and Industry, and the terms were to be 10 years at two percent interest with payment made in timber.

September 19 After less than friendly treatment at the midtown Shelburne Hotel, Cuba's UN delegation moves to the Hotel Theresa on 125th Street in Harlem. Thousands crowd the streets to see and cheer them. The *New York Times* reports that Castro receives "a leader of the so-called Muslim movement among United States Negroes, who calls himself Malcolm X." At the Hotel Theresa, Castro later receives Premier Khrushchev, President Gamal Abdel Nasser of the United Arab Republic (Egypt and Syria), and Prime Minister Jawaharlal Nehru of India as well as many other leading figures such as Langston Hughes. While still in New York, Castro meets with President Kwame Nkrumah of Ghana.

September 26 Prime Minister Castro addresses the UN General Assembly for four and a half hours. He says Cuba was being called "a Red peril" before it "had the opportunity to exchange letters" with the Soviet Union and that Cuba's clash with huge international businesses "was more than the United States government — or rather, the representatives of the United States monopolies — could possibly tolerate." He notes that the OAS resolution of August 28 does not condemn the United States for its air raids and other aggressions against Cuba but instead condemns the Soviet Union which has not committed any aggression whatsoever against Cuba. Castro denounces the way the United Nations has intervened in the Congo (becomes Zaire October 27, 1971), pointing out that Colonel Joseph D. Mobutu (later Mobutu Sese Seko), in concert with the United States, is usurping power from the rightful premier, Patrice Lumumba. He supports independence for Algeria, the Soviet proposal for disarmament, and also the Soviet proposal that China be admitted to the United Nations.

September 28 Returning to Havana, Prime Minister Castro addresses a mass rally at Revolution Plaza. When four bombs explode as he is speaking, he proposes the creation of Committees for the Defense of the Revolution (CDRs), which become a mainstay of Cuban society.

September 29 The U.S. government advises its citizens living in Cuba to send their families home.

September 30 The U.S. government urges its citizens not to travel to Cuba. Prime Minister Castro responds by urging U.S. citizens living in Cuba to stay.

October 7 At the United Nations, Foreign Minister Raúl Roa García states that the CIA is training exiles and mercenaries in Guatemala for aggression against Cuba.

October 8-10 Weapons dropped from a U.S. plane are seized in the Escambray and over a hundred counterrevolutionaries are arrested. The October 20 *New York Times* reports that the weapons were dropped at 2 a.m. on September 29 by an aircraft of U.S. registration coming from the United States and piloted by U.S. "airmen."

October 13 The Cuban consul in Miami, Abelardo León Blanco, is beaten and seriously injured as the consulate is vandalized in broad daylight.

October 14 The U.S. government presents a 10,000-word document to the United Nations in response to Prime Minister Castro's UN speech in September. The document blames Cuba for worsening relations. For example, the United States claims the right to occupy territory at Guantánamo because of the 1934 treaty, and states that there have been "only" five unauthorized flights over Cuba of which the U.S. government possesses any "substantial" evidence.

October 14 The Urban Reform Law goes into effect and ends landlord ownership of housing for profit as it nationalizes all commercially owned real estate. All large industrial, commercial and transportation companies, including 20 owned by the United States, are nationalized. About 200 small U.S. companies remain in private hands.

October 18 Cuba files a formal complaint with the United Nations accusing the U.S. government of aerial aggression.

October 18 Canada says it will not support any embargoes on sales to Cuba.

October 18 Cuba withdraws from the International Bank for Reconstruction and Development (the World Bank) because the economic policy of the bank is "far from being effective" in the process of developing and expanding the Cuban economy, which the Cuban government is carrying out "according to a definite plan." Cuba was an original member of the bank founded in 1945.

October 18 FBI Director J. Edgar Hoover sends a memo notifying the CIA's chief of covert operations, Richard Bissell, that Hoover is aware of Chicago crime boss Sam Giancana's involvement with the CIA in a plot to assassinate Fidel Castro.

October 19 The Eisenhower Administration declares a partial embargo on trade with Cuba, prohibiting all exports except for foodstuffs, medicines, medical supplies and a few items that require special licenses. Vice-President Richard Nixon, the Republican presidential candidate, later describes this policy as an "all-out 'quarantine' — economically, politically and diplomatically — of the Castro regime." Imports continue to be allowed.

October 20 Washington recalls U.S. Ambassador Philip Bonsal for consultations.

October 20 Democratic presidential candidate John F. Kennedy urges aid to the "fighters for freedom" in Cuba and in exile; a freeze on all Cuban assets in the United States; and collective action against communism in the Caribbean by the United States, the OAS and European allies.

October 21 Presidential candidates Richard Nixon and John F. Kennedy meet for a televised debate. Having seen headlines about Kennedy's call for aid to "fighters for freedom," Nixon infers that Kennedy has learned of the invasion plan. Although not formally briefed until after his election in November, Kennedy already has information from sources in and out of the government. The invasion plan is far from secret, especially in Miami. (Through his mistress, Judith Campbell [Exner], Kennedy has been in close contact with crime boss Sam Giancana since April; Giancana, working in Miami with the CIA, could have told Kennedy not only about the invasion but also about the conspiracy to assassinate Prime Minister Castro.) Nixon decides that he must protect the "secrecy" of the invasion. Thus, the U.S. public hears Vice-President Nixon, who knows of the impending invasion, argue that such an act would be "dangerously irresponsible" because it would violate U.S. treaty commitments, probably cost the United States "all our friends in Latin America," lead to condemnation by the United Nations, and cause "civil war" in Cuba with possible Soviet involvement. Kennedy argues that "quarantining" Cuba through economic sanctions would be useless because the United States does not have the support of Latin America and Europe.

October 22   The United States is discussing with Canada ways of preventing U.S. exports from going to Cuba through Canada.

October 24   In direct response to the U.S. embargo of October 19, Cuba nationalizes remaining U.S. property in Cuba.

October 27   On President Eisenhower's orders, the first U-2 spy flight takes place over Cuba.

October 29   In a continuing series of hijacked planes and boats, nine counterrevolutionaries hijack a commercial DC-3 on a flight from Havana to Nueva Gerona in Cuba, killing a soldier and wounding the pilot and a 14-year-old boy.

October 31   At the United Nations, Foreign Minister Raúl Roa García says Richard Nixon and John F. Kennedy in their debate discussed Cuba as if it were a "piece of real estate owned by the United States."

November 1   The UN General Assembly rejects 45 to 29 with 18 abstentions Cuban and Soviet bloc demands for a debate of Cuba's charge that the United States plans to invade. Instead the General Assembly votes to send the matter to committee as the United States and the General Assembly Steering Committee have urged. The U.S. ambassador to the United Nations, James J. Wadsworth, says Cuba's charges are "monstrous distortions and downright falsehoods" and "there is no threat from the United States of aggression against Cuba." Guatemalan representative Luis Coronada Lira denies that the United States is training people in his country for invasion and says Cuba is the one who is guilty of aggression. He cites as an example of this "aggression" Cuba's grant of asylum in 1960 to former Guatemalan President Arbenz, overthrown by the CIA in 1954.

November 13   About half of the Guatemalan Army, led by some 120 officers, rebels against the regime of Miguel Ydígoras Fuentes. One of their motives is objection to the U.S. government's use of Guatemala as a base for the planned invasion of Cuba. In putting down their rebellion, the U.S. government employs some of the

CIA's B-26 bombers piloted by Cuban exiles whom the CIA has trained for use against Cuba.

November 17   President Eisenhower orders the U.S. Navy to protect Nicaragua and Guatemala against possible Cuban invasion. The State Department says Cuba's accumulation of communist-supplied arms has led to fears by Nicaragua and Guatemala that Castro might attempt to "export his revolution." Cuba charges that this is the first step in plans for invasion. The Soviet news agency Tass says, "The message of this military action... becomes clear if one considers that Guatemala and Nicaragua are bases where an attack on Cuba is being prepared."

November 18   CIA Director Allen Dulles and Deputy Director Richard Bissell formally brief President-elect Kennedy about plans for an invasion of Cuba.

December 2   Cuba establishes diplomatic relations with the Democratic Republic of Vietnam (Hanoi).

December 16   President Eisenhower fixes the Cuban sugar quota at zero for the first quarter of 1961.

December 19   Prime Minister Castro announces that socialist countries have ordered four million tons of sugar as their response to the suspension of Cuba's sugar quota in the U.S. market.

December 27   Less than four months before the U.S.-sponsored invasion of Cuba, Cuban authorities arrest 17 members of what was meant to be part of a Fifth Column, charging them with terrorist activities like putting dynamite in cigarette packs and throwing them into stores and theaters. One of those arrested is Armando Valladares, who was a policeman during the Batista dictatorship.

December 30   Diplomatic relations between Cuba and Peru are broken.

December 30   Cuba sets up the Cuban Institute of Friendship with the Peoples (ICAP) to encourage people from around the world to get to know Cuba.

December 31   *La Epoca*, a department store in Havana, is almost completely destroyed by arson.

1961

January 1 Cuba launches a National Literacy Campaign which, in one year, reduces the illiteracy rate from 25 percent to 3.9 percent, becoming a model for other countries.

January 1 From now on, U.S. citizens will need visas to enter Cuba. The Cuban government is imposing this rule because of a lack of reciprocity as well as national security.

January 2 At the UN Security Council, Foreign Minister Raúl Roa García formally charges that the U.S. government is preparing an invasion, denounces the U.S. Embassy in Havana for espionage, and requests that the Embassy staff be reduced to 11 persons, the number in the Cuban Embassy in Washington.

January 3 The U.S. government breaks diplomatic relations with Cuba and arranges for the Swiss Embassy in Havana to assume its diplomatic and consular representation in Cuba. Later the Czechoslovakian Embassy in Washington provides the same service for Cuba.

January 5 The UN Security Council rejects without a vote Cuba's charge that an invasion is being planned by the United States, which formally denies any such plan.

January 5 Conrado Benítez, an 18-year-old volunteer teacher in the National Literacy Campaign, is assassinated in the Escambray.

January 7-9 Quantities of weapons dropped from U.S. planes in Pinar del Río and the Escambray are seized.

January 10 Reporting on military preparations in Guatemala, the *New York Times* describes how Guatemalan authorities insist that they expect an invasion from Cuba "almost any day" while opponents of the government maintain that the operations are being planned, directed and financed by Washington in preparation for an invasion of Cuba. The report notes that the U.S. "Embassy is maintaining complete silence on the subject."

January 12 Cuba reports the torture by U.S. soldiers of Manuel Prieto, a worker at the Guantánamo Naval Base.

January 14 In continuing urban and industrial sabotage, a fire in tobacco warehouses in Havana causes heavy losses.

January 16 The U.S. State Department proclaims that citizens traveling to Cuba must obtain passports specifically endorsed by the State Department for that destination. (*See* June 16, 1958)

January 19 Seven U.S. mercenaries are captured while trying to disembark in Pinar del Río.

January 20 On the day John F. Kennedy becomes president, Prime Minister Castro notes that in his inaugural address Kennedy urged U.S. adversaries to "begin anew the quest for peace." Castro says Cuba is ready to "begin anew" in relations with the United States and will await the next move by the Kennedy Administration. In the belief that the threat of invasion has passed, Cuba begins demobilization of the militia who have been on 24-hour alert for 18 days. But in Washington, CIA Director Allen Dulles begins to give the new president, who had been officially informed as president-elect of invasion plans, intensive briefings on the subject. Soon, Richard Bissell, CIA chief of covert operations, briefs Kennedy Administration officials, including National Security Adviser McGeorge Bundy and Sidney Gottlieb, new chief of the technical services division in charge of the CIA drug experimentation program, on the plan to assassinate Prime Minister Castro.

January 25 At his first news conference, President Kennedy says the United States has no plans to resume diplomatic relations with Cuba.

January 30 In his State of the Union address, President Kennedy speaks of developing an "alliance for progress" in Latin America. Declaring that "communist agents" have "established a base in Cuba," he delivers a clear statement of policy: "Our objection with Cuba is not the people's desire for a better life. Our objection is to their domination by foreign and domestic tyrannies. Cuban social and economic reform should be encouraged. Questions of economics and trade policy can always be negotiated. But communist domination in this hemisphere can never be negotiated."

February According to his testimony in May 1987 at U.S. Congressional hearings about the Iran-Contra Affair, Félix I. Rodríguez (also known as Max Gómez, Félix Ramos Medina, or Frank García) infiltrates into Cuba at this time, two months prior to the invasion, with Cuban exile Rafael "Chi Chi" Quintero, who also turns up years later in the Iran-Contra Affair. Rodríguez's testimony to Congress exemplifies the CIA's use of Cuban exiles and other mercenaries: Rodríguez trains in Central America in 1960 and 1961 before being sent by the CIA to Cuba; most of his infiltration team are killed or captured but he escapes; after the invasion fails, he flees to the Venezuelan Embassy where he stays for five months before getting a safe conduct pass out of Cuba; he and Quintero continue to infiltrate Cuba for years with Thomas G. Clines as their CIA case officer; like many Bay of Pigs veterans, he joins the U.S. Army in 1963 with a special commission from President Kennedy and trains at Fort Benning, Georgia; he then participates, with Quintero, in a "special operation" in two Central American countries against Cuba; that operation terminates in 1965 when he goes to Venezuela; he is sent to Bolivia by the CIA to help capture Che Guevara (*see* October 8, 1967); then he serves in covert operations in Vietnam and again in Central America.

February The CIA delivers to one of their would-be assassins a box of Prime Minister Castro's favorite cigars, contaminated with a botulism toxin so potent that he would die after putting a cigar in his mouth. Colonel Sheffield Edwards of the CIA delivers pills containing the same toxin to crime boss Roselli. The cigar plot is thwarted February 28. The other goes awry, like several other exotic schemes to assassinate Castro and other Cuban leaders.

February 3 The U.S. Armed Forces Joint Chiefs of Staff approve a "Military Evaluation of the CIA Paramilitary Plan — Cuba," with a warning that ultimate success will depend on political factors — "i.e., a sizable popular uprising or substantial follow-on forces."

February 17 Vasco Leitão de Cunha, Under Secretary of Brazil's Foreign Ministry, says he finds the Cuban atmosphere favorable to good relations among the countries of the Western

Hemisphere and offers to mediate between Cuba and the United States.

February 22 Another volunteer teacher in the Literacy Campaign, Pedro Morejón Quintana, is assassinated.

February 23 Che Guevara heads the new Ministry of Industries set up to implement Cuba's industrialization plan.

February 28 For the first time since President Kennedy was inaugurated, Cuban media warn that the United States is continuing its plan to invade. In these weeks prior to invasion, there are rumors that the CIA is interfering with publication of articles that would expose the plan to the people of the United States; for example, a major article by David Kraslow of the *Miami Herald* about the training of Cubans in Florida is not printed.

March The CIA begins to work inside Cuba with Rolando Cubela Secades ("AM/LASH" in CIA cryptonym). This continues until Cubela's arrest in Cuba in 1966 (*see* November 22, 1963).

March 3 The Kennedy Administration rejects Brazil's offer (*see* February 17) to mediate.

March 9 Che Guevara explains how socialist aid differs from U.S. aid: "...whereas we may use the Socialist credit for our industrial development in any way we believe best, the United States gives credit to Latin America in such a manner that the credit is only received if it is invested in a way that the United States accepts or believes convenient. That is the difference between colonial credit and a credit that promotes development."

March 11 Sabotage leaves a large part of Havana without electricity. Urban bombings and fires are common.

March 13 An oil refinery at the Santiago de Cuba port is attacked from a boat.

March 13 President Kennedy formally proposes the Alliance for Progress, "a vast new 10-year plan" for economic development of the Americas. Only a month before the planned invasion of Cuba, the President promises other Latin American countries $500 million for their development as soon as Congress appropriates it.

March 20 In Miami, two Cuban exile organizations — the Democratic Revolutionary Front (the *Frente*, coordinated by Manuel Antonio Varona) and the Revolutionary Movement of the People (the MRP founded and led by Manuel Ray) — select José Miró Cardona, former Cuban prime minister and now a Cuban exile, as head of the new Revolutionary Council; it aims to establish a Cuban provisional government, which must exist on Cuban territory to be recognized by foreign nations. The March 22 *New York Times* reports that these organizations have been carrying out sabotage inside Cuba. Miró Cardona denies that the exile groups get any U.S. aid (*see* April 1963).

March 22   Prime Minister Castro says the establishment of the Revolutionary Council is clearly a prelude to a larger effort by the United States to destroy the Cuban revolution.

March 28   At a mobilization of the Cuban people for the imminent U.S. invasion, Che Guevara calls the recent assassination of Prime Minister Patrice Lumumba of the Congo (later Zaire) "an example of what the empire is capable of doing when the struggle against it is carried on in a firm and sustained way."

March 30   A plane flying over an oil refinery is forced to land; the two men aboard are related to the Somoza family of Nicaragua.

March 31   Continuing the policy of the Eisenhower Administration (*see* December 16, 1960), President Kennedy sets the quota for Cuban sugar at zero for the rest of 1961.

April 3   The U.S. State Department issues a "White Paper" on Cuba, calling it a Soviet satellite and saying the revolution has been betrayed. Written by Arthur Schlesinger under the close supervision of President Kennedy, it urges Cuba to cut ties with communism and says the United States will aid a "free" regime. If Cuba fails to do this, the paper says the Cuban people will "join hands with the other republics in the hemisphere in the struggle to win freedom." It states that the "Castro regime offers a clear and present danger to the authentic and autonomous revolution of the Americas."

April 4   Cuban media call the exhortation in the "White Paper" to break off relations with communist countries an insult to Cuba's sovereignty.

April 7   The *New York Times* runs an article about the plan for invasion. Originally the article was to appear under a four-column headline, but it is cut to one column. The published article omits the original's mention of the role of the CIA. Instead, it refers to "experts" who have been training "anti-Castro forces" in Guatemala, Florida and Louisiana. This training is "an open secret" in Miami, says the *Times*, and couriers' boats "run a virtual shuttle between the Florida coast and Cuba carrying instructions, weapons and explosives."

April 9 The *New York Times* reports that a federal grand jury in Miami has indicted Rolando Masferrer for an abortive invasion of Cuba on October 4, 1960 in violation of the Neutrality Act. The Neutrality Act forbids the launching of military expeditions from U.S. territory against any nation with which the United States is at peace. Noting that the Kennedy Administration opposes pro-Batista exiles like Masferrer while encouraging other anti-Castro groups, the *Times* reports that this indictment raises the question of whether the Neutrality Act may be selectively enforced.

April 11 The *New York Times* reports the Kennedy Administration is divided over "how far to go in helping" Cubans overthrow Prime Minister Castro. The article says that U.S. military aid would violate both the UN Charter and the OAS Charter.

April 12 At a press conference, President Kennedy rules out intervention in Cuba by U.S. Armed Forces under any circumstances. Latin American reaction to this position is highly favorable.

April 13 An explosion destroys a Havana department store, *El Encanto*, killing Fe del Valle, a prominent revolutionary and one of many people killed in these acts of sabotage. Seventeen years later at a tribunal held in Havana, Philip Agee, who by then has left the CIA, relates how CIA agents put dynamite in dolls shelved in the stockroom.

April 14 The new president of Brazil, Janio Quadros, says Brazil supports Cuba's right to self-determination and wants to resolve differences between Cuba and the United States.

April 15 B-26 bombers begin "softening-up" attacks against Cuban defenses. The bombers fly to Cuba from Nicaragua with CIA-paid pilots, but the CIA wants the bombers to look like Cuban planes flown by Cubans; so one pilot, Mario Zuñiga, flies a B-26 to Miami and poses as a defector. At an emergency session of the UN General Assembly's Political Committee, Foreign Minister Raúl Roa García charges that the air attacks are the "prologue to a large-scale invasion" while Ambassador Adlai Stevenson denies U.S. involvement. Stevenson uses a wire photo of the "defector's" fake "Cuban" B-26 to bolster his case. Roa points out that anybody can paint markings on a plane. Meanwhile, journalists show that Zuñiga's story is as full of holes as his B-26, which was shot up by the CIA before it left Nicaragua. Stevenson later calls that UN session the most "humiliating experience" of his public life, saying he felt "deliberately tricked" by his own government. Pro-Cuban, anti-U.S. demonstrations begin around the world, especially in Latin America.

April 16 At a massive funeral for seven Cubans killed in the preceding day's bombings, Prime Minister Castro for the first time defines the Cuban revolution as socialist: "How these events help our people to educate themselves! The lessons are expensive, the lessons are painful, the lessons are bloody, but how the peoples learn by these events.... [The imperialists] cannot forgive our being right here under their very noses or to see how we have made a revolution, a socialist revolution, right here under the very nose of the United States." He says the invasion force is on its way and a landing is imminent.

April 17 Before dawn, a CIA public relations man releases to the press a message supposedly from the president of the Revolutionary Council, José Miró Cardona, but actually written by CIA agent E. Howard Hunt Jr. It announces that "Cuban patriots" have begun "to liberate" Cuba. The CIA's Radio Swan broadcasts to the Cuban people a call to arms. The CIA's invasion force, Brigade 2506 of some 1,200 men, invades at Playa Girón (Girón Beach) on the Bahía de Cochones (Bay of Pigs). (In Cuba, the Bay of Pigs invasion is known as the Battle of Girón.) The invaders are led and commanded by CIA agent Grayston (Gray) Lynch and CIA operative William (Rip) Robertson. Within minutes of the landing, Prime Minister Castro calls a national alert. All militia are put on war footing. In the early morning, two of the U.S.-furnished ships, the *Houston* and the *Río Escondido*, carrying invaders and supplies, are sunk by propeller-driven Cuban planes. The internal support anticipated by the CIA fails to materialize.

April 18 The invasion is going so badly that the CIA director of covert operations, Richard Bissell, authorizes six U.S. pilots to attack with three bombers armed with napalm and high explosives. Four of the pilots are killed. Cubans recover one of the bodies and the following day reveal this as proof of the U.S. role in the invasion.

April 19 Less than 72 hours after the invasion began, Prime Minister Castro announces victory. Among more than 1,000 prisoners are men who had previously owned in Cuba 914,859 acres of land, 9,666 houses, 70 factories, 5 mines, 2 banks and 10 sugar mills.

April 19 José Miró Cardona, who has been a virtual prisoner of CIA forces in Opa-Locka, Florida, during the invasion, is flown to Washington. To keep these exile leaders from being directly involved in U.S. operations during the invasion, the CIA detained along with Miró two other Revolutionary Council leaders, Manuel Antonio (Tony) de Varona Loredo (prime minister during the Prío presidency), the defense minister, and Manuel (Manolo) Ray, the underground coordinator. Angry about their treatment and about the invasion's defeat, these three and two other Council members meet secretly at the White House with President Kennedy. Many exile leaders never get over their bitterness at Kennedy's refusal to provide overt U.S. support. Kennedy argues that such a commitment could and probably would have led to a full-scale U.S. invasion.

April 20 In a speech clearly aimed at placating Cuban exiles, President Kennedy says the United States will not allow communists to take over Cuba.

April 21 Cuban exiles criticize the CIA for inadequate consultation with exile groups and proceeding with an invasion despite some exiles warning in recent weeks that the time was not ripe.

April 21 The Kennedy Administration plans to oppose a Mexican resolution in the United Nations appealing to all states "to insure that their territories and resources are not used to promote a civil war in Cuba."

April 22 President Kennedy asks General Maxwell D. Taylor to head an investigation into what led to the Bay of Pigs debacle.

April 22 President Kennedy and his National Security Council discuss whether or not to impose a total embargo on U.S. trade with Cuba. A sudden halt to imports of about $70 million a year could damage some U.S. businesses.

April 24 White House Press Secretary Pierre Salinger reaffirms President Kennedy's full responsibility for the U.S. role in the invasion.

April 27 Cuba urges the United States to enter into negotiations to establish peaceful coexistence, diplomatic relations and even friendly relations if Washington chooses.

April 28 The Kennedy Administration rejects Cuba's offer to negotiate, repeating that communism in the Western Hemisphere is not negotiable.

May 1 Prime Minister Castro says Cuba must develop a socialist constitution.

May 1 Radio Havana Cuba, founded April 16, is officially inaugurated, broadcasting with powerful transmitters to reach all the Western Hemisphere. Eventually this shortwave radio station broadcasts in Spanish, English, Portuguese, French, Arabic, Creole, Guariní and Quechua plus a weekly program in Esperanto.

May 3 In an interview on Cuban radio, Manuel Artime Buesa, a founder of the Movement for the Recovery of the Revolution (MRR) and a leader of Brigade 2506 who was captured two weeks after the invasion in the Zapata Swamps, acknowledges that the CIA planned and directed the invasion. E. Howard Hunt Jr. recommended Artime to be overall political and military leader of the Brigade, and Artime worked closely in planning the invasion with Hunt and Bernard L. Barker, Hunt's right-hand man. After release from prison, Artime continues his connection with Hunt and Barker, becoming a leader in hit-and-run attacks against Cuba from Florida. Barker, also a Cuban exile, was in General Batista's secret police before the revolution and reported on subversive activities in Cuba to the FBI; he became an informer for the CIA in 1959. From 1963 through 1966, Hunt, Artime and Barker work out of a CIA station housed at the University of Miami with the code name JM WAVE. About 300 employees like Hunt control a few thousand Cuban agents like Barker and Artime. Financed by the Kennedy and Johnson Administrations, they run a campaign of armed attacks, sabotage, infiltration of agents, propaganda, arson, etc., against Cuba. JM WAVE's CIA proprietary company is Zenith Technical Enterprises.

June 6 In a letter to a committee seeking release of the Bay of Pigs prisoners, Prime Minister Castro proposes an exchange for an equal number of political prisoners from the United States, Spain, Puerto Rico, Nicaragua and Guatemala.

June 13 General Maxwell Taylor's review of what happened at the Bay of Pigs recommends that "new guidance be provided for political, military, economic and propaganda actions against Castro."

July African American journalist William J. Worthy Jr. travels to Cuba not only without State Department endorsement (*see* January 16) but without a passport. After he returns in October, he is charged and convicted for violating the federal law that prohibits a citizen from leaving or entering the United States without a valid passport. Worthy traveled to China and Hungary in 1955 despite restrictions against U.S. citizens' traveling to communist countries. In 1957 he was denied a renewal of his passport because he refused to sign a commitment to abide by those restrictions. (*See* February 20, 1964)

July 26 This is one of the dates earmarked for assassination of Fidel Castro, Raúl Castro and Che Guevara, according to a CIA plan, Operation Patty, discovered by Cuban security forces. Seventeen years later at an International Tribunal in Havana, Humberto Rosales Torres, who had been arrested for his part in the plot and given a nine-year prison term, testifies that the plan also included an attack on the Guantánamo Naval Base that would have provided an excuse for sending in the U.S. Marines.

August 8 Che Guevara heads the Cuban delegation to a meeting in Punta del Este, Uruguay, of the OAS, which adopts President Kennedy's 10-year Alliance for Progress. Guevara tells the assembly that they have Fidel Castro to thank for this offer of U.S. aid. Cuba is not invited to join the Alliance. Guevara challenges the OAS to compare Cuba with the rest of Latin America in 10 years to see who accomplishes more.

August 8 Cuban security forces find a forged document prepared for the ongoing disinformation campaign against the Cuban government; the fake document dictates that parental authority should be transferred to the state. That rumor, it turns out, is already in circulation, leading fearful parents to send almost

15,000 children out of the country between late 1960 and 1962 in what becomes known as Operation Peter Pan.

August 17 In Punta del Este, Che Guevara meets informally with Richard Goodwin, adviser to President Kennedy on Latin American affairs, and suggests a hijacking agreement.

September Facing prison in Monroe, North Carolina, Robert F. Williams Jr., who organized his chapter of the National Association for the Advancement of Colored People (NAACP) to defy the Ku Klux Klan (KKK) with armed self-defense, goes into exile in Cuba from where he broadcasts "Radio Free Dixie."

September 2 In Belgrade, Yugoslavia, at the Charter Conference of the Movement of Nonaligned Countries, Cuban President Dorticós says the main issue "should be the self-determination of our peoples, the struggle against imperialism, colonialism and neo-colonialism." He condemns U.S. occupation of Cuban territory at Guantánamo. He urges the Nonaligned to condemn "colonialist genocide" by the Portuguese in Angola and colonial domination of Algeria and Puerto Rico.

September 25 After arresting Louis Torroella, sent to Cuba by the CIA, the Ministry of the Interior reveals the discovery of a plan by him and three other men to assassinate Prime Minister Castro.

October 3 Another volunteer teacher in the Literacy Campaign, Delfín Sen Cedré, is assassinated.

October 4 This is yet another scheduled date for the assassination of Prime Minister Castro, this time by a team headed by CIA assassins Antonio Veciana Blank and Bernardo Paradela Ibarreche. In July 1978, an international audience hears testimony about this plot at the International Tribunal in Havana from one of the participants, Fernando de Rojas Penichet. Veciana, head of an accounting firm in Havana when General Batista was in power, was recruited by the CIA in Cuba in 1960. Realizing that the plot had been discovered, Veciana fled on October 3 to Miami, where, later in the month, he becomes a founding member of Alpha 66, a group that carries out terrorist attacks against Cuba from its base in the United States.

October 6 At an OAS meeting, Cuban Ambassador Carlos Lechuga says there is a U.S. plan to provoke breaks in diplomatic relations between Cuba and other Latin American nations on the pretext that Cuba is intervening in the internal affairs of other states.

Within six months Venezuela, Ecuador, Colombia and Argentina sever relations with Cuba.

October 15 Rubén López Sabariego, a Cuban worker at the U.S. naval base at Guantánamo who was arrested on September 30, dies. Cuba says the cause is torture. In 1963, U.S. columnist Jack Anderson reports that U.S. Marine Captain Arthur J. Jackson was secretly dismissed because of the killing. The United States maintains that Jackson acted in self-defense and that his dismissal was kept secret to avoid international repercussions.

November 1 In a memo to President Kennedy, Richard Goodwin, the White House specialist on Latin America, advises that Attorney General Robert Kennedy would be the most effective commander of a new plan to overthrow Prime Minister Castro: Operation Mongoose. Goodwin and the Attorney General have been joined in planning Operation Mongoose by CIA operative General Edward G. Lansdale, who engineered the presidency of Ramón Magsaysay in the Philippines against the Hukbalahap rebellion and then went to Vietnam where he set up the Saigon regime of Ngo Dinh Diem.

November 11 Venezuela breaks diplomatic relations with Cuba.

November 15 In a memorandum to Attorney General Robert Kennedy outlining the proposal for Operation Mongoose, General Lansdale states that a "picture of the situation has emerged clearly enough to indicate what needs to be done and to support your sense of urgency concerning Cuba."

November 26 Volunteer teacher Manuel Ascunce Domenech and a peasant who was his student, Pedro Lantigua, are assassinated in the Escambray. Although not the first killings of participants in the Literacy Campaign, these two murders become symbolic.

November 29 President Kennedy replaces CIA Director Allen Dulles with John Alex McCone. Within the next three months, Kennedy also fires General Charles P. Cabell, the CIA's deputy director, and Richard Bissell, the head of the CIA's Bay of Pigs operation.

November 30 President Kennedy issues a memorandum to Secretary of State Dean Rusk and others who will be involved in his decision to launch top-secret Operation Mongoose "to help Cuba overthrow the communist regime." This leads to the creation of a new control group, the Special Group (Augmented)

(SGA), to oversee Mongoose: regular Special Group members —
National Security Adviser McGeorge Bundy, Deputy Under
Secretary of State Alexis Johnson, Under Secretary of Defense
Roswell Gilpatric, CIA Director John McCone, and General
Lyman Lemnitzer, head of the Joint Chiefs of Staff — augmented
by Attorney General Robert Kennedy and General Maxwell
Taylor. President Kennedy puts General Edward Lansdale in
charge of coordinating Mongoose operations with those of the
Departments of State and Defense and appoints General Taylor as
SGA chair. Within the next few weeks, William K. Harvey is put
in charge of the CIA's Task Force W, the unit that will take part
in Mongoose. Task Force W will have about 400 people working
at CIA headquarters in Washington and in the Miami CIA
Station. During the coming months, Rusk and Secretary of
Defense Robert McNamara sometimes attend SGA meetings.
Richard M. Helms, replacement for Richard Bissell as CIA chief
of covert operations, becomes a major participant, along with
Richard Goodwin of the State Department, and Ed Murrow and
Don Wilson of the United States Information Agency (USIA).

December President Kennedy continues the suspension of Cuba's
sugar quota through the first half of 1962.

December 2 Prime Minister Castro states his ideology clearly: "I am
a Marxist-Leninist and I shall be a Marxist-Leninist to the end of
my life."

December 9 Colombia breaks diplomatic relations with Cuba.

December 26 Two CIA agents trying to come ashore in Pinar del
Río are captured.

1962

January 3 The U.S. State Department issues another "White Paper" on Cuba, again calling Cuba a Soviet satellite.

January 3 In a diplomatic note to the U.S. government, Cuba protests 119 violations of its territory, 76 by planes from Guantánamo Naval Base.

January 7 Secretary of State Dean Rusk says the OAS meeting later this month will deal with the danger of "Castroism" in the Western Hemisphere and will impose sanctions on Cuba.

January 7 Arms dropped from a plane in Pinar del Río and Las Villas are seized.

January 18 In a top-secret report (partially declassified 1989) addressed to President Kennedy and officials involved with Operation Mongoose, General Edward Lansdale describes plans to overthrow the Cuban government: "The failure of the U.S.-sponsored operation in April 1961 so shook the faith of Cuban patriots in U.S. competence and intentions in supporting a revolt against Castro that a new effort to generate a revolt... must have active support from key Latin American countries.... The preparation phase must result in a political action organization in being in key localities inside Cuba, with... its own voice for psychological operations, and its own action arm (small guerrilla bands, sabotage squads, etc.).... The climactic moment of revolt will come from an angry reaction of the people to a government action (sparked by an incident), or from a fracturing of the leadership cadre within the regime, or both. (A major goal of the Project must be to bring this about.) The popular movement will capitalize on this climactic moment by initiating an open revolt.... The United States, if possible in concert with other Western Hemisphere nations, will then give open support.... Such support will include military force, as necessary." Lansdale lists various political, military and economic policies that are subsequently implemented by the Departments of State, Defense and Commerce.

January 19 The U.S. government circulates a proposal that OAS members order "automatic sanctions" against Cuba "if it does not sever ties with communist countries within 60 days."

January 22-31 OAS foreign ministers meet in Punta del Este, Uruguay. President Dorticós, head of the Cuban delegation, proposes peaceful coexistence and says expulsion of Cuba would be illegal. Fourteen of the 21 members, barely the necessary two-thirds majority, vote to expel Cuba from the OAS; Argentina, Bolivia, Brazil, Chile, Ecuador and Mexico abstain on the grounds that the measure violates the Principle of Non-intervention in the Internal Affairs of another member state, part of the OAS Charter. The expulsion measure says Cuba's "adherence... to Marxism-Leninism is incompatible with the inter-American system." The OAS also votes to suspend sales of weapons to Cuba.

January 23 In response to the OAS, a Peoples' Assembly convenes in Havana with representatives from the continent, including Lázaro Cárdenas, former Mexican president; Salvador Allende, future Chilean president; Francisco Julião, Brazilian peasant leader; Vivian Trías, secretary general of the Socialist Party of Uruguay; and Antonio Parra, rector of Guayaquil University in Uruguay.

January 25-February 1 Pointing out that one task outlined in his January 18 report was to "generate popular support" for the U.S. position at the OAS meeting, General Lansdale issues top-secret score cards of "PRO-COMMUNIST" and "PRO-FREEDOM" demonstrations in the Western Hemisphere (partially declassified 1988-89).

January 28 Cuban authorities arrest a group of saboteurs for plotting to paralyze urban transportation by putting motors out of commission with chemicals and magnetic mines.

February 3 The Kennedy Administration announces a total embargo of trade with Cuba to take effect February 7. Since the prohibition of exports (*see* October 19, 1960), the embargo has become extraterritorial with regulations barring reexport to Cuba of any commodities or technical data that originate in the United States. Congress has passed legislation prohibiting U.S. aid for any country that "furnishes assistance" to the Cuban government.

February 3 Speaking in the Panama Canal Zone, U.S. Defense Secretary Robert McNamara says communist subversion, particularly from Cuba, endangers the security of the Western Hemisphere so the United States and its allies must be prepared militarily to meet that threat.

February 4 From the Peoples' Assembly (*see* January 23) comes the "Second Declaration of Havana." In response to the OAS expulsion and sanctions, the Declaration outlines the history of colonial relations in Latin America and present conditions of widespread poverty, disease and illiteracy, calling on revolutionaries to make revolution.

February 5 At the United Nations, Cuban UN Ambassador Mario García Incháustegui denounces the OAS expulsion and proposes settlement in accordance with the UN Charter. He charges that the U.S. government is preparing another large intervention in Cuba.

February 7 The U.S. embargo on all trade with Cuba, except for the non-subsidized sale of food and medicines, goes into effect.

February 8 Argentina breaks diplomatic relations with Cuba.

February 15 The UN General Assembly rejects a resolution calling on the U.S. government to stop interfering in Cuba's affairs with a vote of 50 to 11 with 39 abstentions.

February 19 Cuba asks for an immediate meeting of the UN Security Council to discuss U.S. aggression. Just as Cuban officials quickly learned about "secret" plans that became the Bay of Pigs invasion, they know that U.S. officials are planning another invasion.

February 20 General Lansdale presents to the SGA a 26-page, top-secret timetable for implementation of the overthrow of the Cuban government (partially declassified 1989). CIA agents or "pathfinders" will be infiltrated to carry out sabotage and organization, including radio broadcasts. Jacqueline Kennedy "would be especially effective in visiting children refugees" in

Florida with USIA coverage. The OAS, NATO (North Atlantic Treaty Organization) and the United Nations will be used for international support. Guerrilla operations will begin in August and September with defections of high officials "to tell the inside story" and "evoke world sympathy with the freedom fighters." Finally in the first two weeks of October: "Open revolt and overthrow of the communist regime."

February 22 State Department official Walt Rostow travels to Europe to persuade members of NATO to join the embargo on trade with Cuba.

February 26 Cuba's Ministry of Public Health, assisted by the mass organizations, carries out a nationwide campaign of vaccination against polio and eradicates the affliction by the end of the year. In April 1995 the World Health Organization formally recognizes Cuba as the pioneer in the elimination of polio in the Americas.

February 26 Answering a request from the Joint Chiefs of Staff about possible responses to a revolt in Cuba, the Commander in Chief of the U.S. Atlantic Command recommends supplying arms covertly until the rebels' military advances reach a level that would justify overt U.S. intervention.

February 27 As in the General Assembly (*see* February 15), the United States has a majority (7 to 4) in the Security Council. The British delegate calls Cuba's charges a "propaganda exercise."

March 14 General Maxwell Taylor, SGA chair, issues detailed "Guidelines for Operation Mongoose" (partially declassified 1989). The document states: "*a*. In undertaking to cause the overthrow of the target government, the U.S. will make maximum use of indigenous resources, internal and external, but recognizes that final success will require decisive U.S. military intervention. *b*. Such indigenous resources as are developed will be used to prepare for and justify this intervention, and thereafter to facilitate and support it."

March 20 By diplomatic note, Cuba protests to the U.S. government about repeated provocations by soldiers at the U.S. naval base in Guantánamo, Cuba.

March 22 At a luncheon meeting, FBI Director J. Edgar Hoover tells President Kennedy that the FBI knows about the connection between Judith Campbell, one of the President's mistresses, and crime bosses John Roselli and Sam Giancana. He warns the President of potential damage if word got out. The affair ends at once and the President no longer uses this particular courier for messages to Giancana.

March 23 The U.S. government extends the trade embargo to imports of all goods made from Cuban materials or containing any Cuban materials even if made in other countries.

March 29-April 7 Cuba tries and convicts the Bay of Pigs invaders. Punishment is loss of Cuban citizenship and a fine of $62 million for the whole group. In lieu of the fine, the prisoners are sentenced to 30 years in prison with physical labor.

April 2 Ecuador breaks diplomatic relations with Cuba.

April 9 Cuba sends another diplomatic note to protest provocations by U.S. soldiers at Guantánamo Naval Base. These incidents are in addition to continual aerial and naval bombardment, sabotage of crops and industry, occasional landings along the coast, and assassinations.

April 14 Cuba releases 60 Bay of Pigs prisoners who were wounded during the invasion. They are flown to Miami.

April 28 Armed Cuban exiles attack the New York offices of Prensa Latina, the Cuban press agency, injuring three employees.

May General Lansdale continues to present detailed plans for Operation Mongoose to the SGA. By May 17, the CIA has managed to infiltrate only four small "teams" into Cuba, far fewer than envisioned earlier. In the coming weeks, Lansdale describes plans for the actual invasion with the cooperation of at least two other Western countries, preferably neither Guatemala nor Nicaragua, both tainted by the Bay of Pigs. In the aftermath of this successful invasion, he cautions, "Care must be exercised" to avoid "indications of possible loss of any gains (housing, land, social benefits) which might have accrued to the peasant and worker groups during the Castro regime."

May The Treasury Department formally rescinds Cuba's "Most Favored Nation" status.

May 7 CIA officials inform Attorney General Robert Kennedy that the CIA has been involved with crime boss Sam Giancana in plots to assassinate Prime Minister Castro. But as testimony by CIA officials reveals to the Senate Intelligence Committee years later, the CIA officials tell the Attorney General that the plots have been halted when in fact they continue.

May 8-18   As part of contingency plans for Cuba, U.S. military forces stage Operation Whip Lash, one of several such exercises during the year.

May 12   A heavily armed ship attacks a Cuban patrol boat, killing three and wounding five crew members. Alpha 66, a Cuban exile group based in Miami, claims credit four days later.

May 30   After conferring with other Cuban leaders, President Castro accepts the offer of a visiting Soviet delegation to provide Cuba with nuclear missiles.

June   In daily radio broadcasts, Cuba maintains that the U.S. government is using Guantánamo Naval Base for espionage and violation of Cuban territory.

June 7   Two infiltrators are killed in Oriente province.

July-October   Aggression against Cuba is an everyday occurrence, including the killing of peasants in the Escambray; the killing of fisherman Rodolfo Rosell Salas by U.S. soldiers from the Guantánamo Naval Base; the killing of a soldier and a militiaman by infiltrators; shots fired, sometimes for several hours, from Guantánamo Naval Base into the surrounding area; hit-and-run attacks by boats along the coast and other constant violations of Cuban territory by boats and planes that carry out espionage, sabotage, hijackings of boats, kidnappings, and infiltration of CIA operatives. Cubans capture many of the infiltrators.

July 2-17   Raúl Castro heads a delegation to Moscow for discussions about the deployment of nuclear missiles. According to later accounts by Cuba, emplacement of the missiles in Cuba begins in July.

July 17   Juan Falcón, who claims to be a leader of the Movement for the Recovery of the Revolution (MRR), is arrested in Cuba. On Cuban television, he describes CIA efforts to destabilize Cuba in advance of another invasion.

Late July   In response to the U.S. invasion plans, Soviet arms shipments to Cuba greatly increase.

July 26   In his speech on the ninth anniversary of the attack on Batista's Moncada Barracks, Prime Minister Castro warns that another U.S. invasion is being planned but assures the Cuban people that Cuba has acquired new weapons for its defense.

August 8 An SGA report about Operation Mongoose says Cuban response to invasion will be determined by "the will of Cuban armed forces to resist, as well as by the weapons available to them and their proficiency in their use." The report points out that Cuba's ability to defend itself will improve if the Soviet Union continues to provide additional military equipment and training. The possibility of a lengthy U.S. occupation after seizing "military control of the island" is mentioned.

August 11 In Camagüey, a group of CIA agents is captured with weapons and explosives.

August 12 According to the Operation Mongoose timetable proposed by General Lansdale (*see* February 20), this date was to be a workers' strike. The CIA's Radio Voice was to "thank them the next day for their splendid response (to shame those who didn't participate by making them feel alone)." The timetable is disintegrating.

August 15 A group of CIA agents is captured in Cuba with radio equipment.

August 20 In a memo to President Kennedy, General Maxwell Taylor says that since the SGA sees no likelihood of overthrowing the Cuban government by internal means without direct U.S. military intervention, the SGA favors a more aggressive program for Operation Mongoose. Richard Helms, CIA director in 1962, testifies to the Senate Intelligence Committee June 13, 1975: "I believe it was the policy at the time to get rid of Castro and if killing him was one of the things that was to be done in this connection, that was within what was expected."

August 22 The *S.S. Streatham Hill*, a British freighter under Soviet lease and bound for the Soviet Union with 80,000 bags of Cuban sugar, docks in San Juan, Puerto Rico, for repair of a damaged propeller. More than 14,000 sacks of sugar are off-loaded to facilitate repairs. CIA agents enter the customs warehouse and contaminate the sugar with a chemical supposedly harmless but unpalatable. When President Kennedy is told, he orders that the doctored sugar not leave Puerto Rico. The Soviet Union never receives this part of the cargo.

August 23 National Security Adviser McGeorge Bundy issues NSAM 181 stating that, at the President's directive, Operation

Mongoose's "Plan B plus should be developed with all possible speed." "Plan B plus" aims at an internal revolt in Cuba.

August 24 Two gunboats operated by the Cuban Student Directorate (DRE) based in Florida shell Havana's Sierra Maestra hotel, the Chaplin theater, and the Miramar residential section, killing about 20 Soviet and Cuban people. On the following day, Prime Minister Castro formally protests to the United Nations. Subsequently, the U.S. Coast Guard impounds the boats. The CIA has trained members of the Cuban Student Directorate in demolition and provided the boats used in the terrorist attack.

August 29 A U-2 spy plane photographs construction of a site in Cuba for a surface-to-air missile (SAM), a defensive weapon.

August 30 The SGA overseeing Operation Mongoose asks the CIA to prepare a list of possible targets in Cuba for sabotage.

August 30 At a press conference, President Kennedy says the Monroe Doctrine means today what it meant to Presidents James Monroe and John Quincy Adams, that is, that the United States opposes all foreign intervention in the Western Hemisphere, specifically what is happening in Cuba.

August 31 Senator Kenneth B. Keating (R-New York) warns on the Senate floor that the Soviet Union may be constructing a missile base in Cuba.

September 2 Cuba and the Soviet Union sign an agreement about military and industrial assistance: "In view of the threats of aggressive imperialist quarters with regard to Cuba, the USSR has agreed to Cuba's request for help by delivering armaments and sending technical specialists for training Cuban servicemen." The arms include medium-range nuclear missiles. The Soviet Union and Cuba have agreed that once the atomic weapons are in Cuba, the Soviet-Cuban agreement will be made public, along with the presence of the nuclear weapons, based on Cuba's right to defend itself. Premier Khrushchev wants to save the announcement for his visit to Cuba scheduled for the end of this year, after U.S. elections. (*See* January 9, 1992)

September 3 The Latin American Free Trade Association votes 7 to 4 with 2 abstentions to exclude Cuba.

September 4 White House Press Secretary Pierre Salinger releases a statement of policy about Cuba from President Kennedy. It includes an expression of concern about recent Soviet arms shipments to Cuba, a report that information received within the previous four days shows that the Soviet Union has provided Cuba with "a number of antiaircraft defense missiles," and an assurance that there is no evidence of offensive ground-to-ground missiles or other significant offensive weapons.

September 8 After U.S. pressure to break relations with Cuba or at least stop financial credit, NATO members stop financial credit.

September 10 In one of many of its hit-and-run attacks by boat, Alpha 66 shells the *San Pascual,* a Cuban steamer, and the *Newlane,* a British freighter, at a Cuban port.

September 11 The Soviet Union warns that a U.S. attack on Cuba or on Soviet ships carrying supplies to Cuba would mean war.

September 13 Knowing that Operation Mongoose calls for an October invasion of Cuba, President Kennedy nonetheless tells a press conference that Prime Minister Castro's "charges of an imminent American invasion" are a "frantic effort to bolster his regime."

September 18 Cuban Armed Forces denounce the increase of U.S. violations of Cuban air space.

September 19 NBC television shows film of Cuban exiles training under U.S. supervision in Florida and Guatemala.

September 26 The U.S. Congress passes a joint resolution giving the president the right to intervene militarily in Cuba if the United States is threatened.

September 27 Another group of CIA agents is captured. With his operatives not making any headway in Cuba, General Lansdale, as he complains years later, has not been able to establish a network inside Cuba to try to complete Operation Mongoose.

September 27 Air Force Chief of Staff Curtis LeMay receives a proposed plan for aerial bombardment of Cuba that would precede landing U.S. troops by air and water. The proposal is approved with a plan to complete preparations for such an attack by October 20.

October 2 Again tightening the embargo, the U.S. government announces new regulations, including: U.S. ports are closed to any country that allows any of its ships to transport arms to Cuba; a ship that docks in any country belonging to the socialist bloc will not be allowed to dock at any U.S. port during that voyage; U.S. aid will be unavailable to any country that allows planes or ships under its registry to transport certain materials to Cuba; shipowners involved in trade with Cuba will not be allowed to transport U.S. shipments of foreign aid supplies. No U.S. ships are allowed to be used in any trade with Cuba.

October 2 In a memo to the Joint Chiefs of Staff, Defense Secretary Robert McNamara describes situations that might require U.S. military force against Cuba, including placement of offensive weapons from the Soviet bloc in Cuba, a Cuban attack against Guantánamo Naval Base or U.S. planes or vessels outside Cuban territory, assistance by Cuba to "subversion" in other countries of the Western Hemisphere, a request for assistance by leaders of a "substantial popular uprising" in Cuba or a "decision by the President that the affairs in Cuba have reached a point inconsistent with continuing U.S. national security." The memo requests that contingency plans emphasize removal from power of Prime Minister Castro.

October 2-3 At a Hemispheric Conference, U.S. officials pressure Latin American officials to isolate Cuba in order to combat "Sino-Soviet intervention in Cuba."

October 4 At an SGA meeting, Attorney General Robert Kennedy reports that the President feels more priority should be given to sabotage and urges "massive activity" within the framework of Operation Mongoose.

October 6 Admiral Robert L. Dennison, chief of Atlantic Forces, receives a memo from Defense Secretary McNamara telling the Joint Chiefs of Staff to start putting into effect OPLAN 314 and OPLAN 316, two contingency plans for invasion of Cuba.

October 8 Speaking to the UN General Assembly, Cuban President Dorticós denounces the October 2 decision about ships trading with Cuba as an "act of war" violating the UN Charter. Anti-Castro demonstrators interrupt his speech several times.

October 8 Britain secretly agrees to a U.S. request to position supplies and equipment for an attack on Cuba at Mayaguana in the Bahamas.

October 14 A U-2 flies over western Cuba, the first Strategic Air Command (SAC) mission since authority for U-2 surveillance flights was transferred from the CIA to the Air Force on October 12.

October 15 The Cuban Ministry of Public Health with the cooperation of the mass organizations begins a national campaign to vaccinate against diphtheria, tetanus and whooping cough.

October 15 Algerian Prime Minister Ahmed Ben Bella arrives in Cuba after meeting with President Kennedy in Washington the day before. Prime Minister Castro calls this state visit an "act of courage." Eight days later, the State Department tells the Agency for International Development (AID) to suspend all economic aid to Algeria.

October 15 Analyzing U-2 photographs taken a day earlier, the CIA informs National Security Adviser McGeorge Bundy that the Soviet Union is constructing sites for intermediate-range nuclear missiles in Cuba.

October 15 A group of Cuban exiles led by Eugenio Rolando Martínez receives instructions in Florida from CIA agents for planting explosives at the Matahambre copper mines in Pinar del Río. Cuban authorities discover and thwart the plan on October 25.

October 16-22 President Kennedy and his closest advisers deliberate on what to do about Cuban sites for nuclear weapons that could be used against the United States. On October 16, Attorney General Robert Kennedy discusses the idea of using the U.S. naval base at Guantánamo in some way that would justify an invasion: "We should also think of, uh, whether there is some other way we can get involved in this through, uh, Guantánamo Bay, or something, or whether there's some ship that, you know, sink the *Maine* again or something." Tapes of at least part of these discussions are made public at the John F. Kennedy Library in Boston in 1983.

October 22 Dependents and non-essential personnel are evacuated from Guantánamo Naval Base. President Kennedy masses U.S. forces in Florida and puts them on alert around the world. At 7 p.m. Washington time, President Kennedy speaks on national television and the world learns that it is on the brink of nuclear war. The President announces that there are nuclear missile sites in Cuba and that he has ordered a naval blockade of the island to prevent deliveries of offensive weapons. He demands immediate dismantling of missile sites and withdrawal of any and all missiles. Eighty minutes before Kennedy's speech, Cuba declares a combat alarm (a higher stage in Cuba than a combat alert) and concentrates antiaircraft batteries and artillery along the Havana waterfront.

In a speech on January 1, 1984, Fidel Castro says that in 1962 "42 medium-range missiles were deployed in Cuba." In 1989 at a conference about the Missile Crisis in Moscow, Soviet officials reveal that at the time of the blockade there were 20 nuclear warheads in Cuba with 20 others on a ship that turned back because of the blockade. No missile to launch the warheads was yet operable. In addition, as a Russian general states at the 1992 conference in Havana, there were 43,000 Soviet soldiers on the island.

October 23 The Soviet Union rejects U.S. demands on the grounds that acceptance would violate Cuba's right to self-determination. The OAS meets and most members agree to prepare an invasion if U.S. demands are not met. In a speech to the Cuban people, Prime Minister Castro reaffirms Cuba's right to strengthen defenses with any weapons it chooses. He does not acknowledge the presence of nuclear missiles. He says all of Cuba's weapons are defensive and Cuba will not allow any type of inspection.

October 23 The U.S. government begins low-altitude surveillance flights over Cuba in addition to U-2 high-altitude flights.

October 24 The U.S. naval blockade around the island of Cuba takes effect at 11 a.m. Washington time.

October 26 The Soviet Union sends a message to UN Secretary General U Thant that it has ordered its merchant ships not to enter the zone of the U.S. naval blockade.

October 26 Reasoning that any U.S. attack on Cuba would involve an attack on the Soviet troops and therefore lead to thermo-nuclear war, Prime Minister Castro writes to Premier Khrushchev (these letters are published by *Granma* in 1990) that if the United States invades Cuba, the Soviet Union "should not allow the circumstances" in which the United States would be the first to use nuclear weapons. Khrushchev receives this letter October 27.

October 26-27 The White House receives two letters from Premier Khrushchev, offering to withdraw Soviet missiles from Cuba and to pledge that the Soviet Union will not interfere in the internal affairs of Turkey if the United States ends the naval blockade, pledges not to invade Cuba, and removes its nuclear missiles from Turkey.

October 27 Because U.S. overflights pose the threat of a surprise attack, the Cuban military command has ordered antiaircraft batteries to fire on planes that violate Cuban airspace, and this information is passed on to the Soviet military. Around noon, a U-2 spy plane is shot down over Cuba, killing the pilot. Although at first there are differing accounts of precisely who downed the U-2, in the 1980s officials from both Cuba and the Soviet Union report that a Soviet officer gave the command. Cuban leaders later point out that "had we had the proper weaponry," Cuba would have shot down the plane "without hesitation." (Cuba later identifies the Soviet commander as Lieutenant General G.A. Voronkov, to whom Cuba awarded the Ernesto Che Guevara Order, first degree, after the Missile Crisis ended.)

October 27 President Kennedy sends a letter to Premier Khrushchev with a proposal that the Soviet Union immediately withdraw its missiles from Cuba while the United States ends the naval blockade and pledges not to invade Cuba. This agreement will be made public. Meanwhile, Attorney General Robert Kennedy meets with Soviet Ambassador Anatoly F. Dobrynin and agrees privately that once the crisis is resolved, the United States will withdraw its Jupiter missiles from Turkey.

October 28 After days at the nuclear brink, the worst of the Missile Crisis ends when Moscow Radio broadcasts Premier Khrushchev's letter to President Kennedy accepting the October 27 proposal. Concerning U.S. aggression against Cuba, Khrushchev's letter says, "I regard with respect and trust the statement you made in your message of 27 October 1962 that there would be no attack, no invasion of Cuba, and not only on the part of the United States, but also on the part of other nations of the Western Hemisphere, as you said in your same message. Then the motives which induced us to render assistance of such a kind to Cuba disappear." Without consultation with Cuba, the Soviet Union begins dismantling the missile sites and withdrawing its missiles. At this point Prime Minister Castro asserts Cuba's position with a demand that the U.S. government end five practices: the embargo, subversive activities inside Cuba, armed attacks against Cuba, violation of Cuban air and naval space, and occupation of Cuban territory at Guantánamo.

October 29   The U.S. government rejects all of Cuba's demands, stressing that removal of the missiles and verification have to precede any negotiations. The U.S. government continues to press for removal of IL-28 bombers from Cuba.

October 30   The SGA orders a halt to all the sabotage activities of Operation Mongoose. However, during the Missile Crisis, William Harvey (*see* November 30, 1961) has continued to dispatch sabotage teams into Cuba so that three six-man teams are presently deployed on the island (*see* November 5 and 8).

October 30   UN Secretary General U Thant arrives in Cuba. U.S. naval and aerial surveillance is suspended during two days of discussion between him and Cuban officials.

November 1   Cuba rejects a Soviet proposal for international inspection and turns down U.S. aerial inspection as proposed by Secretary General U Thant, stating: "...the Soviet Union has the right to remove the weapons that are theirs from Cuban soil, and we Cubans respect that decision. Nonetheless, we have certain disagreements with that decision, but we will discuss those differences with the Soviet leaders in private. It is important to remember that the Soviet Union has given us much help." Cuban leaders regard this refusal to allow inspection plus Cuba's five demands (*see* October 28) as the "20th-century Baraguá."

November 2   President Kennedy announces that the missile sites are being dismantled. However, Kennedy insists that the U.S. government does not plan to end its anti-Cuban political and economic policies even if all offensive weapons are removed.

November 2   Maintaining that the U.S. government demands inspection in order to "humiliate" Cuba, Prime Minister Castro declares: "We do not accept inspection demands; the Soviet promise to withdraw is serious enough. What right has the United States to ask us to submit to inspection? Cuba is opposed to the United States' pledge of 'no invasion' in exchange for the establishment of a means for inspection because the United States has no right to invade Cuba and we cannot negotiate on the basis of a promise that a crime will not be committed."

November 2-26   After talking with U.S. officials in the United States, Soviet Deputy Prime Minister Anastas Mikoyan visits

Cuba and then returns to New York for more discussion with UN Secretary General U Thant and U.S. officials, including President Kennedy and Secretary of State Dean Rusk. Later, Cuban officials state that one outcome of this visit is an agreement with the Soviet Union that a Soviet military contingent will remain on the island.

November 5 In Pinar del Río province, Cuban officials arrest Miguel A. Orozco Crespo, leader of a group of CIA operatives infiltrated into Cuba October 20. Admitting to at least 25 missions in Cuba during 1962, Orozco tells Cuban security officers that his CIA overseers in Florida are Rip Robertson and Robert Wall. He provides information to Cuba about CIA operations on the island.

November 8 One of the CIA teams in Cuba (*see* October 30) blows up its industrial target.

November 15 UN Secretary General U Thant receives a letter from Prime Minister Castro declaring that planes which violate Cuban air space will do so at the risk of being destroyed. The order is to take effect November 17. President Kennedy responds on November 16 by suspending low-level flights while continuing the U-2 flights out of range of Cuban weapons.

November 16 Responding in the UN General Assembly to a Brazilian initiative, supported by the U.S. government, for the denuclearization of Latin America, Carlos Lechuga, who became Cuba's UN ambassador on October 31, says the nuclear powers should guarantee no use of nuclear weapons in Latin America and close their military bases there. He points out the illogic of allowing the U.S. government to have a base at Guantánamo on Cuban territory while Cuba is not allowed to have a base belonging to a friendly country for its defense.

November 16 At Onslow Beach in North Carolina, U.S. military forces stage a practice invasion of Cuba.

November 19 Prime Minister Castro informs UN Secretary General U Thant that Cuba does not object to removal of the Soviet-owned IL-28 bombers from its territory.

November 20 President Kennedy lifts the naval blockade after being assured by the Soviet Union that the IL-28s will be withdrawn from Cuba in 30 days. Kennedy does not insist on removal of MiG fighters and accepts the fact that some Soviet trainers will remain in Cuba. The order to lift the blockade takes effect at 6:45 p.m. but the official end to the naval "quarantine" takes place on the following day.

November 25 President Kennedy demands that there be international inspection of Cuba to see whether the threat to U.S. security has been removed.

November 27 Cuba agrees to allow international inspection if the United States will allow the same for all the bases where Cuban exiles are being trained on U.S. territory.

December 4 As hit-and-run attacks continue unabated, an exile organization called the Second Front of the Escambray fires from two gunboats at the port of Caibarién on the northern coast of Cuba in Villa Clara province.

December 12 Premier Khrushchev sends a letter to President Kennedy in which he asks the United States to honor its agreement not to invade Cuba as the Soviet Union has honored its promise to withdraw missiles. During December, a Soviet military brigade arrives in Cuba to train Cuban forces and help defend the island against invasion (*see* September 9, 1992).

December 23-24 In the first stage of an agreement with the United States, Cuba releases 1,113 Bay of Pigs invaders in exchange for $53 million in medicine and baby food. The former prisoners are flown to Homestead Air Force Base in Florida. Cuba keeps nine of the invaders in prison, releasing the final one in 1986. An additional part of the agreement is that Cuba will allow other Cubans to leave for the United States.

December 29 President and Mrs Kennedy meet the Bay of Pigs invaders at the Orange Bowl in Miami. The former prisoners shout "Guerra! Guerra!" and Jacqueline Kennedy, speaking in Spanish, praises their courage. The President receives their Brigade 2506 flag and promises it will fly over "a free Havana." But in 1976 Bay of Pigs veterans have to hire a lawyer to get their flag back from storage in a museum basement.

1963

January Although Operation Mongoose itself is being dismantled (*see* October 30, 1962), the CIA unit involved in the operation, Task Force W, continues to carry out covert activities against Cuba. When Desmond Fitzgerald replaces William Harvey as head of the task force, he asks his assistant to investigate whether a seashell could be rigged to explode in an area where Castro goes skin diving. Another assassination plot envisions sending Prime Minister Castro a gift of a diving suit with a fungus to cause chronic skin disease and a bacillus in the breathing apparatus to cause tuberculosis. These are described in the 1975 interim report of the Senate Select Committee on Assassinations.

January 11 and 24 Counterrevolutionaries kill an eleven-year-old in one attack and two children in another.

January 21 During a television interview, Secretary of State Dean Rusk says, "The President has said that if Cuba does not become a base for aggression, he will not initiate or permit aggression in the Caribbean. But this also means, as he said, that we will not abandon other measures directed to insuring that Cuba not be a source of infection for the rest of the hemisphere."

February In addition to the ongoing activities of Task Force W, the Defense Department's various branches continue to prepare contingency plans for overthrowing the Cuban government.

February 6 Tightening the embargo, President Kennedy orders that shipments financed by the U.S. government not be transported on any foreign merchant ships that have docked at a Cuban port on or after January 1, 1963.

February 13 Two fishing boats are attacked in Cuban territorial waters, wounding two brothers. This is only one of many such raids in this and following months. Some boats are shelled, some hijacked to Florida. Cuba's Armed Forces Ministry files many reports of U.S. warships harassing Cuban fishing vessels. For example, Cuba reports that a U.S. destroyer pursued and attacked a Cuban schooner at the mouth of Guantánamo Bay.

February 20 The U.S. government charges that Cuban MiGs fired rockets at an unarmed shrimp boat but without injuring anyone. Cuba says the jets flew by the boat but did not fire.

February 21 The Cuban Navy recaptures two hijacked fishing boats, now loaded with weapons to be used against Cuba. Eight of 10 would-be infiltrators are captured.

March 17 An armed boat fires on a Soviet ship docked at a port in north central Cuba. Alpha 66 claims credit for this and another attack that wounds 12 Soviet soldiers. The Soviet Union protests to the United States. At a press conference, President Kennedy says these attacks serve no useful purpose. When the U.S. ship *Floridian* is fired on by two jets a few days later, Cuba quickly apologizes, calling it an error.

March 26 At the Caibarién port, a gunboat attacks and sinks the Soviet ship *Baku* that is loaded with sugar. The Soviet Union and Cuba protest once again.

March 28 A Cuban jet fires at but does not strike a boat flying the U.S. flag about 50 miles north of Cuba. The Cuban government apologizes on the following day.

March 29 President Kennedy orders a halt to exile raids against Cuba. He specifically orders Antonio Veciana of Alpha 66 confined to Dade County, Florida, along with a number of other Cuban exiles. However, it becomes obvious during the coming weeks that exile raids promoted by CIA agents continue whether or not they are sanctioned by the White House.

April President Kennedy ends financial aid of between $100,000 to $200,000 a month to José Miró Cardona and the Revolutionary Council. Miró resigns as head of the Revolutionary Council, charging the United States has broken its promise of a new invasion. U.S. officials deny that such a promise was ever made.

April 17 Reporting on the status of the embargo, Secretary of State Dean Rusk informs President Kennedy that Honduras, Liberia,

Panama and Turkey have barred their ships from transporting cargoes to and from Cuba; West Germany has prohibited ships under its registry from shipping cargoes between Cuba and the Soviet Union; but Britain maintains there is no legal basis for such action.

April 24 In an interview by ABC television (broadcast in the United States May 10), Prime Minister Castro says the exchange worked out with the United States (*see* December 23, 1962) and U.S. efforts to stop raids against Cuba are two steps toward better relations. He says U.S. actions toward Cuba after the revolution forced Cuba to turn to the Soviet Union for help. What the interviewer, Lisa Howard, calls Soviet "troops" in Cuba, Castro calls "technicians." He says the presence of these technicians might be discussed among Cuba, the United States and the Soviet Union but that the United States "wants to discuss it with the Soviet Union without us."

April 25 Secretary of Defense Robert McNamara informs President Kennedy that the last Jupiter missile in Turkey will be removed within a few days (*see* October 27, 1962).

April 27-May 23 Prime Minister Castro visits the Soviet Union. A joint communiqué states that if there were an attack against Cuba "in violation of the commitment entered into by the President of the United States," the Soviet Union would offer Cuba "all the means at her disposal."

May 7 Emilio Víctor Llufrio Bofill, a captured leader of a group called "Triple A," appears on Cuban television to discuss CIA-sponsored plots.

May 10 The Associated Press reports from Miami that a new effort is underway to form a single Cuban exile organization capable of overthrowing the Cuban government. Exile sources say the plan has been discussed with CIA agents. AP identifies Bay of Pigs veteran Enrique Ruiz Williams, reportedly a friend of Attorney General Robert Kennedy, as a leader of the attempt.

May 23 Launching its first internationalist health brigade, Cuba sends 56 medical personnel in response to a request for help from the Algerian government.

June 19 President Kennedy authorizes a new program to foment rebellion from within Cuba.

June 30 A group of U.S. students, accepting an invitation from a student group in Cuba, defies the U.S. travel ban and arrives in Havana via Prague. The United States withdraws their passports when they return.

July Cuban exiles are staging raids against Cuba from a base in Nicaragua.

July 3 The OAS votes 14 to 1 (Chile) with four abstentions (Brazil, Haiti, Mexico and Venezuela) for a hemispheric ban on travel to Cuba and closer cooperation on security. (Bolivia is not present.) The United States is disappointed at the lack of unity, having hoped to get a ban on international communist meetings in the Western Hemisphere. Disunity forces this idea to be postponed for the time being.

July 8 The Kennedy Administration tightens the embargo and at the same time makes most travel to Cuba illegal for U.S. citizens. Using its authority under the Trading With the Enemy Act of 1917, the Treasury Department revokes Cuban Import Regulations and replaces them with Cuban Assets Control Regulations, which implement the essential elements of the embargo. The Trading With the Enemy Act allows the president to prohibit economic transactions between the United States and foreign countries or foreign nationals during time of war or national emergency. The "national emergency" pertinent to these Regulations was declared by President Truman in 1950 at the time of the Korean War because of the "world conquest by communist imperialism." The Regulations prohibit unlicensed commercial or financial transactions between Cuba and U.S. citizens, unlicensed import of or dealing abroad in merchandise of Cuban origin by U.S. citizens, and import of goods made in third countries with Cuban materials. All Cuban-owned assets in the United States are frozen, including an estimated $33 million of Cuban assets in U.S. banks (*see* June 23, 1991). Nobody may participate in unlicensed transactions with Cuba in U.S. dollars. This prohibits spending money for travel expenses inside Cuba or for Cuban airline tickets. These restrictions increase the difficulty of resolving the issue of compensation for land expropriated by Cuba because they make it difficult if not impossible to conduct financial transactions with Cuba.

July 11 State Department representative Richard Phillips says the U.S. government wants Britain, Canada, Mexico and Spain to increase isolation of Cuba in regard to commercial air flights.

July 12 Canada's minister of commerce says Canada does not plan to modify commercial policy toward Cuba.

July 26 Speaking on the tenth anniversary of the attack on the Moncada Army Barracks, Prime Minister Castro says a revolutionary must understand the changes in the correlation of forces that have taken place in the world. Crucial to this change, he says, is the deterrent force of the Soviet Union against U.S. use of atomic weapons to threaten liberation movements around the world.

August 5 Perhaps influenced by the Missile Crisis of 1962, the United States signs the Limited Nuclear Test Ban Treaty with the Soviet Union, banning testing of nuclear weapons in the air, on the ground and underwater.

August 15 A plane bombs a sugar mill in Camagüey. These attacks continue with bombings of oil storage tanks and shellings of an electricity plant and a factory. Homes are damaged by bombs, including one where a man is killed and three of his four sons wounded. According to CIA documents released years later (*see* June 23, 1989), Cuban exile Orlando Bosch takes part in these bombing raids.

September 23 William Attwood, an adviser for the U.S. delegation to the United Nations, tells Cuban UN Ambassador Carlos Lechuga that he plans to request official U.S. authorization for talking with Prime Minister Castro about the possibility of a rapprochement between Cuba and the United States. Ambassador Lechuga responds that he will inform his government and await its decision. Some Kennedy Administration officials consider Attwood's proposal risky with an election coming up in 1964, but he is encouraged to continue his contacts with Ambassador Lechuga.

September 25 Cuba establishes the world's first Solidarity Committee with the Democratic Republic of Vietnam (Hanoi).

October The Special Group, which has replaced the Special Group (Augmented) or SGA, authorizes more covert operations in Cuba.

October 4   Cuba's Second Agrarian Reform Law nationalizes all land holdings of more than five *caballerías* (a *caballería* is 33 acres).

October 21   Cuban soldiers capture three CIA infiltrators in Pinar del Río.

October 24   As a result of William Attwood's continuing efforts to facilitate a rapprochement with Cuba, President Kennedy meets at the White House with Jean Daniel, a French journalist who is on his way to Havana. Kennedy does not give Daniel a formal message but asks him to talk with Castro and then meet again with Kennedy.

November 4   National Security Adviser McGeorge Bundy tells William Attwood that the President is more favorable to negotiations with Cuba than the State Department is.

November 18   Speaking by phone, René Vallejo, an aide to Prime Minister Castro, tells William Attwood that Castro will send UN Ambassador Lechuga instructions for discussing with Attwood an agenda for a meeting between Attwood and Castro. When informed about that conversation, McGeorge Bundy tells Attwood that, once there is an agenda, President Kennedy will meet with Attwood about what he should say to Castro.

November 18   President Kennedy visits Florida. Security is especially strict because of threats against him by anti-Castro Cuban exiles.

November 20   Che Guevara comments on the coup in South Vietnam at the first of this month when President Ngo Dinh Diem and his brother, secret police chief Ngo Dinh Nhu, were assassinated: "...once again the United States demonstrated what happens to puppets who do not obey orders."

November 22   President Kennedy is assassinated in Dallas and Lyndon Baines Johnson becomes president. Lee Harvey Oswald is arrested. Within hours of the murder, there is an attempt to blame it on Cuba. In Havana, French journalist Jean Daniel is with Prime Minister Castro when they hear of the assassination (*see* October 24); according to Daniel, Castro says repeatedly, "Es una mala noticia" ("This is bad news"). Instead of being able to report to President Kennedy on his conversation with Castro, Daniel later meets with McGeorge Bundy.

November 22 CIA agent Nestor Sánchez is in Paris delivering to Rolando Cubela a poison pen to be used for assassinating Prime Minister Castro when the two conspirators receive the news of the U.S. president's assassination.

November 23 In a radio-TV address, Prime Minister Castro says the assassination of President Kennedy "can only benefit those ultra-rightist and ultra-reactionary sectors" in the United States. Responding to the attempt to blame it on Cuba, Castro points out that assassinations are not a "correct weapon of struggle," adding that "it just so happens" that this murder occurred "precisely at a moment when Kennedy was being severely criticized by those who considered his Cuban policy weak."

November 24 Lee Harvey Oswald is shot to death by Jack Ruby while in the custody of the Dallas police. On July 13, 1964, at the Warren Commission hearings on the assassination of President Kennedy, Earle Cabell, brother of CIA Deputy Director Charles Cabell who was fired by Kennedy, testifies that as mayor of Dallas in November 1963 he had no responsibility for the Dallas police department.

December 13 Having decided that it is untenable to prosecute U.S. students for traveling to Cuba (*see* June 30), Attorney General Robert Kennedy proposes to remove the ban on travel, but the State Department opposes the idea.

December 23 National Security Adviser Bundy tells his staff that President Johnson does not want to appear conciliatory toward Cuba because he will be running for president in the 1964 election. Bundy later tells William Attwood that his efforts to negotiate with Prime Minister Castro will have to wait.

December 28-29 During a visit to President Johnson's ranch in Texas, Ludwig Erhard, the West German chancellor, agrees to join the economic embargo against Cuba.

1964

January 7 A British firm, Leyland Motor Corporation, announces the sale of 450 buses to Cuba. The U.S. State Department condemns the sale because it undermines efforts to isolate Cuba and weaken its economy. The British minister of commerce replies, on the same day, that British firms are free to sell their products to whomever they choose. He notes that Britain has never boycotted Cuba and has no reason to change that policy. He points out that buses are not strategic matériel and that the United States sells wheat to the Soviet Union. Terms of the sale extend a five-year credit to Cuba for the purchase with an option to buy 1,050 more buses in 1965-68.

January 10 Agitating for a total embargo of trade by the OAS with Cuba, Secretary of State Rusk says, "Those countries which, for commercial reasons, supply Cuba, especially with goods critical to the Cuban economy, are prejudicing the efforts of the countries of this hemisphere to reduce the threat from Cuba."

January 13-23 Prime Minister Castro makes a state visit to Moscow and concludes a sugar agreement: the Soviet Union will purchase two million tons in 1965, three million in 1966, four million in 1967, and after that five million annually through 1970, all at prices favorable to Cuba.

February 2 The United States seizes four Cuban fishing boats with 38 Cuban crew members, saying the boats were within 1.5 miles of the Florida coast.

February 6 In reprisal for the seizure of the fishing boats, Cuba shuts off the normal water supply to the U.S. naval base at

Guantánamo, stating the suspension will continue until the United States releases the 38 Cubans.

February 7 President Johnson orders the Defense Department to discharge any of the 2,500 Cuban civilian employees at Guantánamo Naval Base who do not choose to live there or spend their earned dollars there. Water shuttles operate between Jamaica and the base. Four days later 700 Cuban workers are fired. A desalinization plant that can process more than a million gallons of water a day is built on the base.

February 12-14 When British Prime Minister Sir Alec Douglas-Home meets with President Johnson in Washington, they do not mention in their joint communiqué their disagreement about British trade with Cuba. At a press conference, the Prime Minister confirms that the British position remains unchanged: "We in Britain have to trade... we do not believe in boycotts."

February 18 As a penalty for continued trading with Cuba, the United States curtails aid to five countries: Britain, France, Morocco, Spain and Yugoslavia.

February 19 The captains of the four fishing boats seized February 2 are convicted and Cuba pays their fines; the other 25 captives are acquitted; seven minors have already returned to Cuba; two of the Cubans ask for U.S. asylum.

February 20 The fishing boat incident ends as 29 Cubans leave Florida for Cuba in their boats.

February 20 The U.S. Court of Appeals for the Fifth Circuit voids the lower court conviction of African-American journalist William J. Worthy Jr. for violating the passport law by traveling to Cuba and returning without a passport (*see* July 1961). The decision declares that the federal law prohibiting a citizen from leaving or entering the United States without a valid passport is unconstitutional.

February 25 Asked why it is U.S. policy to trade with the Soviet Union but not with Cuba, Secretary of State Rusk replies that the United States regards the "Castro regime" as "temporary" and expects "the Cuban people to regain their freedom and rejoin the inter-American system."

March 13 In a statement to the Senate Foreign Relations Committee, Secretary of State Rusk spells out the objectives of the embargo: "1. To reduce Castro's will and ability to export subversion and violence to other American states; 2. To make it plain to the people of Cuba that Castro's regime cannot serve their interests; 3. To demonstrate to the peoples of the American Republics that communism has no future in the Western Hemisphere; and 4. To increase the cost to the Soviet Union of maintaining a communist outpost in the Western Hemisphere." Rusk reveals continuing concern about the allies' trade with Cuba: "We are disturbed when other free world countries supply products that cannot help but increase Castro's capacity for mischief." Referring to the British sale of buses to Cuba, Rusk says those buses "would almost double the public transport of Havana."

March 25 Senator William Fulbright (D-Arkansas), chair of the Senate Foreign Relations Committee, urges that U.S. foreign policy toward Cuba, Panama and the Soviet Union be changed. He says the United States has three options regarding Cuba: invasion, which is not workable; political and economic boycott, which is a failure; and the "acceptance" of the "Castro regime" as a "distasteful nuisance but not an intolerable danger" as long as the countries of the Western Hemisphere are prepared to "meet their obligations of collective defense under the Río Treaty." President Johnson disagrees with Fulbright on Cuba and Panama.

March 25 In a speech at the UN Conference on Trade and Development (UNCTAD) in Geneva, Che Guevara explains how certain international institutions are "essentially at the service of United States imperialism." He says, "The International Monetary Fund [IMF] is the watchdog of the dollar in the capitalist camp; the International Bank for Reconstruction and Development [World Bank] is the instrument for the infiltration of United States capital into the underdeveloped world, and the Inter-American Development Bank performs the same sorry function on the American continent." Out of this UNCTAD conference is born the Group of 77 as a caucus for developing countries.

March 31 A U.S. naval task force assembles in the Caribbean and heads for Brazil as requested by U.S. Ambassador to Brazil Lincoln Gordon. On the following day, a military coup overthrows João Goulart, a civilian who was recently elected president. In 1976 Gordon says his request for U.S. intervention took place in the context of the Cold War and revolutionary activities by Fidel Castro. Brazil's military regime soon breaks relations with Cuba.

April 7 President Johnson tells the Special Group to end CIA participation in raids against Cuba.

April 19 Charging that U-2 flights over Cuba are violating Cuban air space, Prime Minister Castro orders ground-to-air missile crews to be ready if the flights continue.

April 20 The State Department responds that the overflights are necessary "to avoid the deception" that occurred when Soviet missile bases were built in 1962. The U.S. government maintains that the flights substitute for on-ground inspection to which the Soviet Union agreed during the Missile Crisis. Cuba never agreed to such inspection.

April 23 Cuban Foreign Minister Raúl Roa García informs the United Nations of 1,181 aggressions by the United States against Cuba.

May 10 Cuba establishes diplomatic relations with the Congo (Brazzaville), the former French colony that becomes, in 1969, the People's Republic of the Congo and, in 1992, Republic of Congo (not to be confused with the Congo [Kinshasa], the former Belgium colony that becomes Zaire in 1971).

May 13 In Oriente province a boat shells a sugar mill and destroys 70,000 sacks of sugar. Many of these hit-and-run attacks are directed from 1964 to 1975 by Paul Lionel Edward Helliwell, a CIA agent working out of Andros Island in the Bahamas. Helliwell, who was the paymaster for the Bay of Pigs invaders, sets up and basically controls Castle Bank and Trust (Bahamas) Ltd. and Mercantile Bank and Trust Company, both used by the CIA to finance anti-Cuban operations.

May 14 The U.S. Commerce Department issues an order requiring export licenses for the sale of food and medicines to Cuba. U.S. officials claim to be puzzled by Cuban efforts to purchase $10 million to $15 million worth of medicines, which they consider more than necessary.

May 29 The Cuban Armed Forces report that near Sancti Spíritus in Las Villas province a large number of brilliant objects were seen falling from a high altitude. They proved to be globes of various sizes that broke up on contact with the earth, leaving a gelatinous substance that dissolved, similar to the culture broth used for bacteria.

June 2   Prime Minister Castro denounces the use of this unknown chemical on Cuban territory.

June 12   Amid continuing attempts at undermining the Cuban government, Armed Forces Minister Raúl Castro reports that U.S. troops at the Guantánamo Naval Base alone have been responsible for 1,651 acts of provocation since November 1962.

June 12-August 12   Defying the U.S. travel ban, 84 U.S. citizens tour Cuba, arriving via Paris, Prague, Shannon and Gander. On the orders of Secretary of State Dean Rusk, their passports are withdrawn when they return (*see* September 22).

June 19   A plane that bombed a sugar mill is shot down in Las Villas province.

June 29   Juana Castro, sister of Fidel and Raúl Castro, defects. The *New York Times* later reports that Washington sources say she has been on the CIA payroll since 1960.

July 6   The *New York Times* publishes an interview with Prime Minister Castro by Richard Eder, in which Castro continues his willingness to negotiate differences with the U.S. government. Among other things, Castro says Cuba would withhold material support from Latin American revolutionaries if the United States and its allies would agree to end material support for subversive activity against Cuba.

July 7   The U.S. State Department rejects Prime Minister Castro's overture, repeating its position that Cuba would have to make fundamental changes prior to negotiations.

July 19   Frontier Guard Ramón López Peña is killed by U.S. soldiers at the Guantánamo Naval Base.

July 26   The OAS votes 15 to 4 for "mandatory termination of all trade and diplomatic relations" with Cuba following an international U.S.-inspired campaign. Bolivia, Chile, Mexico and Uruguay, the four countries in opposition, are the only OAS members that continue to have diplomatic relations with Cuba.

July 26   Cuba's response to the OAS is the "Declaration of Santiago," saying the OAS has no moral or legal basis of any kind for "judging and sanctioning" Cuba and the declaration is a "shameless call for counterrevolution." Nonetheless, in his annual speech commemorating the 1953 attack on the Moncada

Barracks, Prime Minister Castro again talks about rapprochement with the United States. Once more, the State Department dismisses the suggestion.

August 3 Mexico announces that it will maintain its ties with Cuba despite the OAS embargo.

August 12 Chile breaks diplomatic relations with Cuba.

August 15 In a speech at a workers' rally in Havana, Che Guevara mentions that Vietnam has a brigade known as "Playa Girón" (the Bay of Pigs invasion site), a name that has become a symbol of resistance to U.S. imperialism.

September 7 Launching his election campaign against Republican Barry Goldwater, President Johnson says that "in Cuba and in the waters around Vietnam" (a reference to the Gulf of Tonkin incidents), the Democratic Administration "proved that we would stand firm in the defense of freedom."

September 8 Uruguay breaks diplomatic relations with Cuba.

September 22 A U.S. grand jury indicts nine U.S. citizens on charges of conspiring to organize and promote a trip to Cuba by 84 U.S. citizens who traveled to Cuba in June without permission from the U.S. government (*see* June 12). One of those indicted is Levi Laub, already under indictment for a trip to Cuba the previous summer.

September 27 After 10 months of an investigation into the assassination of President Kennedy, the Warren Commission issues its final report, including a finding that there is no evidence of any Cuban government role.

October 5-11 The Second Summit Conference of the Movement of Nonaligned Countries meets in Cairo and issues a final communiqué that includes a demand that the United States cease its occupation of Cuban territory at Guantánamo.

October 14-15 Premier Khrushchev is ousted in the Soviet Union. Aleksei N. Kosygin replaces him and Leonid I. Brezhnev becomes head of the Communist Party.

December 11 Che Guevara addresses the UN General Assembly in New York. He explains Cuba's attitude about peaceful coexistence: "There cannot be peaceful coexistence only among the powerful if we are to ensure world peace. Peaceful coexistence must be exercised among all states." He condemns the U.S. war against Vietnam and attacks against Cambodia from bases in

South Vietnam. He expresses Cuba's support for struggles of self-determination, including in Cyprus, "so-called Portuguese Guinea" (Guinea-Bissau), Angola, Mozambique, "so-called British Guiana" (Guyana), Southern Rhodesia (Zimbabwe), Southwest Africa (Namibia), and by Arabs in Palestine. He champions the struggle of Puerto Rican nationalists for independence and of the peoples of Guadeloupe and Martinique for autonomy. He calls on the United Nations to do something about the racist situation in South Africa which leads to "murder with impunity." He speaks particularly of the Congo (later Zaire), asking, "How can one forget how the hope that Patrice Lumumba placed in the United Nations was betrayed?" After describing the UN role in the Congo, he says that "free men of the world must be prepared to avenge the crime committed" there. He calls for admission of China to the United Nations and an international conference to arrange complete nuclear disarmament. Turning to Cuba itself, Guevara demands an end to U.S. aggression, including the embargo, the covert war, and U.S. military occupation of Cuban territory at Guantánamo. From outside the United Nations, Guillermo and Ignacio Novo Sampol, two brothers who are members of the Cuban Nationalist Movement (CNM), fire a bazooka at the General Assembly building as a protest against Guevara's presence.

December 21 The U.S. government advises Spain that increasing trade with Cuba could jeopardize the U.S. aid that Spain receives.

1965

January 26 Four CIA infiltrators are captured, among them Eloy Gutiérrez Menoyo, a founder of the exile organization Alpha 66 in October 1961. His team entered Cuba on December 28, 1964. He is tried and sentenced to 30 years in prison. Gutiérrez Menoyo, born in Spain, was part of the Rebel Army that fought against Batista. Breaking with the new government, he left Cuba in January 1961 for exile in the United States.

February 6 Four more infiltrators are captured. Appearing on television, they tell of how they were recruited by the CIA and trained in Nicaragua. Capture of these CIA-trained teams continues to be a common event.

February 26 Che Guevara, at the Economic Seminar of Afro-Asian Solidarity in Algeria, gives his last public speech. He says mutually beneficial trade cannot be based on prices "imposed on underdeveloped countries" by "the law of value and unequal international trade relations."

March-April Che Guevara disappears and rumors fly regarding his fate. A favorite one in some circles is that he has been killed or imprisoned in Cuba. On April 20 Prime Minister Castro tells reporters, "Major Ernesto Che Guevara will be found where he is most useful to the revolution."

April 25 Che Guevara leaves Cuba. He arrives in the Congo (Kinshasa) — later Zaire — in May. Soon after his arrival, 200 Cuban troops join him to fight against the regime of Moise Tshombe, but the rebels are not able to defeat Tshombe's mercenary forces backed by Belgium and the United States. Guevara remains in the Congo (Kinshasa) until late 1965 (Joseph

D. Mobutu — later Mobutu Sese Seko — takes power in November). Before returning to Cuba, Guevara travels to Tanzania and Eastern Europe.

April 28 When a popular movement in the Dominican Republic attempts to restore to office President Juan Bosch, who had been elected and then ousted in a coup, President Johnson sends more than 20,000 troops to quell the movement. Johnson says he is intervening to prevent the formation of another Cuba in the Western Hemisphere.

May 3 In a surprising opinion by Chief Justice Earl Warren in *Zemel* v. *Rusk*, the Supreme Court declines to compel the State Department to validate a passport for travel to Cuba (*see* January 16, 1961). In 1978, Congress remedies this by legislating that there should be no geographic limitations for passports except in time of war or other danger to the traveler.

May 6 Cuban authorities arrest Lawrence K. Lunt, a U.S. citizen who has worked for U.S. intelligence agencies since he moved to Cuba in 1956.

Mid-1965 Rafael Moracén and three other Cubans begin training and fighting alongside guerrillas of the People's Movement for the Liberation of Angola (MPLA) based in Cabinda, Angola. This alliance between Cuba and the MPLA later becomes an important factor in U.S.-Cuban relations.

August 6 Jorge Risquet Valdés departs from Cuba with a battalion of Cuban troops to go to the aid of the Congo (Brazzaville) threatened by the Congo (Kinshasa) and to increase aid to the MPLA, which is headquartered in Brazzaville.

August 26 U.S. Ambassador to Spain Angier Biddle Duke tells a group of Spanish businesspeople of U.S. disappointment that Spain is contributing to the Cuban economy by continuing to trade with Cuba.

September 28 At a rally in Havana, Prime Minister Castro announces that Cubans who wish to leave for the United States may depart from the port of Camarioca beginning October 10.

October 3 Signing a new immigration law, President Johnson says, "I declare... to the people of Cuba that those who seek refuge here in America will find it." He will ask Congress for supplementary funds of $12,600,000 to use for this influx.

October 3 The new Communist Party of Cuba (PCC) is formally proclaimed with Prime Minister Castro as First Secretary. In 1959 there were three main revolutionary groups: the July 26 Movement, the Popular Socialist (Communist) Party and the Revolutionary Directorate. They agreed to unify in 1961 as the Integrated Revolutionary Organizations (ORI). In 1962, the ORI evolved into the United Party of the Socialist Revolution (PURS), which becomes the PCC.

October 3 Prime Minister Castro reads on television a farewell letter he received from Che Guevara in April, with the time of disclosure left to his discretion for security reasons. The letter explains, "Other nations of the world call for my modest efforts." It goes on to say, "If my final hour finds me under other skies, my last thought will be of this people and especially of you."

October 10 A boatlift begins to take Cubans from Camarioca to the United States. When this becomes a nuisance for the U.S. Coast Guard, the United States, through the Swiss Embassy, proposes an airlift.

November 3 Cuba halts the Camarioca boatlift. More than 3,000, perhaps as many as 5,000, Cubans have left. On November 6, Cuba and the United States formally agree to start an airlift for Cubans who want to go to the United States. These flights transport more than 200,000 Cubans before ending in 1973.

November 18 President Johnson sends a letter to John W. Gardner, Secretary of Health, Education and Welfare, supporting federal cooperation with Miami in handling the new wave of Cuban immigrants.

December Che Guevara returns secretly to Cuba and begins preparations for a guerrilla expedition in Bolivia.

1966

January 2 Prime Minister Castro explains that Cuba's migration policy is to permit all those who want to leave Cuba to do so.

January 13-15 At Cuba's initiative, the First Tricontinental Congress meets in Havana to organize a united front of liberation movements across three continents: the Organization of Solidarity with the Peoples of Africa, Asia and Latin America (OSPAAAL).

January 16 The Latin American participants in the Tricontinental Conference form the Latin American Solidarity Organization (LASO), which will be based in Havana.

March 1 Rolando Cubela is arrested, tried, convicted and sentenced on March 9 to 25 years in prison for trying to assassinate Prime Minister Castro in a plot masterminded by Manuel Artime.

May Extending the U.S. embargo, Congress outlaws food shipments to any country that sells or ships strategic or nonstrategic goods to Cuba except for certain circumstances in which the President may allow shipments of medical supplies and nonstrategic goods.

May 5 A Federal District Court dismisses the indictment against Levi Laub for organizing travel to Cuba. The U.S. government appeals to the Supreme Court.

May 21 Luis Ramírez López, a frontier guard at Guantánamo, is shot to death, and Cuba's Armed Forces Ministry charges that the gunfire came from the U.S. naval base at Guantánamo. The Ministry says there was sporadic rifle fire from the base for about two hours. The U.S. Defense Department at first flatly denies the shooting but later says it is investigating.

June 1 A CIA agent is captured while trying to infiltrate in Pinar del Río. Hit-and-run attacks by boats and hijackings of boats and planes, sometimes killing people, continue.

June 11 Three U.S. military planes violate Cuban air space.

September 29 A plane bombs a thermoelectric plant under construction and other facilities in Camagüey.

October 31 President Dorticós and other Cuban officials arrive in Hanoi where Ho Chi Minh greets them.

November 2 President Johnson signs into law the Cuban Adjustment Act, which makes U.S. policy toward Cubans an exception to general migration laws. Any Cuban who has reached U.S. territory since January 1, 1959, will be eligible for permanent residency after two years of being present in the United States. This enables some 123,000 Cubans to apply immediately for permanent resident status.

November 4 Having left Cuba in late October, Che Guevara, in disguise, arrives in Bolivia by way of Europe. On November 7, he begins a daily journal of his campaign to organize a revolution in Bolivia. Accompanied by Cuban and Bolivian guerrillas, Guevara aims to establish a revolutionary base, not only for the liberation of Bolivia but for all of Latin America.

November 12 In a statement released as he signs the Food for Peace Act, President Johnson says there are provisions in the Act which cause him concern, especially the preclusion of food aid to countries that trade with Cuba or North Vietnam. He emphasizes that he opposes trade with either country but believes the president should have "flexibility to use food aid to further the full range of our important national objectives."

December 29 U.S. pilot Everett Jackson is shot down and captured after dropping weapons and espionage equipment in Las Villas province.

1967

January 5 Enrique González Rodríguez, alias El Flaco, is captured as he tries to infiltrate in Las Villas province.

January 10 The Supreme Court upholds the Federal District Court decision (*see* May 5, 1966) in *United States* v. *Laub*, legalizing travel to Cuba for U.S. citizens as long as they follow Treasury Department regulations regarding the exchange of money. (*See* July 8, 1963)

February 14 At a regional meeting of Latin American countries at Tlatelolco, a section of Mexico City, Cuba does not join in the signing of a treaty that bans production, use or storage of nuclear arms in Latin America and the Caribbean. Cuba argues that the treaty gives a monopoly on nuclear weapons to the superpowers and especially to the U.S. government.

March 14 Following the *Laub* decision, the State Department revokes Public Notice 179 of January 16, 1961, and issues a new Public Notice that restricts "travel to, in or through Cuba," saying such travel would impair the conduct of U.S. foreign affairs. The Notice continues the policy that U.S. passports must be specifically endorsed for travel to Cuba. This restriction on travel is subsequently issued annually or biannually until 1977 and again beginning in 1982.

April 12-14 At a Summit Meeting of Western Hemisphere nations in Punta del Este, Uruguay, President Johnson and 18 other leaders agree on goals for development, education, health, technology and trade, most of which never get beyond the planning stage.

April 16 Prensa Latina, the Cuban news agency, publicizes Che Guevara's message "from somewhere in the world" to the Organization of Solidarity of the Peoples of Africa, Asia and Latin America (OSPAAAL). In his only public statement between the time he left Cuba in 1965 and his death, Guevara calls for the creation of "two, three, many Vietnams."

April 29 Combatting the U.S. embargo on technology, Prime Minister Castro denounces the concept of "intellectual property" and international copyright agreements. He asserts the "unequivocal right to reprint all U.S. technical materials that we feel will be useful to us."

May 3 A fragmentation bomb is thrown into the car of Cuban Ambassador to Mexico Joaquín Hernández de Armas, wounding four people. The Ambassador is not in the car at the time.

May 19 In an act that proves to be important later in Cuban history, the UN General Assembly votes 85 to 2 to set up a council to administer Namibia (Southwest Africa) and lead it to independence by June 1968. The United Nations also designates "Namibia" as the official name of Southwest Africa. South Africa, which has been administering Southwest Africa, refuses to deal with the council.

June 26 After attending a Summit Meeting with President Johnson in New Jersey, Soviet Prime Minister Aleksei Kosygin arrives for his first state visit to Cuba.

June 28 Cuba becomes a malaria-free country after the last case is diagnosed on this date. In November 1973 the World Health Organization presents Cuba with a certificate recognizing that it is a country that has rid itself of malaria, which was endemic.

July 16 Armed with high-powered rifles, cyanide bullets, and a plot to assassinate Prime Minister Castro, Francisco Avila and several other exiles take a speedboat from Florida to Cuba. They are captured two days later. Released from prison in 1979, Avila returns to Miami and joins Alpha 66.

July 26 At a mass rally following the Newark rebellion in the United States July 12-17 and during the Detroit rebellion of July 23-30, Prime Minister Castro discusses racial violence, expressing Cuba's sympathies with the struggles of Black and other oppressed people in the United States.

July 31-August 11 At a LASO conference attended by more than 200 journalists and delegates, Cuban officials present nine agents infiltrated into Cuba by the CIA. Stokely Carmichael, former president of the Student Non-Violent Coordinating Committee (SNCC), attends the conference as an honorary U.S. delegate.

August 6 Prime Minister Castro introduces on television the would-be assassins captured July 18.

September 22 At a luncheon in honor of OAS foreign ministers, President Johnson warns of "a virulent form of subversion that is directed from Havana." During their meeting in Washington, these foreign ministers approve a U.S. proposal to deny port facilities and government-financed cargos to countries involved in trade with Cuba. Chile, Colombia, Ecuador, Mexico and Uruguay abstain.

October 8 Che Guevara, the Argentine who went to Bolivia in 1966 to fight as he had fought in Cuba, is tracked down by Bolivian rangers and their CIA advisers, wounded and captured. Thomas Karamessines, chief of CIA covert operations, had presented evidence to CIA Director Richard Helms that Guevara was in Bolivia; the Agency sent various types of personnel to help capture him. For example, John Waghelstein is a trainer and adviser to the Bolivian army unit that helps capture Guevara; later he serves two tours in Vietnam, one with Special Forces and, in 1983, Colonel Waghelstein heads U.S. military advisers in El Salvador. Another CIA agent involved in the capture is Cuban exile Félix Rodríguez. In his testimony in May 1987 to the Congressional hearings about the Iran-Contra Affair, Rodríguez boasts that he was one of those selected by the CIA to track down Guevara. He testifies that he showed a picture of himself with Guevara to Vice-President Bush.

October 9 On the day after his capture, Che Guevara is murdered by his captors.

October 15 Prime Minister Castro tells the Cuban people on radio and television that he has reached the conclusion that the news of Che Guevara's death is true. Cuba declares a 30-day mourning period. In a eulogy three days later, Castro says that, while fighting in Bolivia, Guevara "knew that he was offering Vietnam the highest possible expression of his solidarity." (*See* April 16)

December 20 In *Lynd* v. *Rusk*, the U.S. Court of Appeals for the D.C. Circuit upholds the State Department's regulations that effectively prohibit use of a U.S. passport for travel to Cuba. However, the decision does not prohibit such travel as long as the passport is not presented to Cuban authorities to be stamped with a Cuban visa.

1968

January 24 Urging extension of the Arms Control and Disarmament Agency in a letter to the President of the Senate and the Speaker of the House, President Johnson writes of the historical impact of the Missile Crisis of 1962, recalling how it "brought home to every man and woman the unspeakable personal horror of nuclear war." He continues: "One year later, the world took the first great step toward nuclear sanity — the Limited Test Ban Treaty."

March 5 Arson destroys the "Patrice Lumumba" tannery in Caibarién, Las Villas. In the coming months, arsonists' targets include schools, factories, a boat and a tobacco warehouse.

March 31 With the Tet Offensive in Vietnam dispelling Washington's illusions about victory in Vietnam, President Johnson announces that he will not run for a second term. The year of 1968 is a year of domestic turmoil for the United States, including Black rebellions in 125 towns and cities after the assassination of the Reverend Martin Luther King, Jr., in April; the assassination two months later of Senator Robert F. Kennedy, front-runner for the Democratic presidential nomination; and the controversial nomination of Vice-President Hubert Humphrey rather than peace candidate Eugene McCarthy at the Democratic convention in August.

June Antonio Arguedas, who was Bolivia's Minister of the Interior and a CIA agent at the time of Che Guevara's execution, releases Guevara's diary to Cuba, denounces the regime of René Barrientos, states that he agrees with Guevara's motives, and begins to tell what he knows about U.S. agents in the Bolivian government until he himself is assassinated on a street in La Paz.

June 6 Because the Treasury Department believes that nickel-bearing materials made in Italy may contain Cuban nickel, the Office of Foreign Assets Control announces that Customs agents will hold any nickel-bearing imports from Italy until authorized to release them.

July 1 Cuba publishes Che Guevara's Boliviandiary.

August 23 Calling the Soviet-led intervention by Warsaw Pact nations in Czechoslovakia a "drastic and painful measure" but a "bitter necessity," Prime Minister Castro says, "The essential point... is whether or not the socialist camp could allow a political situation to develop which would lead to the breaking away of a socialist country, to its falling into the arms of imperialism.... Our point of view is... that the socialist camp has a right to prevent this in one way or another." Castro raises a further question: if the intervention is truly based on "unbreakable solidarity against any outside threat," does that commitment also apply to Vietnam, [North] Korea and Cuba if these countries should ask for help?

September Cuban authorities announce the capture of 18 CIA agents who were attempting an espionage raid.

September 16 Because Poland trades with Cuba, Cuban exiles fire a bazooka at a Polish freighter docked at the Port of Miami. Orlando Bosch is tried, convicted, and sentenced in 1970 to ten years for this crime and for sending death threats to the heads of state of France, Italy, and Spain because those countries trade with Cuba. He is paroled in 1972. When subpoenaed to testify about the assassination in Coral Gables on Good Friday, 1974, of José Elias de la Torriente, a controversial exile leader, Bosch flees to Latin America in violation of his parole.

September 18 A Cuban exile group claims responsibility for bombs that go off in a group of stores in Miami's "Little Havana." In recent months bombs have exploded at several U.S. tourist offices and at diplomatic missions of countries that trade with Cuba.

November 19 Two U.S. Marines based at Guantánamo Naval Base are captured on Cuban territory outside the base.

December 2 John Roselli, one of the underworld figures involved with CIA plots to assassinate Prime Minister Castro and four associates are convicted of cheating card players such as Tony Martin and Harry Karl (husband of Debbie Reynolds) at the Friars Club in Beverly Hills.

December 4 Five infiltrators are captured in Pinar del Río.

1969

January 2 Celebrating the tenth year of the Cuban revolution, the throng of people in Havana's Revolution Plaza includes some U.S. visitors who listen to Prime Minister Castro discuss economic problems that he hopes will be alleviated by a 10-million-ton sugar harvest in 1970. The young visitors begin to discuss the idea of organizing U.S. citizens to help with the harvest. Two or three months later, Cuban officials approve their proposal for a "Venceremos Brigade" from the United States.

January 9 Richard Nixon is inaugurated as president. One of his first presidential orders directs the CIA to increase covert operations against Cuba, including raids, sabotage and recruitment of agents. Cuban-born Charles G. "Bebe" Rebozo, his friend and confidant with his own suite in the White House, is a strong link between Nixon and anti-Castro Cubans in Miami. However, the war in Indochina continues to dominate U.S. foreign policy.

March 4 Cuba establishes an embassy in a tent in the Vietnam jungle and names Raúl Valdés Vivo as ambassador to the National Liberation Front of South Vietnam, the first accredited diplomatic representative to the NLF.

April 20 Reading in their churches their first pastoral letter since 1962, Cuba's Roman Catholic bishops call for an end to the U.S. embargo against Cuba. The bishops say the embargo creates economic hardships that "weigh principally" on workers, women, children and the sick.

April 13 Cuban authorities arrest Alejandro Blay Martínez accused of planning to disrupt the sugar harvest on orders from the United States.

May 3 A group of CIA agents, infiltrating Oriente province, is captured.

June 11 Cuba officially recognizes the Provisional Revolutionary Government (PRG) of South Vietnam, established June 10 by the NLF and other opposition groups.

July 14 Prime Minister Castro inaugurates the campaign to marshal Cuba's economic resources for the 10-million-ton sugar harvest to break out of economic underdevelopment despite the U.S. embargo.

August 27 A formal Cuban protest signed by Foreign Minister Raúl Roa García is delivered to UN Secretary General U Thant, stating that the Cuban government knows the CIA is taking steps to establish new camps in Guatemala, Nicaragua and Panama for training "Cuban mercenaries to make lightning raids" against Cuba.

August 29 On a National Airlines flight from Miami to New Orleans, a Cuban immigrant, accompanied by his wife and three children, hijacks the jet to Havana. The airliner with its passengers returns to Florida.

September 1 In West Palm Beach, Florida, police dismantle a bomb at a theater showing "Che," a film about Che Guevara, after a man called the fire department to report that he had set the bomb to go off in 15 minutes.

September 8 Cuba expels Fenton Wheeler, the Associated Press correspondent in Cuba since April 1967. Washington retaliates by prohibiting Cuban news bureaus in the United States, except for the premises of the United Nations.

September 12 CIA agent José A. Quesada Fernández infiltrates Oriente province and is captured with espionage equipment.

September 14 Foreign Minister Raúl Roa García sends a note of protest to the Mexican government upon the discovery that the press attaché in the Mexican Embassy works for the CIA.

October 5 Lieutenant Eduardo Guerra Jiménez, a Cuban Air Force pilot, defects by flying a MiG-17 to Homestead Air Force Base near Miami. Ten years later, he hijacks a passenger jet and returns to Cuba.

October 31 President Nixon tells the annual meeting of the Inter-American Press Association, "We cannot have a peaceful community of nations if one nation sponsors armed subversion in another's territory." Although he is speaking in the midst of the U.S. war in Indochina, he is not referring to Asia but to Cuba, which he says is continuing to "export" revolution and therefore cannot "expect to share in the benefits of this community [of the Americas]." He says the principles of the Alliance for Progress "still guide us" and the "goal for the seventies should be a decade of 'action for progress' for the Americas."

November 7 Because the Treasury Department believes that nickel-bearing materials made in Czechoslovakia may contain Cuban nickel, the Office of Foreign Assets Control announces that Customs agents will hold any nickel-bearing imports from Czechoslovakia until authorized to release them.

November 10 President Nixon releases a report by Nelson A. Rockefeller, Republican governor of New York, on his recent fact-finding trip through Latin America. Rockefeller recommends getting along with governments of all political persuasion but excludes Cuba from this pragmatic approach, maintaining that Cuba continues to export revolution in Latin America. The report contains no documentary evidence to support that claim but includes a short section on the effectiveness of Cuban propaganda.

December The first Venceremos Brigade arrives in Cuba via Mexico to work in the sugar harvest as an act of solidarity with the 10-million-ton goal. These 216 U.S. citizens are the largest group to travel to Cuba from the United States since the imposition of the embargo and the travel ban. Cuba pays their living expenses so that they are not violating U.S. Treasury Department regulations.

December 2 Ten Vietnamese fighters straight from battles with U.S. forces arrive to help with the 10-million-ton harvest. On December 12 they join the U.S. Venceremos Brigade in Cuban cane fields.

1970

February The first Venceremos Brigade returns to the United States by ship via Canada. The second Brigade of 687 U.S. citizens departs for Cuba to harvest sugar, some traveling by ship via Canada, some by plane via Mexico. International brigades to work in Cuba are arriving from many countries, including Chile, Syria, the Soviet Union, Algeria, East Germany, Egypt, Guinea, Lebanon, Bulgaria, Romania, North Korea and the People's Republic of the Congo.

March-April Infiltrators are captured in Las Villas and Camagüey.

March 16 Worried about U.S. citizens on the Venceremos Brigades making friends with Cubans, Senator William O. Eastland (D-Mississippi), chair of the Judiciary Committee and opponent of civil rights legislation, rises to tell the Senate: "We intend to light the shadows that surround this vicious operation — to drive from those shadows the missiles — in human form — which have been fashioned on that communist island and fired at America. We want our people to be aware of the direct chain which reaches from Cuba into our cities, our campuses, our conventions, our lives — and which threatens the life of this Republic."

April The second Venceremos Brigade returns and begins organizing to send a third.

April 17 Alpha 66 transports a team of infiltrators from the United States into Cuba, landing near Baracoa. Before they are captured, they kill four Cubans and seriously wound two others.

May 1 Arson destroys a sugar storehouse in Las Villas as sabotage continues.

May 10 Two Cuban fishing boats, *Plataforma I* and *Plataforma IV*, are disabled in an attack carried out by CIA agent Ramón Orozco Crespo, based in Miami. The 11 fishermen aboard are kidnapped and held on a Bahamas islet. A mass mobilization of Cubans in Havana demands their return. The Cuban Air Force has orders to shoot if attacked while patrolling waters near the Bahamas.

May 18 The kidnapped fishermen are freed. The next day Prime Minister Castro says it is the "solidarity of an entire people" that successfully supported diplomatic moves to free them.

May 19 Calling for the "revolutionary fortitude to turn setback into victory," Prime Minister Castro announces the failure of the 10-million-ton goal for the sugar harvest, which at 8,500,000 tons is nevertheless the largest in Cuban history.

July 26 In his annual speech on the anniversary of the attack on the Moncada Barracks, Prime Minister Castro analyzes economic problems following the failure of the 10-million-ton sugar harvest. Pointing out how the effort disrupted production in other sectors, he offers to resign, but the proposal is rejected by the crowd. Cuban leadership begins a reevaluation of development strategy.

August The third Venceremos Brigade of 409 U.S. citizens arrives in Cuba to work on the Isle of Pines in agricultural and construction projects until October.

August 4 In the midst of U.S. bombing raids deep into Cambodia and the continuing "secret" war in Laos, Cubans form a Committee of Solidarity with Vietnam, Laos and Cambodia.

August 4 Meeting with National Security Adviser Henry Kissinger, the Soviet chargé d'affaires in Washington, Yuli M. Vorontsov, brings up the issue of reaffirming the agreement made by the United States and the Soviet Union with regard to Cuba during the 1962 Missile Crisis. Kissinger takes the matter to President Nixon.

September 8-10 The Nonaligned Movement holds its Third Summit Conference in Lusaka, Zambia.

Mid-September A U-2 surveillance photograph shows construction underway in the harbor of Cienfuegos on the south central coast of Cuba, evidently a submarine tender. National Security Adviser Kissinger and President Nixon discuss what to do.

September 23   Secretary of State William P. Rogers supports President Nixon's desire for "no hysteria" before November elections about Soviet actions in Cuba. However, Nixon does ask for contingency plans for mining Cienfuegos Harbor and blockading Cuba, among other options.

September 25   C. L. Sulzberger in the *New York Times* warns that the Soviet Union may be building a submarine base in Cuba.

October-November   In an exchange of notes with Soviet Ambassador Anatoly Dobrynin, National Security Adviser Kissinger and President Nixon agree to reaffirm the 1962 U.S. pledge not to invade Cuba in exchange for a clearer Soviet commitment not to base offensive missiles in Cuba.

October 5   Cuban exiles and two U.S. citizens land between Moa and Baracoa in eastern Cuba. They are captured.

November 3   Government official Carlos Rafael Rodríguez heads the Cuban delegation at the inauguration of Salvador Allende Gossens, newly elected president of Chile.

November 12   Chile restores diplomatic relations with Cuba, opening a significant crack in the U.S. embargo and the campaign to isolate Cuba.

December 10   Asked at a press conference if he thinks U.S. security is threatened at all by Soviet military activity in the Caribbean, including the submarine base in Cuba, President Nixon answers, "No, I do not."

1971

January 4 In a television interview, President Nixon repeats his position that the submarine tender in Cuba is not a threat to the United States because the Soviet Union has reaffirmed its agreement that there will be no offensive missiles in Cuba.

February 17 While a Soviet nuclear submarine is in Cuban waters, President Nixon tells the press that "if a nuclear submarine were serviced from Cuba or in Cuba" this would violate the U.S.-Soviet agreement but a port call by the submarine is not a violation.

February 24 The U.S. Coast Guard seizes four Cuban fishing boats, saying they were in U.S. territorial waters. Cuba says they were in international waters.

February 25 In an annual report to Congress on U.S. foreign policy, President Nixon says Chile's establishment of diplomatic relations with Cuba challenges "the inter-American system" and makes it necessary to "observe closely the evolution of Chilean foreign policy."

March 2 The four fishing boat captains and 47 fishermen seized in February are fined and returned to Cuba, saying that during their captivity they were interrogated and incited to defect.

April 16 Appearing at the annual convention of the American Society of Newspaper Publishers, President Nixon says there are no plans for changing U.S. policy toward Cuba until Cuba stops "exporting revolution all over the hemisphere."

May 6 The Cuban ship *Sierra Maestra* sails for Peru with workers and equipment to build six rural maternity and children's hospitals in areas devastated by the 1970 earthquake.

May 6 The first swine fever ever found in the Western Hemisphere is detected in Cuba. Six weeks later Cuba has to slaughter half a million pigs to prevent the spread of the disease throughout the nation. African swine fever is a highly contagious, usually lethal viral disease that infects only pigs. In 1977, the U.S. press reveals that a U.S. intelligence source admits the virus was introduced into Cuba when he was instructed to transfer it from Fort Gulick, a U.S. Army Base and CIA training center in the Panama Canal Zone, to a group of Cuban exiles who took it to operatives inside Cuba in March 1971.

May 26 The U.S. Coast Guard arrests eight Cuban fishermen in what Cuba claims are international waters. Four are returned to Cuba five days later. On June 9, the other four are sentenced to six months in jail and a fine of $10,000 each. The prisoners vow they would rather spend years in prison than have the fines paid. The Cuban government decides to put on trial the crew of two boats from the United States that were seized off the Cuban coast and on June 14 fines each of them $20,000. (*See* July 6)

June 16 Cubans form a Committee to Free Angela Davis, an African American activist who is imprisoned in solitary confinement while facing a murder charge in California. (Released on bail in February 1972 after being held in solitary for 16 months, she is acquitted in June 1972.)

July 6 The federal court in Miami suspends the prison sentences of the four fishermen arrested in May and reduces their fines to $2,000 each. Returning to Cuba the next day, they receive a tumultuous welcome.

July 10 Cuba sends a plane carrying medical personnel, equipment and medicines to the aid of earthquake victims in Chile.

July 12 Exiles based in Miami claim responsibility for railroad sabotage in Guantánamo province that causes four deaths and injures 17 others.

July 26 Pointing out that Cuba has been under siege for 12 years, Prime Minister Castro describes the economic effects of the U.S. embargo. He denounces U.S. pressure on third countries not to purchase Cuban nickel or anything containing Cuban nickel. He says imperialism is weaker than it was 12 years ago, due especially to the people of Vietnam.

August 17 Cuban UN Ambassador Ricardo Alarcón de Quesada calls for the inclusion of Puerto Rico's status on the UN agenda. From this time on, Cuba requests every year that the UN Decolonization Committee consider the matter of Puerto Rico. The United States opposes this on the grounds that Puerto Rico is a self-governing territory, not a colony.

September U.S. intelligence agents E. Howard Hunt Jr. (CIA) and G. Gordon Liddy (FBI), both members of the White House "Plumbers" set up to investigate news leaks, use a team of Cuban exiles, Bernard Barker, Eugenio Rolando Martínez and Felipe de Diego, to break in to the office of Daniel Ellsberg's psychiatrist. De Diego is a Bay of Pigs veteran who has participated in raids against Cuba and served in U.S. Army intelligence for four years. Martínez has piloted a boat in more than 350 CIA missions to Cuba. Ellsberg turned the secret history of the U.S. government's initiation and conduct of the war in Indochina, known as the *Pentagon Papers*, over to the *New York Times*, which published them in June. The purpose of the burglary is to try to find detrimental information to use against Ellsberg.

October 11 In a further blow to U.S. efforts to isolate Cuba, the Peruvian government of President Juan Velasco Alvarado invites Cuba to the meeting of the Group of 77, the participants from developing nations in the United Nations Conference on Trade and Development (UNCTAD).

October 12 In a night raid, a speedboat strafes the fishing village of Boca de Samá in Oriente province with medium and heavy machine guns, killing two Cubans and injuring four, including 15-year-old Nancy Pavón, who was asleep at the time and whose leg has to be amputated.

October 26 Soviet Prime Minister Aleksei Kosygin arrives for a state visit in Cuba.

October 27 Foreign Minister Raúl Roa García leads the Cuban delegation to the Group of 77 meeting in Lima, Peru.

November 5 Prime Minister Castro greets a Cuban delegation of 19 sugar technicians on their return from New Orleans, Louisiana, where they had gone without visas to attend an international conference about sugar. The State Department had refused to grant permission for them to attend the conference, but the Cubans went anyway and refused to leave before the conference ended. U.S. authorities detained them and the three crew members of their plane at the Belle Chasse naval air station for more than a week.

November 10-December 4 Prime Minister Castro makes a state visit to Chile, a trip that marks the break in diplomatic isolation of Cuba in the Western Hemisphere. Speaking four or five times a day to enthusiastic audiences, Castro tells them on one occasion that a "revolutionary process is taking place in Chile" but that a "revolutionary process is not yet a revolution." He and President Salvador Allende issue a joint communiqué expressing the "need to find Latin American formulas for unity." On his way home, Castro stops briefly in Peru to meet with President Juan Velasco Alvarado and in Ecuador to meet with President José María Ibarra. Years later it is revealed that Luis Clemente Posada Carriles, a Cuban exile and CIA agent, with the help of Alpha 66 members, including Antonio Veciana, engineered various plans to try to assassinate Castro during his visit to Chile.

December 5 As a result of the attack on October 12, the Cuban Navy captures the *Layla Express*, described by Cuba as a "pirate ship" in the service of the CIA. Its owners are Cuban exiles who took part in the Bay of Pigs invasion. Cuba captures another of their vessels, the *Johnny Express*, on December 15.

December 22 Speaking about the capture of the two "pirate ships," Prime Minister Castro describes the destabilization campaign being waged against Cuba: "They have used all kinds of weapons against us.... the landing of weapons, organization of mercenary bands, infiltration of spies, saboteurs, arms drops of all kinds, caches of arms hidden along our shores.... They have forced us to spend fabulous sums in human and economic resources by all these misdeeds." The captain of the *Johnny Express*, José Villa, admits working for the CIA.

1972

February Cuba publishes the first Spanish-Vietnamese dictionary.

April At a meeting of the UN Conference on Trade and Development (UNCTAD) in Chile, Foreign Minister Raúl Roa García analyzes the results of various "aid" programs since 1950: "The underdeveloped countries' foreign debt amounts to more than $60 billion and the yearly interest alone to $5 billion.... The decapitalization of Latin America... is proceeding at breakneck speed. Its deficit in the current account with the United States today is three times what it was in 1961." Roa says revolutionary change is a prerequisite for development because the United States and other developed countries will not take such agencies as UNCTAD seriously.

April 4 A dynamite explosion at the Office of Cuban Commerce in Montreal, Canada, kills Cuban official Sergio Pérez del Castillo.

May The Center for Cuban Studies, a non-profit organization for distributing information about Cuba, is established by Sandra Levinson and others in New York.

May In an act of solidarity, the 89 crew members of two Cuban merchant ships, the *Imías* and *El Jigüe*, begin a stay in the mined harbor of Haiphong that lasts until the United States and Vietnam sign the Paris Peace Agreements in January 1973.

May 2 The White House "Plumbers" go into action again. Conspiring with G. Gordon Liddy, E. Howard Hunt Jr. asks Bernard Barker to gather a team of Cuban exiles to attack Daniel Ellsberg and Attorney William Kunstler at a rally in Washington. Barker recruits Felipe de Diego and Eugenio Rolando Martínez, who broke into Daniel Ellsberg's psychiatrist's office in

September 1971, plus seven others: Pablo Fernández, Angel Ferrer, Iran González, Virgilio R. González, Humberto López, Reinaldo Pico and Frank A. Sturgis (born Frank Angelo Fiorini), a longtime CIA operative.

May 3 The attempt to attack Daniel Ellsberg and William Kunstler fails although Reinaldo Pico and Frank Sturgis pummel a couple of other people. When the police seize Pico and Sturgis, an unidentified man, probably E. Howard Hunt or G. Gordon Liddy, saves them from arrest by flashing official identification.

May-July Prime Minister Castro makes a 63-day tour of Africa, Eastern Europe and the Soviet Union. Cuba's relations with African countries contribute to frustrating U.S. efforts to increase diplomatic isolation of Cuba; in this year alone, Cuba establishes diplomatic relations with Equatorial Guinea, Mauritania, Sierra Leone, Somalia, South Yemen and Zambia.

May 15 Cuba denounces the U.S. campaign of intensified bombing of North Vietnam and the mining of Haiphong harbor and other northern ports. Cuban doctors and nurses continue to work in North Vietnam.

June 7 The Division for Latin America of the United States Catholic Conference calls for an end to the U.S. embargo against Cuba.

June 17 In arrests that ultimately lead to the resignation of President Nixon, five people working for the White House "Plumbers" are caught breaking into the offices of the Democratic National Committee at the Watergate complex in Washington. Among them are three Cuban exiles, Bernard Barker, Eugenio Rolando Martínez and Virgilio González. Bay of Pigs veteran Frank Sturgis and veteran CIA agent James W. McCord Jr. are also caught red-handed. In September, they are indicted along with E. Howard Hunt Jr. and G. Gordon Liddy, their supervisors. McCord is a prominent member of the Committee for the Re-election of the President (CREEP); his name provides the first link between the burglary and the White House.

June 23 Trying to cover up involvement in the Watergate burglary, President Nixon has a conversation with his aide, H.R. Haldeman, about how to stop the FBI's investigation from reaching the White House. Nixon conspires with Haldeman to threaten exposure of the activities of E. Howard Hunt Jr. and his team of Cuban exiles in order to get CIA Deputy Director Vernon Walters to call FBI Director Patrick Gray and tell him, "Stay to hell out of this." Nixon reminds Haldeman that "we protected [CIA Director Richard] Helms from one hell of a lot of things." Speaking of Hunt, Nixon says, "You open that scab, there's a hell of a lot of things.... This involves these Cubans, Hunt and a lot of hanky-panky that we have nothing to do with ourselves." Nixon instructs Haldeman to tell Walters that "the President believes that [the investigation] is going to open the whole Bay of Pigs thing up again." This cover-up preoccupies much of Nixon's time for the next two years, and this particular taped conversation becomes a piece of crucial evidence in efforts to impeach the President.

July 8 In another blow to U.S. plans, Cuba reestablishes diplomatic relations with Peru.

July 11 Cuba joins the Council of Mutual Economic Assistance (CMEA or Comecon), the economic union of the Soviet Union, the Eastern European socialist countries and Mongolia.

July 26 Nguyen Thi Binh, Foreign Minister of the Provisional Revolutionary Government (PRG) of South Vietnam, is a special guest at the 19th anniversary celebration of the attack on the Moncada Barracks. She expresses the "great emotion and deep gratitude" of the Vietnamese for "the attention, affection and exemplary revolutionary solidarity" that Cuba has always given to Vietnam in its war with the United States.

October 8 Trying to infiltrate in Oriente province, two CIA agents are captured in their high-powered fiberglass launch.

October 10 Two gunboats take over two Cuban fishing boats, *Aguja* and *Plataforma IV*, and blow them up south of the islet Andros of the Bahamas, wounding one of the fishermen. This is evidently part of the operations run by Paul Lionel Edward Helliwell (*see* May 13, 1964). On October 13, a helicopter rescues the 11 fishermen adrift in a small boat. Cuba sends a plane to the Bahamas to bring them home on October 15.

November 7 President Richard Nixon is reelected, defeating the Democratic nominee, Senator George McGovern of South Dakota.

November 19 Cuba accepts a U.S. proposal to begin formal negotiations about hijackings. In the years following the Cuban revolution, the U.S. government sponsored and encouraged hijackings of Cuban boats and planes, welcoming the perpetrators as heroes. In the late 1960s, the situation reversed as many U.S. planes began to be hijacked to Cuba. The Cuban government consistently adheres to a policy of putting hijackers on trial and returning planes with their crews and passengers to the United States (after servicing the planes and occasionally allowing passengers to shop for cigars and souvenirs before takeoff).

December 8 The embargo cracks further as Cuba establishes diplomatic relations with Barbados, Guyana, Jamaica and Trinidad and Tobago.

December 10 Chilean President Salvador Allende receives a huge welcome on a state visit to Cuba.

December 26 Cuban medical teams begin work in Managua, Nicaragua, to aid victims of a major earthquake.

December 29 Cuban delegates are among representatives from 23 Communist, Socialist and People's Parties of Latin America, the Caribbean and North America who condemn U.S. imperialism as "the true master of the repugnant murderer Carlos Arana Osorio," head of Guatemala's reactionary government. They call attention to atrocities — mutilated and bullet-riddled bodies on the highways, opponents' bodies dropped into craters of active volcanos and into the ocean, the daily disappearances — and call for acts of solidarity by the other peoples of the American continent with the people of Guatemala.

1973

January 23 Cuba observes a day of mourning for Amilcar Cabral, head of the Party for the Independence of Guinea (later Guinea-Bissau) and the Cape Verde Islands (PAIGC). At the time of his assassination on January 20, Cabral was the most prominent leader in the struggle to oust Portugal from its colonies in Africa. Cuban advisers have been serving with the PAIGC.

January 27 On the day the United States and Vietnam sign the Paris Peace Agreements, Melba Hernández, head of the Cuban Committee of Solidarity with Vietnam, calls this "a great diplomatic victory" for Vietnam "as the inevitable result of their victories on the field of battle."

January 28 Near the Bahamas, a gunboat attacks the Cuban fishing boat *Plataforma I*, wounding one of the seven crew members.

February Now that the United States has signed the Peace Agreements with Vietnam, the Cuban merchant ships, *Imías* and *El Jigüe*, leave the port of Haiphong where they have remained since May 1972 in defiance of the U.S. mining of the harbor.

February 15 Cuba and the United States sign an anti-hijacking agreement, the only formal agreement existing between the two countries. Each government agrees to prosecute hijackers or return them to the other country.

March A bomb explodes at the Center for Cuban Studies in New York. Sandra Levinson, director of the Center, is the only person present at the time and is uninjured.

March 3 The Ministry of Public Health announces that Cuba has achieved Latin America's lowest infant mortality rate — 28.7 per 1,000 live births in 1972.

April   At the meeting of the UN Economic Commission on Latin America (ECLA) in Quito, Ecuador, Cuba's representative Carlos Rafael Rodríguez analyzes U.S. aid to Latin American countries: while such aid may bring increases in production, it does not spur development and in fact leaves the recipients with the structural deformity of their economies; from 1950 to 1970 the profits leaving Latin America exceeded the investments entering. He notes that although skyscrapers keep rising in some cities, the shanty towns also continue to rise, adding, "You may say that Cuba is again calling for revolution, and I admit it."

May 28   Argentina and Cuba reestablish diplomatic relations.

June 21   In Chile, dynamite is thrown into the Cuban Office of Commerce and a bomb into the home of Cuban official Michel Vázquez.

July   Antonio Veciana (also known as Víctor or Mario), a founding member of Alpha 66 who has been involved in attempts to assassinate Prime Minister Castro, is arrested by the U.S. Drug Enforcement Agency (DEA) on cocaine charges. Sentenced to seven years in prison, Veciana is paroled in 17 months.

July 26   In his annual speech on the anniversary of the attack on the Moncada Barracks, Prime Minister Castro says the "only possible salvation" for the peoples of Latin America is to "free themselves from imperialist domination, make revolution and unite."

August 27   In Santiago de Chile, three bombs are thrown into the homes of officials of the Cuban Office of Commerce.

September 5   Another explosive device is thrown into the home of a Cuban official in Santiago de Chile.

September 5-9   At the Fourth Summit Conference of the Non-aligned Movement in Algeria, Cuba is elected to a 15-member coordinating committee. Nonaligned countries now constitute almost two-thirds of the members of the United Nations, and Cuba's relationship with these nations frustrates U.S. attempts to expand sanctions against Cuba beyond the OAS to the United Nations. For the first time, Prime Minister Castro attends the Summit. On his way, he stopped in Guyana, Trinidad and Tobago and Guinea. Later he continues on to Vietnam with stops in Iraq and India.

September 7   Speaking at the Nonaligned Summit, Prime Minister Castro discusses the theory of "two imperialisms," one headed by the United States and the other by the Soviet Union. He denies that the Soviet Union is imperialist, asking, "Where are its monopoly corporations? Where is its participation in the multi-national companies?" He notes that some "regret the fact that the first socialist state in history has become a military and economic power" but that "underdeveloped and plundered countries must not regret this." He objects to any "attempt to pit nonaligned countries against the socialist camp," stating: "Were it not for the extraordinary containing power of the socialist camp, imperialism would carve up the world all over again, new wars would plague the human race, and many of the independent countries that today belong to the Nonaligned Movement would not even exist."

September 11 Chile's President Salvador Allende is killed in a military coup that reverses all major policies of that country, including its diplomatic and economic links with Cuba. During the coup, Chilean military forces shell the Cuban merchant ship, *Playa Larga.*

September 12-17 Prime Minister Castro makes a state visit to Hanoi. At a time of heightened tensions between the Soviet Union and China, the leaders of Cuba and Vietnam issue a joint declaration calling for regaining and strengthening solidarity among socialist countries.

September 28 At a rally in Havana, Prime Minister Castro points out that in Chile "they tried the electoral way, the peaceful way, and the imperialists and reactionaries changed the rules of the game."

October 2 U.S. authorities detain the *Imías*, the Cuban merchant ship (*see* February), in the Panama Canal by refusing to release it from the locks of the Canal. Cuba protests this violation of the international status of the Canal and stays in touch with the captain and crew by radio. The Panamanian government charges that U.S. authorities are violating the commitment that the Canal will never be used for hostile acts against ships that are using it. U.S. gunboats circle the ship 24 hours a day.

October 4 Two Cuban fishing boats are shelled in international waters, killing one fisherman, Roberto Torna Mirabal, and leaving the others in rubber rafts with neither food nor water.

The next day a helicopter from Cuba's Armed Forces rescues them.

November 5 The Cuban ship *Marble Island* carrying a cargo of sugar donated to Chile arrives in Hanoi after being diverted from Chile following the strafing and bombing of Cuban ships by the Chilean junta's forces. The sugar is now a gift to the Vietnamese.

November 13 U.S. officials tell the captain of the *Imías* that the ship may leave the Panama Canal. By the following morning, the *Imías* has cleared the locks and is on its way.

November 16 The *Imías* arrives to a huge welcoming throng in the port of Havana after being illegally detained for 43 days by U.S. authorities who control the Panama Canal. Captain Luis Céspedes says the crew was prepared to scuttle the *Imías* rather than allow a U.S. boarding party to set foot on the ship.

November 21 In Havana, Vietnamese officials award medals to the 89 crew members of the *Imías* and *El Jigüe* (*see* February).

1974

January 16 Cuba's Maternity Law, a revision of existing legislation, takes effect. Perhaps the most far-reaching maternity law in the world, it provides working women with time off for systematic pre-natal medical care, a leave of absence of six weeks prior to birth and three months afterward, time off for taking the child to the pediatrician, and other benefits.

January 20 A powerful explosion causes considerable damage to the Cuban Embassy in Mexico City. The targets of anti-Cuban terrorism are now frequently Cuban personnel and facilities in countries other than Cuba and the United States.

January 28-February 3 Soviet Prime Minister Leonid Brezhnev makes a state visit to Cuba.

February 4 Pilar Ramírez Vega, an official in the Cuban Embassy in Lima, Peru, suffers serious burns when a letter bomb explodes in his hands.

February 13 A package addressed to the Cuban Embassy in Madrid explodes in the Central Post Office, slightly wounding a postal worker.

March 26 Bombs are thrown at the Cuban Embassy in Kingston, Jamaica.

March 28 In Havana, Prime Minister Pham Van Dong of the Democratic Republic of Vietnam and Prime Minister Castro issue a joint communiqué again calling for unity among socialist countries.

April 9 A powerful bomb destroys the Cuban Embassy in Madrid.

April 15 Algerian President Houari Boumedienne and Prime Minister Castro address a rally in Santiago de Cuba. Castro calls for a "strategy of the nonaligned countries... to oppose the imperialist strategy."

April 18 The Nixon Administration grants export licenses for sales to Cuba to Argentine subsidiaries of General Motors, Ford and Chrysler.

May 4 A bomb explodes in a building adjoining the Cuban Embassy in London.

May 14 Two bombs cause considerable damage to the Cuban Consulate in Mérida, Mexico.

June 20 Pelegrín Torras, Deputy Minister of Foreign Relations, heads the Cuban delegation to the Law of the Sea Conference in Caracas, Venezuela.

June 30 Matanzas province holds the first elections for delegates to new bodies of "People's Power." The success of People's Power in Matanzas leads in 1976 to the establishment of this system of government throughout Cuba.

July 3 A bomb explodes at the entrance to the Cuban Embassy in Paris.

July 6 Praising Cuban achievements in education, agriculture and fishing, Mexican President Luis Echeverría tells foreign correspondents in Mexico City that the "unjust embargo of Cuba must end."

July 10 The U.S. Treasury Department issues regulations that allow scholars, journalists and news correspondents to pay Cuba for travel and living expenses if the traveler first gets a passport validated by the State Department for travel to Cuba. At the same time, Treasury slightly loosens the embargo by allowing the import of gifts of little value; letting libraries, universities and some other institutions as well as some scholars import books, films, microfiche, microfilm, phonograph records, photographs, posters, publications and tapes; permitting commercial businesses to import those items if payment is placed in a blocked account rather than sent to Cuba; and allowing news agencies to import news materials from Cuba.

July 18 Nguyen Thi Dinh, deputy commander of the armed forces of the Provisional Revolutionary Government (PRG) in South Vietnam, arrives in Cuba for a visit.

July 18-21 Frank Mankiewicz, former Peace Corps director for all Latin American programs and Senator Robert Kennedy's press secretary, and Kirby Jones, also a former Peace Corps official, begin a series of interviews with Prime Minister Castro, parts of which later reach a U.S. audience through television, magazines, a book and a documentary film. Mankiewicz delivers a secret message from Secretary of State Kissinger to Castro and returns with a secret reply (*see* October 2).

July 26 Prime Minister Castro says the "isolation of Cuba is slowly withering away." Referring to the ongoing Watergate scandal in Washington, he states: "Mercenaries trained by the CIA to carry out such acts of sabotage, subversion and aggression against Cuba were later used to spy on and steal documents from the Democratic Party headquarters." He maintains that the CIA and its mercenaries have been "much more effective in destroying the presidency of the United States than in overthrowing the Cuban revolution."

August 1 Three CIA agents are captured on a launch containing paraphernalia for espionage and sabotage.

August 5 Faced with an impeachment trial, President Nixon releases the transcript of the taped conversation he had with H.R. Haldeman on June 23, 1972.

August 9 President Nixon resigns at noon and Vice-President Gerald R. Ford becomes president.

August 17 Several shots are fired from cars at the Cuban and Soviet Embassies in Lima, Peru.

August 22 The Panamanian government headed by Omar Torrijos reestablishes diplomatic relations with Cuba.

September 10 The Cuban government congratulates the Republic of Guinea-Bissau as it becomes an independent state.

September 11 Cuban exile Eduardo Arocena and three other men establish Omega 7 to carry out terrorist activities against Cuba. Arocena is the head of Omega 7 and is called "Omar."

September 18 Tanzanian President Julius K. Nyerere arrives in Havana for a state visit, one of many visits from African heads of state defying U.S. efforts to isolate Cuba. This year alone, Cuba has established diplomatic relations with Gabon, Zaire, Madagascar, Senegal and Cameroon.

September 26 An SR-71 "Blackbird" surveillance plane overflies Cuba.

September 26 Honduran Foreign Minister César A. Batres thanks Cuba for its medical aid for victims of Hurricane Fifi, including a field hospital that is functioning 24 hours a day.

September 28 Marking a hint of a thaw in the U.S. official approach to Cuba, Senators Jacob Javits (R-New York) and Claiborne Pell (D-Rhode Island) are in Havana to meet with Prime Minister Castro and other Cuban officials. They are the first representatives or elected officials of the U.S. government to visit Cuba since the United States severed diplomatic relations in 1961. As a result of their request, Cuba releases four political prisoners within a week of the senators' departure.

September 28 Speaking at a rally in Havana, Prime Minister Castro addresses the oil crisis created when the Organization of Petroleum Exporting Countries (OPEC) raised oil prices in 1973-1974, resulting in two opposite effects on Third World economies — more money for oil exporting countries and less for oil importers. Castro maintains that if the underdeveloped countries make the battle of petroleum theirs, then the oil exporters must make the battle of the underdeveloped countries theirs. That is, the oil resources must be invested essentially in the Third World so that the petroleum battle "becomes a banner and a hope" for all marginalized peoples. Castro devotes much of his speech to the recent revelations of U.S. involvement in the military coup in Chile, including millions of dollars paid to opposition forces by the CIA for destabilization before the coup.

October An attempt to land two Cuban exiles in Cuba to assassinate Prime Minister Castro fails because a Cuban agent is operating the boat and takes it first to the Bahamas and then back to Miami. At the August 1978 Tribunal in Havana about U.S. aggressions, José Fernández Santos, an Interior Ministry official who for many years infiltrated the CIA, testifies about the foiled plot.

October 1 About 20 people gather outside the Cuban Mission to the United Nations and threaten to enter while police officers stand by without making any effort to enforce the international law and practice relevant to UN missions and diplomats. On the following day, UN Ambassador Ricardo Alarcón sends a note of protest to Secretary General Kurt Waldheim about the illegal activity at the front door of the Cuban Mission.

October 2 With Dan Rather of "CBS Reports" also participating, Kirby Jones and Frank Mankiewicz continue their interviews with Prime Minister Castro. Among other things, Castro tells them that the "worst crimes have been committed by the North American politicians while invoking some noble, just cause." He says the crime of waging a war in Vietnam that killed millions of people is greater than the crime of Watergate for which Richard Nixon lost his job. Mankiewicz again delivers a secret message to Castro from Secretary of State Kissinger, leading to arrangements for secret discussions.

October 16 François Mitterrand, First Secretary of the French Socialist Party, arrives in Havana, heading a delegation of French Socialists on a five-day visit.

October 22 "CBS Reports" hosted by Dan Rather presents to a U.S. television audience parts of the interviews with Prime Minister Castro. Regarding negotiations between Cuba and the United States, Castro says: "Guantánamo is a piece of Cuba's national territory. It is occupied by the United States. But we do not say that in order to start discussions they must withdraw from Guantánamo. Rather we have posed a single condition: that the economic embargo be ended."

October 22 In an exchange with Chile's ambassador at the UN Commission on Social and Cultural Affairs, Cuban Ambassador Ricardo Alarcón notes that today's *New York Times* publishes new disclosures about additional hundreds of thousands of dollars given to Chilean political parties by the CIA in June 1973 to finance opposition to the Popular Unity Government of President Allende.

November In Mexico, 13 bombs explode in three cities, injuring four people and causing heavy damage to government offices, banks and businesses after reports that the U.S. government may be considering normalization of relations with Cuba. Mexico has promoted diplomatic relations with Cuba throughout the Western Hemisphere.

November 3 Carlos Rivero Collado, Bay of Pigs veteran and son of Andrés Rivero Agüero (*see* November 1958), denounces activities by exile groups that are carrying out orders from the CIA.

November 4 Cuba establishes diplomatic relations with Laos.

November 14-17 A delegation from the Palestine Liberation Organization (PLO), headed by its President, Yasser Arafat, visits Cuba.

November 24 The Latin American and Caribbean Group of Sugar Exporting Countries (GLACSEC) is founded. Cuba is a member.

November 25 Angela Davis, member of the Central Committee of the U.S. Communist Party, heads the U.S. delegation to the Second Congress of the Cuban Federation of Women.

December 18 The president of the UN General Assembly, Abdelaziz Bouteflika of Algeria, confirms the election of Cuba to the Special Committee on Decolonization.

December 29 Cuba and Venezuela announce reestablishment of diplomatic relations.

December 30 In Nicaragua, the Sandinista National Liberation Front (FSLN) agrees to release about 30 hostages seized at a party for the U.S. ambassador in exchange for free passage to Cuba for the eight guerrillas involved, a ransom of $1 million, release to Cuba of 14 political prisoners held by the regime of Anastasio Somoza, and the publication of an FSLN statement. Among the prisoners who arrive in Havana is Daniel Ortega Saavedra.

1975

January Cuba offers to exchange CIA agent Lawrence Lunt for Lolita Lebrón, a Puerto Rican Nationalist imprisoned since a 1954 attack in the U.S. House of Representatives that left five members of Congress wounded.

January Anti-Cuban bombings in Mexico kill five people and injure 27 in three cities. These bombings are evidently aimed at interfering with Mexico's support of ending OAS sanctions against Cuba.

January 4 President Gerald Ford establishes a "blue ribbon" panel to investigate charges that the CIA has been spying within the United States, which is illegal under the CIA charter. Later, the President authorizes the Rockefeller Commission to examine the CIA's role in plans to assassinate foreign leaders, including Fidel Castro. Ford appoints Vice-President Nelson Rockefeller to head the commission of eight members: former California Governor Ronald Reagan; former Treasury Secretary C. Douglas Dillon; NATO Commander General Lyman L. Lemnitzer, a former Chief of the Joint Chiefs of Staff; former Commerce Secretary John T. Connor; former Solicitor General Edwin N. Griswold; former University of Virginia President Edgar F. Shannon Jr.; and AFL-CIO Secretary-Treasurer Lane Kirkland.

January 11 In a coffee shop at LaGuardia Airport in New York, Lawrence Eagleburger, a top aide to Secretary of State Kissinger and Ramón Sánchez Parodi, Prime Minister Castro's special emissary from the Americas Department of the Communist Party, meet secretly to discuss U.S.-Cuban relations. Frank

Mankiewicz (*see* October 2, 1974) and Nestor García from the Cuban UN Mission also attend this session.

January 11 In Angola, the Portuguese government grants independence effective November 11. The three rebel factions meet in Alvor, Portugal, and agree to form a tripartite government until elections to be held after independence. The Popular Movement for the Liberation of Angola (MPLA) led by Agostinho Neto is backed by Cuba and the Soviet Union (Soviet aid is suspended at the time of the agreement). The National Front for the Liberation of Angola (FNLA) led by Holden Roberto, who has been on the CIA payroll since at least 1962, is backed by the United States, China and Zaire. The National Union for the Total Independence of Angola (UNITA), a group that split from the FNLA, is led by Jonas Savimbi and backed by South Africa and China (and later in 1975 by the United States). From various sources after the fact, including John Stockwell, the chief of the CIA's Task Force in Angola during this period, it is clear that the Ford Administration decides to undo the Alvor agreement by financing an FNLA attack against the MPLA. With the MPLA under siege, the Soviet Union resumes aid in March.

January 16 The State Department requests that the Justice Department expand the limit on travel by Cuban UN diplomats to a radius of 250 miles from a radius of 25 miles.

January 18 West Germany and Cuba reestablish diplomatic relations.

January 24-February 4 Frank Mankiewicz and Kirby Jones are again in Cuba, continuing their series of interviews with Prime Minister Castro. Mankiewicz again brings a secret message from Secretary of State Kissinger, calling the January 11 meeting "useful" and requesting another session.

January 27 The Senate sets up a bipartisan Select Intelligence Committee, chaired by Frank Church (D-Idaho), to investigate all aspects of the CIA's foreign and domestic operations as well as those of the FBI and other government intelligence units. Besides Church, there are five other Democratic members: Gary Hart (Colorado), Philip A. Hart (Michigan), Walter D. Huddleston (Kentucky), Walter F. Mondale (Minnesota), Robert Morgan (North Carolina). There are also five Republicans: Howard Baker (Tennessee), Barry Goldwater (Arizona), Charles Mathias Jr.

(Maryland), Richard S. Schweiker (Pennsylvania), John Tower (Texas).

January 28 Cuba attends a meeting of the Latin American Group at the United Nations for the first time since the OAS enacted the trade embargo in 1964. Jamaican Ambassador Donald O. Mills, the Group's chair, called the meeting and proposed that Cuban Ambassador Ricardo Alarcón be officially invited. Despite opposition from the United States and some of its Latin American allies, Cuba has recently been elected by the General Assembly to two UN agencies, the World Food Council and the Decolonization Committee. These votes undermine the OAS sanctions.

February 1 Omega 7, a Cuban exile organization, claims credit for bombing the Venezuelan Mission to the United Nations.

February 11 Omega 7 claims credit for bombing the Town and Campus Banquet Hall in Elizabeth, New Jersey.

February 12 The Ford Administration grants Litton Industries of Canada a license to export $2 million worth of furniture to Cuba. U.S. officials represent this to Cuban officials as a "good will" gesture, but it is more likely due to increasing pressure from the Canadian government for a change in the rule about subsidiary trade (*see* August 21).

February 21 Luciano Nieves, a Cuban exile advocate of U.S. dialogue with Cuba, is assassinated in Miami.

March 4 Senator Edward Kennedy (D-Massachusetts) introduces in the Senate a bill to lift the embargo against Cuba. In Miami, Juan José Peruyero, former president of the Bay of Pigs Veterans Association, says his organization is "under a lot of pressure to undertake some direct action to prevent any rapprochement with Castro since it was Senator Kennedy's brother who bungled our invasion plans." He calls Senator Kennedy's bill "an act of extreme villainy" and says "the reaction that Cuban exile groups... are planning is violent."

March 6 Cuba and Colombia reestablish diplomatic relations.

March 8 On International Women's Day, Cuba's Family Code, a law enacted on February 14, goes into effect with the aim of achieving equality between men and women in all of Cuban life.

March 17 The Nonaligned Movement's Coordinating Bureau holds its first Latin American meeting in Havana. Addressing the group on March 19, Prime Minister Castro renews his plea to oil-producing countries of the Third World to assist underdeveloped countries with oil profits rather than investing in developed countries.

April 7 Guyana's Prime Minister Forbes L. Burnham arrives for a state visit in Cuba.

April 21 Zambia's President Kenneth D. Kaunda arrives for a state visit in Cuba.

May Cuban official Flavio Bravo meets with Angolan MPLA leader Agostinho Neto, who asks for aid in shipping arms and mentions other possible aid by Cuba.

May The Bingham Resolution (initiated by Jonathan B. Bingham, Democrat of New York) to end the embargo is introduced in the House of Representatives. The Ford Administration says no action will be taken on the embargo until OAS sanctions are ended.

May 1 Following the Saigon surrender on April 30, Cubans turn the annual May Day rally into a celebration of the Vietnamese victory.

May 5 Visiting Cuba with his family, Senator George McGovern meets with Cuban officials, including Prime Minister Castro. When he returns to the United States, McGovern calls for an end to the embargo.

May 8 Senator Lowell Weicker Jr. (R-Connecticut) is recommending renewed relations with Cuba. He says that although the U.S. government disapproves of Cuba's communist government, the United States should not fear communism but rely on the strength of the U.S. system.

May 17 Reporting to Secretary of State Kissinger about Cuba policy, Secretary of State for Inter-American Affairs William Rogers writes that there is "a momentum for improving relations." He notes that although Cuban exiles might respond with "terrorist acts," opposition would be isolated. He points out that a recent Harris poll shows 53 percent of the American people favor full normalization of relations.

May 29 Robert A. Maheu testifies to the Senate Select Intelligence Committee about his work with the CIA in its attempts to kill Prime Minister Castro. (*See* August 1960)

May 30 Colonel Sheffield Edwards testifies to the Senate Select Intelligence Committee about CIA involvement in attempts to assassinate Prime Minister Castro. (*See* August 1960)

May 30 In a telephone interview with the Associated Press, retired Major General Edward G. Lansdale says that in 1962, on orders from President John F. Kennedy delivered through an intermediary, he began developing plans to remove Fidel Castro by any means, including assassination. Lansdale's interviews and testimony to the Senate Select Committee on Intelligence reveal Operation Mongoose (*see* November 30, 1961) to the U.S. public for the first time.

June 2 Max Gorman González announces in Miami that he plans to sue the CIA for involving him in a plot headed by Frank A. Sturgis (now a Watergate burglar) to assassinate Fidel Castro in 1968.

June 9 Knowing that the OAS nations will be voting to end sanctions against Cuba, William Rogers and Lawrence Eagleburger tell Secretary of State Kissinger they want to meet with Cuban officials before the OAS meets in July. Rogers points out that the bill sponsored by Senator Ted Kennedy to abolish all sanctions could pass. Kissinger responds, "That would be a great one to veto." But he agrees to try to revive the secret talks.

June 10 The Rockefeller Commission's report on CIA domestic operations is made public. The report does not include information on CIA assassination plots against foreign leaders because President Ford says that investigation is "incomplete and extremely sensitive."

June 18 Trinidad and Tobago's Prime Minister Eric Williams arrives for a state visit in Cuba.

June 19 Sam Giancana, Chicago crime syndicate chief recently in the headlines about his involvement in CIA plans to assassinate Prime Minister Castro, is shot and killed only days before he was to testify before the Senate Select Intelligence Committee. He was also set to testify before a federal grand jury. (*See* September 1960)

June 21 At Washington's National Airport, UN diplomat Nestor García meets with Lawrence Eagleburger and William Rogers and agrees to another secret session.

June 24 Ray S. Cline, CIA deputy director from 1962 to 1966, tells United Press International (UPI) that both the Eisenhower and

Kennedy Administrations allowed the CIA to plan for overthrowing Prime Minister Castro by any means, including assassination. He says the CIA during those years infiltrated Cuban exiles into Cuba to get rid of Castro any way they could.

June 24 Crime boss John Roselli (*see* September 1960) testifies to the Senate Select Intelligence Committee. Among other things, he tells about a 1961 plot to poison Fidel Castro, Raúl Castro and Che Guevara.

June 25 The Ford Administration ends a dispute with the Senate Select Intelligence Committee by providing the Committee with the evidence uncovered by the Rockefeller Commission related to CIA assassination plots. President Ford has authorized the Senate Committee to investigate CIA involvement in plots to assassinate foreign leaders.

June 25 William Harvey, former CIA official (*see* November 30, 1961), testifies to the Senate Select Intelligence Committee.

June 25 Cuba and Mozambique establish diplomatic relations on the day Mozambique becomes independent of Portugal.

June 26 At the CMEA meeting in Budapest, the Soviet Union, Bulgaria, Czechoslovakia, East Germany, Hungary, Poland and Romania agree to help construct the largest nickel plant in Cuba.

June 28 Swedish Prime Minister Olof Palme arrives for a state visit in Cuba, the first time a Swedish head of state has ever visited the island. Palme returns to Cuba occasionally until his assassination in 1986.

July 9 Prime Minister Michael Manley and 160 other Jamaicans arrive for a state visit in Cuba. Manley makes a speech praising the unselfish character of the aid that Cuba offers to other developing countries.

July 9 Meeting at the Pierre Hotel in New York City in another secret session, Ramón Sánchez Parodi, Nestor García, Lawrence Eagleburger and William Rogers agree to meet again in a few weeks.

July 18 Cuba establishes diplomatic relations with Ethiopia.

July 29 The OAS votes 16 to 3 (with two abstentions) to end collective sanctions against diplomatic and consular relations with Cuba, leaving each state "free to normalize or carry on relations with the Republic of Cuba at the level and in the form that each state deems convenient." Mexico and nine other countries called the meeting in order to put an end to the sanctions, demanding that the United States respect their sovereign right to determine trade policies of companies operating from their territory. Chile, Paraguay and Uruguay oppose lifting sanctions. Brazil and Nicaragua abstain. The Ford Administration's delegate, William S. Maillard, votes with the majority, recognizing that sanctions were being lifted anyway by one country after another.

July 29 Richard Bissell (*see* August 1960) says in an interview that Colonel Sheffield Edwards reported directly to him and, he believes, to CIA Director Allen Dulles about the CIA's secret cooperation with crime bosses Sam Giancana and John Roselli. Bissell speculates that the mob wanted to remove Fidel Castro in hopes of reopening their gambling casinos in Havana and perhaps also to build up credit with the U.S. government against future federal prosecution.

July 30 Senator George McGovern releases a summary of documents compiled by Cuban officials outlining 24 CIA-sponsored assassination plots against Prime Minister Castro and other Cuban leaders.

August Cuba continues its practice, begun in 1971, of requesting every year that the UN Decolonization Committee consider the matter of Puerto Rico.

August 17-22 Mexican President Luis Echeverría makes a state visit to Cuba, praising the Cuban people for "coming out on top" despite the embargo. At a joint press conference, Prime Minister Castro, responding to a question about the possibility of peaceful transition to socialism, remarks that he cannot say "it is absolutely impossible, in any given historical period and any given country, for far-reaching social changes to be brought about by peaceful means."

August 21 Following the OAS decision in July, the State Department announces that it will allow — with certain restrictions — exports to Cuba by foreign subsidiaries of U.S. firms, end the practice of withholding aid to countries that trade with Cuba, and cancel the rule that ships engaged in commerce with Cuba cannot refuel in U.S. ports. The ban on direct U.S.-Cuban trade remains in effect.

August 23-30 Foreign Minister Raúl Roa García attends a meeting of the Nonaligned Countries' Coordinating Bureau and then the full Conference of Nonaligned Foreign Ministers in Lima, Peru. On August 25, at the first session of the Conference, President Juan Velasco Alvarado, head of Peru's leftist military government for seven years, gives the keynote address, saying, "If the national oligarchies are an anachronism, so are the international oligarchies." Velasco emphasizes the need for Third World unity, recommending, for example, a joint center for Third World news. Four days later, Velasco is ousted in a bloodless military coup and replaced by General Francisco Morales Bermúdez, who then addresses the Conference's closing session.

August 29 The U.S. Commerce Department revokes the regulation that denied bunker fuel to ships from third countries which planned to call at a Cuban port after leaving the United States or which had called at a Cuban port any time after January 1, 1963.

September 5-7 The International Conference of Solidarity with the Independence of Puerto Rico, called by the World Peace Council, takes place in Havana with 300 delegates and 34 observers from 70 countries.

September 13 Marien Ngouabi, president of the Congo, arrives in Cuba for a state visit.

September 28 Prime Minister Castro responds to statements from Washington that ending the embargo depends on Cuba's attitude toward Puerto Rican independence: "There can be no improvement of relations with Cuba if such improvement presupposes renunciation of any of our basic principles."

October Speaking at the United Nations, Ambassador Ricardo Alarcón says that, at a time when the United States is trying to "pass on the negative side" of its economic problems to underdeveloped countries, it is especially important that these countries "transform their traditionally unfavorable trade relations" with the capitalist world market.

October 4 In addition to Cuban advisers who arrived in recent months, several hundred Cuban soldiers, along with a medical team, begin arriving in Angola.

October 8 The Treasury Department formally revokes the regulation that has made it illegal for subsidiaries of U.S. corporations in third countries (e.g., Canada, Mexico) to trade with Cuba. The Commerce Department takes similar action. Treasury's replacement regulation requires specific licenses for export to or import from Cuba in those third countries. The regulation lifts the prohibition on the use of vessels involved in trade with Cuba. Travel expenses by foreign employees are permitted by specific license but U.S. dollar accounts may not be used and U.S. citizens are not allowed to participate in these transactions.

October 17 Meeting in Panama, Cuba and more than 20 other countries found the Latin American Economic System (SELA).

October 17 A bomb, later attributed to Bay of Pigs veteran Rolando Otero Hernández, goes off at Miami International Airport causing considerable damage but no injuries.

October 23 South Africa invades Angola, driving toward the capital of Luanda.

November Responding to Washington's desire for Cuba to permit Cuban exiles to visit their families, Prime Minister Castro conveys a message to Kirby Jones (*see* January 24) that Cuba is prepared to permit a limited number of such visits for humanitarian reasons.

November In case there is any rapprochement with Cuba in the offing, 50 businesses and individuals form a Joint Corporate Committee on Cuban Claims to make sure their demands for compensation are met before any resumption of trade with Cuba. Lone Star Industries and Bangor Punta Corporation took the initiative in bringing together this group that had large holdings in Cuba at the time of the revolution. Cuba's position is that it would be willing to discuss demands for compensation after the embargo is ended if the U.S. government is willing to discuss compensation to Cuba for economic damage caused by the embargo.

November 3-4 The first meeting of the Caribbean Development and Cooperation Committee as a subsidiary body of the United Nations' Economic Commission for Latin America (ECLA) takes place in Havana with 12 Caribbean countries attending.

November 5 At the request of the MPLA, Cuba decides to send a battalion of combat troops with antitank weapons to help resist the South African invasion. When they arrive, South African troops have advanced more than 435 miles into Angola from Namibia, and Holden Roberto's FNLA forces are only fifteen miles north of Luanda. The Cuban campaign is named "Operation Carlota" (*see* November 5, 1843).

November 11 The MPLA announces establishment of the independent People's Republic of Angola, which is recognized immediately by Cuba.

November 20 The Senate Select Intelligence Committee releases a 347-page interim report on the CIA's involvement with assassination plots against foreign leaders, including at least eight plots to kill Prime Minister Castro from 1960 to 1965. CIA plans also targeted other Cuban leaders for assassination.

November 28 A bomb explodes in the car of Cuban Ambassador to Mexico Fernando López Muiño.

December U.S. media report that the CIA's covert operations in Angola, described as "recent," have in fact existed for at least 12 years. But the State Department and the CIA deny any involvement. Congress asks Secretary of State Kissinger to testify on the issue, but Kissinger sends Deputy Assistant Secretary of State for African Affairs Edward Mulcahy. On December 5, Mulcahy tells a Senate subcommittee chaired by Senator Dick Clark (D-Iowa) that the CIA is not operating in Angola or cooperating with South Africa. Later he says this false testimony was inadvertent because he had been out of the country and was not aware of what the CIA was doing.

December 10 At the United Nations, Ambassador Alarcón says: "What is being decided in Angola today is the fate of Africa."

December 17-18 The Senate holds secret as well as public sessions to discuss U.S. involvement in Angola. "What we are doing in Angola is unknown to most Americans," says Senate Majority Leader Mike Mansfield (D-Montana).

December 17-22 Cuba holds its First Party Congress, attended by 3,000 delegates. Prime Minister Castro, First Secretary of the Communist Party, presents the Party's Main Report, an 11-hour analysis of the history of the Cuban revolution, describing its mistakes as well as its accomplishments, its internal and its foreign policy development. The Congress approves the establishment of People's Power throughout the country and passes a Draft Socialist Constitution for submission to popular referendum. In this reorganization of government, Osvaldo Dorticós steps aside as president, remaining one of Cuba's leaders in the Central Committee and the Political Bureau of the Communist Party. At the closing rally, Castro describes Cuba's internationalism, specifically regarding Angola: "We are a Latin-African nation.... African blood flows freely through our veins.... Without proletarian internationalism the Cuban revolution would never have existed, and without proletarian internationalism we would cease to be revolutionaries."

December 19 By a vote of 54 to 22, the Senate passes an amendment to a Defense Department appropriations bill that would forbid U.S. aid for groups or individuals to conduct military or paramilitary operations in Angola. This amendment, introduced by Senators John Tunney, Dick Clark and Alan Cranston, is known as the Tunney Amendment or the Clark Amendment. (*See* January 27, 1976)

December 20 President Ford says Cuban involvement in Angola precludes any possibility of restoring full diplomatic relations.

December 27 General Vo Nguyen Giap, Vietnam's leader of warfare against both France and the United States, arrives at the head of a military delegation visiting Cuba.

December 29 Another bomb later attributed to Rolando Otero goes off, this time at LaGuardia Airport in New York.

December 31 In Miami, Bay of Pigs veteran José Antonio Prat says he is recruiting Cuban exiles and other Hispanics as mercenaries to fight against Cubans in Angola. "We pay their fares to Africa, and they sign their contracts with UNITA," says Prat, adding, "After Angola, this group would help overthrow Fidel Castro."

1976

January 10-15 General Omar Torrijos Herrera, head of the government of Panama, makes a state visit to Cuba. In the joint communiqué issued by the two countries, Cuba supports Panama's struggle for sovereignty in the Panama Canal Zone.

January 12 In a short, secret meeting at Washington's National Airport, Secretary of State for Inter-American Affairs William Rogers gives Cuban diplomat Nestor García a message from Secretary of State Kissinger saying that Cuba's troops in Angola present an obstacle to resolving issues at this time. García and Rogers discuss the issue of family visits (*see* November 1975).

January 22 Bay of Pigs veteran Rolando Otero is indicted by a federal grand jury on charges of planting six bombs in Miami in 1975. About 100 bombs have exploded in the Miami area in the last 18 months, and police attribute most of them to "anti-Castro" terrorists. On January 5, Otero left the United States for the Dominican Republic, where he was arrested but soon released on orders from President Joaquín Balaguer. He is later found in Chile and deported to the United States.

January 26 Prime Minister Pierre Elliott Trudeau of Canada and his wife, Margaret Trudeau, arrive for a state visit in Cuba.

January 27 By a vote of 323 to 99, the House of Representatives approves the Tunney (or Clark) Amendment to the Defense Department appropriations bill, barring U.S. aid to groups or individuals for conducting military or paramilitary operations in Angola. (*See* December 19, 1975, and June 30, 1976)

February 6 In another secret session with Cuba by the Kissinger State Department, Lawrence Eagleburger meets with Nestor

García to continue the discussion about family visits. García says such visits would be for one time only for up to 60 people with preference given to the aged or ill and to relatives of aged or ill Cubans.

February 7 Cuba and the Soviet Union sign their first five-year trade agreement.

February 8 Campaigning in New Hampshire for the Republican presidential nomination, President Ford repeats that Cuban troops in Angola "have stopped any possibility of U.S.-Cuban relations improving."

February 12 The MPLA announces victory against the South African forces with the crucial help of Cuban troops.

February 15 Cubans vote to approve the socialist Constitution, which will be enacted February 24.

February 18 As a result of the Senate Select Intelligence Committee's exposure of CIA plots to kill Fidel Castro and Patrice Lumumba of the Congo (Zaire), among others, President Ford signs an executive order on intelligence that includes a prohibition on assassinations.

February 22-March 16 Prime Minister Castro makes state visits to the Soviet Union, Yugoslavia, Bulgaria, Algeria and Guinea.

March 14 Meeting in Guinea, Prime Minister Castro and Angolan President Agostinho Neto draw up a program for the gradual withdrawal of Cuban troops from Angola.

March 15 At a rally in Conakry, Guinea, to celebrate Angola's victory against South Africa, President Sékou Touré of Guinea, President Luis Cabral of Guinea-Bissau, President Neto of Angola and Prime Minister Castro all speak. Each African leader expresses gratitude for the internationalist aid of Cuba. Says Touré: "We know that imperialism hates and threatens Cuba... but this did not keep Cuba from placing military forces and powerful matériel at the disposal of fighting Africa." Cabral says: "We know that our enemies are not at all happy over the fraternal aid which the revolutionary people of Cuba gave Angola." He says Portuguese colonialism would not have been expelled from Africa without the help of the Soviet Union and other socialist countries.

April 6 In international waters between Cuba and the United States, another armed attack sinks two Cuban fishing boats, *Ferro 119* and *Ferro 123*, killing one crew member, Bienvenido Mauriz Díaz, and wounding three. Cuban exiles in Miami claim responsibility. Cuba's Foreign Ministry charges the United States with violating international law as well as the U.S.-Cuban hijacking agreement by allowing the use of its territory for such activities.

April 21 Former CIA agent Manuel de Armas provides important information to Cuban officials about CIA activities against Cuba and other Latin American countries.

April 22 Two Cuban officials, Efrén Monteagudo Rodríguez and Adriana Corcho, die as a result of wounds from the explosion of a bomb in the Cuban Embassy in Lisbon, Portugal.

April 26 The Senate Select Intelligence Committee releases its final report on its investigation of intelligence activities, recommending, among other things, that Congress outlaw political assassinations by U.S. government agencies. (*See* February 9, 1978)

April 30 In Miami, Emilio Milián, a radio commentator who has criticized terrorism by rightwing Cuban exiles, loses both legs when a bomb explodes in his car.

May 1 Two hundred U.S. citizens of the Venceremos Brigade march in Havana's May Day parade.

May 24-28 Havana hosts the International Seminar on the Eradication of Apartheid and in Support of the Struggle for Liberation in South Africa, sponsored by the UN Special Committee against Apartheid.

June While George Bush is Director of the CIA, one of its operatives, Cuban exile Orlando Bosch, founds and leads the Commanders of the United Revolutionary Organizations (CORU), an umbrella group for terrorist actions against Cuba and against countries and individuals considered friendly to Cuba. Another founding member is CIA agent and Bay of Pigs veteran Eulalio Francisco (Frank) Castro. As revealed later in FBI and CIA documents (*see* June 23, 1989), CORU is soon involved in more than 50 bombings and, quite likely, political assassinations.

June 4 A *New York Times* article reports that Cuban medical teams are staffing central hospitals in 10 of 16 provinces in Angola.

June 6 Omega 7 claims responsibility for a bomb that explodes outside the Cuban Mission to the United Nations, causing some damage to the inside but no injuries.

June 30 The Tunney (or Clark) Amendment becomes law as part of the "International Security Assistance and Arms Export Control Act of 1976" (Public Law 94-329). This law forbids U.S. "assistance of any kind" to "any nation, group, organization, movement or individual to conduct military or paramilitary operations in Angola," ending legal CIA aid to UNITA or the FNLA. Congress undoes this law in 1986.

July 1 Working closely with CORU (*see* June), Cuban exile Luis Posada plants a bomb at the Costa Rica-Cuba cultural center in San José. Posada has been working with the CIA since at least 1959, trained in Guatemala for the Bay of Pigs invasion, and later became an aide to Venezuela's Interior Minister Carlos Andrés Pérez.

July 9 CORU is responsible for a bomb that goes off in baggage that was to be put on board a Cubana Airlines plane in Kingston, Jamaica.

July 10 CORU sets off a bomb in Cubana Airlines' Barbados office.

July 23 Cuban Artaignan Díaz is killed in Mérida, Mexico, when two men try to kidnap Cuban Consul Daniel Ferrer Fernández, who was with Díaz.

July 26 Angolan President Agostinho Neto shares the speakers' stand with Prime Minister Castro at the annual July 26 celebration in Cuba.

July 27 Mexico informs Cuba about the discovery and prevention of a plot by terrorists in Miami to plant three bombs in the Cuban Embassy in Mexico.

August 7 Crime figure John Roselli's body is found in an oil drum floating in Dumfoundling Bay near North Miami Beach. He testified in 1975 to the Senate Select Intelligence Committee about his involvement with CIA plots to assassinate Prime Minister Castro.

August 16 In a speech at the Fifth Summit Conference of Non-aligned Countries in Sri Lanka, Cuban representative Carlos Rafael Rodríguez says that underdeveloped countries owe foreign debts of more than $140 billion. He calls for a new international economic order to "transform international principles into obligations and commitments for those who have benefitted from our exploitation."

August 18 CORU bombs the Cubana Airlines office in Panama.

August 23   Bay of Pigs veteran Rolando Otero, on trial in Jacksonville, Florida, for Miami bombings, testifies that in preparation for the Bay of Pigs invasion he was trained in explosives by E. Howard Hunt Jr. He is convicted.

September 3   Ambassador Ricardo Alarcón again demands that Puerto Rico be placed on the agenda of the UN Decolonization Committee. He reports that South African authorities have been studying Puerto Rico as a model for establishing "bantustans" and creating in them puppet regimes under the guise of "self-determination."

September 8   Laotian Prime Minister Kaysone Phomvihane arrives for a state visit in Cuba.

September 16   Omega 7 claims responsibility for bombing the Soviet ship *Ivan Shepetkov* in the port of Elizabeth, New Jersey.

September 25   Prime Minister Miguel Anjos Trovoada of São Tomé y Príncipe arrives for a state visit in Cuba.

October 1   Sam Nujoma, president of the Southwest Africa People's Organization (SWAPO), arrives for a visit in Cuba. SWAPO is the guerrilla organization fighting to end the illegal South African occupation of Namibia.

October 4   The Socialist Party of Puerto Rico attributes to Cuban exiles an attempt to dynamite a television station that was showing *La nueva escuela* [The New School], a Cuban documentary about building and staffing dozens of junior high schools in Cuba.

October 6   A bomb planted aboard a Cubana Airlines plane explodes after the passenger jet takes off from Barbados, killing all 73 people aboard, of whom 57 are Cubans. The members of Cuba's fencing team, 11 Guyanese and five North Koreans are among the victims.

October 8   The Cuban Embassy in Caracas, Venezuela, is fired upon.

October 13   President Luis Cabral (brother of Amilcar Cabral) of Guinea-Bissau arrives for a state visit in Cuba.

October 14   Two Cuban exiles, Orlando Bosch and Luis Posada, and two Venezuelans, Freddy Lugo and Hernán Ricardo Losano, are arrested in Venezuela and Trinidad for the October 6 terrorist bombing. Posada has served as an aide to Carlos Andrés Pérez, who is now president of Venezuela. During the subsequent investigation, Venezuelan and U.S. authorities report that a network of terrorists has carried out a "vast" number of attacks in seven countries against Cuba and other countries and individuals deemed friendly toward Cuba (*see* June 1976 and June 23, 1989).

October 15 At the memorial service for the people killed aboard the airliner on October 6, Prime Minister Castro says at least one of the people arrested for the bombing is a known CIA agent and that, as a result of this crime, Cuba will abrogate the anti-hijacking agreement with the United States. He says Cuba will not sign another agreement of this kind "until the terrorist campaign unleashed against Cuba is ended once and for all." U.S. officials, including Secretary of State Kissinger, deny that the CIA, headed by George Bush, had anything to do with the bombing.

October 26 CORU member and CIA agent Aldo Vera Serafín, a Cuban exile, is shot to death in San Juan, Puerto Rico.

November 2 The Municipal Assemblies of People's Power elect delegates to Provincial Assemblies and deputies to the National Assembly of People's Power.

November 2 Democrat James Earl (Jimmy) Carter Jr. wins the presidential election, defeating President Ford.

November 7 A powerful bomb explodes in the offices of Cubana Airlines in Madrid, Spain.

November 15 The House Select Committee on Assassinations holds its first formal meeting to begin an investigation of the assassinations of both President John F. Kennedy and Dr Martin Luther King, Jr. After this Select Committee is established, there is a renewed campaign to connect Fidel Castro with Kennedy's death.

November 30 Angolan Prime Minister Lopo Do Nascimento arrives in Cuba for a state visit.

December 2-3 The National Assembly of People's Power meets for the first time. Fidel Castro is elected president of the State Council, a position which, under the new Constitution, consolidates the previous positions of president and prime minister. The president of the State Council now serves as head of state, head of government, and commander in chief of the Armed Forces.

December 19 The *Los Angeles Times* reports that a federal prosecutor and an FBI agent plan to go to Venezuela in early January to interrogate Cuban exile Orlando Bosch about the September 21 assassination in Washington of Orlando Letelier, who had served as a top official in Chilean President Salvador Allende's government. The Justice Department believes not that Bosch did the actual killing, but that he can corroborate evidence pointing to a murder-for-hire plot in which Cuban exiles assassinated Letelier with a car bomb that also took the life of U.S. citizen Ronni Moffitt and wounded her husband, Michael Moffitt.

1977

January 10 At his confirmation hearings before the Senate Foreign Relations Committee, Secretary of State designate Cyrus R. Vance says it is time to begin to remove obstacles in the way of normalizing relations with Cuba.

January 15 President Castro says Cuba favors détente but does not accept "humiliating conditions" as the price for improved relations.

January 24 Thirty members of the House of Representatives write a letter urging President Castro to release Huber Matos, who was arrested in October 1959.

January 25 The Carter Administration's UN Ambassador Andrew Young says Cuban troops in Angola bring "a certain stability and order" to Southern Africa.

January 31 Secretary of State Vance tells a press conference that the Carter Administration is willing to discuss normalizing relations with Cuba despite the presence of Cuban troops in Angola. But in several statements in February, President Carter says that before actual normalization could take place, Cuba must pay attention to human rights, remove its troops from Angola, and stop interfering with other countries in the Western Hemisphere. In January, Frank Mankiewicz once more serves as the intermediary for arranging secret meetings between U.S. and Cuban officials.

February Cuban UN official Nestor García and State Department Director of Cuban Affairs Culver Gleysteen begin meeting in secret to arrange formal discussions about maritime boundaries and fishing rights.

February 9   In a CBS television interview, President Castro says that if President Carter wishes to talk, "I will with pleasure talk to him."

February 25   Seven Cuban exile leaders tell Secretary of State Vance that they oppose any U.S. negotiations with Cuba.

March 1-April 8   President Castro makes state visits to Libya, South Yemen, Somalia, Ethiopia, Tanzania, Mozambique, Angola, Algeria, East Germany and the Soviet Union.

March 9   At a Libyan-Cuban friendship rally in Tripoli, President Castro warns that "the imperialists will try to isolate the Libyan revolution; they will even try to strangle it as they tried to do with the Cuban revolution."

March 9   Admiral Stansfield Turner succeeds George Bush as CIA director.

March 10-16   During this week of visits to African countries, Cuban officials hold a secret meeting with Ethiopian, Somali and South Yemeni officials at which Somalia pledges not to resort to war as a means of settling differences with Ethiopia on the question of Ogaden. Somalia breaks this agreement in July. Cuba reveals the existence of the secret agreement a year later, in March 1978.

March 19   President Carter does not renew the ban (renewable every six months) on travel by U.S. citizens to Cuba, Vietnam, Cambodia and North Korea.

March 21   As a corollary to ending the travel ban, the Carter Administration lifts the ban on U.S. citizens' spending dollars in Cuba. In addition, surveillance flights over Cuba have been quietly suspended (satellites continue to provide surveillance).

March 21   President Castro holds a news conference in Dar Es Salaam, Tanzania, and responds to charges by Zaire's President Mobutu and his allies that Cuban troops are helping Katangan rebels in the revolt taking place in Zaire. Castro states categorically that not a single Cuban is involved in Zaire and adds that, as far as he is aware, Angolans are not involved either. Asked about U.S.-Cuban relations, Castro responds, "The United States maintains a blockade against Cuba. We don't have a blockade against the United States. The United States has a naval base on our soil by force. We don't have any naval base in U.S. territory. The United States has promoted attacks and subversion against our country — and mercenary invasions. We haven't organized subversion against or sent mercenary invaders to the United States." He says, "These matters must be the political basis for any negotiations," adding, "We will not ask them to renounce capitalism, but, by the same token, we will not agree to any concessions on matters of socialist and revolutionary principle."

March 21 Foreign Minister Isidoro Malmierca Peoli, opening the Second Meeting of the Caribbean Development and Cooperation Committee in the Dominican Republic, explains that, although the economic crisis in the capitalist world has worsened since the first meeting in 1975, in Cuba unemployment has been eliminated, children do not go hungry, the infant mortality rate is comparable to that in developed countries, all children and young people go to school and the vast majority of babies are born in hospitals.

March 24 Vice-Minister of Foreign Relations Pelegrín Torras and Assistant Secretary of State for American Republics Terrence Todman head the Cuban and U.S. delegations that meet secretly in New York for the first of a series of discussions, as arranged by Nestor García and Culver Gleysteen. Among the U.S. participants are Gleysteen and Wayne Smith, who was a junior officer in the U.S. Embassy in Havana from 1957 until Washington severed relations in 1961. After four days, talks adjourn until April.

March 27 At a mass rally in Angola, President Castro refutes in detail the charges of Cuban involvement in Zaire.

March 30 President Castro meets in Angola with Oliver Tambo, president of South Africa's African National Congress (ANC). Since 1960, Cuba has been providing aid to the ANC, primarily educational. In June 1990, Thabo Mbeki, ANC director of international relations who accompanies ANC leader Nelson Mandela on his U.S. tour, tells the *Wall Street Journal* that more ANC doctors were trained in Cuba than anywhere else. During the same 1990 tour, Patford Shuma, also accompanying Mandela, says that after the uprising in Soweto in June 1976, when students protesting apartheid education were shot, Cuba began military training for the ANC.

April 5 In what is widely interpreted as a sign of improving relations between Havana and Washington, Senator and Mrs

George McGovern and Senator James Abourezk (both Democrats from South Dakota) watch from the stands as a basketball team from South Dakota universities — the first U.S. sports team to compete on the island since 1960 — plays the Cuban men's team. During the visit, President Castro tells McGovern that Cuba will not sign another anti-hijacking agreement until the U.S. embargo ends but that Cuba will abide by the agreement anyway because Cuba agrees with it in principle.

April 9 Armed Forces Minister Raúl Castro meets with Senator and Mrs McGovern, Senator Abourezk and Representative Les Aspin (D-Colorado).

April 13 The *New York Times* reports that the focus of the FBI investigation of the assassination of Orlando Letelier in September 1976 continues to be on CORU, the Cuban exile organization founded earlier that year by CIA agent Orlando Bosch and others.

April 15 Cuba formally revokes its anti-hijacking agreement with the United States. (*See* October 15, 1976)

April 25-27 Assistant Secretary of State for American Republics Terrence Todman heads the U.S. delegation that meets with Cuban negotiators in Havana to continue discussions begun in March. They sign an accord on fishing rights in the waters between Cuba and Florida. Effective March 1, the United States unilaterally extended its "fishery conservation zone" to 200 miles offshore, and Cuba reciprocated. Theoretically this would mean that part of Cuba is encompassed by the U.S. zone and part of Florida by the Cuban zone. The new accord draws a maritime boundary halfway between the two countries, which are 90 miles apart at the closest point. The Cuban fishing fleet has regularly sought, and been regularly granted, licenses to fish in waters claimed by the United States. The new accord allows Cuba to fish in U.S. waters for species in abundant supply. Two years later, on January 2, 1979, Armed Forces Minister Raúl Castro points out that the U.S. declaration of a 200-mile limit has implied a reduction of Cuba's traditional fishing zone.

April 28 Two members of the U.S. delegation in Havana for the talks, Wayne Smith and legal adviser Frank Willis, remain in Cuba to visit U.S. citizens in Combinado del Este prison.

May Now that U.S. citizens are free to travel to Cuba, Carras Lines begins the first U.S. cruises to the island since the ban on travel was imposed.

May 5 South Africa attacks Namibian refugee camps in southern Angola, killing more than 500 women, children and elderly people in the Cassinga massacre. Orphaned, the several dozen children who escape are later brought to Cuba to be educated on the Isle of Pines (renamed in 1978 the Isle of Youth).

May 25 A bomb explosion in the Florida offices of Mackey International Airlines leads to cancellation of the airline's plans for charter and regular flights to Cuba.

May 25 The State Department says it has received reports about the arrival of 50 Cuban military advisers in Ethiopia and warns that Cuban military activity there could be an obstacle to improvement of relations.

May 30 Cuba and the United States agree to establish "interests sections" in each other's countries beginning September 1. These will deal primarily with trade and consular matters and will serve as channels of communication. As obstacles in the way of normalization of relations, the Carter Administration cites U.S. claims of more than $2 billion in confiscated property; Cuba's refusal to allow U.S. citizens imprisoned in Cuba and Cubans with U.S. relatives to leave; Cuban troops in Angola; Cuba's demand for an end to the embargo; and Cuba's insistence that U.S. troops stop occupying Cuban territory at the Guantánamo Naval Base. In addition to the release of U.S. prisoners (mostly incarcerated on drug charges), President Carter insists that Cuba should release all political prisoners.

June During a visit to Angola, Armed Forces Minister Raúl Castro delivers a message to President Neto from President Castro, offering four schools where some 2,000 Angolan children could finish elementary school, go through junior high and then enroll in Cuban technological institutes. Mozambican President Samora Moisés Machel asks if his country's children could also have this opportunity. This leads to the opening of the internationalist schools on the Isle of Pines (later the Isle of Youth).

June 3 Cuba announces that it will release 10 U.S. prisoners immediately and review the other dozen or so cases.

June 8 Carras Lines announces cancellation of its cruises to Cuba because of bomb threats.

June 9 An interview of President Castro by Barbara Walters is broadcast on ABC television.

June 10 CBS television presents "The CIA's Secret Army," hosted by Bill Moyers, about the CIA's organization of Cuban exiles for attacks against Cuba for 18 years. Part of the program is an interview with President Castro, who says that there have been at least 24 known CIA assassination plots against him and other Cuban leaders.

June 16 The Senate Foreign Relations Committee rejects a proposal to end the embargo. President Carter had lobbied even against allowing the trade of foods and medicines ostensibly because the State Department argued that this would give away bargaining chips for negotiations expected to take place later this year.

June 16 The head of the Communist Party in the Soviet Union is also the chief of state as Leonid Brezhnev becomes president, replacing Nikolai V. Podgorny who resigned in May.

June 20 In Cuba's territorial waters, the Cuban Border Patrol seizes the *Nita Sue*, a boat carrying a load of marijuana and crewed by Donnie Rebozo, close relative of Richard Nixon's friend Bebe Rebozo, and Byron Moore, both of Miami. (*See* August 11)

July Wayne Smith replaces Culver Gleysteen as director of the State Department's Office of Cuban Affairs.

July 26 In his annual speech on this occasion, President Castro says there are 4,100 Cuban civilians working in other parts of the world and that by the end of the year there will be around 6,000. Their services — medical, educational, agricultural, etc. — will continue to be offered free of charge to those who face serious economic difficulties while those countries with better economic conditions will from now on "compensate in part."

July 28 Joshua Nkomo, president of the Zimbabwe African People's Union (ZAPU) and co-leader of the Zimbabwe Patriotic Union, arrives for a visit in Cuba. ZAPU is one of the two main rebel groups opposing the government of Ian Smith in Rhodesia.

August 11 Returning from Havana to Washington, Senator Frank Church (D-Idaho) says that Cuba has agreed to allow the Cuban families of 80 to 100 U.S. citizens to leave Cuba. He says President Castro told him Cuba had released the *Nita Sue* (*see*

June 20) and another boat recently seized in Cuba's territorial waters. Church asks President Carter for a meeting to convey Castro's views on U.S.-Cuban relations.

August 15 U.S. federal and state agents arrest Bay of Pigs veteran Pedro Gil in Miami and seize three boats, an antitank cannon and other weapons, evidently foiling a hit-and-run raid against Cuba.

September 1 Cuba and the United States open interests sections in the two countries as agreed on May 30. Ramón Sánchez Parodi heads the Cuban Interests Section in the Czechoslovakian Embassy in Washington and Lyle Franklin Lane heads the U.S. Interests Section in the Swiss Embassy in Havana. This represents the first direct diplomatic presence of Cuba and the United States in Washington and Havana since the United States severed diplomatic relations January 3, 1961.

September 23 President Salem Robaya Alí of South Yemen arrives for a state visit in Cuba.

September 28 Speaking to a rally at the First Congress of the Committees for the Defense of the Revolution (CDRs), President Castro lists four developments that indicate a "lessening of tension" during the Carter Administration: halting surveillance flights, signing the fishing and maritime boundaries agreement, lifting the travel ban, and establishing interests sections. He also mentions continuing problems, such as the U.S. embargo and occupation of the naval base at Guantánamo. He repeats that Cuba would be willing to discuss payment of compensation as demanded by some U.S. businesses as long as the United States is willing to compensate for the damage the embargo has caused the Cuban economy.

October 5 The U.S. Businessmen's Conference, at which the Cuban Foreign Trade Ministry is represented, comes out in favor of ending the U.S. embargo.

October 9-13 President Samora Machel of Mozambique makes a state visit to Cuba.

October 15 Oliver Tambo, president of the African National Congress (ANC) of South Africa, heads a delegation that arrives for a visit in Cuba.

October 16-21 President Castro makes a state visit to Jamaica where he and Prime Minister Michael Manley speak at a rally October 17. Manley describes how Cuba moved an army across the

Atlantic "at a time when the racist forces of South Africa were about to overrun a newly independent nation" and how the Cubans helped to defeat South Africans in battle and insured the liberation of Angola, an act that "changed the balance of power in the world."

October 24 In Havana, Cuban jurists host the Third Conference of the American Association of Jurists with participants from the United States, Mexico, Panama, Argentina, Ecuador, Chile, Canada, Jamaica and Puerto Rico.

October 27 Sam Nujoma, leader of SWAPO in Namibia, arrives for a visit in Cuba.

November 13 Somalia expels all Soviet advisers and breaks diplomatic relations with Cuba, citing Soviet support for Ethiopia in Ogaden and the presence of Cuban advisers in Ethiopia.

November 16 In a statement for attribution to a "high-ranking Administration official," National Security Adviser Zbigniew Brzezinski tells reporters that there has been a recent military buildup by Cuba in African countries that makes normalization of relations with Cuba "impossible." He cites an increase of 4,000 to 6,000 Cuban troops in Angola since July, a figure that turns out to be based on a change in CIA bookkeeping, not on an actual increase.

Mid-December Cuba sends combat troops to Ethiopia.

December 20 Omega 7 claims responsibility for explosions in two New Jersey offices (Union City and Elizabeth) of *Almacén el Español*, a company that ships food and clothing relief to Cuba.

December 23 The first contingent of the Antonio Maceo Brigade arrives in Cuba for a three-week visit. The Brigade is composed of young people whose parents took them out of Cuba when they were children. This Brigade becomes a regular event with participants from the United States as well as from other countries to which Cubans emigrated.

December 24 Noting a few changes for the better in relations with the United States during the Carter Administration, President Castro reminds the Second National Assembly of People's Power that "the essential thing" is that the U.S. embargo continues. As for the issue of Cuban troops in Angola, Castro asks, "What moral basis can the United States have to speak about our troops in Africa when their own troops are stationed right here on our own national territory, at the Guantánamo Naval Base?" He says it would be "ridiculous" for Cuba to tell the United States that, to improve relations with Cuba, it must remove its troops from the Philippines or Turkey or Greece or South Korea or any of the other numerous countries where U.S. troops are stationed.

December 26 Omega 7 claims responsibility for a bomb that explodes at the Venezuelan Mission to the United Nations to protest the continued imprisonment in Venezuela of Orlando Bosch for the terrorist bombing that killed 73 people in October 1976.

1978

January The U.S.-Cuban accord on fishing rights goes into effect on a provisional basis, not yet ratified by either country.

January 9 The U.S. Treasury Department allows U.S. residents to provide support payments to close relatives in Cuba of no more than $500 in any three-month period. U.S. residents may also send $500 for the purpose of enabling a relative to emigrate.

January 16-19 Cuban Border Patrol and U.S. Coast Guard representatives meet in Havana to discuss cooperation in rescue operations, drug law enforcement and antiterrorism.

January 21 The State Department approves a one-time sale to Cuba of medical supplies, valued at under $80,000.

February 9 The Senate Select Intelligence Committee proposes legislation to prohibit political assassinations by U.S. intelligence agents. (*See* April 26, 1976)

February 13 U.S. intelligence officials say that Soviet Air Force units have begun to assist Cuba, apparently to free Cuban pilots for service in Ethiopia. At a press conference on February 16, Soviet Deputy Defense Minister Kirill S. Moskalenko calls the report "an invention."

February 27 Secretary of State Vance tells the National Governors' Conference that he does not foresee normal relations with Cuba in the immediate future, citing Cuban troops in Africa as the reason.

March 9 Following a swift Ethiopian advance through Ogaden, President Carter announces that Somalia has agreed to withdraw its troops from Ethiopia's Ogaden region.

March 14 *Granma* publishes a detailed account of Cuba's role in Ethiopia, not previously publicly announced.

March 15 President Castro explains that Cuba did not publicly announce its military role in Ethiopia sooner because it was up to the Ethiopians to make that announcement first, which they have now done. He points out that Cubans knew of it "unofficially."

March 17 In a major speech at Wake Forest, North Carolina, President Carter announces a decision for a military buildup of both nuclear and conventional forces.

March 20-23 U.S. and Cuban fishery officials hold technical talks in Havana.

March 22 Signaling that Cuban troops in Africa will be a key Republican issue in upcoming elections, the chairman of the Republican National Committee, Bill Brock, tells a news conference that the United States should expel Cuban diplomats at the Cuban Interests Section in Washington and bring home its diplomats at the Interests Section in Havana because of Cuban troops in Angola and Ethiopia.

April 14 In Miami, the FBI arrests two Omega 7 members, Guillermo Novo Sampol and Alvin Ross Díaz, on bomb-related offenses. Both have also been connected with the 1976 assassination of Orlando Letelier. Rolando Otero, convicted in Miami of bombing charges, may cooperate in the grand jury investigation of the Letelier murder.

April 15 Before leaving to take another post in the Cuban government, UN Ambassador Ricardo Alarcón tells a press conference in New York City that Cuba will not give up any foreign policy principles for normalization of relations with the United States. Raúl Roa Kourí becomes the new ambassador.

April 21 Ethiopian President Mengistu Haile Mariam arrives for a state visit in Cuba.

April 22 Juan Almeida Bosque, Vice-President of Cuba's Council of State, arrives in New York to head Cuba's delegation at the UN conference on Namibia. While in New York, he meets with UN Ambassador Andrew Young to discuss Africa and U.S.-Cuban relations.

May David Aaron, deputy to National Security Adviser Brzezinski, and José Luis Padrón, soon to be Cuba's Minister of Tourism, meet secretly in New York, following an overture by President

Castro through Cuban exile Bernardo Benes. Padrón raises the possibility of releasing political prisoners provided that the United States agree to accept them. This first meeting is soon followed by others between Padrón and Under Secretary of State David A. Newsom in New York and Washington.

May 8 President Joachim Yhomby Opango of the Congo arrives for a state visit in Cuba.

May 9 The U.S. Treasury Department allows travel-related transactions by Cuban visitors to the United States who possess U.S. visas. Treasury also allows payment, by special license, to Cubans and U.S. citizens for public exhibitions or performances in each others' countries.

May 12 Returning from the first visit to the United States by a delegation of the Cuban film industry, director Santiago Alvarez says, "This visit has made us realize firsthand how poorly informed the U.S. people are about the Cuban reality."

May 16 At a press conference, former Secretary of State Henry Kissinger calls Cuban soldiers in Africa "proxy Soviet troops" and warns that their activity jeopardizes détente with the Soviet Union.

Mid-May When Katangan rebels stage another uprising in Zaire's Shaba province, President Castro calls the U.S. Interests Section and tells Lyle Lane that he had tried to stop the incursion when he first learned of it and that he is ready to help defuse the situation if possible. The *New York Times* reports this development on May 19. But also on the 19th, while the Non-aligned Countries are holding a Ministerial Meeting of the Coordinating Bureau in Havana, the Carter Administration charges that Cuban troops are involved in the uprising. On the following day, Cuba's Foreign Ministry issues a statement vigorously denying any involvement.

May 23 President Carter complains to a group of senators about restrictions (primarily the Clark Amendment) on his ability to aid guerrillas fighting against Cuban troops in Angola.

May 25 President Carter continues to blame Cuba for the Katangan uprising.

May 25 A secret meeting takes place between Secretary of State Cyrus Vance and Vice-President Carlos Rafael Rodríguez.

May 30 Vice-President Rodríguez tells the UN General Assembly's special session on disarmament that eradication of the threat of world war is the most urgent task of the times. Reacting to President Carter's March 17 Wake Forest speech, he points to a "new uneasiness" about the U.S. military buildup.

May 30 At a meeting of NATO heads of state in Washington, President Carter denounces Cuban and Soviet actions in Africa.

June 6 Joshua Nkomo, leader of ZAPU, acknowledges that Cuban advisers are training ZAPU guerrillas to fight against Ian Smith's government in what is still known officially as "Rhodesia."

June 8-9 CIA Director Admiral Stansfield Turner testifies to House and Senate committees about CIA reports of Cuban involvement with the Katangan rebels.

June 9 After making its own investigation, the Senate Foreign Relations Committee declares the CIA's evidence on Cuban involvement with Katangans "inconclusive."

June 9 In an unprecedented action, Tanzanian President Julius K. Nyerere calls the entire foreign diplomatic corps to his office in Dar Es Salaam to hear a 45-minute speech in which he says that Cuban forces in Angola and Ethiopia have been invited by legitimate governments faced with external aggression.

Mid-June After President Castro states publicly that he had informed the United States about reports of an impending Katangan uprising, President Carter acknowledges this but says Castro should have done more.

June 18 ABC television presents an interview with President Castro by Barbara Walters (ABC), Richard Valeriani (NBC), and Ed Rabel (CBS) in which Castro says he would like to see President Carter reelected because he "is the only president in the last 20 years to have made some positive gestures toward us." Castro calls National Security Adviser Zbigniew Brzezinski "irresponsible," saying he "does not master international problems" and "ignores the realities of today's world," adding that "it seems to me he plays with war."

June 22 Zairean President Mobutu announces that Zaire is holding Cuban prisoners captured in Shaba, but U.S. investigators state on the following day that there are no such prisoners.

June 28 Speaking with a group of U.S. mayors in Cuba, President Castro says he would not object to a meeting with President Carter.

June 28 The National Assembly of People's Power changes the name of the Isle of Pines (*Isla de Pinos*) to the Isle of Youth (*Isla de la Juventud*) in honor of the World Festival of Youth and Students that will meet soon in Cuba.

July 6 Jamaican Prime Minister Michael Manley arrives for a state visit in Cuba.

July 9 A group of 1,260 young Ethiopians arrives in Cuba to study on scholarships at the Isle of Youth. Most are children of people killed in the fighting in Ogaden.

July 19 At the Organization of African Unity (OAU) meeting in Sudan, Mozambican President Samora Machel says "imperialism is now unleashing a violent campaign against the internationalist aid that African countries, Cuba and other socialist countries are giving to the struggle of our continent." He praises the "exemplary sacrifices" of Cuba and the Soviet Union. Lt. Gen. Olusegun Obasanjo, head of Nigeria's military government, says Cuba has intervened in Africa "on behalf of legitimate African interests."

July 25-30 As foreign ministers of the Nonaligned Movement meet in Yugoslavia, U.S. media have reported that U.S. officials approached 15 of the members about contesting Cuba's role in the Movement. Egypt tries and fails to get the 1979 Nonaligned Summit Conference either moved from Cuba or postponed. Somalia tries but fails to get Cuba expelled.

July 26 President Castro calls for reactivation of Cuba's Committees of Solidarity with Vietnam now that Vietnam is once again under attack — this time by China.

July 28-August 5 The 11th World Festival of Youth and Students takes place in Havana as 18,500 delegates from 145 countries attend hundreds of events. The conference that attracts the most world attention is the "International Tribunal" where several countries' delegates testify about CIA activities in their nations.

Rolando Cubela, serving a 25-year prison sentence in Cuba, testifies that his work for the CIA included an attempt to assassinate Fidel Castro in 1966. Cuba also unveils double agents who describe their work with the CIA.

July 30 The Nonaligned Movement confirms that its Sixth Summit Conference will be in Havana September 3-7, 1979.

August Both the State Department and the National Security Council send representatives (Newsom and Aaron) to a secret meeting in Atlanta, Georgia, with Cuban officials and reach a preliminary agreement for a release of political prisoners. The Cubans want to announce the agreement but the Carter Administration wants negotiations to remain secret. The U.S. government now refers to those released prior to August 1 as "ex-prisoners" and those released afterward as "prisoners," and says that it can only process "ex-prisoners" after accepting all the "prisoners." This means that many prisoners already released by Cuba will face even lengthier waiting periods before being considered for U.S. visas, a situation that increases emigration pressures within Cuba.

August 1 A federal grand jury in Washington indicts five Cuban exiles from New Jersey for the 1976 assassination of Orlando Letelier and Ronni Moffitt, as well as other crimes. They are Guillermo Novo Sampol, his brother Ignacio Novo Sampol, Alvin Ross Díaz, José Dionisio Suárez and Virgilio Pablo Paz. An unindicted coconspirator, U.S.-born Chilean intelligence agent Michael Vernon Townley, pleads guilty August 11 to murder and becomes the key prosecution witness.

August 2 Eusebio Azcué López, former Cuban consul in Mexico City, testifies to the International Tribunal in Havana about the person claiming to be Lee Harvey Oswald who visited him on September 27, 1963, to request a visa for Cuba: "In no way did the person I saw in film and photographs [after the assassination of President Kennedy] resemble the person who visited me."

August 31 Released from prison by the Somoza regime in response to demands by a Sandinista commando group which had seized the National Palace in Managua and hundreds of hostages, 22 Nicaraguan revolutionaries arrive for safe haven in Cuba.

September Tomás Borge, a leader of the Sandinista National Liberation Front (FSLN), visits Cuba and meets with President Castro.

September 1 Cuba publicly offers to let 500 to 1,000 political prisoners leave for the United States.

September 6   At a press conference with Cuban American journalists and several other U.S. journalists, President Castro indicates that Cuba will soon release around 48 political prisoners in response to efforts by the Cuban community abroad and by others in the United States. Castro proposes a dialogue (*El Diálogo*) between Cuba and Cubans outside the island. This leads to the creation of the "Committee of 75," a group of Cubans (later more than 75) chosen to negotiate on behalf of the estimated 1.2 million Cubans abroad.

September 9   President Adolfo Suárez González of Spain arrives in Havana for the first visit by a Spanish head of state to Cuba.

September 9   Omega 7 claims responsibility for a bomb that explodes at the Cuban UN Mission injuring three people.

September 11-20   President Castro makes state visits to Ethiopia, Libya and Algeria.

September 28   The House Select Committee on Assassinations continues its investigation of the assassinations of both President Kennedy and Dr Martin Luther King, Jr., hearing testimony from Santo Trafficante Jr. (*See* September 1960)

September 29   The UN Security Council approves Resolution 435 regarding Namibian independence, recognizing the Southwest Africa People's Organization (SWAPO) as the sole legitimate representative of the Namibian people. The Security Council in January 1970 and the International Court of Justice (World Court) in June 1971 declared South Africa's occupation of Namibia illegal. Resolution 435 calls for a ceasefire, withdrawal of South African troops, a transitional UN administration backed by UN peacekeeping forces, and UN-supervised elections. South Africa does not comply with this resolution, and it requires another decade of fighting in Angola and Namibia to win this independence.

October   The Justice Department sends a team of FBI, Immigration and Naturalization Service (INS), and State Department officials to Havana to start screening about 50 political prisoners and relatives for entry to the United States.

October   At another secret session with Cuban officials in Mexico, U.S. negotiators insist that Cuba withdraw from Angola.

October 5 Omega 7 claims responsibility for a bomb blast at Madison Square Garden in New York to protest the presence of Cuban boxers.

October 21 Cuba releases 46 political prisoners and former prisoners and 33 of their relatives who fly to Miami.

October 21 In New York, Omega 7 claims responsibility for a bomb blast at the influential Spanish-language newspaper, *El Diario-La Prensa*, where editors get frequent death threats against a Cuban American reporter who has investigated Omega 7 and similar groups.

November 8 President Manuel Pinto da Costa of São Tomé y Príncipe arrives in Cuba for a state visit.

November 9 Joshua Nkomo, leader of the Zimbabwe African People's Union (ZAPU), again visits Cuba.

November 10 Continuing a policy of sharing medical personnel with other countries, 122 Cuban doctors and nurses arrive in Libya to spend two years working there.

November 12 A U.S. SR-71 overflies Cuba to look for Soviet-built MiGs. Cuba states that MiGs have been there for almost a year and must have been detected long before now. The overflight coincides with large-scale U.S. military maneuvers in the area. Cuba puts its defense forces on full alert.

November 20-21 The Committee of 75 and Cuban officials hold the first of two negotiating sessions in Havana, the beginning of "the Dialogue."

December Officials from the State Department (Peter Tarnoff) and the National Security Council (Robert Pastor) meet secretly with Cuban officials in Havana. President Castro receives them and protests the November military maneuvers off the coast of Cuba. Tarnoff and Pastor request the release of the four U.S. prisoners still in Cuba (all convicted of espionage or counterrevolutionary activity). Castro suggests that perhaps an exchange could be made for four Puerto Rican independence leaders imprisoned in the United States since the 1950s.

December 8-9 At its second negotiating session, the "Dialogue" results in agreement on three issues: Cuba will release 3,000 political prisoners (more than 80 percent of the total) plus 600 other prisoners at the rate of at least 400 a month, do its part toward reuniting members of separated families, and allow Cubans abroad to visit relatives.

December 13 Saddam Hussein, second in command of the government of Iraq and of the Ba'ath Party, arrives for a visit in Cuba.

December 29 Omega 7 claims responsibility for two bomb explosions, one at Cuba's UN Mission and another at Lincoln Center in New York, forcing cancellation of performances by the Cuban musical group, *Orquesta Aragón*.

1979

January 1 Cuba implements its new policy of allowing visits from Cubans abroad to relatives. Tens of thousands of such visits take place during the first year.

January 7-9 UN Secretary General Kurt Waldheim visits Cuba for two days.

January 17 The State Department says the aircraft sighted in Cuba (*see* November 12, 1978) are not adapted for carrying nuclear weapons and therefore do not violate the 1962 agreement between President Kennedy and Premier Khrushchev.

January 22 Togo becomes the first of several African countries, including Lesotho, the Sudan and Zaire, with which Cuba establishes diplomatic relations this year,

February 1 At a meeting of the Nonaligned Coordinating Bureau in Mozambique, Foreign Minister Isidoro Malmierca notes that investments by U.S. companies in South Africa exceed their total investment in the rest of Africa and that the U.S. government is trying to set up "new military blocs in the South Atlantic that would link Latin American reactionaries with their South African counterparts across the ocean."

February 11 *Granma* reports that Cuba has more than 2,000 health professionals working in 20 countries of Asia, Africa and the Caribbean.

February 14 In Washington, Omega 7 members Guillermo Novo Sampol and Alvin Ross Díaz are found guilty of the 1976 assassination of Orlando Letelier and Ronni Moffitt (*see* September 15, 1980). Omega 7 member Ignacio Novo Sampol is found guilty of lying about his knowledge of the murder and failing to inform authorities. Omega 7 members José Dionisio Suárez and Virgilio Pablo Paz, also charged, remain at large.

February 20 President Carter submits a report to Congress listing problems in U.S.-Cuban relations: Cuba's African policy; Cuba's failure to pay compensation for U.S. property seized after the revolution; the language Cuba uses about the United States; what may happen during the Nonaligned Summit Conference in September; Nicaragua as "another possible area of contention"; Cuba's "excessively abrasive manner" about Puerto Rico. Carter maintains that the MiGs in Cuba are "an issue of concern" and will be closely monitored but that, at present, the United States is satisfied that they are not adapted for nuclear weapons.

February 21 Cuba holds a national rally in solidarity with Vietnam, invaded by China February 17. President Castro points out that Chinese leader Deng Xiaoping, while in Washington 12 days before the invasion, said Vietnam and Cuba must be "taught a lesson." Castro asks, "Did the government of the United States know about the Chinese plan of aggression and invasion of Vietnam or not?" UN Ambassador Raúl Roa Kourí urges the Security Council to condemn the invasion and demand Chinese withdrawal. At the West Berlin Film Festival, Cuban film directors Humberto Solás (*Lucía*) and Tomás Gutiérrez Alea (*Memories of Underdevelopment*) lead the Cuban delegation in a walkout to protest the showing of *The Deer Hunter*, the U.S. Oscar-winner that portrays Vietnamese as sadistic monsters who victimize innocent U.S. soldiers.

March 13 In Grenada, the New Jewel Movement, a socialist organization headed by Maurice Bishop, overthrows the regime of Eric Gairy in a bloodless revolution. Cuba establishes diplomatic relations with the new government on April 14.

March 20 In Havana, President Castro meets with Ros Samay, General Secretary of the Kampuchean (Cambodian) National United Front for National Salvation, and sends a message to President Heng Samrin congratulating the Kampuchean people on their victory against the Khmer Rouge regime of Pol Pot.

March 25 Omega 7 claims responsibility for three bombings, one in a suitcase moments before it was to be loaded on a TWA flight at New York's Kennedy Airport, injuring four airline workers; another in Union City, New Jersey, at *Almacén el Español* (the second bombing there); and the third in Weehawken, New Jersey, at the office of a Cuban emigrant program directed by Eulalio José Negrín. Suspects are Virgilio Pablo Paz and José Dionisio Suárez, still being sought on charges of assassinating Orlando Letelier and Ronni Moffitt.

March 25-30 The U.S. Surgeon General, Dr Julius B. Richmond, leads a medical delegation for a visit to Cuba at the invitation of the Cuban Public Health Minister, Dr José A. Gutiérrez Múñiz.

April 7 Bulgarian President Todor Zhivkov arrives in Cuba for a state visit.

April 28 Carlos Múñiz Varela, leading participant in both the Antonio Maceo Brigade and the "Dialogue," is shot and dies the following day in San Juan, Puerto Rico. In January, Omega 7 claimed responsibility for a bomb blast in San Juan at his Viajes Varadero Travel Agency, which organizes trips to Cuba.

May 17-18 For the first time since leaving for Cuba on the *Granma* in 1956, President Castro visits Mexico, this time as a head of state. He and President José López Portillo issue a joint communiqué emphasizing the need for strengthening regional cooperation. At a press conference, Castro denies Anastasio Somoza's charge that Cuba is interfering in Nicaragua, calling Somoza himself the "child of U.S. intervention."

May 18 Omega 7 claims responsibility for a bomb that causes extensive damage at the Cuban Interests Section in Washington.

May 19 The State Department assures Cuba that it will conduct a "thorough investigation" of the May 18 bombing.

May 31 Cuba and Suriname establish diplomatic relations.

June 11 For the first time since the anti-hijacking agreement of 1973, a scheduled U.S. passenger airliner is hijacked to Havana. The hijacker is former Cuban Air Force pilot Eduardo Guerra Jiménez, who defected in 1969. Cuba now and in the future continues its policy of returning planes with passengers and crew to the United States while arresting hijackers.

June 19 Representative Ted Weiss (D-New York) introduces legislation to end the embargo against Cuba and to reestablish diplomatic relations.

June 19 Cuba's Foreign Ministry warns of U.S. plans for military intervention in Nicaragua.

June 26-27 Cuban Americans from the United States and Puerto Rico present the State Department with 10,000 signatures of Cuban Americans who want normalization of relations with Cuba and an end to the embargo.

July Cubana Airlines inaugurates flights between Havana and Miami.

July 14 The Second Antonio Maceo Brigade arrives in Cuba with 225 Cuban-born participants from Puerto Rico, the United States, Mexico, Venezuela, Costa Rica and Spain. With them are 94 Maceítos, children of Brigade members and other people from the Cuban community abroad.

July 17 The House Select Committee on Assassinations releases its final report, concluding that the Cuban government had nothing to do with the death of President John F. Kennedy. (*See* November 15, 1976)

Late July Wayne S. Smith replaces Lyle Lane as the chief of the U.S. Interests Section in Havana.

July 26 Cuba's annual celebration of its revolution becomes also a celebration of Nicaragua's triumph on July 19. Guests include Humberto Ortega, Bayardo Arce and Carlos Núñez of the FSLN Joint National Leadership. A medical brigade of 60 doctors, nurses and technicians left Cuba on July 25 to help with the urgent medical needs of Nicaragua.

July 26 A bomb goes off in Miami at the Padrón Cigar Factory owned by a member of the Committee of 75.

July 27 Cuba and Nicaragua reestablish diplomatic relations.

August 24 Cuba and Ecuador reestablish diplomatic relations.

August 24 Cuba and St. Lucia establish diplomatic relations.

August 27 Cuba announces that 400 more political prisoners will be released within a few days, bringing to 2,800 the number freed since the December 1978 agreement. Among the latest group is Rolando Cubela, a CIA agent who plotted to assassinate Fidel Castro.

August 30 As delegates to the Nonaligned Summit Conference gather in Havana, the State Department tells the chair of the Senate Foreign Relations Committee, Frank Church (D-Idaho), that it had misinformed the committee in July by saying that there was no evidence of Soviet combat troops in Cuba. In fact, it says now, there are 2,000 to 3,000 such troops. A Cuban official says the timing of the revelation is another effort to discredit Cuba among the Nonaligned. The issue quickly becomes linked with the Strategic Arms Limitation Treaty (SALT II), already in trouble in the Senate as Church postpones hearings scheduled September 4 to "deal immediately" with the alleged combat brigade. Both Cuba and the Soviet Union maintain that the so-called combat brigade has been in Cuba since the 1962 Missile Crisis and that the CIA must have known about it all these years (*see* November 20, 1962 and December 12, 1962).

September 3-9 Despite U.S. efforts to keep the Nonaligned Summit from meeting in Cuba, the Sixth Summit Conference takes place in Havana with delegations from 138 countries including 94 member states and national liberation movements. As president of the host country, Fidel Castro becomes chair of the Nonaligned Movement until the next summit, an office of substantial international influence. In his opening speech, Castro addresses directly the charge that Cuba seeks to align the Movement with the Soviet Union. Cuba's position is that nonalignment does not mean neutrality between socialism and imperialism.

September 6 President Carter commutes the sentences of Puerto Rican nationalists Oscar Collazo (imprisoned in 1950 for an attack at the Blair House residence of President Truman), Lolita Lebrón, Rafael Cancel Miranda and Irving Flores (the latter three imprisoned in 1954 for an attack at the House of Representatives). They are welcomed as heroes on a visit to Havana November 1.

September 7 Cuba and Jordan establish diplomatic relations.

September 17 Cuba releases the last four U.S. citizens held on political charges, including longtime CIA agent Larry Lunt. (*See* January 1975)

September 17 This issue of *Time* magazine carries a picture described as a "Soviet-built intelligence station in Cuba" that turns out to be an installation built by International Telephone and Telegraph Company (ITT) in 1957.

October President Carter issues Presidential Directive 52 that outlines methods for isolating Cuba by raising charges of human rights violations and reviving fears of Cuba's close relations with the Soviet Union.

October 1 In a television address, President Carter states his "reaffirmation" of President Kennedy's 1963 declaration "that we would not permit any troops from Cuba to move off the island of Cuba in an offensive action against any neighboring country." He lists five things his Administration will do: increase surveillance; aid any country in the Western Hemisphere against "any threat from Soviet or Cuban forces"; establish a Caribbean Joint Task Force Headquarters at Key West; stage more military maneuvers and maintain U.S. forces in Guantánamo; and increase economic aid to the Caribbean. On the same day, 16 U.S. Navy ships arrive off Cuba for maneuvers and the Pentagon announces that it will stage an amphibious assault at Guantánamo.

October 11-14 President Castro is in New York to address the UN General Assembly on October 12 as head of the Nonaligned Movement. His speech is primarily a proposal for a new international economic order to deal with the increasing disparity between developed and underdeveloped countries. He asks that $300 billion of the money budgeted for the arms race be contributed for investment in underdeveloped economies.

October 12 While President Castro is in New York, a letter signed by about 90 people appears in the *New York Times* calling on the Cuban government to release Huber Matos who had smuggled a letter to his wife reporting that he was "old and ailing," had lost the use of his left arm and was almost blind. Released a few days later, he is in good health, arm and eyes intact. By 1984 he is in Nicaragua as part of the Special Operations Command unit under Contra commander Enrique Bermúdez, former colonel in Somoza's National Guard.

October 17 At the Guantánamo Naval Base 1,800 U.S. Marines land for maneuvers and a month of weapons training. There are already 6,000 U.S. military and civilian personnel, including dependents, at the base.

October 20 UPI reports that the FBI's special agent in charge of monitoring Cuban exiles in Puerto Rico says that most of the terrorists known to the FBI feel justified in their anti-Cuban attacks because the CIA trained them for the Bay of Pigs invasion.

October 24 A boat with its crew is hijacked to Florida. U.S. authorities follow the usual procedure of not arresting hijackers of Cuban boats.

October 25 The Cuban Foreign Ministry points out to the State Department that Cuba continues to honor the anti-hijacking agreement but will reconsider that policy if the U.S. government refuses to honor it.

October 27 Omega 7 claims responsibility for a bomb that injures three people at the Cuban UN Mission.

November 6 The first contingent of a total of 1,200 Cuban teachers leaves Cuba on their way to help with the Nicaraguan Literacy Campaign.

November 25 Omega 7 claims responsibility for the assassination of Eulalio José Negrín, member of the Committee of 75 who participated in the December 1978 "Dialogue." He is gunned down in front of his young son outside his home in Union City, New Jersey. After the Cuban emigrant center he directed was bombed in March, Negrín said he had helped about 75,000 Cubans immigrate since 1964.

November 26 At a news conference in New Jersey, the Committee of 75, the Task Force Against Terrorism (organized in October by the Cuban community), and the Cuban American Committee for Normalization of Relations with Cuba call for an investigation of the systematic terror campaign that has now led to the murder of Eulalio Negrín. Rutgers University Professor Lourdes Casal, a member of the Committee of 75, tells the press, "Our lives are being threatened and we still do not see any pattern of action by federal authorities."

December 3 Cubana Airlines makes its one and only charter flight between Havana and New York. A bomb threat forces the return flight to depart from Kennedy Airport rather than Newark Airport. To avoid risking lives, Cubana cancels plans for charter service.

December 4 Some 1,200 Ethiopian children arrive to join the Ethiopians already attending school in Cuba, where more than 10,000 children from Angola, the Congo, Ethiopia, Mozambique, Namibia, Nicaragua and São Tomé y Príncipe study on the Isle of Youth.

December 7   An explosion at the Cuban UN Mission injures two U.S. police officers. Omega 7 claims responsibility for this and for an explosion four days later at the Soviet Mission that injures eight people.

December 17   Cuba hosts the ministerial meeting of the Group of 77, Third World countries of the United Nations now actually numbering 119, as they plan for the 1980 General Conference of the UN Industrial Development Organization (UNIDO). The Group of 77 formulates the "Havana Declaration," demanding that industrialized countries provide $300 billion additional aid for investment in underdeveloped economies as proposed at the General Assembly by Fidel Castro when he spoke as chair of the Nonaligned Movement.

December 19   The UN General Assembly approves the Group of 77's "Havana Declaration" by a vote of 118 to 6 (the United States, France, Great Britain, Japan, Belgium and West Germany) with 16 abstentions.

1980

January Presidential candidate Ronald Reagan suggests a U.S. naval blockade of Cuba as a response to Soviet troops in Afghanistan.

January 25 Another Delta passenger jet is hijacked to Havana by a man who wants to go to Iran. Cuban authorities assist passengers in escaping the plane, treat a woman who suffers a diabetic reaction, negotiate the surrender of the hijacker, and arrest him. Then, in accordance with Cuba's consistent policy on hijackings, the plane with its passengers and crew returns to the United States.

February 16 Armed Cubans hijack a Liberian freighter in Havana and force it to Florida. None of them is arrested. Cuban officials point out that the Carter Administration welcomes Cubans who leave by hijacking vessels, while delaying visas and refusing to establish orderly migration procedures.

February 25 Armed Cubans hijack a fishing boat to Florida, where they are not arrested.

March 8 In a speech to the Federation of Cuban Women, President Castro says if U.S. officials continue to encourage illegal departures from Cuba, welcoming hijackers as heroes, Cuba may turn to a solution like the opening of the port of Camarioca in 1965.

March 17-20 Angolan President José Eduardo dos Santos makes a state visit to Cuba. Prior to his visit, Omega 7 claims responsibility for an explosion at Angola's UN Mission.

March 25 UN Ambassador Raúl Roa Kourí escapes assassination in New York as personnel from the Cuban Mission find an explosive device under his car.

March 26 Jamaican Prime Minister Michael Manley arrives in Cuba for a state visit.

April 1 Twelve Cubans seeking asylum crash a minibus through the gates of the Peruvian Embassy in Havana, resulting in the death of a Cuban guard. Peru allows them to remain. Cuba removes its guards from the Peruvian Embassy April 4. The Peruvian chargé d'affaires announces that anyone who wants can enter the Embassy, leading to an overflow crowd of several thousand seeking asylum. On April 6, Peru asks prevention of further entry, and Cuba closes nearby streets.

April 9 An American Airlines Boeing 727 is hijacked from Ontario, California to Cuba. No passengers are aboard.

Mid-April International news agencies report that the Carter Administration plans massive military maneuvers, "Operation Solid Shield 80," in the Caribbean starting May 8. Civilian personnel would be evacuated while U.S. Marines land at Guantánamo as 1,200 U.S. soldiers are transported there. Protesters in many countries, including the United States, demonstrate against such maneuvers.

April 16-17 About 500 Cubans from the Peruvian Embassy are flown to Costa Rica but Cuba suspends the flights April 18 because those Cubans are leaving or plan to leave Costa Rica for third countries, mainly the United States. Cuba's position is that people should go directly to the country where they plan to settle.

April 17 Cuban Council of State Vice-President Juan Almeida Bosque and other Cuban officials attend Zimbabwe's independence celebration. Cuba and Zimbabwe establish diplomatic relations April 20. Almeida meets with the new prime minister, Robert Mugabe, April 21.

April 18 A *Granma* editorial makes it clear that the Cuban government will not object if Cubans who want to leave go directly to Florida by boat.

April 19 In Havana, more than a million Cubans march past the Peruvian Embassy to show support for the Cuban revolution. In New York City, anti-Castro demonstrators march to support the Cubans inside the Peruvian Embassy.

April 21 Small boats start arriving from Florida to pick up people at Mariel, a port 25 miles west of Havana.

April 22 *Granma* announces that anyone who wants to leave may depart from Mariel. Those who leave during this exodus are called "Marielitos." According to the U.S. government, they are not "refugees" as defined by the Refugee Act of 1980; that is, they are not fleeing "persecution... on account of race, religion, nationality, membership of a particular group or political opinion." The U.S. government classifies them as "Entrants — Status Undetermined" and interns them until claimed by relatives or other sponsors.

April 23 The Carter Administration imposes $1,000 fines against boat captains for each Marielito without a valid visa.

April 23 Ronald Reagan, debating George Bush on television in the campaign for the Republican presidential nomination, again suggests a naval blockade of Cuba and asks, "Don't we have to face up to the fact that our problems in this hemisphere are being caused by Cuba?"

April 27 Cuban Ambassador to Colombia Fernando Ravelo Renedo plays a major role in negotiating today's release of hostages held by Colombia's M-19 Movement in Bogotá. M-19 members then fly to Havana on a Cubana jet with Ravelo, other negotiators, and some of the hostages, including U.S. Ambassador to Colombia Diego Asencio.

April 30 Confronted with international opposition, the Carter Administration announces cancellation of the amphibious landing scheduled for May 8 at Guantánamo.

May 1 At the May Day celebration, President Castro calls cancellation of U.S. maneuvers at Guantánamo a victory and suspends the "Girón 19" maneuvers that Cuba had planned for May 7. Grenada's Prime Minister Maurice Bishop and Nicaraguan leader Daniel Ortega speak at the rally.

May 2 In response to a U.S. promise that visas would be ready for ex-prisoners (*see* August 1978), hundreds of ex-prisoners gather at the U.S. Interests Section in Havana. Fighting erupts between them and supporters of the revolution. Almost 400 Cubans take refuge inside the Interests Section.

May 5 President Carter pledges "an open heart and open arms" for the Cubans. Reports persist that the boatlift is being used to rid Cuba of common criminals and other "antisocial" elements.

May 6 President Carter declares a state of emergency in regions of Florida affected by the influx of more than 17,000 Cubans. National Guard troops rush to Key West to quell fighting among the newcomers.

May 8 Fire caused by arson breaks out in Cuba's largest day care center as 570 children and 156 workers are inside. All are rescued.

May 9-10 The Ku Klux Klan demonstrates against Cubans detained at Fort Chaffee, Arkansas, and Eglin Air Force Base, Florida.

May 14 Changing policy, President Carter opposes the boatlift, proposing an airlift. He orders all boats to return without passengers or face confiscation and fines. Almost 40,000 Cubans have arrived in Florida, setting off debate about discrimination in favor of Cubans as compared, for example, to Haitians.

May 14 Venezuela announces that it will not participate in U.S. naval maneuvers in the Caribbean and will join exercises only on the U.S. mainland.

May 17 For the third time in less than a month, Cubans participate in a mobilization of support for the revolution, with more than half the population of Cuba, over five million people, taking part in marches in several cities.

May 17-19 The arrival of thousands of Cubans who will compete for jobs contributes to the rage of Blacks in Miami as they stage a three-day uprising after the acquittal of four white policemen charged with killing a Black man stopped for a traffic violation.

May 18 In Hanoi, General Nam Khanh says if Cuba requests aid the People's Army of Vietnam will send its soldiers to fight alongside Cubans.

May 19 Cuban officials say they are willing to discuss the U.S. proposal for an airlift if negotiations include the embargo, the U.S. occupation at Guantánamo, and spy flights.

May 19 Eugene Trivits, in charge of health checks at the detention camp at Fort Indiantown Gap, Pennsylvania, reports no serious health problems, saying, "We know Cubans are basically in good health because they have a good public health system there."

May 21 Among Cuban exiles who want to pick up Marielitos in Cuba is Watergate burglar Frank Sturgis.

May 23 The State Department acknowledges that it has refused permission for CBS News to send a report on Cuban economic conditions to the United States via satellite. As part of the embargo, U.S. companies must get special permission from the Treasury Department to pay Cuba for use of transmission facilities. Treasury then asks advice of the State Department. In the past, exceptions have been routinely granted to news media.

May 24 Among the first of many riots by detained Cubans, hundreds at Eglin Air Force Base, Florida, throw stones and fight with Military Police, who call for help from Marines, sheriff's deputies, police, and state troopers, as Cubans rush the gates of "Camp Liberty" shouting "Libertad! Libertad!"

May 28 East German President Erich Honecker arrives in Havana for his second state visit to Cuba.

June Cuban officials meet in Havana with State Department (Peter Tarnoff) and National Security Council (Robert Pastor) officials for secret talks, abbreviated by the disclosure that the U.S. team has been told they can only discuss ending the boatlift.

June 1 During a riot at the Fort Chaffee, Arkansas, detention center, state troopers fire at the Cubans, hospitalizing three. About 2,000 local residents, some armed with rifles and clubs, demand to be let into the camp "to bash heads." The presence of the Cubans in Arkansas becomes an issue in the re-election campaign of Governor Bill Clinton, a campaign he loses.

June 1 The United States, Britain and Costa Rica propose negotiations about emigrants. "Cuba's migration policy," responds Cuba's Foreign Ministry, "pertains exclusively to the sovereignty of the country and is not subject to negotiation with any other."

June 7 President Carter orders the Justice Department to expel any Cuban who committed "serious crimes" in Cuba. Cuba has offered to accept "hundreds of Batista's killers" and "scores of CIA-trained terrorists who have committed crimes against Cuba" if U.S. authorities would deport them.

June 14 President Castro says Cuba is winning the battle against fungus-infected tobacco, smut-infected sugarcane and swine fever, but remains concerned about the outbreak of so many diseases at the same time, particularly since it is known that the United States has used biological warfare against Cuba. (*See* May 6, 1971)

June 26 UN Ambassador Raúl Roa Kourí urges the Security Council to impose sanctions against South Africa, which invaded Angola again on June 7.

July 9 There are reports, according to New Jersey State Police, that some money collected to help Marielitos is actually going to groups like Omega 7.

July 10 A Cuban boat is hijacked and forced to Florida. This becomes the first boat hijacking since the Cuban revolution that U.S. authorities prosecute. A federal judge dismisses the case in December.

July 18 During a reception in Managua at the first anniversary celebration of the Nicaraguan revolution, President Castro talks for 40 minutes with the head of the U.S. delegation, UN Ambassador Donald McHenry, along with U.S. Ambassador to Nicaragua Lawrence Pezzullo and Assistant Secretary of State William Bowdler.

July 22 A Marielito hijacks a Delta Airlines passenger jet to Cuba. He surrenders to Cuban officials and the airplane with passengers and crew returns to the United States.

July 31-August 3 Mexican President José López Portillo makes a state visit to Cuba and issues a joint communiqué with President Castro demanding that the U.S. government end the embargo, violations of Cuban air space, and the military occupation at Guantánamo.

August The UN Committee on Decolonization approves a resolution co-sponsored by Cuba demanding U.S. measures to decolonize Puerto Rico.

August 3 At the Moscow Olympics boycotted by the United States, Cuba is among eight countries with the best overall performances, winning 20 medals, eight gold, seven silver, five bronze.

August 7 In Havana, 83 Cubans at the U.S. Interests Section surrender to Cuban authorities, leaving 204 inside. The Cubans are then allowed to apply for emigration through normal channels.

August 16 Marielitos hijack three U.S. passenger jets to get back to Cuba, raising the total of such hijackings to six in one week.

September State Department official Peter Tarnoff returns to Cuba for secret talks. Cuba agrees to terminate the boatlift and to take other unspecified measures to improve relations.

September 1-6 Cuba hosts the FAO Regional Conference for Latin America attended by 25 Latin American members plus six countries with observer status, including the United States and 18 international organizations.

September 11 Omega 7 assassinates Cuban diplomat Félix García Rodríguez of the UN Mission by shooting him through the open window of his car as he stops for a red light on a busy street in Queens, New York City. García is the first UN diplomat ever assassinated in New York. This act of international terrorism embarrasses the U.S. government and brings high-level demands that the FBI take action against anti-Cuban terrorist groups which seem, to many, to operate with impunity. U.S. Ambassador Donald McHenry calls the murder a "stain on the United States." Secretary of State Edmund Muskie calls it "reprehensible."

September 13 Jamaican Prime Minister Manley arrives in Cuba for a state visit.

September 15 A federal appeals court overturns the convictions of the three Omega 7 members found guilty in February 1979 of assassinating Orlando Letelier and Ronni Moffitt.

September 15-18 Soviet Foreign Minister Andrei Gromyko visits Cuba for the first time in 15 years.

September 16 As Marielitos continue to hijack passenger jets back to Cuba, the Cuban government announces that hijackers will face penal measures and may be returned to the United States for trial. On the following day two Marielitos hijack another plane and they are returned to the United States September 18.

September 17 Senate leaders set aside action on the U.S.-Cuban accord on fishing rights after repeated attempts by Senator Jesse Helms (R-North Carolina) to attach anti-Cuban riders, such as a requirement that all Soviet military forces be withdrawn. Neither country has ratified the agreement.

September 18-26 Arnaldo Tamayo Méndez becomes the first "Cuban in the Cosmos," launched into space aboard the Soviet Soyuz-38.

September 23 The last 11 Cubans in the U.S. Interests Section in Havana surrender to Cuban authorities. With the exception of a few who remain for personal reasons, all who were in the Interests Section emigrate to the United States.

September 26 As agreed at the secret talks earlier in the month, Cuba ends the boatlift from Mariel. Of the approximately

123,000 Marielitos in the United States, some 20,000 are being detained in camps and tent cities. About 2,000 are in prisons, with that number increasing.

September 26 A Venezuelan military court acquits the men accused of bombing the Cuban passenger plane October 6, 1976: Bosch, Posada, Lugo, Ricardo.

September 27 President Castro says the Venezuelan authorities "know they are acquitting the guilty." Cuba maintains diplomatic relations for the moment but closes its embassy in Caracas.

October 13 At a news conference held in the House of Representatives in Washington, Ramón Sánchez Parodi, chief of the Cuban Interests Section, announces that Cuba will release all 33 U.S. citizens now imprisoned. Upon their release two weeks later, three choose to remain in Cuba while 30 are flown to Miami.

October 18 Senator Lowell P. Weicker Jr. (R-Connecticut), who recently spent more than 11 hours talking with President Castro in Cuba, says the embargo against Cuba should be ended.

October 23 Orlando Villalta, Nicaragua's Attorney General under Somoza, and his nephew are indicted in New Orleans for conspiracy to acquire "machine guns, silencers, bombs and explosives." Federal sources tell New Orleans journalists that there was a rightwing plot to assassinate President Castro and several Nicaraguan officials while Castro was visiting Nicaragua last July.

October 28 Canada discloses that Cuba has placed $7.3 million in orders with Canadian tire companies, including subsidiaries of B.F. Goodrich and several other U.S. companies. Under the U.S. embargo, foreign subsidiaries of U.S. firms are required to obtain U.S. licenses for export to Cuba, a practice condemned by Canada. Since B.F. Goodrich of Canada is incorporated in Canada and complies with Canadian laws, the company says it is not obligated to get U.S. clearance.

October 30 In a major setback for Cuba in the Caribbean, Edward Seaga, closely tied to the United States, defeats Michael Manley in the election for prime minister of Jamaica. The next day Seaga asks Cuba to withdraw Ambassador Ulises Estrada.

November 4 Ronald Reagan is elected president. His ideological approach to Latin America and specifically Cuba is grounded in a report ("A New Inter-American Policy for the Eighties") issued in the summer by the Santa Fe Committee (Council for Inter-American Security), which sees the area as part of the Cold War battleground: "The Americas are under attack" by the Soviet Union infiltrating through Cuba, a "Soviet vassal state." The Committee includes Roger Fontaine (who joins the National Security Council), Gordon Sumner Jr. (who joins the State Department), and Lewis Tambs (named ambassador to Colombia and later to Costa Rica, where he becomes a participant in the U.S. "covert" war against Nicaragua).

November 13 The Treasury Department bans import of stainless steel and other metal-alloy products made by Creusot-Loire of France because Cuban nickel is used in its manufacture.

December 17-20 Cuba holds the Second Congress of the Communist Party, attended by 5,000 people including delegates, guests, and representatives of more than 140 political parties and organizations from other countries. In his closing speech, President Castro, responding to threats by President-elect Reagan, calls for a People's Militia to train every Cuban to defend Cuba.

December 22 Cuba and the United States hold secret talks on a wide range of migration issues, including possible repatriation of Marielitos.

1981

January 16 Cuba and the United States hold another session about repatriation of Marielitos but reach no agreement.

January 16 Edward Heath, Britain's Conservative Party prime minister from 1970 to 1974, meets with President Castro in Havana.

January 17 Three days before President Carter leaves office, the State Department injects Cuba into U.S. policy toward El Salvador in a press release announcing $5 million in military aid to the junta: "We must support the Salvadoran government in its struggle against Marxist terrorism, supported covertly with arms, ammunition, training and political and military advice by Cuba and other communist nations."

January 29 At his first presidential news conference, Ronald Reagan replies to a question about Latin American policy: "Well, I think we've seen a great reverse in the Caribbean situation and it came about through Prime Minister Seaga's election.... And I think this opens the door for us to have a policy in the Mediterranean [*sic*] of bringing them back in — those countries that might have started in that direction — or keeping them in the Western world."

February 11 The U.S. government expels Ricardo Escartín, a diplomat at the Cuban Interests Section, for allegedly encouraging U.S. businesses to trade with Cuba.

February 13 The State Department sends Deputy Secretary of State Lawrence Eagleburger to Europe and Ambassador at Large General Vernon Walters to Latin America to show "evidence" to other governments that Cuba, Vietnam, Ethiopia and the Soviet

Union are supplying arms via Nicaragua to the Farabundo Martí National Liberation Front (FMLN) in El Salvador.

February 18 In a briefing about El Salvador, Secretary of State Alexander Haig tells representatives from NATO, Australia, New Zealand, Spain and Japan that the United States must "deal with the immediate source of the problem — and that is Cuba," adding that "we do not intend to have another Vietnam and engage ourselves in another bloody conflict where the source rests outside the target area."

February 20 Three days after General Vernon Walters came to Mexico City to present "proof" that Cuba supplies arms to the FMLN, Mexican President José López Portillo signs an agreement to purchase 100,000 tons of Cuban sugar and describes close ties with Cuba, asking Cuban Minister of Economic Cooperation Héctor Rodríguez Llompart to give "an embrace" to President Castro and "a very fraternal salute" to the Cuban people.

February 22 Asked if there might be a naval blockade of Cuba, White House adviser Edwin Meese replies, "I don't think we would rule out anything."

February 23 The State Department releases a "White Paper" claiming "captured documents" prove that Cuba and other socialist countries are engaged in a textbook case of indirect armed aggression against the Salvadoran government. Months later, after Congress has sent military aid and advisers to El Salvador, a few U.S. media question the "White Paper." The June 8 *Wall Street Journal* reports that Jon Glassman, the main writer, "freely acknowledges" that there were " 'mistakes' and 'guessing'" by intelligence analysts. The *Journal* continues: "Several of the most important documents, it's obvious, were attributed to guerrilla leaders who didn't write them. And it's unknown who did.... Much information in the white paper can't be found in the documents at all." The *Journal* notes that no uncertainty was evident in the February 6 *New York Times* story by Juan de Onis based on the "White Paper," which was leaked to him early.

February 24 President Castro addresses the 26th Congress of the Soviet Communist Party in Moscow. Two days later, President Leonid Brezhnev tells him, "In present conditions, when the U.S.

imperialists have launched another anti-Cuban campaign, the USSR, as before, is siding with socialist Cuba." (*See* October 30)

March   The Treasury Department ends the ban on import of stainless steel and other metal-alloy products made by Creusot-Loire after France agrees to certify that products shipped to the United States contain no Cuban nickel.

March 3   With a flood of mail pouring into Washington in opposition to U.S. military intervention in Cuba or El Salvador and demonstrations around the world, President Reagan explains on television that Secretary of State Haig was at no time suggesting "an assault on Cuba." By calling Cuba the "source" of the problem, Reagan says General Haig meant "the intercepting and stopping of the supplies coming into these countries, the export from Cuba of those arms, the training of the guerrillas as they've done there."

March 16   The United States says it will not attend the 1983 UN General Assembly Conference on Trade and Development (UNCTAD) if it is held in Havana.

March 23   Colombia suspends diplomatic relations with Cuba, charging Cuba has trained and armed M-19 revolutionaries.

March 26   Novelist and journalist Gabriel García Márquez flees his native Colombia and seeks asylum in Mexico after learning of an order for his arrest. He believes Colombia will try to link him to M-19 because of his well-known solidarity with Cuba.

April 6   *U.S. News and World Report* magazine lists actions against Cuba being considered by Secretary of State Haig, including a "selective blockade" to intercept aircraft and ships transporting Cuban troops, fomenting a popular uprising (conceded to be very unlikely), and invasion.

April 21   President Castro calls avoidance of nuclear war the most urgent task of our times. He deplores the world's spending $500 billion a year on the military.

May   Without publicity, the Treasury Department orders U.S. Customs to block delivery of Cuban publications sent to unlicensed U.S. addressees. As U.S. citizens who receive Cuban publications find out what Treasury has done, some begin to organize for a lawsuit.

May 4   State Department official John Bushnell tells the Senate Foreign Relations Committee that the Reagan Administration may resume military aid to Guatemala because of aid to Guatemalan insurgents from Cuba and other countries acting for the Soviet Union.

May 4 Juan Mari Bras, head of the Puerto Rican Socialist Party, arrives in Cuba for a visit.

May 8 Vice-President George Bush, speaking at Duquesne University, says Cuba is the worst human rights offender in the Western Hemisphere and is exporting tyranny and brutal repression.

May 13 Costa Rica breaks diplomatic relations with Cuba ostensibly because of a letter sent by Cuba months ago to the United Nations in response to a letter written in December by Costa Rica to the UN about Cuba's treatment of political prisoners.

May 22 At the UN International Conference on Sanctions against South Africa, Cuban official Jesús Montané condemns the April 30 Security Council veto by Western powers of draft sanctions against South Africa for its illegal occupation of Namibia.

May 30 A federal jury acquits Omega 7 members Guillermo Novo Sampol and Alvin Ross Díaz in their retrial on charges of assassinating Orlando Letelier and Ronni Moffitt in 1976. The jury finds Guillermo Novo Sampol guilty of two counts of lying to a grand jury; he is sentenced June 26 to four and a half years in jail. His brother Ignacio Novo Sampol will not be retried for perjury because he has spent two years in prison.

June President Reagan accepts an invitation to go to a conference on relations between developed and underdeveloped countries in Mexico in October if President Castro is not invited. This would mean that the chair of the Nonaligned Countries is excluded from a meeting to deal with their problems.

June Secretary Haig and his State Department counselor Robert McFarlane urge the Defense Department to present contingency plans for action against Cuba and Nicaragua.

June 3 Vice-President Bush and Assistant Secretary of State for Inter-American Affairs Thomas Enders address the Council of the Americas on U.S.-Cuban relations. Bush calls Cuba the "principal threat to peace in this region." Enders says "Castro personally" unified the various revolutionary factions of "first Nicaragua, then El Salvador, then Guatemala, now Colombia."

June 9   Chester Arthur Crocker becomes Assistant Secretary of State for African Affairs and will thus be in charge of the Reagan Administration's policy of "constructive engagement" toward South Africa. First articulated by Crocker in an article in *Foreign Affairs* (Winter 1980/81), this policy calls for using "friendly persuasion" rather than sanctions toward South Africa, which Crocker argues will lead to Namibian independence within 18 months. He and Deputy Secretary of State William Clark visit Pretoria in June to discuss Namibia. During this visit, Crocker initiates a policy called "linkage," which links South African withdrawal from Namibia to Cuban withdrawal from Angola.

July 4   Five members of Alpha 66 infiltrate Cuba with a plan to assassinate President Castro on July 26 and are captured July 9. In the United States, Humberto Alvarado, a leader of Alpha 66, says another squad has infiltrated with plans to "undermine and destroy Cuban industry, transportation and communication." Some Alpha 66 members say that they have conducted 30 sabotage missions in the last six months, including an attack on a power plant.

July 10   Two men who left Cuba during the Mariel exodus with their wives and children hijack a U.S. passenger jet to take themselves and their families back to Cuba, where the two men are arrested. Cuban authorities will determine the degree of responsibility of the two women while the children stay with relatives.

July 26   President Castro says he suspects that an epidemic of dengue fever that has killed 113 people in recent weeks, including 81 children, was introduced into Cuba by the CIA. This charge is given added credence in 1984 when Omega 7 leader Eduardo Arocena testifies during his trial (on unrelated charges) that he carried "some germs" to Cuba in 1980. Castro says Cuba has asked for a U.S. pesticide to help eradicate the fever-bearing mosquito but has received none.

July 27   State Department official Dean Fischer denies any CIA role in dengue fever and says the Commerce Department on July 17 approved a license for export to Cuba of 300 tons of pesticide. Some journalists note that as early as 1959 the U.S. Army's Fort Detrick, Maryland, biological warfare laboratory included mosquitoes infected with yellow fever, malaria and dengue fever.

July 31 General Omar Torrijos, the Panamanian leader, is killed in a plane crash. Later, *Granma* publishes accounts of why many Panamanians wonder if Torrijos's death was caused by the CIA, especially coming only 10 weeks after a similar crash that killed Ecuadoran President Jaime Roldós.

August Bay of Pigs veteran and Watergate burglar Frank Sturgis participates in a failed attempt to invade Cuba and set up a provisional government.

August 7 President Castro travels to Mexico to meet with President López Portillo for two days of talks which are reported to be primarily about exclusion of Castro from the international development meeting (*see* June). They issue a joint statement saying the exclusion is due to "the well-known position of the United States."

August 14 In Honduras at a conference of six Central American countries, former U.S. Ambassador to El Salvador Robert White says "it is not necessary to go to Moscow or Cuba" to find causes for violence which "can be found here, in unemployment, hunger and injustice."

August 20 Cuba is among the sponsors of a resolution adopted by the UN Decolonization Committee calling for the General Assembly to review the status of Puerto Rico.

August 23 Commenting on why U.S. jet fighters shot down two Libyan planes over the Gulf of Sidra four days earlier, Secretary of State Haig says the time has come when the international community cannot ignore "illicit acts" whether from Libya, Cuba or the Soviet Union.

August 31 Vetoing a UN Security Council resolution to condemn South Africa for its latest invasion of Angola, U.S. delegate Charles Lichtenstein says South Africa invaded because of "foreign combat forces in Angola, particularly the large Cuban force."

September 1 Repeating a claim by Secretary Haig, the State Department announces that "at least some Cuban advisers" are operating in the field with Salvadoran guerrillas.

September 3 In a detailed written statement, the Cuban government responds that "Haig and the government of the United States are lying through their teeth." The statement maintains, "There has never been, nor is there at the present time, a sole

Cuban military or civilian adviser with the revolutionary forces" in El Salvador. Cuba compares the current disinformation campaign to Nazi Propaganda Minister Goebbels's technique of the big lie and calls upon the U.S. Senate to investigate, challenging the U.S. government to "produce even a little bit of proof." There is no response.

September 8 The president of Ford Argentina, subsidiary of the U.S. Ford Motor Company, announces plans to export several thousand vehicles to Cuba.

September 11-12 Omega 7 claims responsibility for bomb blasts that destroy the Mexican consulate in Miami and damage the one in New York.

September 15-23 Despite pressure by the Reagan Administration against such a visit, a Congressional delegation headed by Senator Robert Stafford (R-Vermont) attends the Inter-Parliamentary Union (IPU) Conference in Havana with more than 1,000 delegates from almost 100 parliaments.

September 16 The State Department denies visas to three Cuban officials invited to participate in a symposium about Cuba to be held September 23-24 on Capitol Hill, although eight members of Congress are among the sponsors. In October a visa is denied to Deputy Foreign Minister José R. Viera, setting a pattern of such denials.

September 22 In a letter to Soviet President Brezhnev, President Reagan writes, "The role of Cuba in Africa and Latin America is particularly destabilizing."

September 23 Assistant Secretary of State Thomas Enders and National Security Adviser Richard Allen announce plans to set up Radio Martí, named after Cuban patriot José Martí, to broadcast news about Cuba to Cubans. The originator of this idea is Jorge Mas Canosa of the Cuban American National Foundation (CANF), an organization created by the Reagan Administration after Richard Allen decided that Cuban Americans would be an effective tool for promoting the Administration's policy toward Cuba (*see* April 1982).

October 8 Capitulating to the U.S. demand of March 16, UNCTAD decides not to hold its 1983 conference in Havana.

October 12-14 Vice-President Bush warns audiences in the Dominican Republic and Colombia of Cuban expansionism.

October 19 Columnists Rowland Evans and Robert Novak claim Cuba has sent 500-600 elite troops to Nicaragua with a plan to cut El Salvador in two at the Lempa River.

October 21 Two Cuban teachers, Pedro Pablo Rivera Cue y Bárbaro Rodríguez, and two Nicaraguan peasants are assassinated in a remote area of Nicaragua.

October 26 As U.S. Ambassador Chester Hartman presents his credentials in Moscow, he delivers a statement urging the Soviet Union to deny aid to Cuba because of its "efforts directed against sovereign governments in Africa and Latin America."

October 28 Having learned that Secretary of State Haig is spreading the claim by Evans and Novak (*see* October 19), Cuba challenges Haig "to produce the evidence." None is produced.

October 29 The Seaga Administration in Jamaica breaks diplomatic relations with Cuba.

October 30 U.S. Armed Forces begin unannounced military maneuvers in the Caribbean a day after Secretary of State Haig again hinted at taking measures against Cuba. Haig's threats are especially menacing for Cuba in light of a development that remains a secret until a 1993 interview with Vice-President Raúl Castro (*see* May 5 and 12, 1993): confronted by these threats, Raúl Castro, head of Cuba's Armed Forces, meets in Moscow during the period when Haig is the Secretary of State (January 1981 until July 1982) with Soviet President Brezhnev; when Castro suggests that the Soviet Union reiterate that it would not tolerate aggression against Cuba, Brezhnev responds, "We cannot fight in Cuba because you are 11,000 kilometers away from us. Do you think we're going to go all that way to stick our necks out for you?" Castro also reveals that the Cuban Communist Party's Political Bureau, informed of "an extremely significant" problem "should it ever be divulged," agrees that the secret (the "Pandora Case") should remain known only to Fidel and Raúl Castro "for as long as necessary."

October 31 Cuba goes on full military alert. Around the world there are demonstrations of support for Cuba that continue through November, the duration of the U.S. military maneuvers.

November 9 Daniel Ortega, coordinator of the Nicaraguan junta, says the Reagan Administration needs a pretext for intervention in El Salvador "and that has to be Nicaragua, Cuba and the Soviet

Union." *Pravda*, the Soviet Communist Party newspaper, charges that the United States is preparing to attack Cuba and warns Washington to "immediately end its peace-endangering play with fire." The article reminds the United States that Cuba is part of the socialist alliance and that "aggressive actions against Cuba are fraught with dangerous consequences."

November 11 The *Washington Post* publishes a letter from President Castro describing the current disinformation campaign against Cuba.

November 13 Venezuela asks Cuba for further evidence about Orlando Bosch and the other men accused of the 1976 plane bombing that killed 73 people. Cuba delivers this information December 15.

November 14 Dr Héctor Terry, Deputy Health Minister, announces that dengue fever (*see* July 26) has been eradicated in Cuba. The epidemic killed 188 people.

November 16 On Costa Rican television, Myles Frechette, head of the State Department's Office of Cuban Affairs, says, "This Administration is... definitely going to take action. We're going to make Cuba pay."

November 23 Secretary of State Haig and Vice-President Carlos Rafael Rodríguez hold a secret meeting in Mexico, leading to further unpublicized meetings between U.S. and Cuban officials in early 1982. On his way to Mexico, Haig tells reporters that there is "some evidence" of Soviet MiG fighters "arriving in Cuba destined for Nicaragua" or perhaps for some other purpose.

November 24 More than 100 plaintiffs file a lawsuit charging the U.S. government with violating the First Amendment right to read by not allowing delivery of Cuban publications.

December 1 President Reagan secretly authorizes CIA operations against Cubans in Central America. Part of the CIA's "seed money" finances the "Contras," an armed force that begins with 500 Latin Americans joined by 1,000 other mercenaries trained, mostly by Argentina, in Honduras to overthrow the Nicaraguan government.

December 4 Another Cuban teacher, Aguedo Morales Reina, is assassinated in Nicaragua. This kind of terrorism eventually forces Cuba to withdraw teachers in order not to endanger the lives of Nicaraguans they teach.

December 10   CIA agent Constantine Menges appears before the Senate Foreign Relations Committee to offer supporting evidence for the State Department's latest "White Paper" titled "Cuba's Renewed Support for Violence in the Hemisphere" (released publicly four days later). The next day, three Democratic Senators (Paul Tsongas of Massachusetts, Claiborne Pell of Rhode Island, Christopher Dodd of Connecticut) send a virtually unprecedented written message to CIA Director William Casey, protesting that the briefing "seriously violated" the CIA's responsibility to provide Congress with objective analysis.

December 14   The "White Paper" is released and charges Cuba with subversive activities in almost every Latin country. However, it omits any reference to Cuban troops or advisers in El Salvador.

1982

January 11 UPI reports that Cubans and Nicaraguans are training at a southern California desert camp to overthrow their countries' governments. The FBI and San Bernardino law officers say Alpha 66, which runs the camp, is not doing anything illegal. Similar camps continue to operate in Florida.

January 15 For the first time since the Cuban revolution, the INS deports an emigré from Cuba, saying Andrés Rodríguez Hernández has not proven a well-founded fear of persecution. He rejoins his family in Havana. When Cubans in Miami protest the deportation, some are teargassed and arrested.

January 22 Three members of Congress from New York, Hamilton Fish Jr., Robert García and Benjamin Gilman, meet with President Castro and arrange the release of four U.S. prisoners held for illegal entry and possession of drugs.

January 26 Faced with public opposition and a lawsuit, the Reagan Administration lifts its ban on Cuban publications.

January 26 After meeting with Soviet Foreign Minister Gromyko, Secretary of State Haig says one matter discussed was Cuba, including the possible delivery of MiGs that might be equipped to carry nuclear weapons.

January 27 On CBS television, President Reagan says, "Cuba if it was smart would take another look and see if it didn't want to rejoin the Western Hemisphere." He says the Soviet Union "has been adding to Cuban arms to a greater extent than any time since 1962."

February U.S. news media report about current CIA "covert" operations against Cuba, Nicaragua and the FMLN in El Salvador (*see* December 1, 1981).

February 2 Secretary of State Haig tells the Senate Foreign Relations Committee that Cuba has received a second squadron of MiGs, posing a "growing threat" to the Caribbean. He tells reporters that the threat from Cuba and Nicaragua forced the Administration to triple 1982 military aid to El Salvador.

February 2 A Marielito hijacks a U.S. passenger jet to Cuba.

February 4 Responding to U.S. and South African "linkage" between Cuban troops in Angola and Namibian independence, Cuban Foreign Minister Isidoro Malmierca and Angolan Foreign Minister Paulo Jorge make it clear that Cuban troops will withdraw from Angola whenever the sovereign government of Angola asks them to.

February 10 Regarding MiGs in Cuba, President Castro says Cuba will never acknowledge constraints on its right to purchase any weapons necessary for defense, but that Cuba has not received any type of aircraft different from those it already had.

February 15 The Cuban Council of State enacts a joint venture law, allowing joint ownership by Cuban government organizations and foreign investors.

February 21 Mexican President José López Portillo launches a major effort for negotiating a peaceful settlement of the war in El Salvador and improving relations between the United States and both Cuba and Nicaragua. Nicaragua and the FMLN welcome the initiative.

February 22 President Castro sends a letter to President López Portillo assuring him of Cuban willingness to cooperate if the United States promises not to attack its neighbors, stops its threats, and ends its subversive activities.

February 24 Addressing the OAS in Washington, President Reagan ignores the Mexican proposal. He unwraps the long-awaited Caribbean Basin Initiative (CBI), declaring: "If we do not act promptly... in defense of freedom, new Cubas will arise from the ruins of today's conflict." The OAS audience listens without interrupting once to applaud. President López Portillo tells *Le Monde* that chances for détente in the region declined with

Reagan's failure to address the peace initiative. Reagan's entire speech is published in *Granma*.

February 28 CIA Director William Casey claims the Salvadoran guerrilla war is run from Nicaragua with the help of Cuba, Vietnam, the PLO, East Germany, Bulgaria and North Korea. A day earlier José Napoleón Duarte, president of the Salvadoran junta, proffered a slightly different list: Cuba, Nicaragua, the Soviet Union, the PLO and Grenada.

March General Vernon Walters, State Department Ambassador at Large, travels to Havana for four hours of secret talks with President Castro. Walters lists problems and Castro agrees to discuss these matters. Wayne Smith, chief of the U.S. Interests Section, later says the talks were a charade aimed at making it appear that the Reagan Administration tried to negotiate but found Cuba unwilling — precisely the impression conveyed to Congress on March 25 by Assistant Secretary of State Thomas Enders. (*See* June 28, 1983)

March 12 The State Department calls a press conference where Orlando José Tardencillas, a young Nicaraguan captured in El Salvador in 1981, is expected to describe being trained in Cuba and Ethiopia. Instead, he reports that his previous statements were elicited by physical and psychological torture and that he was never in Cuba or Ethiopia and was in El Salvador on his own. President Reagan suspects the whole thing was "a setup."

March 20 A U.S. "White Paper" claims Cuba and Nicaragua run the FMLN from a command post in Managua. One clue: hangars at an airfield in Nicaragua "resembled those at major Cuban air bases."

March 25 At an emergency session of the UN Security Council requested by Nicaragua, Daniel Ortega says U.S. acts of aggression are "dramatically on the rise" and that Nicaragua, Cuba and the FMLN want to negotiate a peaceful solution to regional conflict.

April President Reagan approves a top secret National Security Council document ("U.S. Policy in Central America and Cuba through F.Y. '84, Summary Paper") outlining a policy aimed at preventing a "proliferation of Cuba-model states" in Central America. (The full text with analysis by Raymond Bonner appears for the first time a year later in the *New York Times*,

April 7, 1983.) It calls for "Incremental increase in Cuban and Nicaraguan effort" (*see* December 1, 1981). A major goal is influencing public opinion; a decision is made to target Congress and "opinion leaders." Policy includes: building public pressure against Cuba by highlighting human rights issues, using Cuban exiles in various countries to carry the message; stepping up military training in the region "with emphasis on multilateralization"; increasing economic pressure; stepping up "efforts to co-opt negotiations issue to avoid congressionally mandated negotiations."

April 5 Three Cubans hijack a U.S. passenger jet to Havana.

April 7 In Jamaica, President Reagan says Cuba is trying to undermine democracy "throughout the Americas." Aides tell reporters that Reagan is not taking seriously Cuba's recent talk of negotiations.

April 8 Meeting with Caribbean heads of government in Barbados, President Reagan says Grenada "bears the Soviet and Cuban trademark," meaning it will try to "spread the virus" of Marxism.

April 9 Prime Minister J.M.G. Adams of Barbados tells reporters he does not see the role of the Soviet Union, Cuba and Grenada the same way President Reagan does. Dominica's Prime Minister Eugenia Charles, who was also present at the meeting with President Reagan, says her country is "inoculated" against this "virus." Both leaders show more concern that the money allocated by the Caribbean Basin Initiative is insufficient to help their financial situation.

April 9 The United States orders a halt, effective April 12, to charter flights from Miami to Havana by American Airways Charter Inc., cutting the major air link between the two countries.

April 10 To show support for Argentina in the Malvinas (Falklands) conflict with Britain, Cuba sends its ambassador back to Buenos Aires after a long absence due to Cuba's objections to the military government that seized power in 1976.

April 12 Argentina returns its ambassador to Cuba.

April 19 The Reagan Administration reinstitutes the travel ban, announcing that, effective May 15, U.S. citizens are prohibited from making expenditures incidental to travel to Cuba, effectively banning such travel for the ordinary U.S. tourist despite the fact that U.S. courts have upheld the constitutional right to travel. Exceptions are made for government officials, people visiting close relatives, and those traveling "for the purpose of gathering news, making news or documentary films, engaging in professional research, or for similar activities." Otherwise, travel is permitted only if Cuba pays all expenses. Use of credit cards and similar transactions are prohibited even for those permitted to spend hard currency.

April 19 The Reagan Administration informs Cuba that the 1977 fishing accord will be allowed to lapse.

April 29 The Defense Department begins military maneuvers in the Caribbean, one of eight such exercises since last October. "Operation Ocean Venture 82" will last until mid-May with participation from 45,000 troops, 350 planes and 60 ships, including a mock invasion of Puerto Rico and a "non-combatant evacuation operation" at Guantánamo Naval Base.

April 30 At the United Nations, Cuba votes for adoption of the Law of the Sea Treaty. The vote is 130 in favor, 4 opposed (the United States, Israel, Turkey, Venezuela), and 17 abstentions. The United States announces July 9 that it will not sign the treaty.

May Cuba and North Yemen establish diplomatic relations.

May 1 As the United States stages military maneuvers nearby, more than a million Cubans participate in the March of the Fighting People on May Day.

May 3-6 Vice-President Carlos Rafael Rodríguez meets in Paris with President François Mitterrand and Prime Minister Pierre Mauroy. The Prime Minister says French and Cuban differences of opinion are natural and should not preclude regular meetings for exchange of views.

June 3 In a measure of how the U.S. alliance with Britain in the Malvinas (Falklands) has affected relationships, Argentine Foreign Minister Nicanor Costa Méndez praises various anti-imperialist victories of the last few decades in Cuba, Algeria, India and Vietnam, accusing Britain and the United States of planning a new South Atlantic alliance that would include South Africa.

June 10 The U.S. Senate passes and President Reagan will sign into law the Intelligence Identities Protection Act making it illegal for anyone to identify a "covert agent." As Floyd Abrams, lawyer and lecturer at Columbia University School of Law, points out in the next day's *New York Times*, it will soon be illegal to identify any agent who might be trying to assassinate Fidel Castro.

June 17 Civil liberties organizations — especially the National Emergency Civil Liberties Committee — and lawyers file a lawsuit, *Regan* v. *Wald*, to challenge the constitutionality of U.S. travel restrictions on behalf of various individuals and organizations.

July 4 The United States expels two Cuban diplomats, Mario Monzón Barata and José Rodríguez of the UN Mission, for "buying and trying to buy large quantities of high technology electronics equipment, much of it subject to strategic trade controls" in violation of the Trading With the Enemy Act. A third Cuban diplomat, Juan Bandera Pérez, also from the UN Mission, is expelled in August on similar charges.

August Wayne Smith resigns as chief of the U.S. Interests Section in Havana. John Ferch takes the job.

August 7-18 The State Department allows Puerto Rico's Olympic team to travel to Cuba for the Central American and Caribbean Games with more than 20 countries, but forbids Puerto Rican spectators to go. Several hundred defy the ban, including Rubén Berrios, president of the Puerto Rican Independence Party. Cuba agreed to host the Games because Puerto Rico, originally scheduled as the site, could not afford to do so.

August 10 The House of Representatives approves setting up Radio Martí to broadcast "the truth" to Cuba. The legislation fails to get Senate approval in this session of Congress.

August 19 Mexico's financial situation causes bankers to meet with Mexican officials looking for ways to prevent debt default, forcing recognition of the debt crisis among Third World countries.

September 2 Omega 7 claims responsibility for bombing the Venezuelan consulate in Miami to protest continued incarceration of Orlando Bosch for the 1976 terrorist bombing that killed 73 people.

September 2 Cuba announces that it has asked 13 creditors (Austria, Belgium, Britain, Canada, Denmark, France, Italy, Japan, the Netherlands, Spain, Sweden, Switzerland and West Germany) to reschedule about $1.2 billion of its debt coming due during the next three years. Recently, the United States has put increasing pressure on banks and governments that deal with Cuba. During the last eight months, international banks have withdrawn more than $550 million from Cuba. In addition to the current international economic crisis, Cuba's economy has been hurt by steep interest rates and crashing prices for nickel and sugar.

September 4 The leaders of Angola, Mozambique, Zimbabwe, Tanzania, Botswana and Zambia reject the U.S. proposal to link a pullout of South African occupation forces in Namibia to withdrawal of Cuban troops from Angola.

September 24 The UN General Assembly votes 70 to 30 with 43 abstentions against placing the status of Puerto Rico on its agenda. (*See* August 20, 1981)

October 2 The FBI arrests four members of Omega 7 on charges of interstate transport of explosives in an attempt to bomb the car of UN Ambassador Raúl Roa Kourí in 1980. They are Andrés García, Alberto Pérez, Eduardo Losada Fernández and Pedro Remón. Eduardo ("Omar") Arocena, the head of Omega 7, is being sought.

October 10 As a Cuban delegation arrives in Bolivia for the presidential inauguration of Hernán Siles Zuazo, the crowd which greets them at the airport cheers Che Guevara, murdered by his captors in Bolivia 15 years ago.

October 11 At the opening session of the UN General Assembly, Uganda's foreign minister calls linkage of Namibian independence with Cuban troops in Angola "a very suspicious scheme indeed." These sentiments are reiterated at the Assembly by representatives of Guinea, Guinea-Bissau, the Congo, St. Vincent and the Grenadines, and others. Nigeria's foreign minister suggests that if Cuban troops had not come to help, apartheid would have recolonized Angola.

October 12 Visiting Kenya, France's foreign minister says France, Canada and West Germany have informed the United States that they oppose linking Namibian independence to withdrawal of Cuban troops from Angola.

October 21 Released from prison by Cuba after almost 22 years, Armando Valladares leaves Havana. Some who sought his release expect to find him paralyzed as he described himself from prison, but on October 22 he walks off a plane in Paris in good health.

November 5 Using as evidence the testimony of Cuban Americans arrested for drug trafficking and granted immunity from prosecution, a federal grand jury in Miami indicts four Cuban officials along with 10 Cuban Americans on charges of conspiring to transport marijuana and methaqualone from Colombia to the United States by way of Cuba. The officials are Admiral Aldo Santamaría, chief of the Cuban Navy; Fernando Ravelo Renedo, Cuba's ambassador to Colombia; Gonzalo Bassols, a diplomat stationed in Colombia; and René Rodríguez, president of ICAP.

November 10 Soviet President Leonid Brezhnev dies. President Castro attends the funeral November 15 and meets on the following day with Yuri Andropov, the new general secretary of the Soviet Communist Party.

November 11 Cuba responds to the November 5 indictments with a lengthy editorial in *Granma*, rejecting "this absurd and unprecedented accusation." The editorial lists examples of Cuba's vigilance against drugs, including arrests of many U.S. drug traffickers. Now, says the editorial, Cuba will "halt all cooperation between our Border Patrol and the U.S. Coast Guard."

November 16 In a speech welcoming Vice-President George Bush to Zimbabwe, Prime Minister Robert Mugabe says Cubans are in Angola to help protect it against South Africa's "incessant invasion" and that Cubans have not set foot in Namibia or South Africa.

November 26 South African Foreign Minister Roelof Botha, in Washington for talks with U.S. officials, says the presence of Cuban troops in Angola would prevent a free election in Namibia.

November 27 In a direct response to Vice-President Bush's attempt to get support for "linkage" during his visit to Africa, foreign ministers from 31 African governments issue a statement condemning U.S. and South African attempts to link withdrawal of Cuban troops from Angola with Namibian independence.

December Foreign Trade Minister Ricardo Cabrisas attends the General Agreement on Tariffs and Trade (GATT) session in Geneva. He meets in London with more than 80 British business leaders and bankers, announcing the establishment of the Anglo-Cuban Trade Council to further bilateral trade. He attends the

International Sugar Organization conference in London and meets with British Trade Secretary Peter Rees.

December 3 Colombian President Belisario Betancur tells President Reagan, in Bogotá for a five-hour state visit, that Cuba should be readmitted to the OAS. Reagan says this can happen only if Cuba "breaks its ties" with the Soviet Union.

December 7 Angolan and South African officials meet in the Cape Verde Islands for their first direct talks since Angolan independence. There are also ongoing discussions between Angolan and U.S. officials.

December 13 The U.S. Supreme Court refuses to hear an appeal by First National Bank of Boston, which sued *Banco Nacional de Cuba* in 1961 to try to recover $1,675,000 owed under letters of credit issued by a First National branch in Cuba, nationalized in 1960. A federal appeals court had rejected First National's argument that Banco Nacional, run by the Cuban government, assumed liabilities of banks nationalized by Cuba.

December 21 The State Department denies visas to two Cubans' who were to have spoken at an American Philosophical Association conference in Baltimore. State Department official Alan Romberg says both Florentino Cruz Miranda and Arnaldo Silva León are members of the Cuban Communist Party's Central Committee and that U.S. law prohibits travel in the United States by "those aliens whose activities could be prejudicial to the public interest." A representative of the American Philosophical Association, Professor Clifford Durand of Morgan State University, says this is "prior censorship of political discussion."

1983

January 5 In an effort to settle Central American conflicts, the foreign ministers of Colombia, Mexico, Panama and Venezuela meet on the Panamanian island of Contadora and draft an initial proposal. The Contadora document calls for an end to all foreign intervention in the region, suspension of all military aid, and negotiations to end El Salvador's civil war and the fighting in Nicaragua between government troops and Contras.

January 11 Cuba and Bolivia reestablish diplomatic relations.

March 1 Thirteen creditor nations agree to reschedule Cuban debt payments due from September 1, 1982, through December 31, 1983. (*See* September 2, 1982)

March 7-12 President Castro attends the Seventh Summit Conference of the Nonaligned Movement in India, turning over the position of chair to Prime Minister Indira Gandhi. In his speech, Castro says the Reagan Administration has instructed the CIA to resume plans to assassinate Cuban leaders. The Nonaligned Countries reject "linkage" between Namibian independence and Cuban troops in Angola.

March 9 The Argentine government calls in U.S. Ambassador Harry Shlaudeman to express concern about a document prepared by the U.S. government and distributed this week alleging Cuban subversion in Latin America. In New Delhi for the Nonaligned Summit, Argentine President Reynaldo Bignone calls a press conference to say that distribution of the document constitutes intervention in Argentina's internal affairs. Shlaudeman says the timing was unfortunate but not intended to destabilize the friendlier relations that have developed between Argentina and Cuba since the Falklands (Malvinas) crisis.

March 23 Launching plans for "Star Wars," President Reagan shows on television some high-technology, aerial photographs of what he calls threatening installations in Cuba, Grenada and Nicaragua, including the airport being built in Grenada, which Reagan maintains is for military use. The United States turned down Grenada's request for aid to build the 9,000-foot runway, the minimum length for accommodating jumbo jets needed to compete for tourism in the Caribbean. Layne Dredging Ltd., a Miami company, working with Cuban engineers, recently completed a $2.9 million dredging contract. Another U.S. company designed the fuel storage tanks shown in the photo. The prime contractor is Plessey Airports, subsidiary of the British conglomerate, Plessey, with a $9.9 million contract underwritten by the British government. Cuban construction workers are providing labor. More than a dozen countries are involved, including Canada.

March 25 With Jorge Mas Canosa as a leader in a committee to intercede for the release of Orlando Bosch from a Venezuelan jail, the Miami City Commission proclaims "Orlando Bosch Day."

March 28 Representative Mickey Leland (D-Texas) leaves Cuba with two Texans arrested in November 1982 for drug trafficking, not the first time that Leland has arranged such a release.

March 29 Senator Lowell Weicker Jr. (R-Connecticut) and Wayne Smith, former head of the U.S. Interests Section, meet with President Castro and arrange the release of three U.S. women jailed for drug trafficking. Later, they report to Assistant Secretary of State Enders that Castro is willing to discuss all the problems between Cuba and the United States. (*See* June 28)

April 18 The State Department denies a visa to Cuban Deputy Cultural Minister Julio Pedro García Espinosa, who had been invited to a Los Angeles film festival. U.S. policy is not to grant visas to Cuban government and Communist Party officials unless the purpose of the visit is to conduct diplomacy or attend meetings of international organizations.

April 18 The U.S. government orders Cuban UN diplomats Rolando Salup Canto and Joaquín Rodobaldo Pentón expelled for spying. Cuba charges that this is part of a systematic campaign against Cuba's permanent UN representation. The diplomats depart April 22.

April 19 With Solid Shield 83 military maneuvers taking place in the Caribbean, an SR-71 overflies Cuba twice. Cuba sends a protest note to Washington.

April 25 Along with 135 other countries, Cuba attends the UN International Conference on Namibia, which calls for unconditional independence for Namibia and for sanctions against South Africa, rejecting attempts at linking Cuban troops in Angola to South Africa's illegal occupation of Namibia. The "Contact Group" (in "contact" with South Africa to negotiate Namibian independence) composed of Britain, Canada, France, the United States and West Germany is criticized for attending as observers rather than as participants.

April 25 The State Department restricts travel by Cuba's UN diplomats to within a 25-mile radius of the United Nations. (*See* January 16, 1975)

April 27 In a televised address to a joint session of Congress aimed at garnering support for his Latin American policy, President Reagan says Cuba and the Soviet Union are conspiring to cause revolution in Central America. He echoes the Carter Administration's "discovery" of a Soviet "combat brigade" in Cuba, a brigade that has been there since 1962. Cuba publishes the speech in *Granma* along with the Democrats' response by Senator Christopher Dodd (Connecticut) calling for negotiated settlements.

May To garner support for Radio Martí which is having some difficulty in getting approval by Congress, the Reagan Administration is considering dozens of ways to retaliate against jamming by Cuba, including "surgical strikes" against transmitters.

May 1 A Cuban who left in 1969 hijacks a U.S. passenger jet back to Cuba.

May 11 President Reagan pardons Bay of Pigs veteran Eugenio Martínez, now manager of a car dealership in Miami, for his part in the Watergate burglary.

May 12 Another U.S. jet is hijacked to Havana.

May 14 Oliver Tambo, President of the African National Congress (ANC), and members of his delegation meet in Cuba with

President Castro and other Cuban officials about strengthening ties.

May 16 In the case of *Regan* v. *Wald*, the First U.S. Circuit Court of Appeals in Boston unanimously rules U.S. restrictions on travel to Cuba invalid. The decision vacates a district judge's denial of an injunction that would have blocked enforcement of the regulations and orders the judge to issue a preliminary injunction. The U.S. government will appeal.

May 19 A Cuban who says he was unable to get medical care in the United States hijacks a passenger jet to Havana.

May 20 In Dade County, Florida, President Reagan addresses 1,500 Cuban Americans at the Cuban American National Foundation's commemoration of the withdrawal of U.S. troops from Cuba in 1902, called "Cuban Independence Day" by some Cuban exiles, including CANF. Reagan announces that "Cuba is no longer independent" but someday "will be free." In an ongoing attempt that continues for at least two more years to counter what Cuba regards as disinformation emanating from the Reagan White House, a *Granma* editorial responds point by point to his speech.

May 22 Senator Barry Goldwater (R-Arizona), chair of the Senate Intelligence Committee, says on national TV ("Face the Nation") that the United States should have already invaded Cuba and suggests that Cuba should be the 51st state.

May 24 Thomas Enders, Assistant Secretary of State, meets with Ramón Sánchez Parodi, head of the Cuban Interests Section, to request that Cuba take back 789 Marielitos imprisoned at Atlanta Federal Penitentiary.

May 24 A Japanese newspaper reports that the United States has notified Japan that as of June it will halt imports of Japanese stainless steel containing Cuban nickel. In June, Japan agrees to certify that none of the alloys it sells to the United States will contain the banned nickel. From 1980 through 1983, Washington has imposed this policy on major importers of Cuban nickel such as France, West Germany, Italy and the Netherlands.

May 27 Omega 7 claims responsibility for the fifth bombing this year in Miami's Little Havana, this one at the Continental National Bank office aimed at the bank's vice-chairman Bernardo Benes, who is active in the "Dialogue."

June 15 A day after another hijacking by a homesick Cuban, Cuba summons an official from the U.S. Interests Section to accept a diplomatic note showing, case by case, how Cuba has sentenced hijackers since 1981 to an average of 15 years as compared with two to five years prior to 1981.

June 15 Vice-President Carlos Rafael Rodríguez tells visiting executives of the Associated Press, newspaper publishers and editors that Cuba wants better relations with the United States but believes the threat of U.S. military force is greater than ever.

June 17 Responding to the U.S. note of May 24, Cuba agrees to discuss return of those Cubans but only as part of negotiations on "normalization of migration." Cuba notes the United States has not granted visas to some 1,500 former political prisoners who were promised entry three years ago.

June 17 The U.S. Supreme Court rules 6 to 3 in favor of Citibank in the case of *Banco Para El Comercio Exterior de Cuba* v. *First National City Bank*, deciding that Citibank was entitled to deduct the value of assets lost when Cuba nationalized banks in 1960 from a commercial debt it owed the Cuban bank.

June 23 Cubans end four days of defense exercises in which, for the first time, provincial and municipal Defense Councils were set up to provide leadership against U.S. invasion.

June 28 President Reagan tells a press conference that "early on in my Administration we made contact with Mr Castro. Nothing came of it and we haven't had much success since." (*See* March 1982)

July 2 Marielitos hijack a U.S. passenger jet to Cuba.

July 3-9 Cuba hosts "Health for All: 25 Years of the Cuban Experience," a conference attended by more than 1,300 delegates from 100 countries, including 150 U.S. participants.

July 5 The State Department publicizes Cuba's policy of 15-year sentences for hijackers, but another passenger jet is hijacked two days later.

July 6 The U.S. Supreme Court grants the Reagan Administration's request for a stay of the May 16 decision in *Regan* v. *Wald*, leaving travel restrictions in effect until the Court decides whether to hear a full appeal.

July 7 The United States tells Cuba that it is ready to hold talks about migration if Cuba first takes back the unwanted Marielitos.

July 7 Speaking to 150 U.S. citizens in Nicaragua, Interior Minister Tomás Borge challenges the United States to send doctors and teachers instead of demanding that the Cubans leave, thereby "doing Cuba a great favor" since "that country is now making an extraordinary effort beyond the call of duty to send us technicians, teachers and doctors."

July 17 Former Senator George McGovern meets with President Castro in Cuba and reports later that "there was absolutely nothing" that Castro would not discuss in negotiations with the United States. (*See* June 28)

July 17 A family of seven people hijacks a U.S. passenger jet to Cuba.

July 17 The presidents of the Contadora Group (*see* January 5) meet in Cancún, Mexico, and issue the Cancún Declaration, calling on President Reagan and President Castro "to join us in this effort" for peace in Central America.

July 18 President Reagan makes a speech that ignores the Contadora Group's appeal, blaming Cuba, Nicaragua and the Soviet Union for the civil war in El Salvador. On the same day, U.S. officials report plans for massive military maneuvers in the Gulf of Fonseca and the Caribbean.

July 19 Another U.S. passenger jet is hijacked to Cuba, the second in as many days. Cuba warns of even stiffer sanctions.

July 22 The FBI arrests Omega 7 leader Eduardo Arocena in Miami, charging him with plotting to assassinate UN Ambassador Raúl Roa Kourí in 1980.

July 24 President Castro writes to the Contadora Group saying Cuba can be counted on for cooperation with negotiated solutions.

July 26 Following publicity about President Castro's letter, President Reagan also writes to the Contadora Group praising their efforts. At a press conference, he says Cuba has thousands of military personnel in Nicaragua.

July 28 In an impromptu news conference with U.S. journalists, President Castro says Cuba will accept the principle of nonintervention in Central America if the United States does the same. He explains that of around 4,000 Cubans in Nicaragua, there are about 200 military advisers, more than 2,000 teachers, 500 doctors, a few hundred other medical workers, a few hundred construction workers, while the rest are agricultural technicians.

July 29 Parts of President Castro's news conference are broadcast on U.S. television.

July 30 Responding to President Castro, President Reagan appears on television, saying the OAS "might be a better forum for finding a negotiated settlement" than the Contadora Group. He suggests that Cuba sever Soviet ties "and become American again." Of a July 28 House vote to cut off "covert" aid to Contras in Nicaragua, Reagan says he "couldn't believe congressmen... talked about Castro wanting peace."

August 3 A bipartisan delegation of House and Senate leaders, after meeting with Secretary of State George Shultz, expects the Reagan Administration will follow up on President Castro's apparent willingness to reach agreement about Central America. But there is no follow-up.

August 4 Another U.S. passenger jet is hijacked to Cuba.

August 10 The State Department says it has again asked Cuba to return hijackers. The United States does not return hijackers to Cuba.

August 18 Another U.S. passenger jet is hijacked to Havana.

August 27 For the first time, Honduras admits fighting Honduran rebels, saying they have been trained in Cuba and Nicaragua.

September 7 In Cuba for work in agriculture and construction, the José Martí Brigade holds a press conference. This is the largest contingent since the Brigade was founded in 1973, with 366 participants from Western Europe: France, Italy, Belgium, Spain, Portugal, West Germany, Austria, Switzerland, Britain, Greece, Luxembourg and Malta.

September 13 The Senate approves Radio Martí. The House does the same on September 29 and President Reagan signs it into law in October. Cubans already listen to National Public Radio, ABC, CBS and NBC, and can pick up Florida TV. In addition, the Cuban American National Foundation has its own station, *La Voz de la Fundación* (Voice of the Foundation).

September 14 President Reagan tells reporters: "As far as I'm concerned that agreement [ending the 1962 Missile Crisis] has been abrogated many times by the Soviet Union and Cuba in the bringing in of what can only be considered offensive weapons, not defensive, there." Questioned about Reagan's remark, White House press secretary Larry Speakes says he meant violations of "the spirit of the agreement" and was speaking of "offensive weapons" that have been "funneled... through Cuba" to Central America.

September 22 Another U.S. passenger jet is hijacked to Cuba.

September 22 Cuba tells the United States that it is prepared to begin negotiations about migration, including discussion of the return to Cuba of Marielitos.

October 1 With some 2,000 U.S. and Latin academics participating, the Latin American Studies Association (LASA), meeting in Mexico City, adopts a resolution calling on the United States to begin negotiations aimed at normalizing relations with Cuba.

October 16 The *Miami Herald* reports that Miami mayoral candidate Xavier Suárez prefers to describe someone like Omega 7 leader Eduardo Arocena, arrested in July for conspiring to kill UN Ambassador Raúl Roa Kourí, "as a freedom fighter, not a terrorist." Suárez, supported by the Cuban American National Foundation, later wins the election for mayor.

October 19 A federal grand jury in Miami indicts 23 people on air piracy charges related to nine hijackings to Cuba from July 22, 1980, to August 18, 1983. All 23 are believed to be in Cuba.

October 20 Following the deaths of Prime Minister Maurice Bishop and other Grenadian leaders on October 19 during a coup, the Cuban government issues a statement saying that "if they were executed in cold blood, those responsible deserve exemplary punishment" and warning that these "grave errors" will be used by the revolution's enemies to "sweep away the revolutionary process in Grenada and subject it anew to imperial and neo-colonial power." While most U.S. media previously portrayed Bishop as too close to Cuba, now he is pictured as the victim of a Cuban-Soviet plot. Former Jamaican Prime Minister Michael Manley, speaking in New Jersey on October 26, calls those allegations a "squalid lie" and says he believes U.S. interests were behind Bishop's overthrow.

October 20 With U.S. warships on the way, Grenada asks for Cuban military aid, but Cuba is still trying to define its relations with Grenada's new regime.

October 22 President Castro tells Grenadian leaders that Cubans in Grenada, mostly construction workers, are too few to be a significant military factor. To Cuban diplomats in Grenada, Castro says he understands how "bitter" it is to risk Cuban lives after the "gross mistakes" by Grenadians but that an evacuation of Cuban personnel while U.S. warships are approaching might seem "dishonorable." He orders Cubans in Grenada to use weapons "only if we are directly attacked" for "defending ourselves, not the government or its deeds." He specifically commands: "If the Yankees land on the runway section [of the airport Cuban workers are constructing] near the university or on its surroundings to evacuate their citizens [at the medical school], fully refrain from interfering."

October 22 Cuba sends a message to the U.S. government requesting that the United States "keep in touch" in order to find "a favorable solution of any difficulty without violence or intervention." Cuba receives no response until after the U.S. invasion begins, nor does the Reagan Administration inform the U.S. public of Cuba's message.

October 25 U.S. military forces invade Grenada, using at least 8,850 ground and airborne troops while another 11,800 stand by offshore to control an island with a population of 110,000 and an army and militia of no more than 2,000. When U.S. troops land at the airport, Cubans remain, as instructed, in their camps and work places. Fighting erupts only after U.S. troops advance on the Cubans. U.S. officials tell the U.S. public that there are hundreds of Cuban troops fighting. Cuba's figures prove to be correct: of a total of 784 Cubans in Grenada, 636 are construction workers while only 43 are members of Cuban armed forces who were advisers before Prime Minister Bishop's execution.

October 25 Lt. Col. Desire Bouterse, head of the government in Suriname, announces he has asked Cuba to lower diplomatic status to that of a chargé d'affaires. The Reagan Administration has been concerned about Suriname's increasing ties to Cuba.

October 26 The U.S. 82nd Airborne Division lands in Grenada at dawn to join the fighting against the Cuban construction workers. The UN Security Council begins a special session on the invasion.

October 26 At an OAS meeting, 13 of the 18 participating countries warn that the U.S. invasion of Grenada violates the principles of self-determination, nonintervention and respect for the territorial integrity of one of the OAS members.

October 26-29 Since the press was first barred from entering Grenada and then only a chosen few were allowed to enter, the U.S. media image of Cubans in Grenada is shaped by Pentagon and Administration sources, who report such things as "captured documents" proving that Cuba planned to take over the island in the near future and was considering taking U.S. hostages. These military sources state that in addition to more than 600 Cubans who have been taken prisoner, there are 800 to 1,000 still at large, "disappearing into the mountains" perhaps preparing to wage "protracted guerrilla war." *Granma* comments, "Now they seem to see Cubans behind every tree and rock." There are even reports of missile silos in Grenada, soon denied by a U.S. military official.

October 27 President Reagan makes a televised speech about two military developments in recent days, minimizing the deaths of 262 U.S. troops in Lebanon on October 23 while maximizing the success of the U.S. invasion of Grenada on October 25. He describes a "Soviet-Cuban colony being readied as a major military bastion to export terror and undermine democracy," announcing "We got there just in time." He reports discovery of a warehouse filled with enough weapons "to supply thousands of terrorists." When asked in January 1984 about the inaccuracy of Reagan's narrative, David Gergen, director of White House communications, says Reagan "went with the best information we had."

October 28 Admiral Wesley L. McDonald, commander of U.S. Atlantic Forces, tells reporters that "captured documents" disclose that at least 1,110 Cubans are in Grenada, all "professional soldiers" who were "impersonating construction workers." Within two days the U.S. estimate is revised down to 784, Cuba's figure. Within five days, U.S. military officials say their interrogation of Cuban prisoners has revealed that most are indeed construction workers.

October 28 White House deputy press secretary Les Janka writes a letter of resignation (effective October 31) because he believes his credibility has been damaged "perhaps irreparably" by the erroneous information he has disseminated about the invasion of Grenada.

October 28 The United States vetoes a UN Security Council resolution deploring the invasion of Grenada and calling for an immediate end to the intervention and withdrawal of foreign troops.

October 28 Deputy Foreign Minister Ricardo Alarcón says that Cuban Ambassador Julián Torres Rizo in Grenada has not yet been able to establish contact with U.S. officials. Colombia and Spain, trying to arrange evacuation of Cubans, have said such contact should be the next step. Meanwhile, 642 Cuban prisoners are being interrogated while surrounded by barbed wire in an open area exposed to sun and rain with just one meal a day and little water.

October 28 The U.S. Senate accepts an amendment to a debt-ceiling measure urging President Reagan to hold Cuban prisoners in Grenada until Cuba agrees to take back Marielitos.

October 29 The Reagan Administration has been saying that the new airport in Grenada was being built for military use (*see* March 23). Now Derrick Collier, general director of Plessey Airports, says there "is absolutely no indication of a military installation at the airport." He says the airport is essential for Grenada and he hopes to finish the project. Plessey, he says, had close relations with Cuban architects in charge of the project and several Plessey technicians were working in Grenada when U.S. troops invaded, damaging much of the construction equipment and perhaps damaging the uncompleted runway.

October 30 British Foreign Secretary Geoffrey Howe says on British television that if an independent government like Grenada (part of the British Commonwealth) accepts the cooperation of Cuba and the Soviet Union, this is no justification for the use of force to topple the government.

October 30 According to Bob Woodward in his 1987 book, *Veil: The Secret Wars of the CIA 1981-1987*, U.S. intelligence analysts on this date distribute to appropriate agencies their assessment about Grenada, including these points: All the Cubans have been killed or captured and none remain in the hills; Cuban workers are actually workers and not disguised troops; weapons found were for use by Grenadian forces and inadequate for use against other governments. Woodward reports that this classified report "is never released publicly." Disinformation continues for years.

October 31   A plane sent by the International Red Cross arrives in Barbados, ready to fly to Grenada to pick up wounded Cubans, some of whom are in urgent need of surgery. U.S. officials refuse to allow it to land in Grenada.

November 1   The Defense Department says a nine-ship task force headed by the aircraft carrier *America* is not headed for the Caribbean but for the "Central Atlantic." But on November 3, the Navy says the task force will arrive in the Caribbean within 24 hours for military maneuvers off Guantánamo Naval Base.

November 1   U.S. troops have surrounded the Cuban Embassy in Grenada, preventing both exit and entry. Governor General Paul Scoon, placed in charge of Grenada by the United States, has ordered Cuban diplomatic personnel to leave Grenada by noon November 2. Two Cuban diplomats are being held in U.S. custody while two others were detained and released. There are 41 people, including 3 children, at the Embassy. Cuba has instructed its diplomats to remain until the United States returns all Cuban prisoners, the wounded and the dead.

November 2   Cuban Ambassador Rizo meets with U.S. Ambassador Charles Gillespie in Grenada. Governor General Scoon backs off the noon deadline. The International Red Cross arranges transport of 57 wounded and sick Cuban prisoners along with 10 doctors to Havana, where they and all those who follow later are met at the airport by President Castro and other Cuban leaders, welcoming them home as heroes.

November 2   By a vote of 108 to 9 with 27 abstentions, the UN General Assembly adopts virtually the same resolution that the United States vetoed on October 28 in the Security Council. The negative votes are cast by the United States and the six Caribbean countries which cooperated in the invasion — Antigua and Barbuda, Barbados, Dominica, Jamaica, St. Lucia, St. Vincent and the Grenadines — plus El Salvador and Israel.

November 6   A full-page article in the *New York Times*, by Stuart Taylor Jr., describes "inaccurate information" and "unproven assertions" disseminated by U.S. civilian and military officials during the invasion of Grenada, much of it about the role of Cuba in Grenada.

November 9 The last prisoners arrive in Cuba along with the last diplomats to leave, including the ambassador. Two diplomats remain in Grenada, chargé d'affaires Gastón Díaz González and communications technician Pablo Mora Lettuce.

November 12 The United States ships 37 bodies to Cuba. Examination reveals 24 are the Cubans killed in Grenada while 13 are Grenadians, who are returned after funeral rites in Cuba.

November 14 President Castro's eulogy at the funeral for the 24 Cubans describes the implications of U.S. foreign policy for the world. He notes that intervention after the murder of Maurice Bishop was the same as if another country had intervened after the murder of John F. Kennedy. He lists 19 lies told to justify the invasion and refutes each one, including that medical students were in danger of being taken hostage. Concerning the impact of the lies on U.S. public opinion, he says if a poll had been taken when Hitler occupied Austria and annexed the Sudentenland, most Germans would have approved. In addition, he points out, many U.S. politicians who initially opposed the invasion then condoned it while the press moderated its complaints and criticisms. Castro warns the United States against invading Cuba. If the 82nd Airborne had to be brought in to fight the last 500 Cubans, he asks, then how many divisions would be needed against millions of Cubans fighting on their own soil?

November 15 The Treasury Department informs the Soviet Union that, starting December 20, it will ban imports of Soviet steel until certification that they contain no Cuban nickel. The Soviet Union's resistance to that demand leads to a suspension of U.S. purchases of Soviet metals containing nickel from 1983 to 1991. In an interview with Pedro Prada in *Granma*, September 7, 1994, María de la Luz B'Hamel Ramírez, director of trade policies with western Europe and North America in Cuba's Foreign Trade Ministry, says the U.S. measure remains in force and continues to affect Cuban trade.

November 20 Cuba takes out ads in major U.S. newspapers for publication of President Castro's November 14 speech.

November 28   In the case of *Regan* v. *Wald*, the U.S. Supreme Court agrees to hear the Treasury Department's appeal. Meanwhile, restrictions on travel to Cuba remain in effect.

December 10   Vice-President Carlos Rafael Rodríguez attends the presidential inauguration of Raúl Alfonsín, marking Argentina's return to civilian government.

December 28   Omega 7 leader Eduardo Arocena is indicted by a federal grand jury in New York on seven charges including the attempted assassination of UN Ambassador Raúl Roa Kourí in 1980 and planting 14 bombs in New York and Miami. The FBI now calls Omega 7 an international terrorist group financed by millions of dollars received for services rendered to drug traffickers.

1984

January The State Department informs Canadian Robert Rutka, the only reporter covering the United States for the Cuban news agency Prensa Latina, that he must get a special license to deal with Cuba because it is an "enemy nation." When Rutka refuses to get the license, he is told to leave the country, which he does.

January Cuba has informed diplomats from several countries that by June it will reduce the number of Cuban troops in Ethiopia from about 10,500 to fewer than 3,000 because Somalia is unlikely to renew its attacks in the Ogaden.

January 1 As the Caribbean Basin Initiative (CBI) goes into effect, every Caribbean country except Cuba is invited to take part in this U.S. economic plan for Central America and the Caribbean. In an effort to prove that U.S. trade can benefit U.S. neighbors, CBI is supposed to increase Caribbean exports through increased investments and trade. (*See* November 20, 1985)

January 5 President Reagan broadcasts a speech to Cuba from Voice of America transmitters, saying Radio Martí will "tell the truth about Cuba to the Cuban people."

January 6 For the second time since South Africa began its latest invasion of Angola December 6, the UN Security Council demands that South Africa withdraw its troops, voting 13 to 0 with the United States and Britain abstaining.

January 7 South Africa issues a military communiqué saying its troops directly engaged Cuban troops in a three-day battle earlier this week near Cuvelai 120 miles inside Angola and continuing to claim that the current invasion is aimed solely at SWAPO bases in Angola.

January 11 The Reagan Administration's Commission on Central America, headed by former Secretary of State Henry Kissinger, presents its report, reinforcing current policy: "The Soviet-Cuban thrust to make Central America part of their geostrategic challenge is what has turned the struggle in Central America into a security and political problem for the United States and for the hemisphere."

January 20 Concerned about the U.S. invasion of a Commonwealth nation, British Prime Minister Margaret Thatcher says the airport that Cubans were helping to build in Grenada presents no more of a threat than those built to attract tourists to several other Caribbean islands.

February 9 Soviet President Yuri Andropov dies. President Castro attends his funeral and meets on February 15 with Konstantin Chernenko, who succeeds Andropov as general secretary of the Communist Party and later (in April) as president.

February 21 Omega 7 members José Ignacio González, Gerardo Necuze and Justo Rodríguez plead guilty to conspiracy to make and explode bombs in Florida between 1980 and 1983. The three agree to cooperate with federal prosecutors.

March A lawsuit is filed challenging the State Department's denial of visas to foreign visitors, including two Cuban women. Argued by the American Civil Liberties Union (ACLU), *Reagan* v. *Abourezk* is joined by New York City because the city's Commission on the Status of Women in 1983 invited the two women, Olga Finlay and Leonor Rodríguez Lezcano, to discuss the role of women in Cuban society.

March 4 Commenting on security at the upcoming Olympics in Los Angeles, *Parade* magazine, which reaches 24 million households every Sunday, reports that there are currently five countries on the U.S. list of "terrorist nations": Cuba, Iran, Libya, South Yemen and Syria. The article says all but Iran will send Olympic teams to Los Angeles, and asks how many "terrorists or suicidal fanatics will be among them."

March 13 Omega 7 leader Eduardo Arocena is charged with the 1980 assassination of Cuban UN diplomat Félix García Rodríguez.

March 17-20 Angolan President José Eduardo dos Santos makes a state visit to Cuba for extensive discussions. On March 19, he and

President Castro state the basic conditions that would have to be met for withdrawal of Cuban troops from Angola: 1) Withdrawal of South African troops from Angola and an end to all aggression or threat of aggression against Angola; 2) Implementation of the 1978 UN Resolution 435 on independence for Namibia; 3) Cessation of foreign aid to armed organizations fighting against the recognized government of Angola.

March 19 To an audience of Cuban Americans, President Reagan maintains he's asking Congress for $93 million in aid to the Salvadoran government to protect Central America from being taken over by the Soviet Union through its proxy, Cuba. "Like a roving wolf," Reagan warns, "Castro's Cuba looks to peace-loving neighbors with hungry eyes and sharp teeth." Indicating that he believes Batista's regime was a democracy, Reagan calls Cuba an example of the United States "pursuing policies that lead to the overthrow of less-than-perfect democracies by Marxist dictatorships."

March 20 In a Nicaraguan port, a Soviet tanker hits a mine, injuring five Soviet crew members. It turns out that the CIA trained teams of non-Nicaraguans — Cuban Americans, Argentines, Salvadorans — to mine the ports, ordering the Nicaraguan Democratic Front (Contras) to say they did it "to prevent the arrival of war materials from Cuba and the Soviet Union."

March 22 The Defense Department announces that it will hold the largest military exercise of 1984 in the Caribbean April 20-May 6, including reinforcement of the Guantánamo Naval Base and a simulated evacuation of dependents. On the following day, Moscow announces that a squadron of Soviet warships will arrive in Cuba on March 25.

March 25 On election day in El Salvador, José Napoleón Duarte, the Christian Democratic candidate for president, appears in a taped interview on CBS's "Face the Nation," claiming he could not appear live because "some kind of death squad organized in Cuba has just arrived to make a suicide attempt to kill me." He pleads for Congress not to cut off aid to his government.

March 28 For the second time in as many days, a U.S. passenger jet is hijacked to Havana.

April 1 *Parade* magazine publishes an interview of President Castro by Tad Szulc.

April 9 The Cuban American National Foundation sponsors a two-day conference in Miami to push for Congressional support for aid to anticommunist forces in Central America. CANF chair Jorge Mas Canosa tells his audience, "We are losing a battle for American public opinion."

April 20-May 6 The Defense Department conducts war game "Ocean Venture" in the Caribbean, including military maneuvers in Cuban land, air and water space at the Guantánamo Naval Base. In the midst of it, Cuba celebrates May Day with the traditional parade in Havana. Speaker Roberto Veiga Menéndez, head of the Cuban Federation of Trade Unions, points out that Cuba has doubled the size of its militia and is ready to defend itself.

April 24 In the case of *Regan* v. *Wald*, the Supreme Court hears arguments for and against restrictions on travel to Cuba.

May 3 Cuba's Foreign Ministry reemphasizes Cuban opposition to the use, production and storage of chemical weapons, calling upon all countries to respect and apply the Geneva Protocol of 1925. The statement refers to President Reagan's announcement on April 4 that the United States must increase its supply of chemical weapons because the Soviet stockpile "threatens U.S. forces."

May 9-13 In a nationally televised speech about Central America on May 9, President Reagan blames Cuba and Nicaragua for the civil war in El Salvador. He says Cuba intends "to double its support to the Salvadoran guerrillas and bring down that newly elected government in the fall." On May 13, National Security Adviser Robert McFarlane, on NBC's "Meet the Press," says the Administration believes that Cuba will "roughly double the level of effort of the rebels in Salvador" with a "Tet-like" offensive in the fall. What actually increases is the amount of U.S. military aid to El Salvador: more than doubling from $81.3 million in all of 1983 to $196.5 million by the end of August 1984.

May 14 A Pentagon report, presented to Congress in early May and made public today, describes plans to spend $43.4 million to improve Guantánamo Naval Base during the next four years. The plans are part of an overall design for upgrading and constructing military installations in Central America and the Caribbean through 1988 while conducting constant military maneuvers in and around Honduras.

May 22   Responding to a U.S. proposal for discussions about migration, Cuba expresses concern about the subject being used as an issue in U.S. election campaigns.

May 23   Cuba's Foreign Affairs Ministry issues a statement in support of the initiative by the presidents of Argentina, Brazil, Colombia and Mexico to convene a ministerial conference of Latin American and Caribbean countries about consequences of the recent rise in interest rates. A rise in the U.S. prime lending rate in early May (the third this year) raised Latin American debt by about $4.5 billion.

May 23   Manuel González Guerra, president of Cuba's Olympic Committee, announces that Cuba will not participate in the 1984 Olympic Games in Los Angeles because of the campaign being mounted in the United States against athletes from socialist countries.

June 22   SWAPO President Sam Nujoma meets with President Castro in Havana about the situation in Southern Africa.

June 22-28   Cuban churches host a Martin Luther King, Jr., Theological Seminar attended by representatives of Black churches in the United States, including Reverend Benjamin Chavis, a civil rights activist wrongfully imprisoned and now director of the Commission for Racial Justice of the United Church of Christ. While in Cuba, Chavis praises Cuba's role in helping U.S. prisoners, saying he himself might still be in a North Carolina prison were it not for Cuba.

June 25   Reverend Jesse Jackson, a Democratic Party presidential candidate, arrives in Cuba with a delegation that includes Representative Mervyn M. Dymally (D-California). Jackson is visiting Cuba, El Salvador, Nicaragua and Panama in an effort to find peaceful solutions to the conflicts in the region. He is the only major presidential candidate who has called for normalization of relations with Cuba.

June 26   At a press conference in Havana, Reverend Jackson announces that President Castro has agreed to reopen discussions about migration provided both major U.S. parties express their desire to begin discussions and agree not to make them a campaign issue. (Jackson has agreed to consult with Walter

Mondale, the likely Democratic nominee, to make sure both parties approve.) Cuba is releasing to Jackson all U.S. prisoners except hijackers.

June 27 Reverend Jackson gets President Castro to accompany him to church, attending the memorial service for Dr Martin Luther King, Jr., held in the Methodist Church in Havana's Vedado District as part of the current Theological Seminar.

June 27 House Foreign Affairs subcommittees hold a hearing on human rights in Cuba, including testimony from Assistant Secretary of State for Human Rights Elliott Abrams and former Cuban prisoner Armando Valladares.

June 28 Reverend Jackson takes back to the United States 22 U.S. prisoners and 26 Cuban political prisoners. Andrés Vargas Gómez, who was released 18 months earlier after serving his sentence as a CIA agent, also leaves Cuba with Jackson.

June 28 In the case of *Regan* v. *Wald*, the Supreme Court votes 5 to 4 to uphold Treasury Department restrictions on travel to Cuba on the grounds that they are part of the embargo rather than political control of the right to travel.

June 29 At the UN Conference on Sugar in Geneva, talks aimed at reaching a new sugar agreement collapse. Cuban Foreign Trade Minister Ricardo Cabrisas says Cuba has worked hard to try to reach an accord since the Conference began work in May 1983. The current sugar agreement expires December 31. The Conference agrees to keep the International Sugar Organization in existence as a means of conducting future negotiations.

June 29 Reverend Jackson briefs about 50 members of Congress on his trip to Cuba and Central America. He also meets with Under Secretary of State Michael Armacost and announces to the press that U.S.-Cuban talks about migration will begin in July.

July 4 In remarks recorded July 2 for release on the Fourth of July, President Reagan questions the legality of Jesse Jackson's diplomatic missions to Cuba and other countries, saying the "law of the land" prohibits private citizens from negotiating with foreign governments. The law involved, the Logan Act, is 185 years old and has rarely been invoked because it is so broadly worded that violations are difficult to prove. Jackson responds that he conferred with the State Department before his trip and that he could not have brought the prisoners into the country if State had not processed the visas and allowed a Cuban plane to land. He points out that the Administration has sent a communiqué to Cuba about discussions on migration to begin later this month. In January, when Jackson went to Syria and brought home a U.S. prisoner, Navy Lt. Robert Goodman Jr., the President called the trip a "mission of mercy."

July 9 President Reagan says he went "astray" in his comments on the legality of Jesse Jackson's trip to Cuba and that there is no evidence that Jackson broke any law.

July 10 Cuba's Foreign Ministry asserts "categorically that not a single MiG plane destined for Nicaragua has ever arrived in Cuba." This statement is a direct reply to a July 6 report in the *Christian Science Monitor* that Cuba had received 10 Soviet MiGs destined for Nicaragua but had opted not to send them because of U.S. threats to punish Nicaragua if it acquires any MiGs.

July 12-13 A Cuban delegation led by Deputy Foreign Minister Ricardo Alarcón and a U.S. delegation led by State Department legal adviser Michael Kozak meet in New York for discussions about migration and repatriation of Marielitos. Alarcón and Kozak continue to head their delegations in subsequent negotiations.

July 18 At the Democratic Party Convention, Walter Mondale is nominated for president on a platform that calls for exploring differences "with a view to stabilizing" Cuban-U.S. relations, but the platform also indicates that Cuba is not sufficiently respectful of "the principle of nonintervention," "human rights both inside and outside of Cuba" and "international norms of behavior."

July 31-August 2 Cuba and the United States hold another round of talks about migration.

August Encouraged by the Supreme Court decision of June 28, the Treasury Department serves two subpoenas upon Marazul Tours, a travel agency that arranges trips to Cuba. One subpoena seeks records, including names and addresses, of all persons who have traveled to Cuba since April 1982 when the Reagan Administration imposed the current restrictions. The second seeks names of some one thousand lawyers to whom Marazul mailed brochures about a legal conference to be held in Havana in September. Strong public opposition to Treasury's action, including critical media reaction, succeeds in forcing Treasury to drop its demand for names.

August 23 Elliott Abrams, Assistant Secretary of State for Human Rights, complains that U.S. news media are not picturing Fidel Castro as "one of the most vicious tyrants of our time."

August 24 The UN Committee on Decolonization approves a resolution, cosponsored by Cuba and Venezuela, that reaffirms the principle of self-determination and independence for Puerto Rico. The vote is 11 to 2 with 9 abstentions.

September 3-9 The League of United Latin American Citizens (LULAC), oldest and largest Hispanic civil rights organization in the United States, sends a six-member delegation to Cuba for discussions with government officials, including President Castro. At a press conference on September 10, LULAC president Mario Obledo calls for U.S. recognition of Cuba as "an equal partner" in diplomatic affairs.

September 4 At the trial of Eduardo Arocena, Omega 7 member Gerardo Necuze, testifying about how Arocena worked as an enforcer for a drug dealer, says he "never thought that the Omega 7 organization... would give the chance to the communist government of Cuba to see us in court, morally destroyed, associated with drugs and looking like garbage."

September 10 Taking the stand as the only defense witness in his trial, Omega 7 leader Eduardo Arocena testifies that he took "some germs" to Cuba in 1980 (*see* July 26, 1981). He makes several references to an "American agency" and U.S. "connections" who trained him, gave him fake identification, and financed him in his efforts to combat communism. He says he was one of at least 2,000 men trained in the Florida Everglades in 1969 for an invasion of Cuba that never happened.

September 12-16 President Forbes Burnham of Guyana makes a state visit to Cuba.

September 20-22 A 13-member delegation of U.S. jurists attends the first Conference on the Cuban Legal System in Havana. (*See* August)

September 22 Omega 7 leader Eduardo Arocena is found guilty of the assassination of Cuban UN diplomat Félix García in September 1980 and the attempted assassination of Cuban Ambassador to the United Nations Raúl Roa Kourí in March

1980. The federal jury in New York City finds him guilty of 25 of the 26 charges against him, including 20 bombings, perjury (lying to a federal grand jury when he denied involvement in the 1979 murder of Eulalio José Negrín) and financing his operations by being an enforcer for a Florida drug trafficker.

September 26 Adolfo Calero, head of the U.S.-backed Nicaraguan Democratic Front (Contras), says in Washington that the FDN plans to intensify its attacks on Cuban advisers in Nicaragua. Cuban teachers have continued to be a special target, and at the end of this year *Granma* reports that Cuba's final contingent of teachers has returned after five years during which these internationalists taught more than 250,000 Nicaraguans, built 784 schools, and repaired another 1,500. (*See* December 4, 1981)

October 14 Former West German Chancellor Willy Brandt arrives in Cuba for talks with President Castro about Central America, reportedly including the matter of withdrawal of Cuban personnel from Nicaragua in the event of a settlement like the one proposed by the Contadora Group.

October 28 The new airport in Grenada is officially opened, although it remains incomplete, seven months later than it was scheduled to open during the Bishop government. Some young Grenadian women hold up signs thanking Cubans for their years of work on the airport.

November 9 Omega 7 leader Eduardo Arocena is sentenced to life plus 35 years. Pedro Remón, the Omega 7 member identified by Arocena as the gunman in the assassinations of both Félix García and Eulalio José Negrín, is in prison for criminal contempt of court but has not been charged with the murders.

November 11-16 Cuba hosts three Pediatric Congresses — the 7th Latin American, the 14th Pan American and the 21st National — which hold simultaneous sessions attended by some 3,000 specialists from all over the world, including the United States. Cuba's Public Health Ministry presents impressive statistics, including an infant mortality rate in 1983 of 16.8 deaths per 1,000 live births, making Cuba the only Latin American country that compares with industrialized nations in this key indicator of a population's health. Later, when the figures for 1984 are completed, Cuba's rate is a new low of 15 for every 1,000 live births, placing Cuba among the 15 countries with the lowest rates in the world. U.S. infant mortality in 1984 is 11.5 — 10.1 for whites (down 4 percent) and 20 for Blacks (up 2 percent).

November 13 At the OAU Summit, Angola proposes a four-party (Angola, Cuba, SWAPO, South Africa) agreement, including an end to logistical support for UNITA, implementation of the UN plan for Namibian independence, and gradual withdrawal from Angola of Cuban troops stationed between the 13th and 16th parallels when only 1,500 South African troops are left in Namibia.

November 28-December 5 Cuban and U.S. officials hold another round of talks about migration.

December 14 The United States and Cuba conclude a migration agreement that calls for repatriation of 2,746 Marielitos and U.S. admission of 3,000 political prisoners (promised entry years ago) and up to 20,000 regular immigrants from Cuba each year.

December 14 In an agreement with nine financial institutions, headed by Crédit Lyonnais of France, Cuba reschedules its 1984 foreign debt to Western commercial banks. Provisions stipulate rescheduling mid-term debt of about $100 million with 110 commercial banks over a nine-year period with a five-year grace period.

December 31 A passenger jet is hijacked to Cuba by a prisoner from the Virgin Islands being transferred to the United States.

1985

January The Reagan Administration plans to send the current head of the U.S. Interests Section, John A. Ferch, to be ambassador to Honduras. Curtis W. Kamman, now the second-ranking official in the U.S. Embassy in Moscow, will succeed Ferch in Havana.

January 10-17 Representatives Bill Alexander (D-Arkansas), Jim Leach (R-Iowa), and Mickey Leland (D-Texas) spend 37 hours talking with President Castro in Havana. When they return to Washington, they urge negotiations with Cuba to improve relations.

January 21-25 Bishop James Malone of Ohio leads a delegation from the National Conference of Catholic Bishops on a visit to Cuba at the invitation of Cuba's Catholic bishops. They meet with President Castro for wide-ranging discussion and give him a list of 250 political prisoners they would like to see released. The bishops call for ending the U.S. embargo and normalizing relations.

February 3 The *Washington Post* publishes an interview with President Castro in which he discusses Cuba's willingness for more constructive relations with Washington. A question about Robert Vesco elicits the first official acknowledgement that the fugitive financier is indeed living in Cuba.

February 4 Responding to the *Washington Post* interview, State Department representative Bernard Kalb states that, to prove it wants normal relations, Cuba must stop its subversion in Latin America, remove its troops from Africa, end its close ties to Moscow, and stop human rights violations at home.

February 5 President Castro meets with Kenneth Skoug Jr., director of the State Department's Office of Cuban Affairs, in Santiago de Cuba to object to use of the U.S. Interests Section in Havana as a base for CIA activities.

February 11 PBS's MacNeil-Lehrer Newshour broadcasts the first of three parts of an interview with President Castro by Robert MacNeil on February 8 in Havana.

February 12 After a two-week trial in federal court in Miami on 23 weapons and conspiracy charges, Omega 7 leader Eduardo Arocena is found guilty on all counts. Codefendant Milton Badía is also convicted. (*See* September 22, 1984)

February 17 The Treasury Department allows any U.S. individual or organization to import single copies of any Cuban publication (newspapers, magazines, books), film, microfilm, microfiche, photograph, poster, phonograph record, tape, or similar materials.

February 18 The Spanish News Agency EFE publishes an interview with President Castro, in which he says Latin America needs "a grace period" of 10 to 20 years on the principal of its $360 billion foreign debt, with interest to be paid according to the country and circumstances. He points out that this would only be "a breather" for the economic crisis, which will have to be solved by establishing "a new international economic order."

February 21 In line with the December migration agreement, the first 23 Marielitos are deported from the Atlanta Federal Penitentiary to Havana.

February 27 President Daniel Ortega announces that Nicaragua will send home 100 Cuban military advisers, beginning in May, in hopes that this will be the first step toward withdrawal of all foreign military advisers in the region.

March 1 Julio María Sanguinetti, first civilian president in Uruguay after 12 years of military rule, announces in his inaugural address that Uruguay will restore diplomatic relations with Cuba.

March 2 After meeting with Nicaraguan President Ortega in Montevideo where both are attending the presidential inauguration, Secretary of State Shultz tells reporters: "We compute that if they have 100 Cubans leave by the end of 1985, which is what they said, at this rate it would take until the middle of the next century for all the Cubans to have left." White House officials estimate there are over 8,000 Cubans in Nicaragua, of whom 2,500 to 3,500 are military advisers. Ortega responds that there are fewer than 1,500 Cuban civilians in Nicaragua and 786 Cuban military advisers.

March 10 Soviet President Konstantin Chernenko dies. His successor as general secretary of the Communist Party is Mikhail Gorbachev. When the Reagan Administration suggests that President Castro's absence from the funeral indicates problems in Cuban-Soviet relations, Castro says relations have never been better.

March 17 Part of a six-hour television interview by Dan Rather with President Castro is broadcast on CBS's "60 Minutes."

March 19 Continuing deportation of Marielitos, the United States flies a second group from Georgia to Havana. A total of 201 are deported before the migration agreement is suspended May 20.

March 21 In an interview published by the Mexican daily *Excelsior* that receives worldwide attention, President Castro proposes a moratorium on debt payments by Latin America and the rest of the Third World. He suggests that the governments of the industrialized powers make themselves responsible to their private banks for the debts, using 10 to 12 percent of military expenditures to pay for the consequent increase in the interest on their countries' debts.

March 27-April 13 In his second federal trial in Miami, Omega 7 leader Eduardo Arocena is convicted of all 24 counts involving seven bombings in Miami from 1979 to 1983.

April 14 Ecuador's President León Febres Cordero makes a state visit to Cuba for two days of discussion about Latin American problems, including the debt crisis and Central America.

April 18 Cuban American Félix Rodríguez participates in capturing FMLN Commander Nidia Díaz in El Salvador by using the "helicopter concept" he developed while working for the CIA in Vietnam. When Rodríguez was trying to convince U.S. officials to let him use this "concept" in Central America, his longtime associate, Jorge Mas Canosa, introduced him to Richard Stone, special envoy to Central America for the Reagan Administration.

May 1 President Reagan orders a trade embargo of Nicaragua, effective May 7, citing as one reason its close military ties to Cuba and the Soviet Union.

May 2 One hundred Cuban military advisers leave Nicaragua.

May 7 Omega 7 leader Eduardo Arocena is sentenced by Judge William Hoeveler of the federal court in Miami to 20 years to be served consecutively with the term of life plus 35 years he is already serving.

May 20 Radio Martí goes on the air. In response, Cuba suspends the December migration agreement.

May 21 Two South Africans are killed and a third captured in an ambush during their attempt to sabotage Gulf Oil installations in Cabinda that are guarded by Cuban as well as Angolan troops. This forces South Africa to admit for the first time, two days later, that it has sent military reconnaissance teams into northern Angola.

May 28-31 UN Secretary General Javier Pérez de Cuéllar and his wife Marcela Temple visit Cuba. The Secretary General meets with President Castro to discuss international problems, including Central America and Southern Africa, Third World debt, and efforts to stop the arms race.

May 29 Visiting Cuba, historian Arthur M. Schlesinger Jr., who was a special assistant to President Kennedy during the Bay of Pigs invasion, discusses the Latin American debt crisis and other issues with President Castro. In a June 12 *Wall Street Journal* article, he reports that Cuba is emerging from political and diplomatic isolation.

June As Cuban exile and longtime CIA operative Rafael "Chi Chi" Quintero testifies later (March 2, 1989, at Oliver North's trial), he meets in Miami with General Richard V. Secord, longtime CIA agent Thomas G. Clines, Contra leader Adolfo Calero, former head of Somoza's National Guard Enrique Bermúdez and Oliver North about "covert" aid to the Contras. With North running the meeting, they deliberate about how 89 percent of Cuba's supplies to the Nicaraguan government come up the Rama River; it is suggested that a barge be sunk in the river to block the aid.

June 2 Jonas Savimbi, head of UNITA, tells a news conference in Jamba, Angola, that he rejects any partial withdrawal of Cuban troops and wants them all out. The news conference is called after Savimbi and leaders of insurgent movements in Afghanistan, Laos and Nicaragua unite to form the Democratic International, organized by multimillionaire New Yorker, Lewis E. Lehrman.

Savimbi calls on the U.S. Congress to repeal the Clark Amendment. One of his principal allies in the effort to repeal the amendment is Jorge Mas Canosa.

June 14 In response to Cuba's suspension of the migration agreement (*see* May 20), the State Department announces that as of June 18 no more Cuban immigrants will be accepted, immediately affecting about 1,000 Cubans who have been granted visas but will now be prevented from entering. The decision does not apply to illegal immigrants, who continue to be accepted.

June 19 Meeting in Brazil, the Latin American Parliament accepts Cuba as a member by a vote of 140 in favor, 25 opposed (12 Salvadorans, 12 Paraguayans, one Peruvian), with 3 abstentions (Hondurans).

June 19 The UN Security Council calls for South Africa to implement Resolution 435 for Namibian independence or face "appropriate measures." Britain and the United States abstain, with U.S. delegate Warren Clark reiterating the policy of linking Namibian independence to withdrawal of Cuban troops from Angola.

June 19 Preston Martin of the U.S. Federal Reserve Board calls reporters to the New York Federal Reserve Bank and presents ideas similar to President Castro's proposal of March 21, including investment banker Felix Rohatyn's idea that some international agency (the World Bank, for example) purchase debt owed to banks by developing countries in return for bonds guaranteed by the agency. The next day Federal Reserve Board chair Paul Volcker, in Tokyo, calls Martin's remarks "incomprehensible." Volcker issues a statement opposing any suggestion of "unorthodox approaches" to the debt problem.

June 27-July 30 The 15th contingent of the Nordic Brigade from Denmark, Finland, Iceland, Norway and Sweden works in agriculture and construction in Cuba.

June 30 In an editorial about his recent trip to Cuba, *New York Times* editor Karl E. Meyer calls for an end to the U.S. embargo.

July 8 In a speech before the American Bar Association in Washington, President Reagan claims five nations — Cuba, Iran, Libya, Nicaragua and North Korea — have formed a "confederation of terrorist states" intending "to expel America from the world." He states that "these terrorist states are now engaged in acts of war against the government and people of the United States. And under international law, any state which is the victim of acts of war has the right to defend itself."

July 10 The House of Representatives repeals the Clark Amendment that made U.S. aid to anti-government forces in Angola illegal.

July 13 Angola suspends talks with the United States, calling repeal of the Clark Amendment further evidence of "the complicity which has always existed" between the United States and South Africa. Angola resumes these negotiations in November.

July 26 President Castro accuses the United States of trying to sabotage the conference about Latin American debt to be held later this summer in Havana by attempting to persuade U.S. airlines not to fly delegates to Cuba.

July 28 In an announcement enthusiastically supported by many Third World countries, including Cuba, President Alán García in his inaugural address says Peru's debt payments will be limited to 10 percent of export income for the next year.

July 29 At a press conference in Guatemala, U.S. Treasury Secretary James A. Baker 3d says talk about "political solutions" to the debt problem is "counterproductive" because it will make banks less willing to make new loans.

July 30 Meeting in Lima, Peru, the foreign ministers of 20 Latin American nations, including Cuba, call for linking foreign debt payments to export earnings.

July 30-August 3 Havana hosts a conference on the debt crisis attended by more than 1,200 political leaders, government officials, academicians, economists, union leaders, church representatives, and students from 37 Latin American and Caribbean countries. Delegate after delegate describes crippling effects of the region's foreign debt of $360 billion. Interest payments alone in the next 10 years, by conservative estimate, will run to $400 billion. The delegates call for a basic restructuring of the relationship between debtor and creditor nations.

August In a continuing wave of attention by U.S. media, *Playboy* features interviews with President Castro, which took place last spring — first by Representative Mervyn M. Dymally (D-California) and Jeffrey M. Elliot, professor of political science at North Carolina Central University in Durham, North Carolina, and later by Kirby Jones, who was in Cuba to film a PBS documentary. Topics range from the debt crisis to one of Castro's favorite books, *Don Quixote.*

August 8 An SR-71 again violates Cuba's airspace. In a note to the U.S. Interests Section in Havana, Cuba's Foreign Ministry protests this violation, the fifth since 1983, as well as a series of sonic booms during the overflights.

August 8-9 Cuba stages large military maneuvers as part of its preparations to be ready for any U.S. invasion.

August 14 The UN Decolonization Committee approves a resolution, sponsored by Cuba and Venezuela, to "reaffirm the inalienable right of the people of Puerto Rico to self-determination and independence" in accordance with the General Assembly's 1960 declaration on decolonization. The vote is 11 to 1 (Chile) with 10 abstentions. The United States is not a member of the committee, but on August 12 the United States' UN ambassador, Vernon Walters, guided by the U.S. position that Puerto Rico is not a colony, sent a letter calling the discussion "totally inappropriate."

August 22 Luis Posada, arrested for the 1976 bombing of a Cubana airliner that killed 73 people, escapes from a maximum security prison in Caracas, Venezuela, by walking out the main door after his jailers evidently received substantial bribes.

August 22 Marielitos riot at a federal minimum-security prison in Florence, Arizona, demanding to be returned to Cuba.

September 5 In federal court in Washington, a Spanish company, Piher S.A., pleads guilty to transferring almost $2.5 million in U.S. manufacturing equipment to Cuba and the Soviet Union from 1979 to 1982. The U.S. Justice Department reports that Piher agreed in 1978 to build an electronics factory (evidently never completed) in Cuba and then bought its equipment from U.S. companies, saying it was for use in Spain.

September 9 A federal indictment charges Omega 7 members Pedro Remón, Andrés García and Eduardo Losada Fernández with the 1980 assassination of Cuban UN diplomat Félix García Rodríguez; the 1980 attempt to kill Raúl Roa Kourí, then Cuban UN ambassador; and a plot to kill Ramón Sánchez Parodi, head of the Cuban Interests Section. It charges Remón and García with participating in the 1979 murder of Eulalio José Negrín. The indictment also includes bombing charges and names Omega 7 leader Eduardo Arocena as an unindicted coconspirator.

September 19 Crédit Lyonnais, the state-owned French bank which heads Cuba's debt coordinating committee, says Cuba has rescheduled $90 million owed to foreign commercial banks in 1985. The agreement stretches the payments over a 10-year period with six years grace and includes about $375 million in short-term credit lines to Cuba's National Bank that will be extended for a year until September 1986.

October In the first two weeks of this month, three African leaders make state visits to Cuba: Tanzanian President Julius K. Nyerere, Zimbabwean Prime Minister Robert Mugabe and Zambian President Kenneth Kaunda.

October 4 President Reagan issues Proclamation 5377 banning entry for officials or employees of the Cuban government or the Cuban Communist Party, with the final decision about visas to be made by the State Department. The proclamation does not apply to Cubans on official business at the Cuban Interests Section, the UN Mission, or the United Nations itself. Questioned about their "silence" in response to the decision, Cubans point out that it is nothing new, but only a continuation of the policy already being implemented.

October 8 In response to the Third World debt crisis, Treasury Secretary James Baker 3d proposes to the joint annual meeting of the World Bank and the International Monetary Fund (IMF) that international commercial banks lend $20 billion in the next three years to a group of 15 heavily indebted developing countries, mainly in Latin America. He also calls for a 50 percent boost of loans in the same period from agencies like the IMF and the World Bank. The Baker Plan is a policy of lending more while continuing to demand payment on all the debt. In less than three years, it is defunct.

October 17 Cuba and Uruguay reestablish diplomatic relations.

October 21-22 Indian Prime Minister Rajiv Gandhi, chair of the Nonaligned Movement since the assassination of Indira Gandhi, makes a state visit to Cuba.

October 25 As a result of a prisoner exchange between the Salvadoran government and the FMLN, 96 war-wounded guerrillas, including Commander Nidia Díaz and three political prisoners are flown to Havana for asylum and medical care.

October 27 In New York for the opening of the UN General Assembly, Soviet Foreign Minister Eduard A. Shevardnadze takes a side trip to Cuba for a three-day visit.

October 31 An SR-71 again violates Cuban airspace. Cuba again protests.

October 31 Asked during an interview by Soviet journalists if the United States would leave Guantánamo Naval Base if the Cuban people were to vote in a referendum that it should leave, President Reagan answers, "No, because the lease for that was made many years ago, and it still has many years to run, and we're perfectly legal in our right to be there. It is fenced off. There is no contact with the people or the main island of Cuba at all."

October 31-November 1 Continuing a series of meetings, Soviet and U.S. officials meet in Washington to discuss the Caribbean and Central America, reportedly with emphasis on Cuba and Nicaragua.

November 1 CIA director William Casey meets with General Manuel Antonio Noriega, the Panamanian leader, in Washington and complains about Noriega's part in trade with Cuba that facilitates circumvention of the embargo.

November 4 A Reagan Administration official says a spy plane was sent over Cuba October 31 because there was a "serious increase" in Soviet arms being sent to Nicaragua through Cuba. During the week of October 20, according to this account, there was a buildup of equipment at Mariel, which was confirmed by the SR-71. The *Washington Times*, owned by Reverend Sun Myung Moon's Unification Church, reports that Cuba fired at the SR-71; this report is carried by media such as CBS News. It turns out that the SR-71 "sensed" the firing of weapons that were part of military exercises taking place in Cuba at the time and not aimed at the plane.

November 16 A delegation from the Cuban Ecumenical Council begins a visit to the United States at the invitation of the National Council of Churches and its Latin American Cooperation Committee. They meet with Assistant Secretary of State for Inter-American Affairs Elliott Abrams and National Security

Adviser Robert McFarlane. Meanwhile, a U.S. religious
delegation, invited by the Ecumenical Council, visits Cuba and
issues a statement opposing the U.S. travel ban and pledging to
work for an end to such barriers.

November 19-20 For the first time in six years, Soviet and U.S.
leaders meet at a Summit Conference. General Secretary
Gorbachev and President Reagan talk in Geneva. *Granma* headlines its coverage "A Nuclear War Must Never Be Fought."

November 20 Vice-President Bush blames the failure of the
Caribbean Basin Initiative on the countries it was supposed to
help, saying they "have got to do more than they are doing."

December 2 At an OAS meeting in Colombia, one objective is to
study changes in the OAS Charter that would lead to the
readmission of Cuba. Secretary of State Shultz tells reporters at
the conference that Cuba's "behavior has not improved and, if
anything, has deteriorated, so I don't see any case for
readmission."

December 5 Elliott Abrams, Assistant Secretary of State for
Inter-American Affairs, testifies to a House Foreign Affairs subcommittee that Cubans are fighting in Nicaragua. He does not
mean the Cuban exiles who are fighting in Nicaragua on the side
of the Contras.

December 10 In his annual International Human Rights Day
speech, President Reagan names Cuba as the worst example in the
Western Hemisphere of a country "where institutionalized
totalitarianism has consistently violated" citizens' rights.

December 10 Speaking in London, Secretary of State Shultz
provides the Administration's perspective of the state of war and
peace in the coming years: "In the 1980s and beyond, most likely
we will never see a world in a total state of peace — or a state of
total war.... But day in and day out, we will continue to see a
wide range of conflicts in a gray area between major war and
millennial peace." Explaining that there are sometimes openly
military problems, he offers five examples of which two involve
Cuba: "a massive Soviet and Cuban military intervention in
Africa" and "Cuban combatants using Soviet weapons in
Nicaragua."

1986

January The third contingent of the Southern Cross Australian Brigade (60 Australians and three New Zealanders) picks citrus fruit in Cuba.

January 29 The Reagan Administration welcomes Jonas Savimbi, head of UNITA, to Washington with the kind of top-level reception usually reserved for a head of state. Some Congressional members argue that giving aid to UNITA compromises the U.S. position as "mediator" in negotiations regarding Cuban troops in Angola. The fanfare for Savimbi has been criticized by the Washington Office on Africa, the Congressional Black Caucus, the TransAfrica organization, and in a petition signed by 500 specialists on Africa from universities in 38 states and the District of Columbia.

January 29 The Roman Catholic Archbishop of Havana, Msgr. Jaime Ortega Alamino, appeals to Florida Governor Bob Graham to stop the execution of Cuban emigrant Omar Blanco, who was convicted of killing a man during a 1982 burglary. Graham says he will not grant clemency.

January 31 At a news conference in Washington sponsored by *Foreign Policy* magazine, Jonas Savimbi says that Chevron's Gulf Corporation unit in Angola is "a target" of UNITA and that his forces are waiting for an appropriate time to strike. Gulf employs about 150 U.S. citizens in Angola in addition to some 400 Angolans. Its facilities in Cabinda are guarded by Cuban troops.

February 3-7 Jonas Savimbi gives talks sponsored by the Cuban American National Foundation, the American Enterprise Institute (where he is hosted at a seminar by former UN

Ambassador Jeane Kirkpatrick), the Heritage Foundation, Georgetown University's Center for Strategic and International Studies, and Freedom House. UNITA's public relations are handled by Black, Manaford, Stone, Kelly, Inc., of Alexandria, Virginia.

February 4 At the Third Party Congress, the Main Report, presented by President Castro, includes serious criticism of developments in the previous five years. The main economic objective of the next five-year plan, through 1990, is rapid industrialization within the framework of the CMEA.

February 7 Omega 7 members Pedro Remón, Andrés García and Eduardo Losada Fernández have each accepted a plea bargain that drops the charge of assassinating UN diplomat Félix García in 1980 in exchange for pleading guilty to the attempted murder of then UN Ambassador Raúl Roa Kourí in 1980 and bombing the Cuban UN Mission in December 1979.

February 18 Testifying before the Senate Foreign Relations Committee, Assistant Secretary of State for African Affairs Chester Crocker admits publicly for the first time that the Reagan Administration has decided to provide "covert" military aid to UNITA. The amount of at least $15 million will come from the CIA's funds, which are never publicly disclosed. Both Senate and House Intelligence Committees advise against the move. Some observers of the African situation maintain that the CIA never stopped aiding Angola even when it was illegal from 1976 until 1985 (see July 10, 1985).

February 26 President Castro addresses the 27th Congress of the Communist Party of the Soviet Union. After his visit in the USSR, he travels to North Korea where he meets with President Kim Il Sung.

February 28 Sweden's Prime Minister Olof Palme is assassinated and Cuba's Council of State decrees three days of official mourning. Palme was strengthening ties between Cuba and Sweden, which had never joined the embargo against Cuba despite U.S. pressure.

March When the State Department refuses a visa to film director Pastor Vega to attend the Third World Film Festival in Atlanta, Mayor Andrew Young proclaims the week of the festival, March 2-8, "Cuban Film Institute Week."

March 4 South Africa proposes that August 1, 1986, be set as a date to begin granting independence to Namibia on the condition that an agreement be reached before that date on withdrawal of Cubans troops from Angola. Angola rejects the proposal because South Africa includes no indication that it would stop aiding UNITA.

March 25 UNITA claims its forces have attacked and seriously damaged the Gulf Oil complex in Cabinda, but a Gulf representative says there was "shooting outside the camp" that "did not affect anybody or anything to do with our operation." There is speculation that Jonas Savimbi needs to convince the Cuban American National Foundation and other U.S. supporters that he is successfully combatting Cuban troops in Angola.

March 31 Congressional and private sources report that the Reagan Administration has decided to provide UNITA with several hundred "Stingers," state-of-the-art shoulder-fired antiaircraft missiles. Previously the U.S. has preferred to supply "freedom fighters" in various countries with Soviet- and Chinese-made weapons (purchased on the international arms market or from U.S. allies) so that there is no direct evidence of U.S. involvement in covert operations. However, "covert" aid to UNITA and to the Afghan guerrillas has become so "overt" that conservative legislators argued successfully, especially at a March 5 meeting with Secretary of State Shultz in Senator Robert Dole's office, that "effectiveness" rather than secrecy should be the goal. UNITA will also receive TOW antitank missiles.

April During a visit to Cuba, a delegation from the U.S. National Council of Churches, led by Bishop Phillip Cousin of the African Methodist Church, calls for normalization of U.S.-Cuban relations.

April 10 Manhattan U.S. District Judge Robert L. Ward sentences Omega 7 members Pedro Remón, Andrés García and Eduardo Losada Fernández to 10 years in prison but expresses sympathy for the avowed goal of Omega 7: to unseat the government of Fidel Castro.

April 19 President Castro explains how the weaker dollar adversely affects Cuba because of the U.S. embargo. Although Cuba's exports are denominated in dollars (the universal practice), Cuba, which is not allowed to buy U.S. products, must use its dollars to buy from Japan and Europe where the dollar buys less against the mark, franc, yen and pounds sterling.

May 2 In the wake of the Chernobyl nuclear plant disaster in the Soviet Union in April, Representative Michael Bilirakis (R-Florida) writes to President Castro requesting guarantees about the safety of the nuclear power plants that Cuba has begun to build with Soviet help.

May 2 In the latest of a series of visa denials, the State Department bars entry to Rogelio Martínez Furé of the *Conjunto Folklórico Nacional de Cuba*, invited to New York to spend three months with the Schomburg Center for Research in Black Culture under the terms of a Ford Foundation grant.

May 20 At a benefit in Miami for the Cuban American National Foundation, Vice-President Bush makes a speech that is broadcast to Cuba by Radio Martí, saying Fidel Castro "has humiliated Cuba before the world." Urging his audience of 1,200 to support the Contras in Nicaragua and UNITA in Angola, he concludes with a cry of "*Viva Cuba libre.*"

May 20 The State Department issues a report on human rights in Cuba, stating that "freedom is abridged in almost every aspect of life."

June Cuba clarifies its migration policy, explaining that for "strictly humanitarian reasons," almost 1,200 Cuban Americans have been granted visas since May 1985, when the migration agreement was suspended, to allow them to visit seriously ill relatives or to mourn a close family member who has died. It is "also the policy," the statement continues, that "on an exceptional basis and not to exceed 2,500 per year" Cuban Americans not involved with counterrevolutionary organizations may visit Cuba.

June 8 After intercession by Senator Edward Kennedy, Cuba releases Ricardo Montero Duque, the next to the last of the prisoners taken during the Bay of Pigs invasion. Of the nine invaders who were kept in prison after the others were released in December 1962, one died, seven have been released, and one remains in prison. Having served 25 years of his 30-year sentence, Montero is flown to Homestead Air Force Base in Florida.

June 12 Seymour Hersh reports in the *New York Times* that senior State Department, White House, Pentagon and intelligence officials say that General Manuel Ortega Noriega, head of

Panama's armed forces, has been providing intelligence information to both Cuba and the United States for 15 years and that he
is "a secret investor in Panamanian export companies that sell
restricted American technology to Cuba and Eastern European
countries." Noriega later says that U.S. officials turned against
him because he refused a December 1985 request by Admiral
John M. Poindexter, National Security Adviser, to cooperate in a
U.S. plan to invade Nicaragua.

June 12 President Castro responds to Representative Bilirakis's
letter of May 2, describing current construction of four nuclear
power plants. Construction of the first reactor began in 1983.
The project conforms to safety regulations of such agencies as the
International Atomic Energy Agency. Castro tells Bilirakis that
detailed information on the type of reactor has appeared for some
years in the annual publications of the International Atomic
Energy Agency on reactors in operation and under construction,
as well as in other international publications. He offers to maintain an exchange of information with Bilirakis as a neighbor in
Florida and hopes that Bilirakis will in turn send information
about nuclear power plants in Florida.

June 14 President Reagan campaigns for Republican Senator Paula
Hawkins in Miami where there is an uproar over the State
Department's announcement that it would accept Cuban political
prisoners only under "exceptional circumstances." Reagan
expresses surprise upon hearing that the United States would ever
refuse entry to former Cuban prisoners and promises to make
"any effort" to admit them.

June 18 Bay of Pigs veteran and Watergate burglar Frank Sturgis is
arrested and charged with accepting stolen property. He is
acquitted on November 6; a juror says the deciding factor was
U.S. Customs Agent John McCutcheon's testimony that Sturgis
often worked for him.

June 23 Kenneth Skoug Jr., head of the State Department's Office of
Cuban Affairs, sends a note to Ramón Sánchez Parodi, head of
the Cuban Interests Section, proposing talks between Cuba and
the United States. This proposal is the result of an exchange of
letters between Senator Edward Kennedy and President Castro in
which Kennedy urged restoration of the 1984 migration agreement and Castro then indicated that Cuba was prepared to drop

its demand that Radio Martí be halted in exchange for U.S. recognition of Cuba's right to broadcast to the United States over an AM frequency. Kennedy's office provided Castro's response to Secretary of State Shultz.

June 25 Cuba and Brazil reestablish diplomatic relations, a development made possible when José Sarney in 1985 became the first civilian president since the 1964 coup.

July 1 Cuba suspends payments on its medium- and long-term debt to Western banks until negotiations for rescheduling the debt are completed. Later in July Cuba also suspends payments on its short-term debt to Western banks because of a shortage of foreign capital. The amount of interest owed to Western banks this year is $50 million; principal repayments due this year total $100 million. Cuba's overall debt to Western banks is about $3.3 billion.

July 3 Cuba accepts the June 23 proposal for talks.

July 7-12 The International Pediatric Congress meets in Honolulu, Hawaii, without the Cuban delegation, who were denied visas by the State Department.

July 8-9 Cuba and the United States hold talks in Mexico City about migration and radio broadcast rights but reach no agreement. Chief negotiators are Deputy Foreign Minister Ricardo Alarcón and State Department legal adviser Michael G. Kozak. Before the talks, there seemed a possibility that the United States would cooperate with Cuba's request for broadcasts to the United States since the United States broadcasts to Cuba on Radio Martí.

July 12 The *Miami Herald* reports that the U.S. Attorney's Office in Miami believes at least one load of weapons was illegally shipped to the Contras in March 1985 by Cuban Americans in Florida.

July 23 Seymour Hersh reports in the *New York Times* that Britain and the United States have exchanged intelligence reports with South Africa for years and that South Africa has reciprocated, reporting, for example, on the Cubans in Angola. The Reagan Administration requested weekly reports on Cuban activity rather than the monthly reports previously received. South Africa specifically asked the United States to monitor international travel by Oliver Tambo, head of the African National Congress, and report when he was taking flights aboard Cuban or Soviet airliners.

July 30 Cuban UN Ambassador Oscar Oramas Oliva, addressing the Security Council, demands an end to U.S. aggression against Nicaragua. On June 25 the House of Representatives reversed an April vote and approved aid to the Contras, the first time the House openly supported military aid. On June 27 the World Court ruled that U.S. aid to the Contras violates Nicaraguan sovereignty and international law. The Reagan Administration says the Court has no jurisdiction. U.S. Ambassador Vernon Walters tells the Security Council that it is "fascinating" and "odd" to be lectured on justice by the ambassador from Cuba, "a country which has been for more than 25 years a vast concentration camp." On the following day, the Security Council votes 11 to 1 with 3 abstentions for a resolution calling for full compliance with the World Court decision. The United States casts the veto vote.

August Cuba has granted asylum to U.S. Army Captain Hugo Romeu Almeida, who defected in Stuttgart, West Germany, as an act of opposition to U.S. policy toward Central America.

August Two U.S. officials from the INS and the State Department go to Havana to screen prisoners, former prisoners and relatives of prisoners who have applied for visas. The list includes prisoners whose release was offered by President Castro to a delegation of U.S. Roman Catholic bishops in 1985, former prisoners who were released in the spring after intercession by Jacques Cousteau and 22 relatives of prisoners who left for the United States with Reverend Jesse Jackson in 1984.

August 7 In its first U.S. appearance in 26 years, the Cuban national baseball team, the world champion, defeats Team USA 13 to 8 in Durham, North Carolina.

August 12 Following a fact-finding visit to Angola, Andrew Young, Atlanta mayor and former UN ambassador, holds a news conference in Washington to denounce covert U.S. aid to UNITA because he believes UNITA is acting in the interests of South Africa.

August 22 The Treasury Department issues a press release announcing new measures to tighten the embargo, including "crackdowns on trading with Cuban front companies located in Panama and elsewhere" and "closer controls on organizations which organize or promote travel to Cuba." Treasury is trimming limits on cash and gifts Cuban Americans can send to relatives in Cuba and increasing regulation of companies that ship food and care packages to Cuba from Cuban Americans.

September 1-7 President Castro attends the Eighth Summit Meeting of the Nonaligned Movement in Zimbabwe. Speaking on September 2, Castro points out that South Africa continues to occupy Namibia eight years after passage of UN Resolution 435.

September 10 During a state visit to Angola, President Castro speaks to some 3,000 Cubans in Luanda, saying the 40,000 Cubans now in Angola will remain until South Africa withdraws from Angola and Namibia. After leaving Angola, Castro also makes state visits to Algeria and Yugoslavia.

September 15 The United States accepts 112 former prisoners and relatives of prisoners, who are then flown from Cuba to Florida.

September 17 The House of Representatives votes 229-186 to approve continued funding for UNITA.

September 24 A House Foreign Affairs subcommittee holds a hearing about U.S. delays in processing visa applications from released prisoners and their families in Cuba. The House Judiciary Committee is also criticizing the Administration's linking normal immigration to the issue of Cuba's acceptance of more than 2,000 Marielitos in U.S. prisons. Representative Henry J. Hyde (R-Illinois) says the United States "can use all of the anti-communist Latinos we can get."

September 25 At a ministerial meeting of the International Atomic Energy Agency, Soviet officials agree to give U.S. officials information about Soviet-made nuclear reactors in Cuba.

October Marine Lieutenant Colonel Oliver North keeps notes about paying $5,000 to any Contra who captures a Cuban or Sandinista officer in Nicaragua, while the Contra leadership would receive $200,000 for every five such captives. This money would come from arms sales to Iran. The plans for these bounties are revealed when the House-Senate report on the Iran-Contra Affair is released November 19, 1987.

October 5 Soviet Foreign Minister Eduard A. Shevardnadze meets with President Castro and other Cuban officials in Havana.

October 9 Eugene Hasenfus, a U.S. mercenary captured in Nicaragua, tells a news conference in Managua the names of two Cuban exiles who direct Contra supply operations for the CIA from El Salvador: Max Gómez, whose real identity is Félix Rodríguez and Ramón Medina, actually Luis Posada. Rodríguez and Posada first met in 1963 at Fort Benning, Georgia, where they received their training. Hasenfus states that Rodríguez says he reports directly to Vice-President Bush. This is the first time that Posada's name has surfaced publicly since his escape from Venezuela in 1985. Vice-President and former CIA Director Bush later denies knowing about Rodríguez's Contra connection, although he admits meeting with him a few times to discuss El Salvador. Hasenfus was part of the crew of one of the supply aircraft when it was shot down October 5. His capture leads to Congressional investigation of what becomes known as the Iran-Contra Affair.

October 10 El Salvador is struck by a devastating earthquake but President Duarte refuses Cuba's offer of a completely equipped mobile hospital with 160 beds and the capacity for 400 outpatient consultations and 30 surgical operations daily along with a medical team of 43 people.

October 11-12 President Reagan and Secretary General Gorbachev hold a Summit Meeting in Reykjavik, Iceland.

October 12 INS agents arrests Patricia Lara, a journalist for Colombia's leading newspaper *El Tiempo*, as she arrives at New York's Kennedy Airport on her way to attend a dinner for recipients of journalism prizes at Columbia University. She is held for five days and then deported for allegedly being a member of M-19 and serving as a liaison between M-19 and Cuba. In 1991, Lara settles a lawsuit against the U.S. government by accepting a visa.

October 18 Cuba releases Ramón Conte Hernández, the last prisoner taken during the Bay of Pigs invasion. Before the revolution, Conte was part of Batista's secret police, a member of Special Group 5 led by the notorious Colonel Carratalá. Senator Edward Kennedy was instrumental in getting him released.

October 18-19 Argentine President Raúl Alfonsín makes a state visit to Cuba.

November 1 *Granma* reports that the State Department has denied visas to five Cuban orthopedic specialists who were planning to attend the Latin American Orthopedic and Traumatological Society conference in San Juan, Puerto Rico.

November 9 President Castro arrives in Moscow for a meeting of the leaders of the Communist Parties from CMEA countries.

November 13-16 Spanish Prime Minister Felipe González makes a state visit to Cuba. One of the agreements reached is that Cuba will pay $40 million in hard currency and products over the next 15 years to about 3,000 Spanish citizens whose property was expropriated by Cuba 25 years ago.

November 30-December 2 Cuba holds the Deferred Session of the Third Party Congress (the first session was held in February).

December 8 An SR-71 again overflies Cuba. Cubans hold a three-day protest in front of the U.S. Interests Section, climaxed by a rally of 800,000 people December 11.

December 20 Cuba releases Eloy Gutiérrez Menoyo from prison after the intercession of Spain's Prime Minister Felipe González during his recent visit to Cuba. Gutiérrez Menoyo was born in Spain and is flown there after he leaves prison, but in 1988 he becomes a member of the U.S. delegation at the UN Human Rights Commission meeting in Geneva.

1987

January Cuban American José Sorzano moves from his position as president of the Cuban American National Foundation to a job in the Reagan Administration as director of Latin American Affairs for the National Security Council.

January A group of Cuban Interior Ministry officials attempt their first drug trafficking operation only to have their speedboats captured by the U.S. Coast Guard. These drug operations end in scandal and the executions of four government officials in 1989. The smuggling evidently began after Cuban exile Reinaldo Ruiz, who left Cuba in 1962, suggested last year to his cousin in the Interior Ministry, Captain Miguel Ruiz Poo, that they collaborate in a drug deal. The smugglers operate through the Interior Ministry's "Department MC," established to bypass the U.S. embargo by acquiring products otherwise unavailable.

January 23-26 Ovidio Díaz, president of Panama's National Assembly, heads a delegation of Panamanian legislators to Cuba. Their meeting with Deputy Foreign Minister Ricardo Alarcón is primarily concerned with the Contadora peace process. Díaz tells a *Granma* reporter that a peaceful settlement of the conflicts in Central America is vital to Panama in order to avoid a pretext that could be used by the U.S. government to undermine the Torrijos-Carter agreements on handing over possession of the Panama Canal to Panama by the year 2,000.

January 29 Curtis Kamman, head of the U.S. Interests Section, meets with President Castro before leaving his post in Havana. Castro tells Kamman, "We have come to the conclusion that, regarding the Interests Section, political matters are not what most interest the U.S. government.... The U.S. government's main interest in the Interests Section and its top priority is information, intelligence, and if you want, I will be even more precise: espionage."

January 30 Thirty-nine FMLN war-wounded arrive in Cuba for medical treatment. Commander Nidia Díaz, who arrived in 1985 and is still recovering from her wounds, officially welcomes them.

February Senator Claiborne Pell, the new chair of the Foreign Relations Committee, favors normalization of relations with Cuba.

February 1 John Mike Joyce, second in command at the U.S. Interests Section, becomes acting chief as Curtis Kamman departs.

February 13 The State Department denies visas to Cuban artists Rebeca Chávez and Senal Paz, invited to New York for three months by the Center for Cuban Studies under the terms of a Ford Foundation grant.

March 5 Eight White House participants in the 1962 Missile Crisis meet in Florida with scholars of the period for a four-day conference to share information. This all-American meeting leads to a series of conferences with Soviet and Cuban participation.

March 11 The UN Human Rights Commission rejects by a vote of 19 to 18 with 6 abstentions a U.S. resolution condemning Cuba for alleged human rights violations. One of the U.S. delegates is Armando Valladares, granted U.S. citizenship by President Reagan so that he could be an official representative.

March 21 U.S. officials announce plans for the largest military maneuvers yet in the Caribbean and Central America, including a simulated evacuation of Guantánamo Naval Base. The main goal of Solid Shield '87 is to practice response to a Honduran call for assistance against an invasion by Nicaragua. The exercise at Guantánamo is to practice response to Cuba's projected reaction to the invasion of Nicaragua. After this announcement, the Soviet Union sends five submarines to hold an exercise in April in the western Atlantic near Bermuda, the largest deployment in that area since 1985. NATO officials say that four or five long-range Soviet bombers arrive in Cuba for this exercise.

April 3 Three men are indicted in Miami for allegedly selling more than $1 million worth of high-tech computer equipment in 1985 to Siboney International in Panama, identified as a Cuban "front."

May The Cuban Interior Ministry drug traffickers use a new pilot, former Nationalist Chinese Air Force fighter pilot Hu Chang, once a contract pilot for the CIA in Southeast Asia. Arrested in the United States for drug smuggling, he is now an informant for the DEA. Later, he records hours of conversation with Cuban exile Reinaldo Ruiz about his Cuban drug deals.

May Kenneth Skoug Jr., head of the State Department's Office of Cuban Affairs, holds secret talks with Cuban officials in Havana. Cuba gets permission to fly Cubans in chartered planes directly from Havana to Indianapolis for the Pan American Games in August. The United States gets permission to use chartered planes for supplying the U.S. Interests Section in Havana.

May 11 In his opening testimony before the Congressional hearings about using money from the sale of arms to Iran for "covert" aid to the Contras (the Iran-Contra Affair), Robert McFarlane, former National Security Adviser, testifies, "There's little doubt in my mind that if we could not muster an effective counter to the Cuban-Sandinista strategy in our own backyard, it was far less likely that we could do so in the years ahead in more distant locations."

May 27-28 Bay of Pigs veteran and CIA operative Félix Rodríguez testifies at the Congressional investigation of the Iran-Contra Affair that Vice-President Bush's national security adviser, Donald P. Gregg, helped him get a job in counterinsurgency in El Salvador in 1985 because Gregg and Rodríguez had worked together during the Vietnam War in Air America, one of the "covert" CIA airlines, while Gregg was CIA chief of Saigon Region Three. Rodríguez testifies that later in 1985 Lieutenant Colonel Oliver North told him that "somebody" would be calling him about organizing the Contra airlift; that "somebody" turned out to be another Cuban exile with whom Rodríguez had previously worked in the CIA — Rafael Quintero. Rodríguez also testifies that he brought CIA agent Luis Posada from his prison escape in Venezuela in 1985 to El Salvador to help with these "covert" activities. At the conclusion of his testimony, several Congressional members thank Rodríguez for his brave fight against communism. (*See* February 1961)

May 28 Brigadier General Rafael del Pino Díaz, a hero during the Bay of Pigs invasion and in Angola, defects by flying a Cessna to Florida, taking along his third wife and some of his children. Interviews with del Pino are soon featured on Radio Martí.

June Another group of 98 FMLN war-wounded arrives in Cuba for medical treatment.

June 6 Major Florentino Azpillaga defects from the Cuban Embassy in Czechoslovakia and shocks U.S. intelligence officials by informing them that more than 90 percent of the CIA's covert operations in Cuba have been taken over and controlled for years by Cuban intelligence (DGI).

June 8 The U.S. Catholic Conference says Cuba has agreed to release another 348 current and former political prisoners for emigration to the U.S. in response to a request from the Conference.

June 28-29 Italian journalist Gianni Minà interviews President Castro for Italian television. The interview is shown in Spain, Canada, France, Hungary and many other countries and is published as a book, *Un encuentro con Fidel* [*An Encounter with Fidel*], in more than 20 countries, including the United States.

July 6 Deputy Foreign Minister Ricardo Alarcón delivers to the U.S. Interests Section in Havana a note informing the State Department that Cuban television, "starting tonight," will begin a series of programs showing evidence of CIA activities by people based at the Interests Section. The television programs present on-the-spot footage of espionage activities. Cuba names 89 CIA agents who have operated from the Interests Section in the past 10 years. Several Cuban double agents appear on television to tell their stories.

July 14 The State Department responds with a note protesting the public naming of U.S. officials as CIA agents and ordering the expulsion of two Cuban officials, Bienvenido Abierno and Virgilio Lora, from the Cuban Interests Section in Washington by July 25.

July 16 The Cuban Foreign Ministry responds to the July 14 note, pointing out that the State Department does not deny Cuba's evidence of espionage and yet orders expulsion of two Cubans without offering any evidence of wrong-doing.

August 7 Orlando Bosch is acquitted by a Venezuelan military court for the third time on charges of taking part in the 1976 bombing of a Cuban passenger jet, killing all 73 people aboard. He is released from prison but not allowed to leave the country, pending appeal by the prosecution. An August 16 *Granma* editorial says pressure to release Bosch increased after Cuban American Otto Juan Reich, head of the Office of Public Diplomacy that specialized in disinformation or "white propaganda" for Oliver North, became U.S. ambassador to Venezuela.

August 8-23 Cuba sends a delegation of approximately 600 people to the Pan American Games in Indianapolis, by far the largest contingent of Cubans to be sent together to the United States since the revolution. Some groups, including the Cuban American National Foundation and Soldier of Fortune, encourage defections, but the only defectors are eight athletes from the Dominican Republic. Cuba wins 175 medals, 75 of them gold, second only to the United States. At the closing ceremony, José Ramón Fernández, Minister of Education and Sports, accepts the torch as host of the next Games in 1991.

August 12-13 Nicaraguan President Daniel Ortega flies to Havana to confer with President Castro about the peace accords known as "Esquipulas II" (also called "the Arias plan" and "the Guatemala plan") signed by Ortega and the presidents of four other Central American countries (Costa Rica, El Salvador, Guatemala, Honduras) August 7. Castro endorses the peace plan. Although Esquipulas II does not mention foreign military advisers, Ortega's office in Managua issues a statement after his meeting with Castro saying the two leaders agree that an important contribution to peace in Central America would be a regional agreement to end all foreign military presence in the area.

August 24 U.S. media report that the U.S. Customs Service is investigating the role of Panamanian leader General Manuel Noriega in selling U.S. "high-tech" equipment, such as IBM personal computers, to Cuba.

September 14-17 The American Jurists Association meets in Havana with 1,164 jurists from 31 countries, including a large U.S. delegation. One of the main topics is human rights.

September 15   Representative Robert Torricelli (D-New Jersey) calls for a federal investigation of a Contra training camp in New Jersey run by Cuban and Nicaraguan exiles, including Alpha 66 member Humberto Alvarado, who is "operations chief."

September 16   John J. Taylor, a career diplomat, arrives in Havana to head the U.S. Interests Section.

September 16   Hilda Inclán, who resigned this month as Radio Martí's Miami bureau chief, charges that the station uses staff for intelligence-gathering rather than news-reporting. Michael W. McGuire, speaking for the Voice of America that oversees the station's programming, says the charge is "completely false."

September 17   At a ceremony in Havana, officials from two Bolivian universities give President Castro honorary degrees from their Schools of Law and Political Science.

October   The presence in Cuba of Assata Shakur, formerly Joanne Chesimard, becomes publicly known. A Black political activist, she was convicted by an all-white jury in March 1977 for the murder of a New Jersey state trooper in May 1973. A fugitive after her 1979 escape from a New Jersey prison, in 1984 she arrived with her daughter in Cuba, where she has been granted political asylum.

October 7-8   Soviet Foreign Minister Shevardnadze meets with President Castro in Havana.

October 11-13   Participants in the Soviet and U.S. Governments at the time of the Missile Crisis of October 1962 meet for three days at Harvard University to exchange ideas about why the crisis happened and how it was resolved. When Cubans later contend that they should be represented at these conferences, they are invited to the 1989 meeting in Moscow.

October 11-15   Cuban Foreign Trade Minister Ricardo Cabrisas chairs the 23rd Plenary Meeting of the Group of Latin American and Caribbean Sugar Exporting Countries (GLACSEC) in Havana. Sugar prices continue at roughly half the cost of production. In 1987 the average price has been 6.7 cents a pound while the production cost of the most efficient producers is around 12 cents.

October 19   With a tie vote (3-3), the U.S. Supreme Court lets stand a federal appeals court decision of May 1986 that limits the Administration's power to bar entry to foreigners solely because of affiliation with communist organizations. If communist affiliation is the sole reason, then the State Department must recommend granting a visa or certify to Congress that the visit is a threat to national security, as stipulated by a 1977 law (the McGovern Amendment to the Immigration and Nationality Act). Two of the four people involved in the case, *Reagan* v. *Abourezk*, are Cubans: Olga Finlay and Leonor Rodríguez Lezcano.

November 5 In Venezuela, the deadline for filing an appeal in the case of Orlando Bosch passes without action by the prosecutors. This allows Bosch to leave Venezuela.

November 6-8 In Moscow for the 70th anniversary of the October Revolution, President Castro meets with General Secretary Gorbachev.

November 10 Swedish Foreign Minister Sven Andersson meets with President Castro in Havana and then tells reporters that Cuba would be willing to have the president of the International Red Cross investigate the status of human rights in Cuban prisons.

November 11 South Africa admits for the first time that its troops have been fighting alongside UNITA inside Angola to save UNITA from defeat by Angolan and Cuban troops.

November 13 In another of a series of secret contacts and exchanges, Cuban and U.S. diplomats meet in Montreal to discuss reinstating the 1984 migration agreement and Cuba's right to make radio broadcasts to the United States. These informal meetings lead to the formal session on November 19-20.

November 15 Because of South African attempts to take Cuito Cuanavale in Angola, Cuba agrees to send reinforcements.

November 19-20 At an unannounced meeting in Mexico City, Cuba and the United States reach two agreements: to reinstate the December 1984 migration agreement and to continue talks early next year to "find a mutually acceptable solution" to the situation created by Radio Martí in which the United States broadcasts to Cuba while Cuba is deterred from broadcasting to the United States because such broadcasts would interfere with U.S. stations. Cuba's negotiators are Deputy Foreign Minister Ricardo Alarcón and José Antonio Arbesú Fraga, deputy chief of the Americas Department of the Communist Party Central Committee. U.S.

negotiators are State Department legal adviser Michael Kozak and Kenneth Skoug Jr., head of the Office of Cuban Affairs. The agreement is made public November 20.

November 23 Cuban reinforcements leave Cuba by air and sea heading for Cuito Cuanavale, Angola.

November 25 Cuban delegate Pedro Núñez Mosquera participates in the UN Security Council debate that leads to a unanimous vote demanding South Africa's unconditional withdrawal from Angola.

November 26-29 At a Summit Meeting of the Río Group of Latin American countries in Mexico, Uruguayan President Julio María. Sanguinetti proposes that Cuba be included in the regional bodies from which it has been excluded. Brazilian President José Sarney says the presidents are trying to find ways to integrate all Latin American countries without ideological discrimination and that there is "a consensus among the presidents that we ought to struggle for the total integration of Cuba into the inter-American system." For the regional organizations to function normally, Sarney continues, Cuba's participation is "indispensable." The Río Group also includes Argentina, Colombia, Panama, Peru and Venezuela.

November 30 The State Department says Cuba must halt "subversion of democratic governments in the hemisphere" before the U.S. government will support its readmission to the OAS.

December 5 The first Cuban reinforcements, about 300 advisers and fighters, arrive in Cuito Cuanavale, Angola.

December 8 The Intermediate-range Nuclear Forces (INF) treaty signed today in Washington by President Reagan and General Secretary Gorbachev to eliminate U.S. and Soviet medium- and shorter-range missiles is hailed by a *Granma* editorial as an "unprecedented historical step that for the first time opens up the possibility for disarmament." After the signing, Alexei Obukhov, deputy head of the Soviet delegation at the Soviet-U.S. talks on nuclear weapons in space, travels to Havana to discuss with Cuban leaders what happened at the Summit Meeting.

December 15 Angola announces that it has adopted a new policy of asking Cuban troops to patrol in southern Angola with orders to engage South African troops in combat. Meanwhile, a captured

UNITA rebel says U.S. personnel are piloting supply flights from Zaire into southeastern Angola and supervising the deliveries on the ground while U.S. advisers are training UNITA forces at a Zairian base. President Mobutu Sese Seko denies that he is allowing Zaire to be used for supplying and training UNITA.

December 15-16 The House and Senate approve legislation that prohibits the U.S. government from denying visas, from January 1, 1988, through February 1989, to foreigners because of their political beliefs, thus negating part of the McCarran-Walter Act of 1952. The legislation excepts people suspected of terrorism.

December 15-18 Cuban and U.S. officials meet in Havana to discuss practical aspects of the November migration agreement.

December 22 The U.S. Congress approves $100,000 to determine what technical problems, costs and legal questions would be involved in setting up television broadcasts to Cuba.

1988

January Cuba's Ministry of Health announces that the infant mortality rate dropped to 13.3 deaths per 1,000 live births in 1987, continuing to be the lowest rate in Latin America.

January 12-13 Cuban and U.S. officials meet in Mexico City to discuss the migration agreement reinstated in 1987.

January 18 To reschedule debt payments, Cuban officials meet in Paris with representatives of the Western countries to which Cuba owes $2.4 billion. Cuba also owes $3.1 billion to Western banks and suppliers. Cuba rescheduled debt payments four times in the 1983-86 period. The schedule arranged in 1986 has not been implemented because of Cuba's financial difficulties.

January 18 U.S. Secretary of the Navy James H. Webb Jr. writes in a *Wall Street Journal* article that "it is reasonable to assume that we will lose our lease on Guantánamo Bay in 1999."

January 22 On the grounds that they are employees of a terrorist state, the State Department denies visas to two Cuban artists, Professor Consuelo Castañeda and Arturo Cuenca.

January 28-29 Cuba officially joins negotiations about Angola and Namibia, participating with Angola's delegation in a new round of talks with the United States in Luanda. These negotiations continue through the coming months. After this round, the State Department portrays Angola's statement that Cuban troops will withdraw under certain conditions as a breakthrough. Manuel Pacavira, Angola's chief UN delegate, points out that Angola has always said Cuba would withdraw its troops given certain conditions: South Africa and the United States end their aid to UNITA; South Africa withdraws its forces from Angola; and

South Africa grants independence to Namibia in accordance with UN Resolution 435.

February 3 The State Department refuses visas to the Tropicana Review because the dancers and their entourage are employees of the Cuban government. This decision is reversed in April.

February 5 In one of two U.S. indictments of General Manuel Antonio Noriega of Panama on drug charges, federal prosecutors imply some relation between drug trafficking and President Castro, but admit they cannot prove any connection. Based on testimony by José Blandón (former head of Panamanian military intelligence), the Miami indictment alleges that in June 1984 Noriega met secretly in Havana with Castro, who mediated a dispute between Noriega and the Colombian Medellín drug cartel (*see* February 24).

February 16 Cuban exile and CORU leader Orlando Bosch arrives in Miami from Venezuela and is taken into custody for violating parole in 1974 (*see* September 16, 1968; June 23, 1989).

February 22 *USA Today* carries a front-page interview with President Castro.

February 24 In a televised interview with Maria Shriver of NBC (broadcast later in the United States and Cuba), President Castro says he would be willing to visit the United States to discuss a number of issues with the Senate, including the embargo and occupation of Cuban territory at Guantánamo by U.S. military forces. He rejects José Blandón's charge (*see* February 5) and invites the Congressional committee which heard Blandón's testimony to visit Cuba to receive evidence that Blandón was lying to Congress. Castro denies that the Medellín drug cartel has ever trafficked drugs through Cuba to the United States. In 1989, after the drug scandal emerges, Cubans refer to this denial as an example of how drug trafficking by Cuban officials hurt Castro and Cuba.

February 24 In Miami, two federal indictments charge that Cuban exile Reinaldo Ruiz and 16 other people smuggled Colombian cocaine to Florida through Cuba. Five days later Reinaldo Ruiz is captured in Panama and transported to the United States.

February 26-March 5 Board members of the Institute for Policy Studies (IPS) in Washington lead a delegation to conduct an inquiry into present prison conditions in Cuba. According to an agreement between IPS and the National Union of Cuban Jurists, the inspection is to be reciprocal. Relying upon good faith efforts to achieve reciprocity, Cuba waived the condition that U.S. visas for the Cubans be obtained prior to the IPS visit. (*See* May 12)

March 11 The annual UN Human Rights Commission meeting in Geneva ends without the United States being able to persuade the 43 member nations to condemn Cuba for human rights abuses. The U.S. resolution was withdrawn on a motion, proposed by four Latin American countries (Colombia, Argentina, Mexico and Peru) and carried unanimously, that contained Cuba's invitation for a UN committee to visit Cuba later this year to observe the human rights situation. *Granma* points out that the United States has some 2,000 people on death row.

March 23 South Africa makes a fifth major offensive against Cuito Cuanavale in Angola and is defeated for the fifth and decisive time, suffering heavy casualties. The battle for Cuito Cuanavale, which Cubans call the African Battle of Girón (Bay of Pigs), changes the course of negotiations.

March 29 As Reverend Jesse Jackson takes the lead in popular votes in the Democratic presidential primaries, his message includes frequent reiteration that "If we can have relations with China and Russia, certainly we can negotiate with Castro in Cuba." Albert Gore Jr., a distant third in the race, today begins to try to use Jackson's 1984 trip to Cuba against him, claiming to be "dismayed" by Jackson's "embrace" of Castro.

April 1-22 The U.S. Defense Department stages military maneuvers, Ocean Venture '88, in the Caribbean with 40,000 troops, 28 warships and dozens of aircraft. Evacuation of U.S. residents is rehearsed at the Guantánamo Naval Base. Ocean Venture maneuvers take place every other year, alternating with Solid Shield.

April 7 Cuban Guillermo García, who won second place in the New York Open chess tournament in March, leaves for home without his $10,000 prize. The Treasury Department says that sanctions against Cuba require that the money go into a blocked, interest-bearing account in the United States in García's name. He may have access to the money only if he establishes permanent residence in some country other than Cuba that is not sanctioned.

April 12 President Castro becomes the only head of government in the world to receive the Health for All medal awarded by the World Health Organization (WHO) in recognition of what he has done for health not just in Cuba but around the world.

April 17 Brigade 2506 veterans dedicate a Bay of Pigs museum in Miami.

April 18-22 A visit by John Cardinal O'Connor of New York, the highest-ranking U.S. Catholic official to travel to Cuba since the revolution, includes a long meeting with President Castro.

April 22 The Cuban Museum of Arts and Culture in Miami holds an auction of Cuban paintings but sells only pre-1963 works because the Treasury Department warned the Museum that a special license is required to sell any work of art created after July 8, 1963.

May U.S. officials visit a nuclear power plant under construction in Cuba and Cuban officials tour a similar facility already operating in North Carolina.

May Cuba celebrates 25 years of internationalism since sending its first medical brigade to Algeria in 1963. Some 3,000 Cuban doctors now serve in 30 countries. More than 20,000 educators have served abroad. About 15,000 students from 37 countries study on the Isle of Youth. Another 24,000 students from 80 Third World countries attend Cuban universities on scholarships. In the last 10 years, Cuban construction workers have built 158 major projects in 14 countries, including hospitals, factories, apartment buildings and bridges. This month, eight doctors and 94 health technicians travel to Ecuador to combat a dengue epidemic, leading two months later to an official expression of gratitude from Ecuador's National Congress for "decisive" work in wiping out the disease.

May-June In an interview in the May-June issue of the journal *Africa Report*, Massachusetts Governor Michael Dukakis, campaigning for the Democratic presidential nomination, says, "As president, I will stop U.S. aid to the UNITA rebels in Angola, recognize the Angolan government, and work toward creating conditions that will lead to the withdrawal of Cuban troops from Angola and improved relations between Angola and the West." On linkage of the withdrawal of Cuban troops to independence for Namibia, he comments, "UN Resolution 435 makes no reference to the withdrawal of Cuban troops and the current Administration's insistence on formally linking the two issues has simply handed the South Africans an excuse to stall on withdrawal until the Cubans leave." In the same issue, Reverend Jesse Jackson, also running for the nomination, says he "would end all CIA military assistance to UNITA" and "establish full diplomatic relations with Luanda." He says, "The Cubans first came to Angola in 1975 to help repel a South African invasion. They have since remained to help defend Angola against constant South African intervention and bombardment."

May 3 In Miami, a pipe bomb shatters the front door of the Cuban Museum of Arts and Culture, involved in controversy over whether to show or sell works by artists who have not broken with Cuba even though such works have been exhibited previously at the museum.

May 3 For the first time, South Africa joins the negotiations about Angola and Namibia.

May 12 Deputy Secretary of State John C. Whitehead writes Adrian W. DeWind, chair of Americas Watch (a human rights organization), denying visas to Cuban penal experts invited by the Institute for Policy Studies to tour five U.S. prisons. (*See* February 26)

May 13 José Sorzano, the highest-ranking Cuban American in the Reagan Administration, leaves his job as head of the Latin American Affairs Office of the National Security Council after senior officials began to lose confidence in him because his ideological position interfered with his judgment.

May 13 Proposing U.S. military forces "go in and get [General Manuel Noriega] out" of Panama, Senator Alfonse D'Amato (R-New York) claims Noriega has been importing Cuban personnel and weapons and now has Cuban bodyguards. Appearing on the same ABC-TV program as D'Amato, Panamanian Foreign Minister Jorge Ritter calls the "Cubanization" issue a U.S. lie.

May 20 The Cuban American National Foundation and the INS agree on a unique arrangement that allows up to 4,000 Cubans from third countries to enter the United States each year if sponsored by CANF. "Operation Exodus" brings the first group to Miami from Costa Rica and Panama in September. CANF promises to pay all resettlement expenses, but in 1991 the Cuban Exodus Relief Fund (CERF) is certified a "voluntary agency," entitling it to $588 of federal funds for each emigrant. In the same year, the Office of Refugee Resettlement of the Department of Human Health and Services authorizes $1.7 million for 2,000 more Cubans under another CERF program for settlement of Cuban immigrants. This arrangement increases both the number of CANF supporters and the amount of money that CANF receives from the federal government.

May 25 The UN Social and Economic Council elects Cuba and Panama to represent Latin America on the UN Human Rights Commission, a setback for U.S. efforts to discredit Cuba on the issue of human rights. (*See* January 1, 1989)

May 26 In Coral Gables, Florida, a bomb explodes at the home of Maria Cristina Herrera, a Miami-Dade Community College professor who heads the Institute of Cuban Studies. The Institute and the Johns Hopkins School of Advanced International Studies in Washington are cosponsoring a conference on Cuban-U.S. relations scheduled for later in the day. After the hotel where the conference was to meet denies entrance for fear of being bombed, the conference is allowed to take place at the University of Miami's faculty club.

May 31 The International Red Cross begins to visit 15 Cuban prisons and to interview all political prisoners in Cuba.

May 31 At a Summit Meeting in Moscow, President Reagan and General Secretary Gorbachev set September 29 as a target date for a settlement in Angola. Evidently unable to recall the name "Angola," Reagan states at Moscow University: "Well,... in South Africa, where Namibia has been promised its independence as a nation, it is impossible because of a civil war going on in another country there. And that civil war is being fought on one side by some 30,000 to 40,000 Cuban troops who have gone from the Americas over there and are fighting on one side with one kind of authoritative government."

June The Cuban Studies Program of the Johns Hopkins School of Advanced International Studies publishes a study called *Opportunities for U.S.-Cuban Trade*, describing what the embargo against Cuba costs U.S. firms and the benefits that could result from resuming trade.

June 2 Vice-President Carlos Rafael Rodríguez meets with Cardinal O'Connor in New York to discuss releasing political prisoners in Cuba, sending AIDS specialists to Cuba, and shipping medicines to Cuba. There are now 429 political prisoners in Cuban prisons; 385 will soon be released; 44 will remain imprisoned because of the especially serious nature of their crimes. U.S. AIDS experts are expected to visit Cuba to exchange information.

June 7 After more than four years of litigation in the case of *Reagan v. Abourezk*, Judge Harold H. Greene of the federal court in Washington rules that the U.S. government must grant visas to the four people involved, including two Cubans, Olga Finlay and Leonor Rodríguez.

June 24 Guillermo (William) Morales of the Puerto Rican independence movement is released from prison in Mexico and arrives in Cuba. Mexico rejected a U.S. extradition request on the ground that Morales is a "political fighter for the independence of Puerto Rico" who has been persecuted for political reasons. Arrested in New York in 1978 on weapons possession charges and sentenced to up to 99 years in prison, Morales escaped from a hospital in 1979.

June 24-25 The four-party negotiations about Angola and Namibia are joined by a Soviet observer. For the first time, South African Foreign Minister Roelof F. Botha takes part.

July Cuba asks for discussions with the United States about cooperation in combatting drug trafficking.

August 8 Angola, Cuba and South Africa announce an agreement that could lead, in stages, to withdrawal of South African troops from Angola, independence for Namibia, and withdrawal of Cuban troops from Angola. The accord includes an immediate ceasefire in Angola and Namibia. Although not directly involved in the talks, SWAPO says it will observe the ceasefire as of September 1 if South Africa observes it. Implementation of this agreement and problems that arise necessitate continued negotiations.

August 9-13 President Castro makes a state visit to Ecuador for the presidential inauguration of Rodrigo Borja, speaking with Ecuador's Congress for almost five hours. Castro is received by enthusiastic crowds wherever he goes.

August 10 The U.S. Drug Enforcement Agency (DEA) proposes discussions with Cuba about cooperation in combatting drug trafficking. Later, at a meeting of officials from the DEA, the State Department, the Defense Department, the Justice Department and the Coast Guard, the DEA continues to support cooperation, but the State Department does not follow up on Cuba's request for discussions.

August 22 Indictments unsealed in Fort Lauderdale, Florida, charge six Cuban Americans with violating the Neutrality Act from July 1983 until September 1986 by training mercenaries at a camp in the Everglades to fight against the Nicaraguan government.

August 23 President Reagan signs into law a Trade Act eliminating restrictions on imports and exports of books, films, phonograph records and other informational material to and from Cuba. Since 1962 it has been necessary to obtain a license from the Commerce Department to import more than a single copy of any educational material. No exports to Cuba have been allowed. The State Department told Congress it did not object to the measure sponsored by Representative Howard L. Berman (D-California). However, when Reagan vetoed an earlier version of the trade bill, he called the measure a limitation on presidential powers.

September 8-15 Eleven legislators from the Honduran National Congress spend a week in Cuba at the invitation of the National Assembly, and call for improved relations between Honduras and Cuba.

September 16-25 The UN human rights investigating team observes the human rights situation in Cuba. (*See* February 24, 1989)

September 21 Foreign ministers and representatives of 30 Latin American and Caribbean countries, including Cuba, meet in Venezuela for informal discussion about foreign debt as the IMF and the World Bank are set to hold their annual meeting in West Berlin. This takes place against the background of a September 1 regional conference on poverty that declared the debt unpayable and called for global talks. In a statement September 23, President Castro says the Third World's foreign debt is the main threat to the already shaky state of the international economy. Throughout the IMF/World Bank meetings in West Berlin, tens of thousands of people demonstrate to protest the plight of debtor nations, including a huge march on September 25 and running battles with riot police on September 26-27 with hundreds of arrests.

September 22 In a speech on the Senate floor, Senator Tom Harkin (D-Iowa) says the American people "deserve a full accounting" of Vice-President Bush's "knowledge of Luis Posada's role in the secret Contra supply operation." This does not become an issue in the Bush-Dukakis presidential campaign even though longtime CIA agent Posada was involved in multiple acts of terrorism against Cuban targets in 1976 when Bush was CIA director.

September 28 Congress approves $7.5 million for operating TV Martí for a 90-day trial period.

October Representative Mickey Leland (D-Texas), who has met with President Castro a dozen times or more, helps negotiate the release of three political prisoners and their families.

October 1 The Supreme Soviet confirms Mikhail Gorbachev as president. A shakeup of top leadership began September 30 with the goal of promoting *perestroika*, which will restructure the Soviet economic and political system.

October 1 The Festival Cine San Juan in Puerto Rico begins without the Cuban film delegation because the State Department denied them visas. The State Department also refuses to allow three Cubans to attend the Denver International Film Festival in October.

October 2 Almost 2,000 Cuban Americans attend a Miami breakfast hosted by the Cuban American Committee for Family Rights, a group founded six months ago to support U.S.-Cuban negotiations.

October 13 In the second and final Bush-Dukakis debate of the presidential campaign, Vice-President Bush says, "It now looks, because of steady negotiation, that we may have an agreement that will remove the Cubans from Angola." He does not mention the independence of either Namibia or Angola. Bush calls Armando Valladares, a former policeman during General Batista's regime, one of his American heroes.

October 25 Cuban American Francisco Aruca, owner of Marazul Charters and Marazul Tours in Miami and New York (later New Jersey), announces that Cuba has amended its travel regulations so that Cuban immigrants who arrived in the United States after

December 31, 1978, previously not granted visas by Cuba, are permitted to visit relatives.

October 31 Mexican President Miguel de la Madrid Hurtado is in Cuba for a state visit.

November President Castro informs the U.S. Catholic Conference that Cuba will release the 44 political prisoners who were to be kept imprisoned. About 3,000 prisoners, former prisoners and their closest relatives have arrived in the United States from Cuba since the migration agreement was reinstituted last November.

November 19 Jonas Savimbi, head of UNITA, tells reporters that, after the U.S. election on November 8, President-elect Bush gave assurances that U.S. aid to UNITA will continue until Cuban forces leave Angola and the Soviet Union stops providing arms to the Angolan government.

November 20-23 Representatives Robert Torricelli (D-New Jersey) and Mel Levine (D-California) of the House Foreign Relations Committee visit Cuba and have a long meeting with President Castro. After he returns to the United States, Torricelli tells reporters, "Living standards are not high, but the homelessness, hunger and disease that is witnessed in much of Latin America does not appear evident."

November 24-28 Senator Claiborne Pell, chair of the Senate Foreign Relations Committee, visits Cuba and afterward recommends "a more rational and normalized relationship with Cuba."

November 27-December 2 Four officials of the Port Authority of New York and New Jersey visit Cuba to discuss resumption of trade relations between the two countries.

November 30-December 4 President Castro makes a state visit to Mexico for the presidential inauguration of Carlos Salinas de Gortari, his first trip to the capital city since he was in exile. As in Ecuador, he is received enthusiastically. He tells a press conference that "the battle for the region's survival has become even more imperative than the emergence of a revolution in some country."

December A poll taken from September to November by the Cuban Studies Program of the Johns Hopkins School of Advanced International Studies indicates that 73 percent of Cuban Americans favor normalization of diplomatic relations between Cuba and the United States. For 86 percent, the primary issue is easing travel restrictions.

December 2 The United States deports five Marielitos to Cuba, the first deported since 1985.

December 7 Addressing the UN General Assembly, President Gorbachev says the Soviet Union "is prepared to institute a lengthy moratorium of up to 100 years on debt servicing by the least developed countries, and in quite a few cases to write off the debt altogether." This presumably would apply to Cuba, which owes approximately $8 billion to CMEA countries. While in New York City, Gorbachev confers with President Reagan and President-elect Bush. When a major earthquake strikes Armenia on December 8, Gorbachev immediately returns to the Soviet Union, canceling the rest of his itinerary, including a visit to Cuba.

December 14 Representative Charles Rangel (D-New York), chair of the House Select Committee on Narcotics, heads a delegation from the House Narcotics Committee to Cuba during a tour of the Caribbean, meeting with President Castro. Rangel says afterward that Cuba will cooperate in anti-narcotics operations at sea and in the air and will share information about drug trafficking with the United States.

December 22 Cuba, Angola and South Africa sign an agreement that provides for implementation of UN Resolution 435 for Namibian independence to begin April 1, 1989 (Namibia actually becomes independent on March 21, 1990). At the same ceremony, Cuba and Angola sign a separate agreement on the withdrawal of Cuban troops to begin by April 1989 and to be completed by July 1991.

December 23 The Treasury Department tightens restrictions on travel to Cuba from the United States by requiring the traveler to provide a written statement of why the proposed trip falls within the rules for permissible travel.

1989

January Cuba's infant mortality decreased to 11.9 per 1,000 live births in 1988, ranking among the top 20 countries in the world. Cuba's tuberculosis rate of 5.9 per 100,000 people is now below that of the United States and Canada.

January 1 Cuba begins its three-year term on the UN Human Rights Commission to which it was elected May 25, 1988.

January 10 The first detachment of Cuban soldiers leaves Angola.

January 17 At the Senate confirmation hearings for James Baker as Secretary of State, Baker says the incoming Bush Administration "will be watching carefully to be sure that Cuba does carry out its obligations" to withdraw troops from Angola. Senator Claiborne Pell tells Baker he hopes the new Administration will reexamine conduct toward Cuba, noting that the 30-year policy "to embargo, to isolate, to invade, and even to assassinate" has failed.

January 18 Two days before leaving office, President Reagan pins a presidential medal on Armando Valladares.

January 26 On the eve of a conference about the 1962 Missile Crisis, a lawsuit by the National Security Archive, a Washington-based research center, forces the U.S. government to make public some declassified documents about Operation Mongoose.

January 27-29 Cuban, Soviet and U.S. officials who were involved in the 1962 Missile Crisis meet in Moscow to discuss the event. Cuban official Jorge Risquet tells the conference that 270,000 Cuban and Soviet troops were ready to defend Cuba against the expected invasion in October 1962 that was part of Operation

Mongoose. (This is why Cubans call the crisis the "October Crisis" rather than the "Missile Crisis.")

January 29 Speaking to reporters at the conference on the Missile Crisis, Jorge Risquet says, "Cuba believes it ought to have been advised" about the decision to remove the missiles because the "missiles were stationed on our territory." Anatoly Dobrynin, then the Soviet ambassador to the United States, replies that there was not enough time for consultation.

January 30 The annual meeting of the UN Human Rights Commission, of which Cuba is now a member, opens in Geneva. The Bush Administration continues the Carter and Reagan Administrations' policy of making human rights in Cuba a major agenda item. Armando Valladares heads the U.S. delegation but UN Ambassador Vernon Walters has to fly to Geneva in March to try to get enough votes to keep Cuba on the agenda.

February 1-4 President Castro attends the presidential inauguration of Carlos Andrés Pérez in Venezuela. Cuban American Otto Reich, the U.S. ambassador, tried to persuade Venezuela not to invite Castro. Because of public demand, Castro's first television interview is repeatedly broadcast. A letter from 800 Venezuelan intellectuals salutes Castro for what he has done "on behalf of the dignity of the Cuban people and therefore of all Latin America." Cuba and Venezuela agree to exchange ambassadors for the first time since 1980. During the visit, Castro meets for over two hours with former President Jimmy Carter.

February 2 To comply with the trade bill enacted last August, the Treasury Department's Office of Foreign Assets Control issues regulations that allow U.S. companies to pay Cuba for the rights to informational materials, such as magazines, newspapers, books, posters, records, photos, microfilm, microfiche and tapes.

February 8 Delivering the annual State Department report on human rights to Congress, Richard Schifter, Assistant Secretary of State for Human Rights and Humanitarian Affairs, calls Cuba and North Korea the world's worst violators of human rights in 1988.

February 9 The United States deports eight Marielitos (called "excludables" by U.S. officials) to Cuba.

February 23-24 Cuba, Angola and South Africa hold their first session as the joint commission set up in December to discuss any problems that arise with the settlement in Angola and Namibia. Soviet and U.S. observers are present.

February 24 At the annual UN Human Rights Commission meeting, the UN team that observed human rights in Cuba last September presents its report.

March 4 Cuban exile Reinaldo Ruiz pleads guilty in Miami to heading a smuggling ring that shipped cocaine into the United States via the Cuban Air Force Base at Varadero. Shortly after this, President Castro asks the Interior Ministry to investigate to see if any Cuban officials are involved in drug trafficking.

March 9 The United States fails for the third year in a row to persuade the UN Human Rights Commission to label Cuba a human rights violator. The Commission votes for a motion, presented by Latin American countries and supported by Cuba, that thanks the Cuban government for inviting and facilitating the September 1988 visit by UN human rights observers.

March 18 Responding to U.S. denial of visas to the mayors of Havana, Managua and Panama City for a conference on drugs in New York, Bogotá's mayor, Andrés Pastrana Borrero, says that neither he nor New York's mayor, Ed Koch, were in favor of that decision.

March 24 The Bush Administration and Congressional leaders of both parties announce an unprecedented "bipartisan accord" on continued "humanitarian aid" to the Contra army based in Honduras, including the following: "The United States believes that President Gorbachev's impending visit to Cuba represents an important opportunity for both the Soviet Union and Cuba to end all aid that supports subversion and destabilization in Central America."

March 28 The Associated Press reports that Secretary of State James Baker has sent a confidential memo to U.S. embassies in Latin America with the message that the Administration is not considering improved relations with Cuba.

March 29 U.S. media report that the Bush Administration, through a variety of channels, has been telling President Gorbachev that he can improve relations by using his upcoming visit to Cuba for conciliatory action vis-a-vis Nicaragua.

March 31 Cuban Trade Minister Armando Blanco says that 70 percent of Cuba's trade is with the Soviet Union, 18 percent with other socialist countries, and 12 percent with capitalist countries, including Canada, Japan and Western European nations.

April In Bolivia, a delegation from Cuba's Health Ministry delivers a third children's intensive care ward.

April Deputy Foreign Minister Ricardo Alarcón is denied a visa to attend a conference at the Johns Hopkins School of Advanced International Studies in Washington though he has been in and out of the United States during the past year for negotiations about Namibia and Angola.

April 2-5 President Gorbachev, accompanied by his wife Raisa, makes a state visit to Cuba, the first since Leonid Brezhnev's in 1974.

April 8-May 19 The joint commission of Cuba, Angola and South Africa meets steadily until they negotiate an end to the resumption of fighting between South Africa and SWAPO. U.S. and Soviet observers attend the sessions.

Mid-April The State Department denies visas to four Cuban singers invited to a Puerto Rican festival.

April 30 After serving as head of the Cuban Interests Section in Washington ever since it was established in 1977, Ramón Sánchez Parodi returns to Havana to become Deputy Foreign Minister for American Affairs. His successor is José Antonio Arbesú, formerly a vice-chief of the Central Committee's Americas Department.

May 1 Marking its 20th anniversary, the Venceremos Brigade of more than 200 people participates in Havana's May Day celebration.

May 5 U.S. Customs agents raid the home of Ramón Cernuda in Florida and confiscate more than 200 paintings from Cuba, claiming the paintings were smuggled into the United States. Cernuda, a Cuban American book publisher, was vice-president of the Cuban Museum of Art and Culture when it exhibited paintings by Cubans who are still in Cuba (*see* May 3, 1988). Dennis Lehtinen, the U.S. Attorney General in Miami responsible for the raid, is the husband of Ileana Ros-Lehtinen (*see* August 29). In "Campaign for Democracy," shown on PBS television in October 1992, Cernuda names Jorge Mas Canosa as the instigator of the raid on his home; he plays a tape that has Mas Canosa saying he plans to continue to try to get an investigation of Cernuda and "20 other Cernudas." Mas Canosa denies responsibility for the raid on the PBS broadcast. On CBS's "60 Minutes," also in October 1992, Cernuda, asked how Mas Canosa gets his influence, replies that the Reagan Administration chose him as "the president" of the Cuban American community and from that flows his power. (*See* September 18)

May 1-26 The Defense Department carries out its annual Global Shield military exercises, simulating nuclear war. In 1988 President Reagan suspended the exercises due to an upcoming Summit with President Gorbachev. President Bush not only renews the exercises but stages a more massive mock air raid against Cuba than in previous years, sending F-4, F-15 and F-16 fighter planes followed by B-52 strategic bombers directly from Florida toward Cuba's coast east and west of Havana. Cuba puts its defense forces on alert.

Mid-May The State Department continues to deny visas to Cubans, including theatrical director Huberto Llamas; the orchestra, Aragón; and two athletes invited to Puerto Rico.

June 11 Cuba detects a U.S. submarine in its territorial waters 12.4 miles from Cienfuegos.

June 12 Speaking to reporters in Guatemala, Vice-President Dan Quayle warns that "the axis of Cuba, Nicaragua and Panama" opposes the United States and democracy in the region.

June 16 In response to Cuba's arrest of high-ranking officials on drug charges, Senator Claiborne Pell, chair of the Foreign Relations Committee, and Representative Charles Rangel, chair of the House Narcotics Committee, urge cooperation with Cuba to combat drug trafficking. The State Department argues that any direct approach to Cuba would signal a change in the official policy of no dialogue.

June 22 *Granma* reports that from January 1987 through April 23, 1989, the Interior Ministry group of drug dealers helped smuggle about six tons of cocaine to the United States for which they received about $3.4 million. Fourteen officials are subsequently convicted and four are executed on July 13.

June 23 The U.S. Justice Department rules that Orlando Bosch should be deported because of his terrorist activities. Bosch plans to appeal. The deportation order cites FBI and CIA reports that Bosch "has repeatedly expressed and demonstrated a willingness to cause indiscriminate injury and death," including 30 acts of sabotage in the United States, Cuba, Puerto Rico and Panama from 1961 through 1968. In a review of Bosch's record, U.S. District Judge William Hoeveler was allowed to study in secret hundreds of government documents. Noting Bosch's leadership of the Coordination of United Revolutionary Organizations (CORU) founded in 1976, Hoeveler wrote: "These organizations through (his) leadership and association have been responsible for numerous terrorist operations, including bombing attacks against Cuban territory; setting off a bomb in front of the Panamanian embassy in Caracas, Venezuela; blowing up the Viasa (Venezuela's airline) office in Puerto Rico; setting off a bomb at the Mexican Embassy in Buenos Aires, Argentina; and planning the murder of two Cuban diplomats in Argentina who subsequently were kidnapped and disappeared." Later, the CIA releases 1,700 pages of documents that link Bosch to air strikes against Cuba in the early 1960s (*see* August 15, 1963). In the most notorious charge against Bosch, 73 people were killed when a bomb blew up a Cuban passenger jet October 6, 1976. (*See* May 21, 1992)

July After seven months of negotiations, Mexico becomes the first country to sign up for a "debt-reduction" agreement called "the Brady plan" (for its author, U.S. Treasury Secretary Nicholas Brady). Venezuela, Argentina, Chile and Uruguay soon sign such agreements. Under the Brady plan, the debtor country must first get the International Monetary Fund to approve a restructuring of the economy that assures payment of new interest by instituting even more severe domestic austerity measures. After the IMF seal of approval, creditor banks agree either to reduce the country's debt by up to 35 percent or to reduce interest payments on current debt.

July 9 President Castro tells the Council of State that U.S. officials had at least two names of Cuban officials (Miguel Ruiz Poo and Antonio de la Guardia) involved in drug trafficking and should have told Cuba confidentially just as Cuba promptly reported to the U.S. government when it learned that a rightwing group planned to assassinate President Reagan.

July 12 Representative Charles Rangel says the Bush Administration is "playing anticommunist politics" by not taking advantage of Cuba's efforts to cooperate about drug traffickers.

July 20 Senator Connie Mack (R-Florida) introduces an amendment that would again make it unlawful for subsidiaries of U.S. companies in foreign countries to trade with Cuba, even in goods of local origin (*see* August 21, 1975). Cuba trades with U.S. subsidiaries in 12 Latin American countries, 11 European countries, Japan and Australia. Mack introduces this proposal every year until the passage in 1992 of the "Cuban Democracy Act" (CDA), which incorporates the Mack Amendment. After the passage of the CDA, Jorge Mas Canosa, in a statement published by the *Miami Herald*, says, "Without Senator Mack opening the way for three years with the Mack Amendment, the Cuban Democracy Act would have had a more difficult time becoming law."

July 25-27 The House Select Committee on Narcotics Abuse and Control and the Senate Foreign Relations Subcommittee on Terrorism, Narcotics and International Operations hold hearings on Cuba and drug trafficking, with most witnesses favoring cooperation with Cuba to combat the drug trade.

July 26 In his annual speech on the anniversary of the attack on the Moncada Barracks, President Castro says that if "the socialist community were to disappear" the "imperialist powers would set upon the Third World like wild beasts" and "divide up the world all over again."

August 1-2 The House Foreign Affairs Subcommittee on Western Hemisphere Affairs holds hearings on U.S.-Cuban relations. Deputy Assistant Secretary of State Michael Kozak says the Bush Administration is concerned about Cuba's ties to the Soviet Union, "support for terrorism" (examples he gives are the FMLN, M-19, Guatemalan guerrillas and the Nicaraguan government), and domestic "human rights abuses and political repression." Questioned about the U.S. travel ban, Kozak says the U.S. government does not have "a constitutional obligation to allow Americans to support the Cuban tourism industry."

August 15 In response to the U.S. Justice Department's June 23 order that Cuban-born Orlando Bosch be deported, the Cuban government requests that he be returned to Cuba.

August 16 At a fund-raiser in Miami for Republican State Senator Ileana Ros-Lehtinen's Congressional campaign, President Bush tells his predominantly Cuban American audience that there will be no improvement in relations with Cuba as long as Castro, "almost alone in the entire world now, swims against the tide that is bringing sweeping change and democracy and freedom to closed societies around the world."

August 20-21 Performances by Cuban pianist Gonzalo Rubalcaba and his band, Grupo Proyecto, in New York are canceled because the State Department refused to grant them visas.

August 21 An editorial in the daily *Granma* warns of imminent U.S. aggression against Panama.

August 29 Ileana Ros-Lehtinen becomes the first Cuban American elected to Congress. During her campaign, managed by the President's son, Jeb Bush, she championed Orlando Bosch as a hero.

September 4-8 Speaking at the Summit Meeting of the Movement of Nonaligned Countries in Yugoslavia, Armed Forces Minister Raúl Castro calls for democratizing the United Nations by eliminating the veto power of the five permanent members of the Security Council because the present system means that the vote of one country can be more decisive than the will of more than 150 member countries.

September 7 Cuba announces that its remaining troops in Ethiopia will be coming home since conditions have changed. Cuba and Somalia, which Cuban troops had opposed, recently restored diplomatic relations.

September 18 In the case of *Cernuda* v. *Heavy*, a Federal District Court in Florida rules that original oil paintings are included in the protection of the Trade Act of August 1988. The Treasury Department, which had confiscated Cuban paintings imported by Cuban American Ramón Cernuda, will not appeal.

September 20-21 In a continuing series of Congressional hearings about Cuba, the House Subcommittee on Western Hemisphere Affairs listens first to testimony about human rights in Cuba and, on the second day, to opinions from Cuban American organizations. Three of the four Cuban American representatives support U.S. dialogue with Cuba. The president of the board of the Cuban American Committee Research and Education Fund, Dr Dagmaris Cabezas, testifies that most Cuban Americans are afraid to speak for fear of terrorist retaliation by the minority that opposes U.S.-Cuban relations.

September 23-24 At a meeting with Soviet Foreign Minister Shevardnadze, Secretary of State James Baker continues the pressure about Cuba by stressing that the Soviet Union should use its influence with Cuba to end arms shipments to Nicaragua.

September 25 *Wall Street Journal* editor David Asman reports that Cuban exile Reinaldo Ruiz, in cooperation with DEA officials, was arranging for the defection of two Cuban officials involved with him in drug trafficking, Miguel Ruiz Poo and Antonio de la Guardia, before their arrests on drug charges.

September 27 The House Subcommittee on Western Hemisphere Affairs and the Subcommittee on International Economic Policy hold a hearing on the embargo against Cuba.

October 5 Soviet Foreign Minister Shevardnadze meets with President Castro in Havana.

October 7 Forty-six wounded and disabled FMLN guerrillas are flown to Cuba for medical care.

October 12 At the end of a two-day Summit of the Río Group in Peru, the presidents of Argentina, Brazil, Colombia, Mexico, Peru, Uruguay and Venezuela recommend that the OAS readmit Cuba.

October 18 The UN General Assembly elects Cuba as one of the 10 nonpermanent members of the Security Council for a two-year term starting January 1, 1990. Cuba receives the largest vote in the history of the United Nations: 146 of a possible 156.

October 27 Confirming news that first broke in the *Los Angeles Times* a week earlier, the Treasury Department announces that General Manuel Antonio Noriega, head of Panama's armed forces, has been designated an agent of Cuba. Since the U.S. embargo outlaws trade with Cuban agents, this means that U.S. citizens are prohibited from doing business with Noriega. Noriega's wife and 32 Panamanian companies are also designated Cuban agents. Treasury calls this "another step" in efforts "to neutralize Cuban commercial activities in Panama that serve to circumvent the U.S. trade embargo."

October 27-28 Cuba is not invited to attend a "Hemispheric celebration of democracy" hosted by Costa Rican President Oscar Arias. President Bush attends along with his two guests, opposition leaders Violeta Barrios de Chamorro of Nicaragua and Guillermo Endara of Panama.

November 4 Representative Matthew Rinaldo (R-New Jersey) calls for release of three political prisoners in Cuba: Alfredo Mustelier Nuevo (imprisoned for murder in 1969; released in March 1990), Ernesto Díaz Rodríguez (arrested as part of an Alpha 66 infiltration group in 1968; released in March 1991), and Mario Chanes de Armas (arrested for trying to assassinate Fidel Castro; released when his sentence expires in July 1991). These three are the last of the *plantados*, long-term prisoners who refused to wear prison garb and rejected the "rehabilitation" program.

November 6 A Senate-House conference committee approves U.S. broadcasts on TV Martí if a feasibility test shows that it will not interfere with domestic broadcasts.

November 8 The Justice Department order that Orlando Bosch be deported is upheld in federal court.

November 13 Addressing the OAS foreign ministers in Washington, Secretary of State James Baker says the biggest obstacle to full improvement in U.S.-Soviet relations is "Soviet behavior toward Cuba and Central America."

November 15 The State Department says the Soviet Union has shipped advanced MiG-29s to Cuba despite the fact that Cuba is under no U.S. threat.

November 16 The *Los Angeles Times* reports that the Bush Administration and Congressional intelligence oversight panels recently agreed that the United States may participate in covert operations that might lead to violence or death of foreign leaders. Assassination would not be approved overtly but it would no longer be illegal.

November 20 The Treasury Department's latest restrictions on travel to Cuba take effect, including a $100 per day limit on travel-related expenditures (not including money already paid to a travel agency nor money spent on "informational materials").

November 22 In his Thanksgiving address to the nation, President Bush declares that the "winds of change" are "transforming the Americas" with "some exceptions: Panama, Nicaragua and Cuba."

December Ramón Cernuda's publishing offices in Hialeah and Miami are raided by INS officials searching in vain for undocumented workers. He is also being harassed constantly by the IRS.

December 1 The Treasury Department informs ABC that it will be allowed to broadcast the 1991 Pan American Games in Havana only if it puts the money owed to Cuba in a "blocked account" available to Cuba if relations with the United States improve. ABC takes the matter to court on December 4. ABC agreed in April to pay $8.7 million to the Pan American Sports Organization, coordinator of the Games. PASO would pay the Cubans 75 percent of that. Treasury says this would violate the embargo. The U.S. government plans to allow the U.S. Olympic Committee to send more than 500 athletes, coaches, trainers and officials to participate in the event.

December 2 President Bush and President Gorbachev hold a Summit Meeting aboard a Soviet ship in the Mediterranean. After it ends on December 3, President Bush tells reporters that "there is no doubt in [Soviet leaders'] minds that their assistance to Cuba and their lip service for the Sandinistas give us a considerable amount of difference with them. I mean, so it's very clear — well, until we see a free Cuba, self-determination and the people deciding what they want, Cuba will stick out until that date, as a tiny country, but swimming against Mr Gorbachev's own tide."

December 20 More than a million Cuban citizens converge outside the U.S. Interests Section in Havana to protest the U.S. invasion of Panama that began at 1 a.m.

December 21 U.S. troops in armored personnel carriers surround the Cuban, Nicaraguan and Libyan Embassies in Panama City on the pretext that Manuel Noriega may be inside one of them, although both General Thomas Kelly and Rear Admiral Ted Sheafer of the Joint Chiefs of Staff acknowledge on U.S. television that there is no evidence that Noriega has sought asylum in any of them. Cuban UN Ambassador Oscar Oramas Oliva sends a letter to the UN Secretary General to be distributed to the Security Council, describing how the United States has positioned tanks in front of the Cuban Embassy and stationed troops on the roofs of adjacent buildings.

December 23 The UN Security Council votes 10 to 4 with one abstention (Finland) to condemn the U.S. use of force in its invasion of Panama. The United States, Britain and France use their veto powers to block the resolution. Canada also votes against the resolution.

December 23 Cubans end four days of protest at the U.S. Interests Section in opposition to the invasion of Panama.

December 24 In addition to continuing to surround the Cuban Embassy in Panama City, U.S. troops surround the residence of Cuban Ambassador Lázaro Mora Secade, preventing Cuban diplomats from leaving or entering. Deputy Foreign Minister Ricardo Alarcón calls a news conference in Havana and tells reporters that at no time had General Noriega been in the Cuban Embassy or the Cuban ambassador's residence. He says a number of Panamanians have asked for and received political asylum since the invasion, adding that if Noriega had asked for political asylum, Cuba would have granted it without hesitation. Cuba generally grants political asylum to those who request it. It turns out that Noriega is inside the papal nunciature in Panama City.

December 26 Cuba calls for an urgent meeting of the UN Security Council because U.S. troops at the Cuban ambassador's residence in Panama are harassing Cuban diplomats. Cuba says the officer in charge of those troops continues to say he has orders to arrest any Cuban diplomat who tries to leave and to prevent anyone from entering, contradicting assurances given earlier by State Department officials in Washington. The United States opposes taking up the matter in the Security Council. Cuba and Nicaragua are trying to reconvene the General Assembly.

December 28 The UN General Assembly meets in emergency session. Cuba and Nicaragua introduce a resolution that "strongly deplores the intervention in Panama by the armed forces of the United States of America which constitutes a flagrant violation of international law and of the independence, sovereignty and territoriality of states."

December 28 Inspecting cars coming and going from the Cuban Embassy, U.S. troops detain Ambassador Mora and his first secretary, Alberto Cabrera, for an hour.

December 29 The UN General Assembly votes 75 to 20 with 40 abstentions for a resolution similar to the one vetoed in the Security Council. It "strongly deplores" the U.S. invasion of Panama as a "flagrant violation of international law and of the independence, sovereignty and territorial integrity of states" and demands immediate withdrawal of U.S. forces with strict observance of the "letter and spirit" of the 1977 Carter-Torrijos treaties.

December 29 U.S. troops detain Jorge Sosa, second secretary of the Cuban Embassy in Panama, as he is entering the residence of the Cuban ambassador. Ambassador Mora accompanies Sosa in order to defend his diplomatic rights. Both are released later in the day. When Cuba protests, the State Department assures Cuba that these problems are going to be resolved.

December 31 Cuba announces that it will not recognize the government of Guillermo Endara who was sworn in as president of Panama at a U.S. military base in the middle of the first night of the invasion.

1990

January Explaining that U.S. policy is to maintain but not significantly upgrade telecommunications with Cuba, the State Department informs Representative George Crockett (D-Michigan) that it has denied AT&T permission to upgrade phone service to Cuba through the use of a fiber optic cable that has been in place since April 1989.

January 1 Cuba takes a seat on the UN Security Council, which it will hold through 1991.

January 4 Journalists observe U.S. troops, still surrounding the Cuban Embassy in Panama City, stop and check occupants of cars leaving the Embassy. Outside the Cuban ambassador's residence, U.S. troops seize Cuban diplomat Victor Hernández González but release him within an hour. A Cuban airliner is permitted to take more than 60 Cubans from Panama City to Havana.

January 9 At a meeting of the CMEA, the Soviet Union proposes to begin trading on January 1, 1991, on a hard-currency basis at real market prices.

January 14 For the third time since the invasion, U.S. troops stop Cuban Ambassador Mora's car in Panama City and demand to search it. Mora refuses to allow the search, citing diplomatic immunity. After almost two hours, the troops return Mora's passport as well as those of the three aides with him.

January 18 U.S. troops withdraw from around the Cuban Embassy and the residence of Cuban Ambassador Mora in Panama City, which they had surrounded for four weeks.

January 23 The U.S. battleship *Wisconsin* arrives at Guantánamo Naval Base. Along with the earlier arrival of the amphibious assault ship *Wasp*, this constitutes a considerable buildup of U.S. military force on Cuban territory.

January 25 Cuba's Foreign Ministry announces a temporary suspension of the withdrawal of troops from Angola because of a UNITA attack January 21 that killed four Cuban soldiers who were guarding a water purification plant. The Ministry states that ultimate responsibility for UNITA's actions rests with the U.S. government, which supplies and advises UNITA. Cuba has withdrawn 31,138 troops, and resumes its withdrawal February 24.

January 26 Cuban television begins regular broadcasts of the weekly news series, "CNN World Report." Cuba is one of the founders of the program, prepared with material sent in by reporters in some 120 countries.

January 26 In Texas, Dan Snow is found guilty of violating the Trading With the Enemy Act by arranging fishing trips to Cuba. In April, his five-year sentence is suspended on condition that he serve 90 days in jail, pay a $5,000 fine and carry out 1,000 hours of community service. He is also placed on five years' probation.

January 30 In the international waters of the Gulf of Mexico, the U.S. Coast Guard cutter *Chincoteague* begins to follow the Cuban freighter *Hermann*, bound from Moa, Cuba, for Tampico, Mexico, with a routine cargo of chrome. According to the Coast Guard, the freighter matches its "profile" of a possible drug-runner. The *Hermann* is chartered by a Cuban company, registered in Panama, and flies the Panamanian flag. The Coast Guard asks Washington to obtain permission for boarding from Panama, where the United States has just set up a new government. Permission is granted. When Captain Diego Sánchez Serrano continues to refuse boarding, the *Chincoteague* sprays water down the stacks of the *Hermann*, which continues toward Mexico.

January 31 Shortly after midnight the State Department contacts José Antonio Arbesú, head of the Cuban Interests Section in Washington, to inform him that at 4:00 a.m. the Coast Guard plans to board the *Hermann*. This decision was made by an interagency committee that includes the National Security

Council and the Departments of State and Defense. Told of this development, President Castro calls Arbesú and tells him to inform the State Department that Cuba will not submit to such a search but will allow Mexican officials to search the ship in Mexican territorial waters. Shortly after 6:00 a.m., the Coast Guard attacks with machine guns and a cannon causing serious damage, but the *Hermann* enters Mexico's territorial waters, forcing the Coast Guard to give up the chase. Mexican anti-narcotics police search the vessel for hours and find no trace of drugs.

February President Bush signs legislation that essentially voids a major provision in federal law allowing exclusion of foreigners solely on the basis of political belief. The State Department may still deny visas if it deems there is a threat to national security.

February Florida's governor, Republican Bob Martínez, appoints a "Free Cuba Commission" of 18 members to study how the ouster of President Castro would affect Florida. Appointed chair of the Commission, Jorge Mas Canosa of the Cuban American National Foundation advises the governor on policy toward Cuba.

February 1 UN Ambassador Ricardo Alarcón becomes president of the Security Council for the month of February.

February 4 Cuba cooperates with the U.S. Coast Guard to go to the rescue of a Cypriot merchant ship on fire off the coast of Cuba.

February 8 Another 32 wounded FMLN guerrillas arrive in Cuba for medical treatment.

February 9 The UN Security Council takes up the issue of the U.S. attack on the *Hermann*. Lasting only one hour, the discussion is limited to a speech by Ambassador Alarcón, a response by U.S. Deputy Ambassador Alexander F. Watson and a Cuban rebuttal. Watson does not rule out a repetition of such an incident, claiming that it has been done before (though not with Cuba involved). Alarcón responds that the fact that it has been done before does not make it legal. The Council reaches no decision, declaring only that the issue will be reconsidered if similar incidents are submitted for consideration in the future. Afterward, Alarcón says the biggest accomplishment is that the United States was unable to prevent the meeting.

February 20 The State Department says Cuba has received a new shipment of Soviet MiG-29s.

February 27 The United States again makes the question of human rights in Cuba central to the agenda of the annual meeting of the UN Human Rights Commission in Geneva. The head of the U.S. delegation is Armando Valladares.

March The SR-71 Blackbird surveillance planes are being retired from service by the U.S. Defense Department in favor of spying by satellite. (They are reactivated in 1995.)

March The first group of Ukrainian children to be treated in Cuba for effects from the Chernobyl nuclear plant disaster arrive in Havana.

March Ernesto Betancourt, appointed the director of Radio Martí at its inception, is reassigned to a different USIA job two days after saying that, even if technical difficulties can be overcome, the U.S. government will not be able to begin broadcasts of TV Martí without violating international agreements. Betancourt charges that his ouster is the result of his opposition to TV Martí and his attempts to defend the integrity of Radio Martí from the influence of powerful Cuban Americans in Miami. Since the creation of both Radio Martí and TV Martí, Jorge Mas Canosa has headed the presidential advisory board for both stations. Betancourt says Mas Canosa seeks programs favorable to the Cuban American National Foundation. Periodically, workers at Radio Martí complain about Mas Canosa's control of what is supposed to represent balanced reporting.

March 6 Adopting a resolution cosponsored by the United States, Poland and Czechoslovakia, the UN Human Rights Commission votes 19 to 12 with 12 abstentions to examine Cuba's human rights record again next year.

March 7 President Castro says Cuba will not comply with the resolution passed by the UN Human Rights Commission because it is treating Cuba differently than any other country.

March 13 Visiting Argentina, Vice-President Dan Quayle urges President Carlos Saúl Menem to put pressure on President Castro to end aid to the FMLN.

March 14-20 President Castro makes a state visit to Brazil to attend the presidential inauguration of Fernando Collor de Mello. He is warmly received in Brasilia, São Paulo and Río de Janeiro.

Mid-March Davidoff International, manufacturer of prestigious Havana cigars since soon after World War II, formally ends relations with Cuba. By switching operations to the Dominican Republic, Davidoff can sell more cigars in the United States.

March 23 Cuba broadcasts a radio speech by President Castro picked up by AM stations along the Florida coast and as far away as Nashville, Tennessee.

March 27 At around 1:30 in the morning, the United States launches its first test of TV Martí, broadcasting for three hours to Cuba on Channel 13. Cuba blocks almost all of the test by electronic jamming. A Voice of America official says tests are being conducted in predawn hours to avoid interference with Cuba's regular programming that would violate international agreements.

April Visiting Angola after his release from prison in February, ANC leader Nelson Mandela calls Cuba an "inspiration" and praises its love for human rights and liberty. (*See* June 28)

April 2 The International Frequency Regulation Board of the International Telecommunications Union, which regulates television, notifies the U.S. government that TV Martí violates the 1982 Nairobi International Telecommunications Convention, to which both the United States and Cuba are parties.

April 2 The *Miami Herald* reports that AFL-CIO members have been meeting in Miami with Cuban American leaders who have asked them to support dissident activities in Cuba. Lane Kirkland, president of the AFL-CIO, is developing a Labor Committee for a Free Cuba.

April 3 President Castro holds a long press conference in Havana attended by 246 journalists, including 53 from the United States. He says the U.S. government "is experiencing a great euphoria" stemming from its invasion of Panama, the electoral defeat of the Sandinistas in Nicaragua in February, and recent events in Eastern Europe, noting, "The United States can't contain... its feeling of being the master of the world."

April 11 After almost 12 years as a fugitive charged with the assassinations of Orlando Letelier and Ronnie Moffitt in Washington, Cuban exile José Dionisio Suárez, an Omega 7 member at the time of the murders, is arrested in Florida. Two other Omega 7 members indicted with Suárez in 1978, the brothers Guillermo and Ignacio Novo Sampol, are now working for Jorge Mas Canosa in the "Information Commission" of the Cuban American National Foundation.

April 13 One week after a large pro-Cuba demonstration in New York City by a coalition of groups called "Hands Off Cuba," the New York police shut down Casa de las Américas, one of the main organizing groups, for violation of Fire Department regulations. Francisco Medina comments later on the kinds of harassment faced by Casa members; for example, Radio América in New York broadcasts their home addresses and telephone numbers. Casa later reopens.

April 14 The *Washington Post* reports that Alpha 66 leader Francisco Avila is training in the Florida Everglades.

April 17 Cuba begins broadcasting on a new Radio Taino station on the 1180 kilohertz band. The U.S. Federal Communications Commission reports in May that the new station interferes with broadcasts from Radio Martí as well as with two U.S. commercial radio stations, all three operating on the same 1180 kilohertz band.

April 25 Education Minister José Ramón Fernández heads Cuba's delegation to the inauguration of Violeta Chamorro as president of Nicaragua.

April 29 Cuba's Defense Ministry announces that the U.S. Defense Department will conjoin three threatening military maneuvers in early May. In previous years there have been large consecutive maneuvers in April, May and June, but this year Ocean Venture, which began April 20, will coincide with Global Shield while Guantánamo Naval Base practices evacuation of civilian personnel.

May 7 Cuba begins 24-hour jamming of Radio Martí in Havana and plans to extend the jamming to the entire country.

May 22-24 A seminar called "Malcolm X Speaks in the 90's" takes place in Havana. President Castro meets with U.S. participants on the final day.

May 31-June 3 President Bush and President Gorbachev hold a Summit Meeting in Washington and at Camp David, Maryland.

June Deputy Assistant Secretary of State for Inter-American Affairs Michael Kozak meets with Deputy Foreign Minister Ramón Sánchez Parodi and UN Ambassador Ricardo Alarcón in New

York to discuss migration issues. The migration agreement, reinstated in 1987, calls for the United States to accept 20,000 Cubans each year, but since 1987 the INS has accepted only about 6,000, leaving almost 30,000 waiting with exit visas in Havana. This situation leads to increased illegal immigration from Cuba.

June 4 The last known Omega 7 fugitive, José Ignacio González, is arrested upon arrival in Miami after he was expelled from Guatemala. He has been sought since 1984 on perjury and bombing charges.

June 4 U.S. Assistant Secretary of State for African Affairs Herman J. Cohen is in Havana as an observer at the latest meeting of the joint commission regarding the settlement in Angola and Namibia.

June 5 Gustavo Arcos, a dissident in Cuba, calls for dialogue of dissidents inside and outside the island with Cuban officials. Arcos has the backing of some officials in the U.S. State Department.

June 5 The National Emergency Civil Liberties Committee (NECLC) based in New York files suit in federal court to overturn the Treasury Department's ban on importation of some Cuban art. Despite passage of the Berman Amendment in 1988 and the *Cernuda* v. *Heavy* decision in 1989, Treasury has taken the position that paintings, drawings and sculpture are not informational materials. NECLC is acting on behalf of individual artists, critics, galleries, collectors, the Chancellor of the City University of New York and the Center for Cuban Studies.

June 11 Reflecting a growing response within the United States to Cuba's worsening economic situation, the Presbyterian Church votes to work to reduce the U.S. restrictions on trade and travel.

June 14 A bomb causes considerable damage to the Cuban Museum of Arts and Culture in Miami, under attack for exhibiting art by Cubans still in Cuba.

June 25 CNN broadcasts an interview of President Castro by Ted Turner.

June 27 President Bush announces another U.S. attempt to enhance relations with Latin American countries. The Enterprise for the Americas Initiative (EAI), reminiscent of President Kennedy's Alliance for Progress, aims to widen trade and investment and reduce debt.

June 27 Three former prisoners to whom the INS has refused to grant entry are on a hunger strike in Havana, appealing to various nations and the Vatican to intercede on their behalf with the U.S. government.

June 28 Tens of thousands attend an antiapartheid rally for ANC leader Nelson Mandela in Miami, but local officials retaliate for his praise of Cuba (*see* April) by refusing to give him the key to the city, leading to a Black-led tourism boycott of Dade County. Some anti-Mandela demonstrators carry placards with a picture of Jonas Savimbi, head of UNITA, as their choice in Africa.

June 29 In *Capital Cities/ABC, Inc.* v. *Brady*, a federal judge rules that the Treasury Department can use the Trading With the Enemy Act to prohibit Capital Cities/ABC Inc. from broadcasting the 1991 Pan American Games in Cuba, deciding that in this case constitutional concerns about free speech are outweighed by the executive branch's right to conduct foreign policy. (*See* December 19)

July 9 The U.S. Justice Department reverses itself and allows Orlando Bosch to be freed without deportation despite being identified as a terrorist by both the FBI and CIA. The reversal is evidently a result of lobbying by the Cuban American National Foundation and Republican officials such as Senator Connie Mack and Representative Ileana Ros-Lehtinen, both from Florida, as well as Jeb Bush, the President's son who is active in South Florida politics. Bosch agrees to 14 conditions, including renunciation of terrorism. But at a news conference immediately after his release on July 17, Bosch calls the deal with the Justice Department "ridiculous" and "a farce," saying, "They purchased the chain but they don't have the monkey."

July 12 The USIA announces plans to consolidate its broadcasting division under Voice of America, meaning that Radio Martí and TV Martí will be part of a new and more powerful broadcasting unit of the USIA. Cuba jams TV Martí and also jams Radio Martí in 90 percent of the island. Cuba makes no attempt to jam regular U.S. radio stations, but regards Radio Martí as a special case of U.S. aggression.

July 27 Cuba and Jamaica reestablish diplomatic relations.

July 27-August 2 More than 150 Cuban athletes participate in the Goodwill Games in Seattle, Washington, but the State Department refused to grant a visa for Education Minister José Ramón Fernández, who was to lead the Cuban delegation.

August 2 Cuba joins the UN Security Council's condemnation of Iraq's invasion of Kuwait and demand for Iraq's withdrawal. The vote is 14 to 0 with Yemen abstaining.

August 6 Cuba and Yemen abstain when the UN Security Council votes 13 to 0 for a trade and financial embargo of Iraq and occupied Kuwait except for medicine and, in humanitarian circumstances, foodstuffs. In the coming months of UN debate about the situation in the Middle East, Ambassador Ricardo Alarcón argues consistently for territorial integrity; against use of force by the United States and its coalition of allies; for an international conference to negotiate a peaceful solution to regional conflicts, including Israeli occupation of various territories; and against withholding food, medical supplies and other essentials from Iraqi civilians.

August 7 President Castro writes a letter to Arab leaders (sent as well to other leaders around the world) warning that the Security Council resolution of August 6 "creates ideal conditions for an escalation of the conflict and the probable use of the most powerful war machinery on the planet for the unquestionable purpose of entrenching [U.S.] hegemony in the region."

August 15 Cuba joins the majority on the UN Decolonization Committee in approving a resolution, sponsored by Venezuela, to continue monitoring the United States regarding the political status of Puerto Rico. Norway casts the only vote against the measure.

August 25 Cuba and Yemen abstain as the Security Council votes (13 to 0) for the first time in the history of the United Nations to authorize military action for the purpose of enforcing an embargo on all maritime trade with a nation (Iraq).

August 27 President Bush says TV Martí has passed a five-month preliminary test and will be permanent.

August 29 Citing a shortfall in Soviet oil shipments (one-fifth of what was expected), Cuba announces drastic nationwide fuel restrictions and other economic measures.

September 10 José Dionisio Suárez (*see* April 11) pleads guilty to plotting to detonate the car bomb that killed Orlando Letelier and Ronni Moffitt in 1976. Virgilio Paz, a fugitive in the case, remains at large. Suárez is sentenced in November to 12 years in prison.

Mid-September Alan H. Flanigan, a career diplomat, replaces John J. Taylor as head of the U.S. Interests Section in Havana.

September 28 In a major speech, President Castro declares there is no doubt that Cuba is entering "a special period during peacetime" when the unreliability of former CMEA trading partners creates scarcities in Cuba of a magnitude similar to what would be caused by a wartime naval blockade. CMEA members have been accounting for 85 to 88 percent of Cuba's trade.

October 10 Nine former Kennedy Administration officials file affidavits in the Federal District Court of Washington, D.C., asking for release of hundreds of documents about the 1962 Cuban Missile Crisis. The affidavits support a motion filed by American University Professor Philip Brenner and the National Security Archive in Washington asking the court to compel the State Department to provide more information about the documents and the basis for withholding them.

October 18 As the United States and the Soviet Union issue a joint statement calling upon the Salvadoran government and the FMLN to intensify negotiations, a State Department official tells reporters that he is certain the Soviets are conveying their view to Cuba that no arms should be sent to the guerrillas.

October 26 Congress passes a trade bill, the Export Administration Act, that includes the Mack Amendment. The Cuban American National Foundation is a major supporter of the Mack Amendment even though most trade with Cuba by foreign subsidiaries involves exports of food to Cuba. Alicia Torres, executive director of the Cuban American Committee Research and Education Fund based in Washington, opposes the Amendment because it would make the embargo even more harmful to Cuban relatives of the Cuban American community.

October 31 In response to the Mack Amendment, Canadian Attorney General Kim Campbell issues an order to block any attempt by the U.S. government to restrict trade with Cuba by U.S.-owned subsidiaries in Canada. Campbell says Canada will decide what laws and policies govern Canada-based companies.

November Armando Valladares resigns from his position on the U.S. delegation to the UN Human Rights Commission, reportedly under pressure from the State Department because of his opposition to Gustavo Arcos (*see* June 5).

November 7 Angolan President Eduardo dos Santos says the U.S. government continues to encourage UNITA to fight even though the presence of Cuban troops, previously cited by Washington as a barrier to diplomatic relations with Angola, has been reduced to 12,000, with Cuba following the timetable for total withdrawal set by the 1988 agreement.

November 12 *Variety* reports that ABC and the Treasury Department are "inches away from a deal" that would allow ABC Sports and Turner Broadcasting to telecast the Pan American Games from Havana in August. According to *Variety*, the "deal would not include a broadcast rights fee" but would include payment for essentials necessary in housing the production team.

November 16 President Bush pocket-vetoes the trade bill containing the Mack Amendment (*see* July 20, 1989). Soon after meeting (during his re-election campaign earlier this year) with members of the Cuban American National Foundation, Senator Claiborne Pell, chair of the Foreign Relations Committee, reversed his long-held position on trade with Cuba and now supports the Mack Amendment.

November 18 The German Minister of Development Aid, Juergen Warnke, says the newly unified nation of Germany will end all development aid that East Germany has been providing to Cuba.

November 19-21 President Bush and President Gorbachev, along with other leaders of NATO and the Warsaw Pact, hold a Summit Meeting in Paris, signing a treaty that pledges a "new era of democracy, peace and unity."

November 23 In response to an allegation made in the posthumous memoirs of Nikita Khrushchev that Fidel Castro suggested a pre-emptive nuclear strike by the Soviet Union against the United States during the 1962 Missile Crisis, *Granma* publishes the relevant letters between Castro and Khrushchev. (*See* October 26, 1962)

November 28 Foreign Minister Isidoro Malmierca and Secretary of State James Baker meet for 90 minutes to discuss the UN Security Council resolution scheduled for a vote on the following day. Cuba rejects the U.S. appeal for its support in authorizing the use of force to oust Iraq from Kuwait if Iraq does not withdraw by a specified date in January.

November 29 With Secretary of State Baker presiding, the UN Security Council votes 12 to 2 (Cuba and Yemen) with one abstention (China) for Resolution 678 authorizing the use of "all necessary means" to expel Iraq from Kuwait if Iraq does not withdraw by January 15, paving the way for the war that begins January 16.

December The State Department denies visas to four Cuban artists invited by Francisco Aruca to perform at a concert in Miami.

December 19 ABC senior vice-president Stephen Solomon announces that ABC Sports has settled its suit with the Treasury Department and has reached an agreement with Cuba to broadcast the 1991 Pan American Games. Turner Broadcasting will provide cable coverage. Solomon refuses to comment on whether the agreement with Treasury allows any payment to Cuba because, he says, none of the details can be made public.

Late December The new anticommunist Czechoslovakian government announces that it will no longer provide diplomatic and consular representation for Cuba in the United States.

1991

January Despite severe economic problems, Cubans decreased their infant mortality rate from 11.1 in 1989 to 10.7 in 1990.

January 1 Reflecting drastic changes in the CMEA, the dollar replaces the ruble as the accounting unit. In February, the CMEA formally disbands, ending the cycle of five-year socialist economic plans in which Cuba has been an integral participant. For Cuba, this is a cataclysmic change because 85 to 88 percent of its trade has been with CMEA countries.

January 1 Directed by Francisco Aruca, Radio Progreso goes on the air in Miami. Threats from rightwing Cubans against the ten members of the station's staff begin immediately. Aruca is the president of both Marazul Tours and Marazul Charters, which arrange trips and air flights to and from Cuba. He established his travel agency in 1979 after President Carter lifted the travel ban. His Miami office was bombed twice in 1989.

January 3 Representative Ted Weiss introduces a bill that would remove the U.S. embargo on export of medicines and medical supplies. Originally introduced in 1989 by the late Mickey Leland, the bill died for lack of action. The Weiss legislation is referred to the House Foreign Affairs Committee chaired by Dante Fascell (D-Florida), closely aligned with Jorge Mas Canosa of the Cuban American National Foundation that opposes any contact or trade with Cuba.

January 3-7 A meeting of Cuban, Soviet and U.S. officials and scholars takes place in Antigua, the fourth in a series of conferences about the 1962 Missile Crisis. Prior to this meeting, the

Soviet Union declassified more than 200 pages of related documents.

January 16 As U.S. planes attack Iraq, UN Ambassador Ricardo Alarcón, representing Cuba on the Security Council, says that the Council's obligation is "to meet and to end this war."

January 31 The Security Council resists an attempt to have public debate about a ceasefire in the Gulf War. At the request of several UN delegations from countries that are not members of the Security Council, Cuba and Yemen have tried for more than a week to get the Council to allow debate. U.S. diplomats tell the *New York Times* that they have firm instructions not to let such a public debate take place.

February Preparing the way for the U.S. resolution at the UN Human Rights Commission session in March, the Senate and House pass resolutions condemning Cuba for human rights violations.

February 7 Esteban Lazo, a member of the Communist Party's Political Bureau, represents Cuba at the inauguration of Jean-Bertrand Aristide as president of Haiti.

February 11 Switzerland announces it will replace Czechoslovakia as the formal sponsor of the Cuban Interests Section in Washington beginning April 1.

February 12 Tele Caribe begins a system of rapid telephone calls from Miami to Cuba. On March 15, the Treasury Department prohibits Tele Caribe's communications.

February 13 Just before dawn in Iraq, U.S. planes bomb a civilian bomb shelter killing hundreds of people, mostly women and children. At the United Nations, Cuba and Yemen again ask the Security Council for public debate about how to achieve a ceasefire, but the Council votes 9 to 2 with 4 abstentions for a closed session.

February 21 As tourist flights from Montego Bay in Jamaica to Havana are about to start, the U.S. Embassy in Kingston informs its staff that it is illegal for any U.S. citizen or permanent U.S. resident to spend money for travel to Cuba for purchases of goods or services without special permission from the Treasury Department. Increasing numbers of U.S. citizens are by-passing travel restrictions by going via third countries. Cuba is expanding its tourist industry to obtain hard currency. Last December, the

Cuban government announced that, in some areas such as tourism, it will allow foreign ownership of more than 50 percent of joint ventures.

March   Namibian President Sam Nujoma makes a state visit to Cuba and invites President Castro to the celebration of the first anniversary of independence on March 21.

March 8   The UN Human Rights Commission ends its annual session, having voted 22 to 6 with 15 abstentions for a U.S.-sponsored resolution to appoint an independent expert to examine conditions in Cuba. Deputy Foreign Minister Raúl Roa Kourí, Cuba's chief delegate at the session, states that Cuba will not accept this resolution because the Human Rights Commission is treating Cuba in a different manner than it treats other countries.

March 18   The *Wall Street Journal* reports that a federal grand jury in Atlanta is investigating whether Cargill Inc., the largest privately held company in the United States, violated the Trading With the Enemy Act when it sold Cuban sugar to Venezuela in 1988. Cargill International, based in Geneva, was licensed to trade in Cuban sugar but only if the transactions did not involve bankers or Cargill employees in the United States. It seems that fake documents showed two shiploads of sugar sailed from Galveston, Texas, and a third from Mobile, Alabama, when in fact they sailed from Cuba.

March 18 and 20   Personnel from the Cuban American National Foundation's Exodus program, along with INS officials, go to Ecuador and Grand Cayman to arrange for Cubans living there to move to the United States. To date, more than 7,500 Cubans have taken advantage of this means of migration. Exodus has become the primary and sometimes the only legal means of entry into the United States by Cubans in third countries. (*See* May 20, 1988)

March 20   Air Force Major Orestes Lorenzo Pérez flies a Cuban MiG to the U.S. military base at Key West and asks for political asylum, the first defection in a fighter plane since October 1969. State Department representative Douglas Gray says the plane will be returned to Cuba.

March 22   Cuba and Yemen try but fail to have all restrictions on food and humanitarian aid to Iraq formally abolished, as UN

Under Secretary General Martti Ahtisaari recommended in a report a day earlier. The report says Iraq is in a pre-industrial condition, "near apocalyptic."

March 27 To resolve the lawsuit filed June 5, 1990, the Treasury Department agrees to end its ban on the sale of Cuban art in the United States, and issues a new regulation allowing importation, with the exception of sculpture valued at more than $25,000.

March 29 Rodolfo Frometa Caballero is released from a Cuban prison and flies to Miami in April. He was arrested in Cuba in 1981 while trying to carry out an Alpha 66 plot against President Castro.

April 1 The Cuban Museum of Arts and Culture in Miami faces eviction from a city-owned building today. On March 28, the Miami City Commission voted not to renew the lease. The Commission includes Mayor Xavier Suárez, closely allied with the Cuban American National Foundation.

April 9 A U.S. State Department official informs Cuba that the U.S. government has evidence that Cuba is supplying the FMLN in El Salvador with SAM-16 portable antiaircraft missiles. On April 11, Cuba officially issues a categorical denial to the U.S. government.

April 12-14 To check on preparations for the Pan American Games scheduled for August in Cuba, a U.S. sports delegation travels to Havana. The participants meet with President Castro on April 13.

April 19 Speaking in the Karl Marx Theater in Havana on the 30th anniversary of the Bay of Pigs invasion, President Castro says, "Today many people in the world, especially in the Third World, are realizing how important the existence of the Soviet Union was for them and how the mere existence of that country checked the United States' zeal for domination."

April 23 Cuban exile Virgilio Pablo Paz Romero (*see* September 10, 1990) is arrested as a result of a phone tip from a viewer of TV's "America's Most Wanted."

May The U.S. State Department denies visas to Cuban engineers Alejandro Bilbao Alfonso and Rafael Soler Deschapells to attend the annual convention of the World Association of Nuclear Operators in Atlanta. They were planning to report on the Juraguá nuclear plant in Cienfuegos.

May The U.S. government tells Empresa Brasileira de Aeronautica that if it goes ahead with a deal to sell five of its 30-passenger planes to Cuba, it will no longer be allowed to purchase spare parts for the plane from the United States. The Brazilian company cancels the sale.

May Scholars from the Cuban exile community travel to Havana for the annual meeting of the Caribbean Studies Association.

May 14 A group of Cuban Americans, calling themselves "Brothers to the Rescue," holds a press conference to announce that they are flying single-engine planes over the Straits of Florida searching for Cubans in rafts or small boats and then notifying the U.S. Coast Guard, which can come to the rescue. Because of the worsening economic situation in Cuba and the slow rate at which the U.S. authorities process visas, increasing numbers of Cubans are trying to reach Florida on unseaworthy vessels.

May 20 In the White House Oval Office, President Bush meets with Cuban Americans and delivers a message to be broadcast to Cuba on Radio Martí. He lists the current conditions for normalization of relations: free elections, freeing political prisoners, putting "democracy to a test."

May 20 In the *Washington Post*, columnists Rowland Evans and Robert Novak claim U.S. spy satellites have discovered one or more Soviet SS-20 missiles in Cuba. White House spokesperson Marlin Fitzwater denies the report.

May 21 Federal Judge James Lawrence King enjoins the city of Miami from evicting the Cuban Museum of Arts and Culture.

May 25 Cuba's last troops in Angola leave for home, five weeks before the deadline of June 30 and a week before the Angolan government and UNITA are scheduled to sign armistice accords.

May 27 At a ceremony to honor returning troops and to officially close Operation Carlota, Armed Forces Commander Raúl Castro says Cuba lost 2,077 troops in the war.

June 5 In a letter published in the *Washington Post*, José Antonio Arbesú Fraga, chief of the Cuban Interests Section in Washington, responds to the May 20 Evans and Novak column alleging that Cuba has Soviet SS-20 missiles. With both the White House and the State Department denying any evidence that would validate that story, Arbesú charges that Evans and Novak are promoting "the ridiculous and dangerous belief that Cuba poses a nuclear threat to the United States."

June 9 *Granma* announces that Cuba has been reelected to the UN Human Rights Commission. Cuba's current term ends December 31. Now it will have another three-year term beginning January 1, 1992. Cuba's election was supported by 38 of the 54 members of the Commission.

June 13 In Washington seeking money, Salvadoran President Alfredo Cristiani, member of the rightwing Arena Party, says he believes Cuba supplied Soviet-made surface-to-air missiles (SAM-16s) to the FMLN. On June 17, the Cuban Foreign Ministry states that, since its April 9 accusation, the U.S. government "has avoided presenting proof to back this imputation because there is no such proof."

June 19 Five Cubans steal a crop duster and fly to Miami International Airport. The U.S. government files no hijacking charges.

June 20 Appearing before the House Subcommittee on Western Hemisphere Affairs, Assistant Secretary of State for Inter-American Affairs Bernard Aronson testifies that Soviet aid to Cuba will not cease because Cuba is too valuable strategically. He says the intelligence facility at Lourdes, Cuba, is run by a Soviet brigade of 2,800 military personnel and is Moscow's most sophisticated intelligence facility outside its borders. He notes that the Soviet Union relies on Cuba for sugar, nickel, citrus fruit, seafood and medical care, including treatment for the victims of the Chernobyl nuclear accident.

June 20 For four and a half hours, ABC television's Jim McKay meets with President Castro for an interview to be broadcast July 28. Castro says ABC offered $10 million to Cuba for the right to broadcast the Pan American Games but that the State Department informed ABC that it could not pay any money to Cuba.

June 20 Eight of the ten Cuban American state legislators from Dade County, Florida (home to 54 percent of Cuban immigrants in the United States), urge President Bush to demand that the Soviet Union oust President Castro from Cuba in exchange for U.S. aid. At a news conference in Little Havana, they say that Moscow must do three things to qualify for aid: suspend aid to Cuba; pull Soviet troops from Cuba; and help overthrow or "eliminate" President Castro. The word "eliminate" is used by

Florida State Senator Lincoln Díaz-Balart, who is elected to the House of Representatives in November 1992.

June 22 Visiting Cuba, a Puerto Rican brigade issues a resolution to increase their opposition to the U.S. embargo.

June 23 The *Miami Herald* reports that the U.S. government holds about $134 million in 1,300 frozen accounts belonging to Cubans (*see* July 8, 1963). Treasury Department officials say owners or heirs can request the money if they have permanently moved out of Cuba.

July Cuban Deputy Foreign Minister Ramón Sánchez Parodi participates as a guest at the meeting of the Caribbean Community and Common Market nations (CARICOM) on St. Kitts-Nevis.

July 1 The Warsaw Pact, the alliance of socialist nations (Bulgaria, Czechoslovakia, East Germany, Hungary, Poland, Romania and the USSR) that was founded in 1955 as a counterweight to NATO, ceases to exist.

July 2 UN Secretary General Pérez de Cuéllar announces the appointment of Colombian diplomat Rafael Rivas Posada as the official observer of human rights in Cuba.

July 2 In a *New York Times* opinion piece, Sergo Mikoyan, son of Anastas I. Mikoyan, writes that "no self-respecting country would accept" the proposition that the Soviet Union "abandon Cuba so that the U.S. can more easily bring it to its knees." He remarks that "social conditions in Cuba are incomparably better than in those countries that U.S. troops so splendidly defended from Saddam Hussein's arbitrariness."

July 7 Thirty miles from Miami, the Coast Guard stops a leaky fishing boat carrying 161 Haitians and two Cubans whom the Haitians had rescued from a raft. The Cubans are quickly allowed to enter the United States. But the Coast Guard returns 152 of the Haitians to Haiti. Among the other nine, six are taken to Miami hospitals and three are being considered for political asylum.

July 10 Mikhail Gorbachev, now the president of the Union of Soviet Sovereign Republics (new name of the former Union of Soviet Socialist Republics), attends the inauguration of Boris Yeltsin as president of the Republic of Russia.

July 16 In his confirmation hearing before the Senate Foreign Relations Committee, Ambassador-designate to the Soviet Union Robert S. Strauss testifies that he will oppose Soviet "support for Castro's brutality in Cuba."

July 17 On the eve of an historic Ibero-American Summit Conference, it is announced in Mexico that Cuba is reestablishing consular relations with Colombia and Chile, a step toward full diplomatic relations.

July 18-19 President Castro attends the First Ibero-American Summit Conference in Guadalajara, Mexico, along with leaders from 20 other Spanish- and Portuguese-speaking countries. OAS Secretary General Mario Baena Soares says, "It's time to reconsider the reincorporation of Cuba into the OAS. The conditions of the 1990s are not the same as those of the 1960s."

July 26 ANC leader Nelson Mandela gives a speech at Cuba's annual celebration of the Moncada attack. He says the world should maintain economic sanctions against South Africa. President Bush removed most U.S. sanctions July 10. Again praising Cubans for the victory at Cuito Cuanavale in Angola in 1988, Mandela says that historic victory gave Angola the possibility of peace; enabled Namibia to achieve independence; destroyed the myth of the invincibility of South Africa's apartheid regime; and created the conditions that led to his own release from prison.

July 29 The State Department calls a halt to new applications for U.S. tourist visas in Havana, blaming this on a backlog created by Cuba's decision to lower age limits for travel. Within a few days of the decision, Cuba lowers the age even further, allowing travel abroad for anyone aged 20 or over. (*See* May 1, 1992)

July 30 In Federal District Court in Washington, Cuban American Virgilio Paz Romero pleads guilty to conspiring to assassinate Chilean diplomat Orlando Letelier in 1976. On September 12, he is sentenced to 12 years in prison. An Omega 7 leader at the time of the murders of Letelier and Ronni Moffitt, his aliases include Virgil Romero, Alejandro Bontenpi and Frank Baez.

July 30 On the opening day of a Summit Meeting between President Bush and President Gorbachev in Moscow, Bush praises Gorbachev for introducing reforms that have changed the world. Urging an end to Soviet aid to Cuba, Bush says, "The United

States poses no threat to Cuba. Therefore, there is no need for the Soviet Union to funnel millions of dollars in military aid to Cuba."

July 31 *New York Newsday* editorializes for an end to the U.S. ban on travel to Cuba.

July 31 Speaking at a hearing before the Foreign Relations Committee's Subcommittee on Western Hemisphere Affairs, Jorge Mas Canosa proposes a "Cuban Democracy Act" that would tighten the embargo. Aiming to forestall any rapprochement between Washington and Havana as the Soviet Union collapses, the Cuban American National Foundation is collaborating with the office of Representative Robert Torricelli, chair of the subcommittee, to make sure that U.S. policy toward Cuba does not veer from its consistent aim of controlling Cuba. (*See* February 5, 1992)

July 31-August 3 The Latin American Parliament meets for its 13th Regular General Assembly in Cartagena, Colombia. On August 2, it votes 154 to 27 with 30 abstentions for a resolution expressing "solidarity with the people of Cuba" and asking for an end to the U.S. embargo. The Parliament unanimously elects Cuba to preside over the Standing Commission on Health, Labor and Social Security.

August 2-18 The Pan American Games, for which Cuba bid in 1986 before its current economic difficulties could be foreseen, take place in Havana and Santiago de Cuba with the participation of about 5,000 athletes from 39 countries. Some 20,000 foreigners are present. The United States wins the most medals, 352, while Cuba comes in second with 265; Cuba wins more golds, 140, while the United States has 130. According to the *New York Times* on February 3, 1992, the Bush Administration shares intelligence information with Cuba to thwart a terrorist plot to plant a bomb at the Games.

August 9 The *Miami Herald* reports that, with the increase of travel, CBT Charters joins Marazul Charters and ABC Charters in offering flights between Miami and Havana.

August 19 Cuban Ambassador Alarcón asks the United Nations to place the issue of the U.S. embargo against Cuba on the agenda to be discussed by the General Assembly, which opens its next session in September.

August 20 At the height of an abortive coup against President Gorbachev, President Bush claims that Cuba "supported what's happening in Moscow." UN Ambassador Ricardo Alarcón responds, "President Bush is not well informed on this matter or [he is] practicing an old American game, which is simply to lie. We have not expressed any position."

August 21 The State Department declares that the embargo against Cuba is not an appropriate topic for discussion at the UN General Assembly. In response, Ambassador Alarcón submits official U.S. documents showing how Washington interrupted or provoked cancellation of various trade agreements between Cuba and firms from third countries to obtain equipment and medical products.

August 29 The *Boston Globe* editorializes for ending the embargoes against travel and trade with Cuba, urging Washington to "extend a neighborly hand to the hard-pressed Cubans" and concluding: "Renewing ties would be good for them and for us."

September 6 Conducting the trial of former Panamanian leader Manuel Noriega in Florida, Judge William M. Hoeveler rules that the defense will be allowed to introduce evidence that Noriega "regularly acted as an intermediary between the United States and Cuba, often meeting with [President Castro] at the behest or with the approval of the United States."

September 11 Soviet President Gorbachev announces he intends to withdraw the Soviet training brigade from Cuba. The Cuban Foreign Ministry states that Gorbachev's remarks "were not preceded by consultations or any prior notice, which constitutes inappropriate behavior from the point of view of international standards as well as the agreements existing between the two states." Bush Administration officials say they hope this will lead to the downfall of President Castro. On the following day, Soviet Foreign Minister Boris Pankjin says the Soviet Union wants the United States to match the Soviet military withdrawal from Cuba by removing U.S. troops from Guantánamo Bay and halting military maneuvers in the region.

September 18 As requested by Cuba, the organizing committee of the UN General Assembly unanimously approves putting the embargo on the General Assembly's agenda.

September 22 Responding to the Soviet plan to remove troops from Cuba, *Granma*, in a long editorial, reports the history of the Soviet brigade in Cuba and its relationship to the U.S. military occupation of Cuban territory at Guantánamo. The editorial states that "we could be moving toward a world order in which small Third World countries like Cuba, whose social system is not to the liking of the United States, have no alternative except to risk disappearing; and in which there is no room for ideological loyalties or even the most elemental ethical principles, without which our civilization will be threatened with the possible emergence of a new barbarism based on the United States' technological might and hegemonic delirium."

September 23 Addressing the UN General Assembly, President Bush calls President Castro "the lone holdout in an otherwise democratic hemisphere, a man who hasn't adapted to a world that has no use for totalitarian tyranny."

September 24 Covering the trial of Manuel Noriega in Florida, the Associated Press reports, "Testimony by Manuel Noriega's former aide [Lt. Col. Luis del Cid] fell apart under defense questioning yesterday, casting doubt on the government's charge that Fidel Castro mediated a drug dispute between the Panamanian leader and [drug] traffickers." The AP story continues, "Del Cid then admitted his account was wrong. 'It was an error, it was a mistake on my part,' he said." Nevertheless, del Cid's earlier, erroneous account continues to be used during the following years by U.S. media, including the *New York Times*, to indicate some connection between President Castro and drug trafficking.

September 27 The Treasury Department's Office of Foreign Assets Control tightens the embargo by limiting the amount of money that U.S. citizens may send to Cubans for financing travel to the United States to $500, including $200 to $250 for an airplane ticket. The same limit is placed on the amount that U.S. citizens may pay to the Cuban government for travel to Cuba. The new rules also cut from $500 to $300 the amount that relatives may send to family in Cuba for general support over a three-month period and prohibit Cuban visitors from returning to Cuba with more hard currency than they brought to the United States.

September 28 The *Washington Post* reports that the Soviet Union plans to keep personnel at Lourdes, an intelligence post in Cuba. About 2,100 Soviet technicians are there now.

October 10-14 The Fourth Congress of the Cuban Communist Party takes place in Santiago de Cuba with 1,667 of the 1,800 delegates in attendance. The Congress proposes various measures to try to deal with the dire economic conditions that Cuba faces while at the same time liberalizing election laws (*see* July 10-12, 1992) and other aspects of Cuban society, including a decision to allow religious believers to join the Communist Party.

October 11 Seeking to sell CNN International and TNT South in 13 Cuban hotels, the Turner Broadcasting System files a lawsuit in the Federal District Court in Washington to force the Treasury Department to allow it to sell news and entertainment programming in Cuba. Two weeks earlier the Treasury Department turned down Turner's request for a license on the grounds that selling the satellite programming would be "contrary" to U.S. foreign policy. In 1988, Congress exempted informational materials from the embargo. The Treasury Department argues that satellite transmissions remain covered by the embargo while Turner argues that they should be treated like videotapes, which are now allowed to be sold in Cuba. The Treasury Department currently permits Turner to exchange news transmissions with Cuba; Turner pulls Cuban news feeds from a Soviet satellite while Cuba pulls unscrambled CNN feeds from a U.S. satellite. The September letter to Turner Broadcasting officers from R. Richard Newcomb, director of the Treasury Department's Office of Foreign Assets Control, declared the new request a "substantially different arrangement" because TNT South in hotels would "result in the enhancement of Cuba's tourist industry, contrary to the objectives of the embargo."

October 23 In Cozumel, Mexico, at the invitation of the presidents of the Group of Three — César Gaviria of Colombia, Salinas de Gortari of Mexico and Carlos Andrés Pérez of Venezuela — President Castro meets with the three leaders to discuss, as *Granma* puts it, "the integration of Cuba into the Latin American context."

October 30 The House of Representatives approves the Export Administration Act that includes the Mack Amendment. Already approved by the Senate, the legislation now goes to a House-Senate conference committee.

October 30 Cuban consul Omar Morales arrives in the Colombian capital, marking resumption of relations after a ten-year freeze.

November 10 Estonia and Cuba establish diplomatic relations. The Baltic states of Estonia, Latvia and Lithuania have all declared their independence from the Soviet Union.

November 13 UN Ambassador Alarcón postpones discussion of the U.S. embargo at the General Assembly for one year because of pressure on Cuba's friends in the UN that would prevent them from taking a position against the United States at this time. By the time the embargo is discussed and condemned by the UN General Assembly in November 1992, the "Cuban Democracy Act" to tighten the embargo has already become law.

November 25 Following the military coup that ousted President Aristide in Haiti, the Bush Administration authorizes a military task force to go to Guantánamo Naval Base to build a tent city for housing Haitian refugees. The Coast Guard takes Haitians picked up at sea to Guantánamo. Speaking of this policy on December 6 before the Federation of University Students, President Castro says, "What an empire of hypocrites that talks about human rights and international law while converting the Guantánamo Naval Base, an illegally occupied Cuban territory, into a Haitian concentration camp."

December The Bush Administration initiates new negotiations about migration with Cuba.

December 2-3 During his first visit to Cuba, Senator Larry Pressler (R-South Dakota), a member of the Foreign Relations Committee, meets with President Castro in Havana for more than five hours.

December 8 The leaders of Russia, Ukraine and Byelorussia (soon Belarus) announce the death of the Union of Soviet Sovereign Republics and invite the other republics to join them in the "Commonwealth of Independent States" (CIS). As more republics join, they agree Russia will assume the former USSR's permanent seat on the UN Security Council while the other states will seek separate UN membership. Boris Yeltsin becomes the most powerful figure of the Commonwealth. With nothing left to govern, Mikhail Gorbachev resigns on December 25.

December 9-12 The Methodist Church in Havana's Vedado district is the site of the Continental Meeting for Pastoral Accompaniment with Cuba's Churches and People, attended by more than 130 delegates and guests from the Americas, including the United States. President Castro and other Cuban leaders meet with the participants, who issue a statement opposing the U.S. embargo.

December 29 After landing a boat carrying weapons, three members of Comandos L — Pedro De la Caridad Alvarez Pedroso, Eduardo Díaz Betancourt and Daniel Santovenia Fernández — are captured near Jucaro in Matanzas province. Founded by Tony Cuesta in 1962, Comandos L has carried out dozens of raids against Cuba. The three men on this raid are convicted January 11, 1992. The Cuban Supreme Court upholds the death sentences for two of them. The Council of State commutes one of the two death sentences on January 19. Díaz Betancourt is executed by firing squad on January 20. The other two are sentenced to 30 years, the maximum prison sentence for anyone in Cuba. With evidence of illegality so obvious, the FBI says it is investigating Comandos L.

Late December The Bush Administration authorizes payment to Cuba by AT&T of a limited share of telephone tolls. In 1990, the State and Treasury Departments approved payment to Cuba of $620,000 for installation and maintenance of the fiber optic cable to Cuba that has been in place since April 1989, but had held up permission for a toll share. On February 6, 1992, AT&T announces that Cuba is refusing the deal. The main obstacle is U.S. refusal to turn over more than $80 million in a blocked escrow account for revenue owed to Cuba from phone calls made since 1966 when AT&T was exempted from the U.S. embargo.

1992

January 1 Cuba's second three-year term on the UN Human Rights Commission begins.

January 3 Cuban pilot Germán Pompa steals a helicopter and flies 33 of his relatives and friends to Miami.

January 9-12 Cuban, Russian and U.S. officials meet for the fifth in a series of conferences to discuss the 1962 Missile Crisis, with President Castro taking part for the first time. Castro says Cuban leaders in October 1962 did not know how few missiles the Soviet Union possessed and therefore did not realize that placing missiles in Cuba changed the global strategic situation.

January 18 Even before Representative Torricelli introduces the "Cuban Democracy Act," the *Miami Herald* editorializes against it.

January 20 As a result of the January 18 editorial, Jorge Mas Canosa launches a campaign against the *Miami Herald* and its sister publication, *El Nuevo Herald*, accusing the newspaper's publisher, David Lawrence Jr., and other executives of being tools of Fidel Castro. Death and bomb threats follow against Lawrence and the other *Herald* executives. The newspaper's vending machines are vandalized and smeared with feces.

January 25 Thousands of people fill the Jacob Javits Convention Center in New York City to overflowing for a rally calling for normalization of relations with Cuba, an end to the embargo, and the right of U.S. citizens to travel to Cuba.

January 26 *Granma* reports that Cuba's infant mortality rate in 1991 remained at 10.7, the same as in 1990.

February 3 In his opening argument for the defense in the trial of Manuel Noriega (*see* September 24, 1991), Attorney John May says Noriega met with President Castro in July 1984 not to mediate a drug dispute as the indictment alleges but to discuss the volatile political situation in Central America; Noriega informed the CIA of the meeting ahead of time, brought up the points that the CIA wanted Castro to know, and was debriefed by the CIA afterward.

February 4 Scenarios prepared by the Defense Department and issued to the U.S. Armed Forces imagine possible future conflicts for which the U.S. military must be prepared, including some "irrational" act by Cuba as it faces "intense crisis." On February 18, the Defense Department follows up with a draft "Defense Planning Guidance," including: "Cuba's growing domestic crisis holds out the prospect for positive change, but over the near term, Cuba's tenuous internal situation is likely to generate new challenges to U.S. policy. Consequently, our programs must provide capabilities to meet a variety of Cuban contingencies which could include an attempted repetition of the Mariel boat-lift, a military provocation against the U.S. or an American ally, or political instability and internal conflict in Cuba."

February 4 The Mack Amendment contained in the Export Administration Act has reached a joint Senate-House conference committee (*see* October 30, 1991).

February 5 Representative Torricelli (D-New Jersey) introduces the "Cuban Democracy Act" (*see* July 31, 1991) in the House of Representatives. Bob Graham (D-Florida) introduces the same legislation in the Senate. The bill would tighten the embargo in many different ways, including punishment of third nations which trade with Cuba and prohibition of trade with Cuba by U.S.-owned subsidiaries in third countries, thus incorporating the Mack Amendment (*see* July 20, 1989). Cuban Americans divide sharply over this legislation. While the Cuban American National Foundation helped write the CDA, many Cuban Americans, even those who oppose President Castro, believe that tightening the embargo will only lead to more economic hardship for the Cuban people. For Torricelli, this is precisely the purpose; later, he tells a Georgetown University audience that he wants to "wreak havoc on that island."

February 16 Cuban police capture three Cuban Americans — David Quero Martínez, Lázaro Bitón Martínez, Alan Pico Treto — and charge them with drug trafficking and illegal entry. The police seize 629 pounds of cocaine which, according to the three, was dropped from an airplane and hidden on the island. The exiles arrived in a fast launch with, according to their story, the aim of picking up the drugs.

February 23 Three men break into the radio station in Miami from which Francisco Aruca buys air time for Radio Progreso, beat an employee and damage equipment.

March According to newspapers in India, U.S. Agriculture Secretary Edward Madigan has informed the Indian government that one reason the U.S. government will not sell subsidized wheat to India is that India has supplied rice to Cuba.

March 3 In Geneva, the UN Human Rights Commission votes 23 to 8 with 21 abstentions and one absentee for a U.S.-sponsored resolution accusing Cuba of suppressing political opposition and calling on it to cooperate with the UN special investigator. The role of the special investigator, Rafael Rivas Posada, is upgraded to special rapporteur, a level appointed by the Commission only for extremely serious cases, but he soon resigns.

March 5 Jorge Mas Canosa shares the dais with President Bush at a $1,000-a-plate fund-raiser for Bush's re-election campaign. Bush has not endorsed either the Mack Amendment or the "Cuban Democracy Act" because both would outlaw trade with Cuba by U.S. subsidiaries in third countries, a measure opposed by allies such as Britain, France and Canada.

March 8 Jorge Mas Canosa has dinner with Representative Stephen Solarz (D-New York), one of the co-sponsors of the "Cuban Democracy Act," and offers to provide help for the presidential campaign of Arkansas Governor Bill Clinton in Little Havana if Clinton will endorse the CDA.

March 25 At a House Foreign Affairs Committee hearing about the "Cuban Democracy Act," several Cuban Americans testify against the legislation, including Alfredo Durán and Ramón Cernuda. Durán, a Miami attorney who works closely with dissidents in Cuba, testifies that his main concern about the CDA is that Cubans might interpret the provisions as an attempt by the U.S. government to unduly influence the choice of successors to Fidel Castro. Cernuda is the representative in the United States for the Cuban Committee for Human Rights and National Reconciliation, a coalition of dissident groups in Cuba that oppose the CDA.

April The Cuban Studies Program of the Johns Hopkins School of Advanced International Studies publishes a new study, *New Opportunities for U.S.-Cuban Trade*, by Donna Rich Kaplowitz and Michael Kaplowitz. A follow-up to the June 1988 study, the report concludes that U.S. corporations could engage in between $1.3 billion and $2 billion worth of bilateral trade with Cuba during the first year after the embargo is lifted. Cuban trade with U.S. subsidiaries in third countries, a target of both the Mack Amendment and the "Cuban Democracy Act," has increased from $292 million in 1980 to $718 million in 1991. Almost 75 percent of this trade is in food and medicines. Cuba has more than 200 agreements with foreign companies for joint ventures.

April 1 The battle for the airwaves escalates when TV Martí makes its daytime broadcast debut by broadcasting at 1:30 p.m. on Cuba's Channel 13 for two and a half hours (and again the next day). Cuba jams the broadcast within seconds. The usual predawn broadcasts continue from 3:45 to 6:00 a.m. They are also jammed. Because Cuba has had to limit daytime broad-casts due to its energy shortage, USIA seized this opportunity. In turn, Cuba begins broadcasting Radio Havana on some frequencies on the AM band in the United States, heard as far away as Iowa.

April 2 Cuba charges that TV Martí violated international broadcast laws when it made its daytime debut.

April 2 The *Miami Herald* reports that Cuba's membership will be discussed at the next board meeting of the Caribbean Tourism Organization in June because Cuba recognized the government of Grenada in March.

April 3 The *Washington Post* editorializes against the "Cuban Democracy Act," calling for a "transition to democracy" that "is accomplished peacefully and by Cuban not American means."

April 6 For the second time, Federal Judge Sterling Johnson Jr. of Federal District Court in Brooklyn rules that Haitians held at Guantánamo have the right to legal counsel. The Bush Administration argues that, since U.S. forces are holding the Haitians on

Cuban territory — not U.S. territory — they are not entitled to legal rights of people in the United States and its territories.

April 7 Cuban Americans Andrés Gómez of the Antonio Maceo Brigade and Walfrido Moreno, head of the Alliance of Cuban Workers, present to the chairs of the House Foreign Affairs and Senate Foreign Relations Committees — Democrats Dante Fascell of Florida and Claiborne Pell of Rhode Island — 18,500 signatures of Cuban Americans in the Miami area who favor an end to the embargo. Growing numbers of Cuban Americans are opposing the embargo because of the effects of what is called the "double embargo" — the continuing U.S. embargo plus the loss of CMEA trade.

April 13 As Cuba is broadcasting a test pattern on its Channel 13 frequency, TV Martí interferes. Cuba promptly jams the U.S. broadcast and protests the interference.

April 14 The USIA halts TV Martí daytime transmissions. Tony Navarro, head of the Office of Cuba Broadcasting that oversees both TV Martí and Radio Martí, says he hopes Cuba will not retaliate for the April 13 interference.

April 14 Cuba and Kazakhstan establish diplomatic relations. According to the April 18 *Miami Herald*, Cuba has formalized relations with 12 former Soviet republics since the breakup of the Soviet Union.

April 18 President Bush announces that he is asking the Treasury Department to formulate regulations to forbid ships that contain Cuban goods or goods in which Cuba has an interest from loading or unloading at U.S. ports. These regulations are issued by the Treasury Department on April 24. At the same time, Bush authorizes family-to-family shipments of food, medicines, toiletries and other "humanitarian" items via charter flights directly from Miami. The value of the packages cannot exceed $100 and fees paid to Cuba cannot exceed five dollars per pound. No more than two bottles of medicine can be sent in each package and there can be no more than one package a month. Bush's implementation of these two measures that are also part of the "Cuban Democracy Act" is evidently aimed at placating CDA supporters without endorsing the legislation.

April 21 Deputy Foreign Minister Raúl Roa Kourí says Cuba will not cooperate with the special rapporteur appointed by the

United Nations to investigate human rights in Cuba because the appointment is "discriminatory treatment," part of a U.S. "vendetta."

April 22 Spain's new consul in Miami, Fermín Pireto Castro, says protests by Cuban exiles over Spanish investments in Cuba are understandable but that such investments cannot be limited without infringing on principles of free enterprise. Exile protests have intensified because President Castro plans to attend the second Summit Meeting of Latin American leaders in Seville in July. Alpha 66 is attempting to organize a consumer boycott of Spanish products and the Spanish airline, Iberia.

April 23 As Bill Clinton arrives in Miami to attend fund-raisers, a *Miami Herald* editorial asks him to "please think twice" about embracing the "Cuban Democracy Act." But, running low on campaign funds following the New Hampshire primary, presidential candidate Bill Clinton endorses the legislation at a fund-raising banquet in Miami hosted by the Cuban American National Foundation. This affair contributes $125,000 to his campaign in addition to the $150,000 raised at a private fund-raiser earlier in the day in Coral Gables.

April 23 The *Wall Street Journal* reports about a new Florida law that requires any firm wishing to issue securities in Florida to reveal whether it or any subsidiary does business in Cuba. Florida State Senator Lincoln Díaz-Balart acknowledges that U.S. firms are anxious about losing ground to foreign companies that are trading with Cuba but urges them to "be patient." He warns that those "who are now collaborating" will be at the end of the line after the current Cuban government falls.

April 24-May 2 Participants in the 23rd contingent of the Venceremos Brigade work in construction and agriculture.

April 27 In a letter to the UN Security Council, Ambassador Alarcón asks that the U.S. government extradite Orlando Bosch and Luis Posada Carriles and that the Security Council take action about terrorist acts against Cuba by groups trained and based in the United States. (*See* May 21)

May 1 Saying the backlog of applicants has been cleared, U.S. State Department representative Margaret Tutwiler announces that the United States will resume processing general non-immigrant visas in Cuba May 26. (*See* July 29, 1991)

May 4 Reuters reports that Cuban journalist Nicanor León Cotayo, who specializes in the U.S. embargo against Cuba, says the embargo has cost Cuba more than $20 billion in lost trade and financing, the equivalent of about three times Cuba's debt to western countries and Japan. Deputy Foreign Trade Minister Alberto Betancourt says Cuba's convertible hard-currency debt to those creditors is a little over $7 billion. Negotiations about the debt have been blocked since 1986 because Cuba says it cannot afford to repay without first receiving guarantees of fresh money from creditors. Betancourt points out that the U.S. government tries to keep Cuba out of world markets for nickel and biotechnology products.

May 6 The *Miami Herald* reports that the Bush Administration has reached agreement with the Cuban American National Foundation and key House Democrats (like Democratic Representatives Torricelli and Fascell) on the "Cuban Democracy Act." Democratic presidential candidate Bill Clinton's endorsement of the CDA on April 23 precipitated this change.

May 6 At the White House, Armando Pérez Roura, news director of Miami's WAQI-Radio Mambi, heads a group of Cuban Americans who present a petition to President Bush asking for an end to the ban on armed action against Cuba from U.S. soil, exempting Cuba from the Neutrality Act. Immediately afterward, Bush writes to Pérez Roura and Andrés Vargas Gómez, leaders of the petition drive: "I will do everything I can to support those striving within the law to free Cuba from Castro's illegitimate, desperate grip." He says "there is nothing in the Kennedy-Khrushchev understandings" that prevents Cubans from removing President Castro and freely electing new leaders. Pérez Roura is among the Cuban Americans invited by the Bush Administration to attend the signing of the "Cuban Democracy Act" in October. In 1991 he co-founded *Unidad Cubana* (Cuban Unity), a coalition of about 80 anti-Castro groups, with the aim of using militant methods such as military force to overthrow the Cuban government.

May 7 Former KGB operative General Oleg Kalugin urges Washington to increase propaganda against President Castro, who, he says, has no more than three years left in power. He tells reporters that Russian President Boris Yeltsin should take a stronger stand on condemning human rights abuses in Cuba.

May 13 The General Accounting Office (GAO), the non-partisan investigative arm of Congress, issues a report saying TV Martí appears to be a waste of taxpayers' money and is not presenting balanced programs. The GAO says it is being seen by few Cubans and "doesn't practice the pluralism that it preaches." The Voice of America overseer of TV Martí, Antonio Navarro, defends a January 27 program that three GAO consultants call skewed: TV Martí spent 20 minutes covering the January 25 counter-demonstration sponsored by the Cuban American National Foundation outside the Javits Center and only two minutes on the larger rally inside. Navarro points out that the *New York Times* and the major television networks also emphasized the CANF demonstration. TV Martí's current budget is $18.4 million a year for three hours of predawn programming (jammed in Havana).

May 18 At a news conference, Cuban Vice-President José Ramón Fernández reports that Coca-Cola Co., an official sponsor of the 1992 track and field World Cup in Cuba on September 25-27, will not be able to supply soft drinks for the event because of the U.S. embargo. The Mexican subsidiary of Coca-Cola was to have sold soft drinks, T-shirts, sun shades and other promotional items. Coca-Cola is one of 12 designated sponsors for the competition, among eight international teams, including one from the United States. Alberto Juantorena, vice-president of the Cuban National Sports Institute, tells reporters that Cuba is demanding the right to receive the same sponsorship benefits as any nation that hosts international sports events.

May 18 The Indian government announces that it will sell 10,000 tons of rice to Cuba despite U.S. disapproval.

May 20 The *Miami Herald* reports that David Moya, who left Cuba in July 1991 and now lives in Miami, has received a $60,000 grant from the National Endowment for Democracy (NED) to publish *Joven Cubano*, the first magazine aimed at fomenting dissent among Cuban youth. NED was established by the Reagan Administration in 1983 to promote "democratic" institutions around the world through grants of federal funds. The Cuban American National Foundation receives hundreds of thousands of dollars from NED through groups associated with it — for example, the European Coalition for Human Rights in Cuba.

May 21 In the House Foreign Relations Committee, Representative Ted Weiss successfully includes an amendment to the "Cuban Democracy Act" that would exempt the sale of medicines and medical equipment from the U.S. embargo (*see* June 4). Without this change, the CDA would allow only donation of medicines to nongovernment organizations, which in Cuba amount to less than 10 percent of the public health sector. The chair of the committee, Dante Fascell (D-Florida), adjourns the session rather than allow a vote on a second amendment, proposed by Representative Bill Alexander (D-Arizona), that would allow sales of food and agricultural products to Cuba.

May 21 The UN Security Council takes up the subject of the bombing of the Cuban passenger jet in 1976 and Cuba's request for the deportation of Orlando Bosch and Luis Posada. Ambassador Alarcón gives the Council a copy of a U.S. Justice Department document dated June 23, 1989, in which Acting Associate Attorney General Joe D. Whitley outlined his decision to deport Bosch, writing, "The October 6, 1976, Cuban airline bombing was CORU operation under the direction of Bosch. CORU is the name of Bosch's terrorist outfit." Whitley concluded, "We could not shelter Dr Bosch and maintain our credibility in this respect." The Justice Department's decision was upheld in Federal District Court, but both have been overruled by President Bush. The meeting ends without a vote.

May 24 President Bush authorizes the U.S. Coast Guard to repatriate all Haitians stopped at sea to Haiti without offering any opportunity for political asylum or for continuing their voyage. They may apply for asylum only at the U.S. Embassy in Port-au-Prince.

June 4 President Bush sends a letter to House lawmakers supporting the "Cuban Democracy Act" with minor differences.

June 4 The House Foreign Affairs Committee approves the "Cuban Democracy Act" on a voice vote. Before the vote, Representative Torricelli thwarts the May 21 Weiss amendment with the passage of another amendment that would require on-site monitoring by U.S. officials of the use of any U.S. medical supplies imported by Cuba. Torricelli argues that there is no way of knowing that

President Castro would not misuse medical products by, for example, converting medical equipment into torture devices.

June 6 More than a dozen waves of F-16 fighter planes drop 500-pound explosives into the waters off Key Largo, Florida. Environmentalists had protested against the plan to bomb because of dolphins, whales, turtles and other wild ife. According to an Air Force official on June 8, these waters may be a regular target for bombing.

June 9 The Caribbean News Agency reports that St. Vincent and the Grenadines and Cuba have established diplomatic relations.

June 10 In Havana, President Castro welcomes about 125 foreign businesspeople, many from the United States, on their arrival for the Euromoney conference, briefings on investment opportunities that remain largely forbidden due to the U.S. embargo. Arranged by the London-based Euromoney Publications as a three-day seminar on investing and trading with Cuba, the conference began by meeting June 8-9 in Cancún, Mexico. During the Havana day trip, the Cuban government pays for all expenses so that the U.S. participants are not violating the embargo. About 80 U.S. companies or subsidiaries participate, including Boeing; Scott Paper Co. Costa Rica; Pfizer; Squibb; Kodak Panama; SmithKline; Ralston Purina; Philip Morris; Federal Express; and Joseph Strain, director of marketing and sales for the Jacksonville (Florida) Port Authority. Executives from Japan, Europe, Latin America, Taiwan and Hungary are also present. Kirby Jones, who chairs the conference, arranged trips to Cuba for more than 200 representatives of U.S. companies in the late 1970s and early 1980s.

June 11 The Miami City Commission votes unanimously to evict the Cuban Museum of Art and Culture so that Miami can convert its building into a fire station.

June 11 In Rio de Janeiro, President Castro arrives for the Earth Summit (the UN Conference on Environment and Development) in which some 35,000 delegates from 78 countries are participating. On the following day, according to the June 13 *New York Times*, Castro "drew cheers when he strode to the platform to denounce the industrialized countries as guilty of most of the world's environmental problems." Speaking on the same day at the Summit, President Bush says he has no apologies for his environmental record. Castro signs the biodiversity treaties while Bush does not.

June 14 In a speech at a Cuban American rally in Union City, New Jersey, broadcast to Cuba over Radio Martí, Jorge Mas Canosa calls on Cuba's Armed Forces to revolt against Fidel Castro and not allow him to return from Brazil. Representative Robert Torricelli (D-New Jersey) tells the audience that in the history books Mas Canosa will be known as the "liberator" of Cuba.

June 15 The *New York Times* editorializes against the "Cuban Democracy Act," calling it "misnamed" and pointing out that there is "something indecent about vociferous exiles living safely in Miami prescribing more pain for their poorer cousins."

June 16 The U.S. Supreme Court rules that U.S. agents can legally kidnap suspects abroad and bring them to the United States for trial. Later, the Cuban Foreign Ministry calls the ruling "a flagrant violation of the principles and norms of international law."

June 16 Representative Howard Berman (D-California) introduces the "Free Trade in Ideas Act" that would end restrictions on travel to any country by U.S. citizens.

June 17 Addressing a joint session of Congress in Washington, Russian President Yeltsin says, "We have corrected the well-known imbalances in relations with Cuba. At present that country is one of our Latin American partners. Our commerce with Cuba is based on universally accepted principles and is conducted to mutual benefit using world prices."

June 18 The first direct shipment of "humanitarian" packages arrives in Havana aboard a flight by ABC Charters, the first company to receive a license under the order signed by President Bush on April 18. The Cuban Ecumenical Council will distribute the medicines and canned pork sent by the U.S. National Council of Churches of Christ. Cuba is making a distinction between shipments of donated materials and the Bush Administration's proposal of family-to-family shipments. Cuba maintains that family packages and mail should be delivered on regularly scheduled commercial flights.

June 19 The Caribbean Tourism Organization approves membership for Cuba.

June 19 The largest daily newspaper based in Representative Robert Torricelli's New Jersey district, the *Record*, editorializes against Torricelli's "Cuban Democracy Act."

July The State Department continues to regularly deny visas to Cubans, including the head of Cuba's Finlay Institute, Concepción Campa, invited to an International Workshop on Immunology in Atlanta to discuss Cuba's vaccines against meningitis.

July 1-6 The international conference of the Women's International League for Peace and Freedom in La Paz, Bolivia, passes a resolution calling for an immediate end to the U.S. embargo against Cuba.

July 2 The *New York Times* reports that Marine General Richard I. Neal, commander of the U.S. task force at Guantánamo Naval Base, told the *Times* that the number of Haitians remaining in the camps at Guantánamo has dropped from more than 12,000 in June to 848. Of 36,985 Haitians processed at the base since last November, 10,736 have been approved for asylum in the United States. The others either have been or will be returned to Haiti. Within about two weeks, there will remain about 300 Haitians at Guantánamo — those who have tested positive for the HIV virus and their relatives.

July 4 A U.S. Coast Guard cutter enters Cuban waters to rescue four members of Comandos L whose heavily armed boat malfunctioned during one of their secret missions to infiltrate Cuba. The four are led by U.S. citizen Tony Bryant. In August, UN Deputy Ambassador Carlos Zamora presents a protest of this raid to the UN Security Council. Zamora says the U.S. Coast Guard entered Cuban waters without permission and did not notify Cuban authorities until two hours afterward.

July 10-12 The National Assembly of People's Power meets and approves constitutional revisions, recommended by the October 1991 Fourth Party Congress, including omission of references to a non-existent Soviet Union; the addition of the ideas of Martí alongside those of Marx, Engels and Lenin; guarantees for foreign investments (for example, instead of owning all means of production, the state owns the fundamental means of production); legalization of nongovernmental organizations (NGOs); and liberalization of election laws (*see* October 29).

Cuba becomes the first nation to include resolutions of the Earth Summit in its Constitution.

July 15   In Havana, Marazul Charters delivers a shipment of pediatric antibiotics sent by the U.S.-Cuba Medical Project, based in New York. The antibiotics will be distributed by the Cuban Red Cross to three children's hospitals.

July 22   Unofficially launching his re-election campaign in Bergen County, New Jersey, President Bush vows to a rally at the Three Saints Russian Orthodox Church that if reelected he will be the first U.S. president to "set foot on a free and democratic Cuba." He says the "Castro dictatorship" is "on its last legs."

July 23-24   In Madrid, President Castro attends the Second Summit Meeting of 19 Ibero-American heads of state.

July 25   In Barcelona, President Castro attends the opening ceremony of the Olympics.

August   The State Department refuses to grant a visa to Cuban cosmonaut, Colonel Arnaldo Tamayo Méndez, invited to Washington for a meeting of astronauts from all over the world.

August 3   For the first time, Americas Watch (a wing of Human Rights Watch) and the Fund for Free Expression report on political conditions in a U.S. city — Miami. The report documents how Miami Cubans who are opposed to the Cuban government harass political opponents with bombings, vandalism, beatings and death threats.

August 17   In Havana, Cuban American Francisco Aruca of Radio Progreso interviews Ricardo Alarcón, recently appointed Foreign Minister of Cuba, for a program to be broadcast August 20. Speaking directly to the Cuban American community, Alarcón calls for both Cubans and Cuban Americans to create conditions that would permit normalization of their ties to each other.

August 20   Accepting his party's nomination for re-election, President Bush again predicts that he will be "the first President to visit a free, democratic Cuba."

September 2   Cuba suspends work on the Juraguá nuclear power plant near Cienfuegos because of rising costs that Russia is insisting be paid in hard currency rather than through the subsidized barter agreements of past practice. But in 1995, plans are made to continue the work with the help of companies from Russia, Italy, England and Brazil.

September 4 Speaking to Reuters in Jakarta, Indonesia, where he is attending the Nonaligned Movement's Summit Meeting, Foreign Minister Ricardo Alarcón charges that private armies are training in the United States to infiltrate Cuba and he suspects that the Bush Administration is backing them. He notes that a U.S. Coast Guard cutter entered Cuban waters in July (*see* July 4) in answer to a distress call from a U.S. private boat carrying explosives, automatic weapons and ammunition. So far, Alarcón points out, U.S. authorities have done nothing to stop such activity.

September 5 In Cienfuegos, President Castro gives a major speech about the Cuban economy. Cuba's purchasing power has fallen from $8.1 billion in 1989 to $2.2. billion in 1992. Imports have fallen 70 percent since the end of CMEA aid. The sugar harvest reached seven million tons, higher than expected, but the harvest had to be lengthened by two months because of the necessity of using manual labor rather than machines.

September 6 Organizing Cuban American Republicans for Bill Clinton in Dade County, Florida, Cuban American María Victoria Arias, wife of Hillary Rodham Clinton's brother Hugh Rodham, is present as 13 of them endorse his candidacy. A supporter of the "Cuban Democracy Act," Arias says that, as a relative, she has an influence on Clinton's attitude toward Cuba that no adviser could have.

September 7 The final declaration of the Tenth Summit Meeting of the Nonaligned Movement demands an end to the U.S. embargo and the military occupation of Guantánamo, and condemns U.S. violations of Cuban territorial waters, air space and airwaves and the broadcast of Radio and TV Martí. The resolution follows an address by Cuban Vice-President Juan Almeida. Forty heads of state and 95 delegations are present.

September 8 Running for Congress, Florida State Senator Lincoln Díaz-Balart wins the Republican primary. Since there is no Democratic candidate, he becomes the second Cuban American in Congress without having to compete in the general election.

September 9-14 Cuba and Russia agree on withdrawal of a contingent of troops that has been in Cuba since the 1962 Missile Crisis. The troops withdraw in stages until the final departure on July 3, 1993. Former Soviet personnel continue to staff an electronic intelligence station at Lourdes, Cuba.

September 12 Enforcing the April 24 regulations (*see* April 18) for the first time, U.S. authorities refuse to allow a freighter flying the Greek flag to enter Long Beach Bay, California, for servicing because it is carrying Chinese rice destined for Cuba.

September 13 *Granma* reports that Cuba will not repair telephone lines damaged by Hurricane Andrew in August until the U.S. government pays Cuba the money in the escrow account (*see* late December 1991). To bypass damaged lines, AT&T has rerouted calls from the United States to Cuba through third countries. Cuba says this is unacceptable because it disrupts outgoing calls and ties up phone lines from countries that pay Cuba for long-distance service.

September 18 By voice vote, the Senate approves the "Cuban Democracy Act" as part of the Defense Authorization Act. The House can vote on the bill as an amendment to the Defense Authorization Act or its original sponsor, Representative Torricelli, can put the bill before the full House on its own, which is what he plans to do. Democratic presidential nominee Bill Clinton sends a statement to the House of Representatives urging passage of the CDA.

September 24 In a vote taken under a suspension of rules process that requires a two-thirds vote for passage, the House of Representatives approves the "Cuban Democracy Act" by a vote of 276 to 135. Even if it had failed at this point, it would have passed anyway in the Defense Authorization Act that is on its way to the House from the Senate. In fact, this version of the bill does not become law; the language in the Defense Authorization Act becomes law.

October 3 Congress gives final approval to the "Cuban Democracy Act" and sends it to President Bush for signing.

October 6 Cuban Roman Catholic bishops issue a statement opposing the "Cuban Democracy Act" as "contrary to the values of the Gospel."

October 7 Reacting to Congress's approval of the "Cuban Democracy Act," the European Community lodges a diplomatic protest against the attempt to expand the embargo to U.S. companies based in EC countries.

October 7 From an offshore speedboat, a group from Comandos L fires shots at the Hotel Melia on Varadero Beach. Owned jointly by Cuba and Spain, the Melia is one of Cuba's main resort hotels.

October 14 The *Miami Herald* reports that Comandos L faxed this "war communique" to the *Herald*: "On the evening of October 7, 1992, Comandos L attacked a military objective off the coast of the province of Matanzas, Cuba." The fax does not mention that the "military" target is a tourist hotel and that the "military objective" would be to scare tourists away from Cuba. Comandos L leader Tony Cuesta told the *Herald* on October 13 that he does not know if the target was a hotel. He said the four-man team returned safely to its base. The *Herald* notes that the FBI has been investigating Comandos L for months with no arrests. The article reports that Justice Department representative Julie Reside said the department will check to see if this attack violated U.S. neutrality laws.

October 14 Cuba sends a letter formally protesting the October 7 terrorist attack to the State Department, which refers the protest to the Justice Department, which in turn asks the FBI to investigate. Cuban officials present to the chief of the U.S. Interests Section in Havana two volumes of evidence, including eyewitness accounts, photographs and bullets taken from the Hotel Melia.

October 21 When the U.S. Coast Guard boards the yacht *Nautilus* that has run aground on Anguilla Cay in the Bahamas, they spot suspicious activity on the beach and detain three Comandos L members — Rubén Castro, Jesús Morales and Iván Rojas — evidently burying something on the beach. Bahamian authorities arrive by helicopter and arrest the exiles on explosives and weapons charges.

October 23 In Miami at a ceremony attended only by Republicans, President Bush turns the "Cuban Democracy Act" into law by signing the Defense Authorization Act. He says, "We are not going to listen to those editorials that tell us how to run the foreign policy of this country." Earlier in the day, Bush attended a fund-raiser at the home of Fort Lauderdale cardiologist Zachariah Zachariah, where guests paid $10,000 for lunch — a total of $550,000 for Bush's re-election campaign.

October 29 The National Assembly of People's Power finalizes the constitutional changes approved at its July session. From now on, provincial and national deputies will be elected directly by the voters (municipal deputies are already elected by direct vote). The National Assembly will elect members of the Council of State and the Council President.

October 31 The FBI subpoenas Alejandro Pérez, a new member of Comandos L.

November Meeting in Washington, the American Public Health Association (APHA) passes a resolution that says the "Cuban Democracy Act," if implemented, would contribute "directly to death, disability and suffering of the Cuban people." The State Department denied a visa to Cuban Health Minister Julio Teja Pérez, invited by APHA to attend its meeting. APHA elects him, in absentia, to a second term as vice-president of APHA for Latin America.

November 3 Cuba and Russia sign new trade and shipping accords and agree to maintain the Lourdes intelligence station in Cuba.

November 3 Bill Clinton wins the presidential election, but President Bush carries Florida by a margin of two percent, including 75 percent of the Cuban American vote. Democrat Robert Menéndez of New Jersey becomes the third Cuban American in the House of Representatives; all are close to the Cuban American National Foundation.

November 8 On charges related to the July raid on Cuba, U.S. authorities arrest Tony Bryant of Comandos L in Delray Beach, Florida, for possession and transport of firearms by a convicted felon.

November 10 The State Department expels Cuban diplomat Carlos Manuel Collazo Usallán from the UN Mission, demanding he leave the country within 48 hours. In a series of interviews in early November with Spanish-language TV station WSCV in Miami, Francisco Avila of Alpha 66 claimed he was a double agent. In October, WSCV videotaped Avila at a New York City restaurant with Collazo.

November 10 New Cuban Assets Control Regulations become effective. Among other things, the latest rules make it more difficult to travel to Cuba to do research and limit to $500 per year the amount that a Cuban American can spend for travel-related costs paid to Cuba.

November 13 The Sun Company says its Sun Refining and Marketing Company unit and two executives did not know that two 1986 shipments of oil would be diverted to Cuba. But Sun and the two officials have agreed to pay $60,000 in civil penalties for the illegal export of 7,000 metric tons of aviation oil to Cuba.

November 20 Without requesting a license from the Treasury Department and despite harassment, including a few arrests (and one later conviction), the first U.S.-Cuba Friendshipment Caravan takes about 12.5 tons of powdered milk, medical supplies, bicycles, school supplies and Bibles across the U.S. border at Laredo, Texas, into Mexico, to be loaded aboard a Cuban cargo ship at Tampico, Mexico, for delivery to Havana. Reverend Lucius Walker of the Interreligious Foundation for Community Organizations (IFCO), the sponsor of this Pastors for Peace project, leads the group of 103 people traveling in 43 vehicles. The participants visited 90 U.S. cities before converging at the border. Risking fines and jail terms to challenge the embargo, the Caravanistas fly from Mexico to Havana, where they are met by Reverend Raúl Suárez and other members of the Martin Luther King Center and later by President Castro. IFCO continues to organize these Caravans, two more across the Mexican border in 1993 and 1994 and two across the Canadian border in 1994 and 1995. Each time, when the Treasury Department finally allows the Caravan to cross the border, its representatives claim that Caravan members received a license and therefore have not violated the embargo. However, no Caravan member ever signs or accepts any license.

November 24 The UN General Assembly approves a Cuban resolution opposing the U.S. embargo with a vote of 59 to 3 (U.S., Israel, Romania), 71 abstentions and 42 absentees. During the discussion before the vote, Cuban UN Ambassador Alcibíades Hidalgo says the embargo has cost Cuba $30 billion in more than three decades. U.S. Deputy Ambassador Alexander Watson calls Cuba's effort a propaganda exercise and claims the embargo is a bilateral issue not a multilateral issue that affects the international community. Britain's UN Ambassador Thomas

Richardson, speaking for the European Community, criticizes the "extraterritorial application of U.S. jurisdiction."

November 26 Responding to the General Assembly's opposition to the U.S. embargo, State Department official Joe Snyder says that only UN Security Council resolutions, not those of the General Assembly, are binding.

November 29 The Minneapolis *Star Tribune* editorializes against the "Cuban Democracy Act."

November 30 *New York Newsday* editorializes against the "Cuban Democracy Act."

December The European Parliament supports a resolution calling on President-elect Clinton and the U.S. Congress "to remove from the statute books the Cuban Democracy Act." Canada has passed a blocking order that will penalize subsidiaries of U.S. companies in Canada that comply with the "Cuban Democracy Act."

December 2 Tony Cuesta dies. As leader of the terrorist group, Comandos L, Cuesta sanctioned at least eight raids against Cuba since last December, three of which became public, forcing an FBI investigation. Tony Bryant becomes head of Comandos L.

December 4 Ten days after receiving the report of the UN Human Rights Commission's special rapporteur on Cuba, Carl Johan Groth, the UN General Assembly approves a U.S. resolution condemning human rights abuses in Cuba 64 to 17 with 59 abstentions. Because Cuba refused entry to Groth (*see* April 21), he interviewed Cubans who contacted him either directly or through U.S. representatives.

December 6 The Newark, New Jersey, *Star-Ledger* reports that Representative Torricelli (D-New Jersey) wrote a letter to President Bush last week urging him to monitor the oil-for-sugar trade agreement between Russia and Cuba. Torricelli warned that reports of the trade agreement indicate a subsidy to Cuba "above world prices for sugar of some $100 per ton."

December 15 At the celebration of the end to the 12-year civil war in El Salvador, rebel leader Shafik Handal thanks Cuba and the Nicaraguan Sandinistas for supporting the rebels. Vice-President Quayle looks on.

December 19 Former Cuban Air Force pilot Orestes Lorenzo Pérez, who defected in 1991, flies a small plane onto a Havana highway to pick up his wife and two sons with whom he flies back to Florida.

December 20 Of Cuba's eligible voters, 93 percent go to the polls to elect 13,865 delegates to Cuba's 169 Municipal Assemblies, the local bodies of People's Power.

December 29 Cuban pilot Carlos Cancio Porcel and several other people with their families hijack a Cuban airliner to Miami. They overpower and tie up the copilot and chloroform and handcuff a security guard. On the following day, a Cuban plane lands at Miami International Airport to pick up those Cubans who were kidnapped during the hijacking and who wish to return to Cuba: the copilot, his wife and daughter, the security guard and a stewardess. A Cuban pilot flies the hijacked plane back to the island. Cancio is detained. The other 48 Cubans are granted immediate asylum, leading to a hunger strike by more than 150 Haitians who are not being granted asylum but instead are being kept at the Krome detention center in Miami. On September 29, 1993, Cancio is released after the U.S. Justice Department rules that seizing an airliner, overpowering the copilot, kidnapping passengers, and diverting the plane to another country is not hijacking as long as the pilot is the perpetrator because one cannot hijack one's own plane.

1993

January The Cuban Health Ministry announces that the infant mortality rate decreased from 10.7 in 1991 to 10.2 in 1992.

January 6 In Florida, felony charges against Tony Bryant, head of Comandos L, are dismissed by Federal Judge James Lawrence King before the case could go to a jury. The next day's *Miami Herald* reports the judge's reason: "Bryant didn't act like he committed a crime."

January 7 At a news conference, Tony Bryant announces plans for more raids against targets in Cuba, especially hotels. Warning tourists to stay off the island, he declares, "From this point on, we're at war," adding, "The Neutrality Act doesn't exist."

January 7 A group of 14 Cubans on a supposed fishing trip tie up the boat's captain and sail for Key West. Three days later, the U.S. Coast Guard tows the fishing boat into Key West. The captain asks to return to Cuba. After interviewing the hijackers, U.S. officials from the INS, the FBI and the U.S. Attorney's office release them to the Cuban Migrant Transit Center in Key West that helps Cuban emigrants contact relatives in the United States. FBI agent Paul Miller says, "The U.S. Attorney's office discussed the matter and decided there was no basis for prosecution."

January 18 Accompanied by Bernardo Benes and Alfredo Durán, Eloy Gutiérrez Menoyo, who has left Alpha 66 and renounced violent methods of trying to change Cuba, announces at a Washington press conference the creation of a new Cuban American group, *Cambio Cubano* (Cuban Change), committed to ending the embargo, increasing U.S. tourism to Cuba, and constructing "a future without revenge and without hatred."

January 18 Two days before the inauguration of President Bill Clinton, the *Miami Herald* reports that prominent Cuban American attorney Mario Baeza, partner in the New York law firm, Debevoise & Plimpton, is about to be nominated as Assistant Secretary of State for Inter-American Affairs. Jorge Mas Canosa immediately informs key legislators about his opposition to the choice of a Black Cuban American unaffiliated with the Cuban American National Foundation. CANF, which favors no contact whatsoever with Cuba, objects to Baeza's participation in the Euromoney conference held in 1992 in Cancún and Havana. Democrats Senator Bill Bradley (New Jersey), Senator Bob Graham (Florida), and Representative Robert Torricelli (New Jersey) inform President-elect Clinton of their opposition to Baeza. The next day, Baeza's name is crossed off the list of nominees being sent to Congress.

January 21 The Black Congressional Caucus takes a position of support for the nomination of Mario Baeza. The January 22 *Miami Herald* quotes Representative Charles Rangel (D-New York): "The reason he was taken off the list (of nominees) was strictly political. When it became clear color was a factor, it was clear we had to fight for him." Despite protests against allowing the Cuban American National Foundation the power to veto an appointment in the new Democratic Administration, Baeza's name remains off the list.

January 27 As more Ukrainian children arrive to be treated in Cuba for effects from the Chernobyl disaster, Ukraine's Deputy Health Minister, Dr Vladimir Maltsev, accompanying this latest group, says no country has helped Ukrainian, Byelorussian, Armenian and Russian children as Cuba has. This experience has enabled Cuba to assist in the care of hundreds of Brazilian children affected by radiation from mishandled Cesium 137.

January 29 Traveling to Cuba with a delegation arranged by the U.S.-Cuba Medical Project based in New York City, pediatrician Dr Benjamin Spock and his wife, writer Mary Morgan, deliver $75,000 worth of medicines for Cuban children and call for President Clinton to end the embargo. While on the island, Mary Morgan says she will invite Hillary Rodham Clinton, head of the

Clinton Administration's Health Task Force, to visit Cuba and study its social policies: "Maybe she'll be able to apply some of the health programs operating in Cuba to the United States." One of several groups in the United States that are sending to Cuba humanitarian aid for which they receive a special license from the Treasury Department, the U.S.-Cuba Medical Project continues to send regular donations — for example $5 million worth in September 1995.

February 1   A Cuban newspaper, *Trabajadores* [Workers], reports that workers at Varadero, a resort area, will be allowed to keep hard-currency tips for use in tourist shops, where only dollars may be used. This replaces a policy that required workers to pool hard-currency tips, which were exchanged for pesos and divided among them.

February 1   The *Miami Herald* reports that the U.S. Coast Guard has arrested five men — believed to be members of Frank Sturgis's Democratic National Unity Party (PUND) — on a heavily armed fishing boat.

February 10   The School of Humanities of the Dominican Republic's Autonomous University of Santo Domingo awards an honorary doctorate to President Castro at a ceremony in Santiago de Cuba.

February 18   Speaking in Atlanta at a press conference during a meeting of the Carter Center's International Negotiation Network, former President Jimmy Carter says he favors free travel, free trade and tourism between Cuba and the United States.

February 23   Representative Torricelli tells the Center for Strategic and International Studies in Washington, "A group of Cuban patriots at some point in the near future is going to recognize that no matter what the risk to themselves, it is time to take Cuba's future in their own hands." He predicts: "The end of that government will be measured in months and not years."

February 24   Of Cuba's 7,872,806 registered voters, 99.62 percent go to the polls to elect by direct and secret ballot 1,190 delegates to 14 Provincial Assemblies and 589 delegates to the National Assembly (*see* July 10-12, 1992). Jorge Mas Canosa has waged a massive campaign on Radio Martí — 452 appeals, including a message from Florida Governor Lawton Chiles — during the 16 days prior to the elections to persuade Cubans to demonstrate opposition to the current Cuban government by spoiling their ballots. More than a dozen other radio stations, including short-wave stations, also urged opposition. But according to the Cuban Electoral Commission, 92.8 percent vote for the ticket while only 7.2 percent spoil their ballots or leave them blank. Because there are no opposition parties on the ballot, many analysts agree that the vote is in effect a plebiscite — one that reveals strong support for the Cuban government. Speaking on television, President Castro calls the elections a "referendum for socialism" in this difficult period "when the socialist camp and the Soviet Union have disappeared." Some 200 foreign journalists, including U.S. reporters, are in Cuba to observe the electoral process.

February 25 Diane Sawyer of ABC News interviews President Castro, and ABC broadcasts a brief segment March 4 while Cuba broadcasts the whole session March 5. Sawyer asks if Castro believes that a U.S. president could end the embargo and resume relations as long as he is in power. Castro responds that if he were the obstacle, he would be willing to "give up not only my positions and responsibilities but even my life." He says that he would never negotiate the revolution, socialism, or Cuban sovereignty and independence.

February 25 In Geneva, the UN Human Rights Commission reappoints the special rapporteur on Cuba for another year by a vote of 27 to 15 with 10 abstentions.

February 26 In a Washington snowstorm outside the White House and the Treasury Department, Cuban Americans demonstrate against the embargo. Andrés Gómez, head of the Antonio Maceo Brigade, delivers to the White House a petition against the embargo signed by 35,000 Cuban Americans from Miami.

March U.S. Coast Guard officials meet for two days in Havana with their Cuban counterparts about how to cooperate in matters such as search and seizure procedures.

March 2 President Clinton nominates Alexander Watson as Assistant Secretary of State for Inter-American Affairs. Unlike Mario Baeza, Watson, a career diplomat, has the approval of the Cuban American National Foundation, partly because Watson's top aide will be Richard Nuccio, who, as an aide to

Representative Torricelli, helped devise the "Cuban Democracy Act."

March 8   In Washington, the signing of the Women's Peace and Justice Treaty of the Americas lacks the participation of two representatives of the Federation of Cuban Women because the State Department denied visas to María Isabel Acevedo and Rebeca Cutié. The treaty has been developed by the Women's International League for Peace and Freedom.

March 19   *Cambio Cubano* publishes a full-page ad in the *Miami Herald* titled "For Cuba, For Change," signed by Eloy Gutiérrez Menoyo, and calling for dialogue with President Castro.

March 23   Asked at his first White House news conference if he would meet with President Castro and if there might be a change in policy toward Cuba, President Clinton replies, "I have no change in Cuba policy except to say that I support the Cuban Democracy Act and I hope someday that we'll all be able to travel to a democratic Cuba."

April 1   Representative Howard Berman (D-California) reintroduces the Free Trade in Ideas bill (*see* June 16, 1992).

April 2   Off Cuba's northern coast, gunmen fire from a speedboat at a Cyprus-registered tanker carrying fuel oil to Cuba.

April 15   The UN General Assembly adopts a resolution introduced by Belize calling on all nations to aid Cuba in the wake of the March 13 storm that killed five people and caused more than one billion dollars in damages. Shipments of aid from all over the world arrive during the following months.

April 24   A flotilla of boats carrying humanitarian aid, licensed by the Treasury Department, sails for Cuba from Key West. John A. Young, head of the organizing group, *Basta!* [Enough!], tells the media that a fire set in their warehouse two days earlier did little damage. The flotilla arrives at the Hemingway Marina west of Havana on the following day. The group repeats the humanitarian voyage in October.

April 29   Representative Charles Rangel (D-New York) introduces the Free Trade with Cuba Act that would end the U.S. embargo against Cuba. (*See* May 20)

May   Former U.S. Attorney General Ramsey Clark, Pulitzer Prize winner Alice Walker, and American Indian Movement (AIM) leader Dennis Banks lead a delegation to Cuba to deliver $75,000 worth of medical supplies and call for an end to the embargo. Banks compares the U.S. government's policy to its post-1868 policy toward Native Americans: negotiate or starve. Walker speaks of her gratitude to Cuba for its inspiration to the civil rights movement in the United States.

May 3 Richard Newcomb, director of the Treasury Department's Office of Foreign Assets Control, advises Attorney Michael Krinsky that persons wishing to help Cuba recover from the March storm's damage may make checks or money orders payable to "Licensed Tropical Storm Relief" and send them to a Chemical Bank "lock box" set up to facilitate processing contributions for credit to UN relief efforts on the island.

May 5 and 12 *Granma* prints, in two parts, an important interview by Mario Vázquez Raña with Vice-President Raúl Castro, first published in *El Sol de México*. One revelation concerns what the Cubans call the Pandora Case, so threatening that it has remained secret for more than a decade (*see* October 30, 1981).

May 8 The *New York Times* reports that prominent dissidents in Cuba have sent a letter pleading for an end to the embargo. Rolando Prats, president of the Cuban Democratic Socialist Current, delivered the letter to Clinton Administration officials in early May during a visit to the United States. In addition to Prats, signers include Elizardo Sánchez and Vladimiro Roca. Many dissidents in Cuba argue that the continuing embargo allows the Cuban government to blame all problems on the United States and therefore delays reforms desired by dissidents.

May 11 Foreign Minister Roberto Robaina accompanies foreign and Cuban journalists to the Malones observation post where they see and hear U.S. planes dropping bombs at the Guantánamo Naval Base, close to the Cuban towns of Caimanera and Boquerón. Malones has recently been opened for tourists by Cuba's Gaviota corporation.

May 12 The Strategic Studies Institute of the U.S. Army War College publishes "The United States and Cuba: From a Strategy of Conflict to Constructive Engagement" by Donald E. Schulz, recommending that the U.S. government repeal the "Cuban Democracy Act" or at least "enforce it to the minimal extent possible."

May 13   Representative Jerrold Nadler (D-New York), who has replaced the late Representative Ted Weiss, introduces legislation, like that introduced repeatedly by his predecessor, to make an exception to the U.S. embargo for export of medicines and medical supplies to Cuba.

May 13   The *Wall Street Journal* reports the end of a boycott of Miami area tourism that began as a protest of the Miami Commissioners' treatment of African National Congress leader Nelson Mandela when he visited in June 1990. Black leaders of the protest agreed to end the boycott after negotiating an economic development program for Black business owners and Black workers in the tourist industry.

May 13-25   A delegation of Cuban Protestants visits 40 U.S. cities, including Miami, calling for dialogue between Havana and Washington.

May 20   Representative Charles Rangel presents a revised version of his Free Trade With Cuba Act.

May 20   In the White House Rose Garden, President Clinton celebrates what some people call "Cuban Independence Day" (*see* May 20, 1902) with a group of invited Cuban American and Congressional supporters of the "Cuban Democracy Act." Hillary Rodham Clinton expresses "special thanks" to her brother Hugh Rodham and his wife María Victoria Arias Rodham (*see* September 6, 1992) for making the Clintons "even more acutely aware" of Cuban issues.

May 20   In Florida, at a luncheon hosted by the Cuban American National Foundation, Governor Lawton Chiles signs into law the Free Cuba Act that authorizes local government bodies in Florida to revoke occupational licenses of companies doing business with Cuba. Moreover, the law legalizes shutting down any Florida business owned by a foreign company which does business with Cuba even though the U.S. branch of the company makes no transactions involving Cuba. In June, the law is challenged in court by Marazul Tours and five other companies on the basis that the Florida law preempts federal law. Michael Krinsky, partner in the New York law firm Rabinowitz, Boudin, Standard, Krinsky and Lieberman that represents the Cuban government and its agencies in the United States, writes in the summer issue of *CUBA Update*: "Federal law does not prohibit or even purport to regulate third-country companies doing business with Cuba unless those companies are owned or controlled by United States persons."

May 20 Nine Alpha 66 members are arrested as U.S. Customs agents board their weapons-laden speedboat in the Florida Keys. The head of the terrorist organization, Andrés Nazario Sargén, not among those arrested, tells the press that they were on their way to attack Cuba and spark a rebellion. On June 9, State Department official Joseph Snyder issues a statement saying the U.S. government "does not support, condone or encourage any such illegal activities" and will prosecute anybody who organizes attacks against Cuba in violation of the Neutrality Act.

May 25 More than 60 workers at Radio Martí send a petition to Joseph D. Duffey, the new USIA director who oversees all foreign broadcasting for the United States, requesting that Radio Martí "be maintained above any competing political factions existing within the Cuban exile community." The petition is the latest in a series of complaints by some of the station's personnel about programming that reflects primarily the views of the Cuban American National Foundation.

June IMF official Jacques de Groote, executive director for nine European countries, meets informally with Cuban officials in Havana, a preliminary visit leading to formal discussion in November.

June In Paris, 130 French doctors, including Nobel Prize winner Jean Dausset, appeal to the international community to help end the U.S. embargo against Cuba. The doctors maintain that the "Cuban Democracy Act" contributes to worsening conditions for the Cuban people.

June 3 A.B. Laffer, V.A. Canto & Associates publishes "A Transition Program for a Post-Castro Cuba" by Jorge Mas Canosa.

June 6-11 A delegation of the American Public Health Association makes a fact-finding trip to Cuba. As a result, APHA publishes *The Politics of Suffering: The Impact of the U.S. Embargo on the Health of the Cuban People*, explaining how the embargo threatens Cuba's exemplary health care system and calling for "a new vision in U.S. policy toward Cuba."

June 8 In Brooklyn, New York, Federal District Judge Sterling Johnson Jr. orders an end to U.S. detention of Haitians at the Guantánamo Naval Base. The 158 Haitians still being detained behind barbed wire include 143 who have tested positive for the HIV virus, two adults who are HIV negative, and 13 untested minors. On June 21, the last of these Haitians are flown to Miami.

June 9-12 Leading a delegation of U.S. physicians and other health workers on a visit to Cuba, Wayne Smith, former head of the U.S. Interests Section in Havana, says the group is assessing the effect of the embargo as well as studying how best to help Cuba cope with the effects of the March storm.

June 9 and 16 *Granma* reprints an interview by Mario Vázquez Raña with Dr Carlos Lage Dávila, originally published in *El Sol de México*, in which he discusses at length the U.S. embargo. Lage is the architect of Cuba's new economic policy, having devised in 1991 a plan for "mixed enterprises" to attract foreign capital. In March, the National Assembly made him Second Vice-President of the Council of State, the third-highest position in Cuba. In the interview, he states that, by conservative estimates, Cuba has lost $40 billion dollars because of the embargo and then offers corroborating facts and figures. For example, he mentions the increase in transportation expenses for markets that are far away. Lage notes that the U.S. government has aimed at controlling Cuba since the beginning of the 19th century.

June 15 Prensa Latina reports that Ernesto Meléndez, president of Cuba's State Committee on Economic Cooperation, says Cuba is willing to negotiate reparations for U.S. properties expropriated in the 1960s as part of broader talks on normalizing relations. This has been Cuba's consistent position on compensation. The State Department says 5,911 Americans lost $1.8 billion in expropriations, a figure that is now about $6 billion due to inflation and interest.

June 16 Addressing the World Conference on Human Rights in Vienna, Foreign Minister Roberto Robaina says the so-called new world order "continues to be founded on disrespect for our rights.... Efforts are being made to give the [UN] Security Council the role of world policeman, based on the designs and interests of a superpower and its allies who aim to establish new procedures and mechanisms with this end in mind."

June 21 In a decision that will later prove relevant to Cubans, the U.S. Supreme Court rules 8 to 1 that it is legal for U.S. authorities to repatriate Haitians intercepted on the high seas without allowing them to have asylum hearings. The Court decides that U.S. refugee law applies only to migrants who reach U.S. territory.

June 29-July 2 Wayne Smith is again in Cuba at the head of a delegation — this time an unofficial U.S. military group, including Admiral Eugene Carroll Jr., director of the Center for Defense Information, Army General Kermit Johnson, Air Force General Jack Kidd, all retired, and Jack Mendelsohn, formerly of the State Department and currently deputy director of the Arms Control Association. They meet with officials from Cuba's Armed Forces to discuss ways the two countries can improve relations. The visit is sponsored by the Center for International Policy based in Washington.

July 2 The Newark, New Jersey, *Star-Ledger* reports that, because the U.S. government will not release escrow funds of more than $80 million owed to Cuba (*see* late December 1991), AT&T has been forced to cut 400 jobs in Pittsburgh at the calling center that handles all of AT&T's U.S.-Cuba phone calls.

July 7-10 During a four-day visit by a high-level delegation, Vietnamese Prime Minister Vo Van Kiet discusses with President Castro Vietnam's efforts to change its economy to a market-oriented system and at the same time maintain socialism.

July 11 The *New York Times* reports that State Department officials plan to close communications services that allow people in the United States to make phone calls to Cuba via Canada. The State Department has asked the Treasury Department to determine if Canadian "resellers" are violating the embargo by sharing revenues with Cuba.

July 11-19 Pittsburgh declares "U.S.-Cuba Friendship Week" and the City Council encourages citizens to support the second Friendshipment Caravan that is challenging the embargo by taking aid to Cuba without requesting permission from U.S. authorities. Lois Grimes, president of Communication Workers of America local 13550, reminds the media that the embargo recently cost Pittsburgh 400 jobs (*see* July 2).

July 15   In Cancún, Mexico, at the Euromoney conference of businesspeople, mostly from the United States, Cuban officials announce that all Cubans will be allowed to possess dollars and that foreigners may open joint-venture banks. The conference moves to Havana for one day on July 16, as it did in June 1992. The number of foreign firms with investments in Cuba has increased from some 100 in 1987 to almost 500 in 1993.

July 16   In Brazil, President Castro attends the third annual Ibero-American Summit that includes leaders from Latin American countries and Spain and Portugal.

July 23   U.S. officials say that the Clinton Administration has decided to permit U.S. telephone companies to expand communications links to Cuba and share some of their revenues with the Cuban government. This could net Cuba $50 to $60 million a year. But $80 million in escrow will remain frozen.

July 26   In a speech in Santiago de Cuba, President Castro, announcing profound economic changes, explains why Cuba is legalizing possession of dollars. Describing the economic situation, he says Cuba will have sufficient hard currency to import only $1.7 billion this year (down from $8.4 billion in 1989).

July 27   Cuban American Representative Robert Menéndez (D-New Jersey) introduces his Free and Independent Cuba Assistance Act, promising rewards after the ouster of Fidel Castro.

July 28   The *Miami Herald* reports that Cuba plans to lift restrictions on travel to Cuba for exiles and will allow them to carry an unlimited amount of dollars, buy things for their relatives in dollar shops, and return as often as they like. Local charter agencies follow up by announcing an expansion of airline flights to meet the increased demand. United Airlines plans to supply the extra planes.

July 28   Joseph G. Sullivan replaces Alan Flanigan as head of the U.S. Interests Section in Havana.

August   The CIA issues a classified "National Intelligence Estimate" warning President Clinton that he could face a major crisis in Cuba "virtually at any time."

August A new exile group, the Cuban Committee for Democracy (CCD), is formed to advocate a change in U.S. policy toward Cuba by "easing" the embargo and opening negotiations.

August 4 In response to the plan for increasing airline flights to and from Cuba (*see* July 28), Deputy Assistant Secretary of State for Inter-American Affairs Robert Gelbard tells a House subcommittee that the U.S. government will review the situation to see if the flights violate the embargo. Representatives Lincoln Díaz-Balart and Ileana Ros-Lehtinen — both Republican Cuban Americans from Florida — and Representative Robert Torricelli (D-New Jersey) are present for the hearing and oppose the increased contact with Cuba. Lonnie Jones, an attorney for ABC Charters, tells the press that no supporter of expanding flights was invited to the hearing.

August 5-9 President Castro attends the inauguration of Bolivia's new president, Gonzalo Sánchez de Lozada. This is the first time that Castro has visited Bolivia, where Che Guevara was murdered in 1967. From Bolivia he travels to Colombia.

August 9-11 President Castro meets with Colombian President César Gaviria in Cartagena.

August 20 While most members of the second Friendshipment Caravan are already in Cuba, President Castro visits with dozens of Cubans holding a hunger strike outside the U.S. Interests Section in Havana in solidarity with hunger strikers aboard a "little yellow school bus" being held by U.S. Customs agents at the U.S.-Mexican border in Laredo, Texas. Later in the day, in the midst of media attention and widespread protests, the school bus is released, ending the 23-day hunger strike.

August 22 *New York Newsday* reports that the Transportation Department has approved an application by ABC Charters of Miami to add extra flights to Cuba. A day later, the State Department puts approval on hold. Deputy Assistant Secretary of State Robert Gelbard says the Administration wants to make sure travelers would not spend more than $100 a day in Cuba. Havana is proposing that every traveler to Cuba must purchase a $100-a-day hotel package, but later drops that restriction.

August 24 In Miami, Federal Judge James Lawrence King dismisses weapons charges against six of the nine Alpha 66 members arrested May 20. On the following day, a jury finds the other three not guilty of weapons charges. Their attorneys argue that the defendants did not know that there were illegal weapons aboard their boat. Says Attorney Paul Lazarus, "Nobody knows who put what where or how anything got where it was found."

August 30 At a luncheon meeting with President Clinton, leaders of five Caribbean nations — the Bahamas, Barbados, Guyana, Jamaica and Trinidad — discuss CARICOM's efforts to establish trade relations with Cuba. An agreement for increased trade and technical cooperation with Cuba, discussed at CARICOM's Summit Meeting in July, is being finalized. Representatives Torricelli and Menéndez (both New Jersey Democrats) and Representatives Díaz-Balart and Ros-Lehtinen (both Florida Republicans) this month sent a letter to CARICOM warning that the agreement could adversely affect trade relations between its members and the United States.

September Representatives of three U.S. telephone companies, Sprint, MCI and AT&T, go to Havana to negotiate increased telephone service to Cuba.

September The U.S. government sends a cable, "Buyer Beware," to all U.S. embassies and consulates ordering diplomats to inform host governments that the U.S. government "strongly urges" them to dissuade their citizens from investing in Cuban property that could be part of $1.8 billion in U.S. claims for expropriations. Such warnings were issued in 1991 as well.

September The World Health Organization announces that an epidemic of neuropathy in Cuba seems to have ended. In the last five months, Cuban health workers have distributed 1.5 billion vitamin pills to combat the affliction. The Pan American Health Organization (PAHO) and medical groups from several countries, including the United States (for example, the Centers for Disease Control in Atlanta and the Orbis Project), have sent teams to attempt to identify the precise cause of the problem. Of the 50,000 cases, the symptoms in all but 1,300 have been eradicated. But the causes remain elusive.

September 7 Northern Technical University in Ibarra, Ecuador, awards an honorary degree to President Castro.

September 9 Cuba authorizes limited private enterprise in more than 100 trades and services.

September 10 In Miami, Federal Judge James Lawrence King sentences Iván Rojas, who pleaded guilty in July to one firearms violation, to probation. Comandos L member Tony Bryant and Frank Sturgis of the Democratic National Unity Party (PUND) are in the courtroom to support Rojas. On March 16, 1995, the Eleventh U.S. Circuit Court of Appeals in Atlanta rules that Judge King must sentence Rojas to time in prison in accordance with the National Firearms Act that mandates a sentence of up to 30 months for the firearms charge. (*See* October 21, 1992)

September 14 Cuban Roman Catholic bishops issue a pastoral letter (dated September 8) criticizing the Cuban government and calling for a national dialogue that would include the exile community to discuss Cuban problems. The letter also renews the bishops' opposition to the U.S. embargo. On September 30, Protestant clergy, including Baptists, Methodists and Presbyterians, and some Catholic lay persons issue a statement warning the Cuban people not to be misled by those who want to return "to a past of racism, illiteracy and inequality" and calling for discussion of problems in a spirit of support for the Cuban government's efforts to preserve Cuba's socialist project. The Oscar Arnulfo Romero Catholic lay group demands that the bishops lift the ban they have imposed on those who disagree with their analysis.

September 15 Foreign Minister Roberto Robaina calls the first visit by a high-level official of the Clinton Administration "satisfactory and constructive." Dennis Hays, head of the State Department's Office of Cuban Affairs, was in Cuba for a week. Hays, closely allied with the Cuban American National Foundation's positions regarding Cuba, maintains that the cornerstone of policy toward Cuba should continue to be the embargo.

September 17 Cuban pilot Enio Ravelo Rodríguez defects in a Cuban MiG-23 jet fighter to the Naval Air Station in Key West. On September 23, a Cuban pilot, flown to the base from Cuba along with a maintenance crew, flies the MiG back to Cuba while the maintenance team returns on their transport plane.

September 18 In an example of steadily growing U.S.-Cuban cooperation against drug trafficking, Cuba hands over to the Drug Enforcement Agency two Cuban Americans arrested in August for smuggling cocaine, and they are flown to Miami for prosecution. DEA officials say the two, Jorge Roberto Lam Rojas and José Angel Clemente Alvarez from Miami, picked up several bales of cocaine dropped into the Straits of Florida by a plane tracked from Colombia. As a U.S. Army helicopter chased their boat, they tossed the bales overboard and crossed into Cuban waters, where they were arrested after their boat ran out of fuel. U.S. officials offered to turn the recovered 720 pounds of cocaine over to Cuba as evidence, but Cuba preferred that the United States prosecute.

September 23 For the second time this month, a Cuban pilot defects in a MiG-23 jet fighter. Captain Leonides Basulto Serrano lands at the U.S. naval base at Guantánamo. The plane is returned to unoccupied Cuba.

September 28 In New York to address the UN General Assembly, Foreign Minister Roberto Robaina says that as long as the Clinton Administration respects Cuban sovereignty, Cuba will continue to improve cooperation in areas like migration, drug smuggling and telecommunications. He says Cuba is studying expansion of cultural, scientific, sports and journalistic exchanges with the United States. While in the United States for three weeks, Robaina meets with various groups. On October 10 in New York, while speaking with more than 150 Cuban Americans from around the United States, he issues an invitation to another meeting in Havana next year to discuss matters of mutual interest. Robaina and Reverend Lucius Walker of Pastors for Peace lead a march in Harlem, starting at the Hotel Teresa where Fidel Castro and Malcolm X met in 1960, in protest against the U.S. embargo.

October Cuba is elected to the board of governors of the International Atomic Energy Agency.

October 6 Representatives from some 40 different U.S. agencies convene to plan responses to political crisis in Cuba. Agencies include the National Security Agency, the State Department, the Defense Department, the Immigration and Naturalization Service (INS), the Coast Guard, the Federal Emergency Management Administration (FEMA), and the Agency for International Development (AID). One topic is how to handle a potential wave of emigrants.

October 6 The first United Airlines flight to Havana (*see* July 28) arrives with 125 passengers. In addition to seven already in operation by travel agencies with chartered planes, United plans to offer four weekly flights.

October 9 Thousands of Cuban Americans march in Little Havana to oppose dialogue with Cuba and to support the rebellion they claim is taking place in Cuba. Jorge Mas Canosa says the march will help unify Cubans in the United States and Cuba. Representative Torricelli (D-New Jersey) proclaims, "This march marks the beginning of the end. We're in the last few months of our great battle." Marchers include Senator Mack and Representatives Ros-Lehtinen and Díaz-Balart, all Republicans from Florida, and Jeb Bush.

October 10-17 Exercising the constitutional right to travel, the Freedom to Travel Campaign, a coalition of 50 organizations, makes its first challenge to the travel ban as 175 U.S. citizens visit Cuba without requesting permission from the U.S. government. Upon their return, Customs officials confiscate the passports of 65 members of the group, as well as some of their property. All recover their passports by the time the second challenge takes place in June, 1994.

October 11 The Associated Press reports that Cuban exile "training camps operate freely in the Everglades" of Florida. Andrés Nazario Sargén, head of Alpha 66, is quoted: "There is already a rebellion inside Cuba." He claims, "We are in a countdown. It's a matter of 80 or 90 days." He boasts that Alpha 66 has staged five recent missions inside Cuba. Tony Bryant, chief of Comandos L, is also quoted: "We are in the process of learning where every general lives" and they "will be targeted to be eliminated." He plans to smuggle surface-to-air missiles and explosives into Cuba. Federal District Judge James Lawrence King, who has been acquitting Alpha 66 and Comandos L terrorists, has this question about laws against such actions: "Did Congress have in mind a person who had intense convictions — patriotic in nature — but which would not have any direct possibility of hardship [to U.S. citizens]?" A Customs official, speaking on condition of anonymity, says Customs cannot act against training camps "without support from the Department of Justice."

October 13 *Granma* reports that, in addition to Radio and TV Martí, 14 other radio stations broadcast to Cuba for 1,112 hours a week on 18 frequencies, urging Cubans to rebel against the government and encouraging acts of terrorism, including assassination.

October 15 Preparing to use Guantánamo Naval Base in Cuba as a staging area, if necessary, for possible use in Haiti, President Clinton orders 450 to 600 troops of the Marine Expeditionary Force based at Camp Lejeune, N.C., to go on standby at Guantánamo.

October 15 In a close race with his Republican rival in the November 2 election for governor, New Jersey Governor Jim Florio meets with Jorge Mas Canosa, New Jersey Democratic Representative Robert Menéndez and other Cuban Americans in Princeton to announce the formation of the New Jersey Free Cuba Task Force to plan for the state's role in Cuba after the ouster of President Castro. This wins the endorsement of Jorge Mas Canosa but Florio loses the governorship.

October 19 In response to investments in Cuba led by Honduran businessman Miguel Facusse, the U.S. government sends a letter to the Honduran government warning that investments in Cuba may face legal challenges once Fidel Castro is ousted.

October 19 The Associated Press reports that Cuban authorities have arrested José Marcelo García Rubalcaba at the Havana airport after finding grenades and Alpha 66 propaganda in his luggage. Rubalcaba is a Mexican citizen currently living in the United States. Later, at his trial, he admits that he was attempting to carry out a smuggling mission for Alpha 66.

October 26 Speaking at a luncheon hosted by the Cuban American National Foundation, Assistant Secretary of State for Latin American Affairs Alexander Watson delivers the Clinton Administration's first major policy statement on Cuba, supporting the "Cuban Democracy Act" and assuring his audience that President Clinton does not plan "to soften" policy toward Cuba. He says the U.S. government has no intention of taking military action and will prosecute those who violate U.S. neutrality laws.

October 28 Cuba and Colombia resume full diplomatic relations.

November Accompanied by his assistant Frank Moss, IMF official Jacques de Groote returns to Cuba to spend six days discussing with senior Cuban officials the experiences of transition to a market economy in former communist countries of Eastern Europe. De Groote's report on his visit says the U.S. embargo will continue to impair Cuban growth potential.

November 1-2 Cuba's minister of health, Dr Julio Teja Pérez, cannot attend a conference in Washington to discuss control and treatment of AIDS and other communicable diseases because the State Department refused to grant him a visa.

November 3 For the second year in a row, the UN General Assembly approves a Cuban resolution that calls for an end to the U.S. embargo against Cuba. The vote is 88 to 4 (Albania, Israel and Paraguay vote with the United States) with 57 abstentions.

November 5 According to a report in the December 2 *El Diario*, Humberto Pérez of Alpha 66 says clandestine members of Alpha 66 inside Cuba would make "uso de la violencia" [use of violence] and mentions "la posibilidad de secuestrar a turistas para exigir rescates" [the possibility of kidnapping tourists to demand ransoms].

November 6 The Cuban government announces it is opening state enterprises to private investment.

November 8 The *New York Times* again editorializes against the "Cuban Democracy Act."

November 15 A pilot employed by Cuba's agriculture department pulls a gun on security guards and steals a 1950s-era biplane in which he flies with 12 other Cubans to Opa-Locka airport in a Miami suburb. According to Mario Miranda of the Cuban American National Foundation, the Cubans are all friends from Camagüey.

November 18 Following a visit to China by National Assembly President Ricardo Alarcón, Chinese President Jiang Zemin spends a day in Cuba. Traveling with him, Chinese Foreign Minister Qian Qichen calls for an end to the U.S. embargo against Cuba.

November 18 The UN Human Rights Commission urges the United States to lift the embargo against Cuba, an appeal based on special rapporteur Carl Johan Groth's report which concludes that a policy based on isolating Cuba is "the surest way of prolonging an untenable internal situation."

November 21 Howard W. French reports in the *New York Times* that a new 674-page study called "Transition in Cuba, New Challenges for U.S. Policy," commissioned by the State Department, paints a grim picture of Cuba now and in the future with one scenario envisioning U.S. military intervention to remove the Castro government. Prepared by 17 academics during two years and turned over to the State Department in May, the study was supervised by Lisandro Pérez, director of the Cuban Research Institute at Florida International University, and funded with a half-a-million-dollar grant from the State Department.

November 30 In response to the latest threats against tourists in Cuba from terrorists based in the United States, the State Department issues a statement saying, "Acts of violence against U.S. nationals may be punishable under U.S. law, as may be conspiring or threatening to carry out such acts."

November-December During the XVII Central American and Caribbean Games in Costa Rica, some 40 Cubans defect out of 881 in the delegation. Cuban athletes are the overwhelming winners of the contests.

December In Santiago de Cuba, U.S. and Cuban officials meet to discuss migration.

December 1 The *San Francisco Chronicle* reports that musicians and artists in San Francisco have filed a lawsuit against the U.S. government for denying visas to Cuban musicians from the fusion group Mezcla, who had been expected to accompany Lázaro Rós, a founder of Cuba's Grupo Folklórico Nacional, on a December tour in the United States. Guitarist Carlos Santana has spearheaded the protest because Grupo Mezcla is his favorite Cuban band. The founder and leader of Mezcla is Pablo Menéndez, son of U.S. singer Barbara Dane.

December 9-12 Accompanied by Wayne Smith and Alfredo Forti, ten Congressional aides depart from Washington for Havana on a visit organized by the Center for International Policy. They meet with National Assembly President Ricardo Alarcón, Finance Minister José Luis Rodríguez and several National Assembly deputies. President Castro and other Cuban leaders attend a reception for the delegation. They also visit Marianao municipality and confer with local government officials. Senate aides come from the offices of Democrats Claiborne Pell (Rhode

Island) and Edward Kennedy (Massachusetts) and Republicans Jim Jeffords (Vermont) and Frank Murkowski (Arkansas). House aides come from the offices of Democrats John Conyers, Jr. (Michigan), Charles Rangel (New York), Howard Berman (California), Jim McDermott (Washington), Cynthia McKinney (Georgia), and Republican Constance Morella (Maryland).

December 13 Trade Minister Ricardo Cabrisas Ruiz meets with CARICOM members in Guyana to sign the agreement for a CARICOM-Cuba Joint Trade Commission.

December 20 The UN General Assembly unanimously creates the post of High Commissioner for Human Rights whose office will be based in Geneva. Earlier, the UN voted 62 to 18 with 52 abstentions to approve a U.S. resolution demanding that Cuba "cease the persecution and punishment of citizens for reasons related to political expression and peaceful association" and to halt retaliation against citizens seeking to leave Cuba.

December 24 Invited by the Martin Luther King Jr. Ecumenical Council, Reverend Jesse Jackson and Dennis Rivera, chair of the Rainbow Coalition, arrive in Havana for a four-day visit, including a meeting with President Castro. New Jersey Democratic Representatives Robert Menéndez and Robert Torricelli object to their trip. At a press conference on December 26 in Havana, Jackson urges the United States to end its embargo and says he plans to talk with agricultural and pharmaceutical companies interested in establishing trade relations with Cuba.

1994

January The Cuban Health Ministry announces that the infant mortality rate for 1993 was 9.4 per thousand live births.

January 1 The North American Free Trade Agreement (NAFTA) among Canada, Mexico and the United States takes effect.

January 6 After years of litigation, Dan Walsh and Lincoln Cushing travel to Cuba as the first recipients of a special Treasury Department license that permits travel to Cuba to conduct business about import and export of informational materials, specifically posters and graphics. Previously, the U.S. government's restrictions made it virtually impossible to carry out the import-export deals legalized by the Trade Act of August 23, 1988. The license is good for only one year and mandates submitting to the Treasury Department plans for all travel, including inside Cuba.

January 9 On the third and final day of a Congressional Workshop sponsored by the Greater Miami Chamber of Commerce in Coral Gables, Dennis Hays, head of the State Department's Office of Cuban Affairs, tells the 16 participating members of Congress that the Clinton Administration is updating contingency plans for dealing with potential crises in Cuba: "There are a number of worst-case scenarios we are working on, from civil war to calls for U.S. intervention and humanitarian assistance."

January 13 Public Health Ministry official Dr Manuel Santín Peña announces a change in the controversial policy of quarantining those who are HIV-positive. The program to combat AIDS, in effect since April 1986, has been effective in preventing an AIDS epidemic on the island but has been criticized — especially in the

United States — as a violation of human rights. The new plan allows Cubans with the AIDS virus to live at home and return to their jobs if they choose, while receiving free outpatient care at special clinics. Those proven to be irresponsible will be returned to treatment in sanitoriums.

January 28 In a major speech at the Fourth Latin American and Caribbean Meeting in Havana, President Castro analyzes the situation of the Third World as imperialism's "neoliberalism" goes unchallenged by what used to be the Second World (the socialist bloc). Many of those socialist nations, Castro remarks, have now joined the Third World of underdeveloped countries.

February Latin America sends the largest volunteer brigade in the history of the region to work in Cuba's citrus harvest — about 240 people from Argentina, Bolivia, Brazil, Chile, Ecuador, Uruguay and Venezuela.

February 1 The Senate passes a nonbinding "sense of the Senate" resolution introduced by Senator John Kerry (D-Massachusetts) stating that the President should not restrict travel for educational, religious or humanitarian purposes or restrict information or cultural exchanges. Later in the month, the State Department recommends ending most travel restrictions to embargoed countries *except* for Cuba and North Korea. (*See* April 30)

February 3 The Clinton Administration ends the U.S. trade embargo against Vietnam, leading to increased questioning of the embargo against Cuba.

February 4 Businesspeople from around the United States announce at a press conference the founding of the Association for Free Trade with Cuba. Myron Simmons, the president of the new group, owns two companies in Pennsylvania that he maintains would be more profitable if allowed to trade with Cuba.

February 14 Foreign Minister Roberto Robaina calls for a conference April 22-24 to begin a dialogue with the Cuban community from around the world about family unification, including migration issues, and other mutual problems (*see* September 28, 1993).

February 14 The *Miami Herald* reports that airlines may expand service to Cuba because ten weekly charter flights are not sufficient for current demand.

February 16   UN human rights special rapporteur Carl Johan Groth of Sweden issues his latest report about Cuba to the UN Human Rights Commission in Geneva. Critical of human rights violations on the island, he once again concludes that the U.S. embargo impedes Cuba's efforts toward economic and political changes.

February 21-23   With the cooperation of the Cuban Institute of Friendship with the Peoples (ICAP), Cuban American Professionals and Entrepreneurs, based in Miami, sponsors its second seminar in Havana since it was founded in 1993. Some 30 to 40 Cuban Americans discuss business prospects in a post-embargo Cuba. Roberto Solís, the president of CAPE, says the organization favors an end to the embargo and normalization of relations.

February 24   At a Washington rally sponsored by *Unidad Cubana*, Representative Torricelli tells his Cuban American audience, "We will rally again" soon — in Havana. Hillary Clinton's brother, Hugh Rodham, addresses the rally as a representative of the President's family. Other speakers include both Florida senators and about 14 House members, including the three Cuban Americans. Afterward, as some participants harass people at the entrance to the Cuban Interests Section, Secret Service agents eventually intervene to prevent people from throwing rocks and scaling the fence.

February 26   The *Miami Herald* reports that the FBI is investigating complaints about threatening letters signed by three Alpha 66 leaders — Andrés Nazario Sargén, Diego Medina and Hugo Gascón Góngora. Received by a number of people, the letters warn that all those who visit Cuba or "dialogue" with the Cuban government "directly or indirectly" will become military targets of Alpha 66. Medina acknowledges that he and two other Alpha 66 leaders signed the letters.

February 28   An article titled "Fidel's New Friends" in *Forbes* magazine warns its readers that Cuban Americans traveling to Cuba are "adding as much as $100 million a year to the island's foreign exchange reserves." The magazine's publisher and one of the wealthiest people in the world, Malcolm Stevenson (Steve) Forbes Jr., is honorary chair of the Cuban American National Foundation's Blue Ribbon Commission on the Economic

Reconstruction of Cuba and in September 1995 announces plans to use $25 million of his personal fortune to run for president of the United States.

February-March Traveling through some 140 U.S. and Canadian cities, more than 250 people join the third Friendshipment Caravan, challenging the travel ban and the trade embargo by delivering medicines, seven buses and other humanitarian aid to Cuba.

March 9 The UN Human Rights Commission votes 24 to 9 with 20 abstentions for a U.S. resolution, presented by Geraldine Ferraro, that condemns Cuba for denying basic freedoms to its people.

March 10 The *Wall Street Journal* reports that Williams Company's telecommunications subsidiary says it has signed a memorandum of understanding with Cuba's telephone company that will allow WilTel and other phone companies to establish direct, high-quality phone links between the United States and Cuba. According to WilTel, the project complies with State Department guidelines encouraging improved communications between the two countries. The link will be located between the southern tip of Florida and a point near Havana. But the March 14 *Wall Street Journal* reports that the State Department has said it will not approve the agreements that Cuba has reached with U.S. companies (MCI, WilTel, IDB, LDDS) because Cuba charges a $4.85 surcharge for collect calls. This is considered normal practice in many countries but the State Department says that in the case of Cuba it would violate the "Cuban Democracy Act." (*See* October 5)

March 10-12 More than 30 scholars from Cuba attend the Latin American Studies Association meeting in Atlanta. LASA passes a resolution condemning the U.S. embargo and urging support for Representative Rangel's legislation, the Free Trade with Cuba Act.

March 11 U.S. media report that President Clinton plans to invite all of the Western Hemisphere's heads of state except for President Castro to a December Summit Meeting in Miami, the first such summit since 1967 in Uruguay. (President-in-exile Jean Bertrand Aristide will be invited to represent Haiti.)

March 17 At a hearing on Capitol Hill before the House Ways and Means Committee, more than thirty witnesses testify for and against the Free Trade with Cuba Act that would end the embargo against Cuba. Representative Charles Rangel, who introduced the bill and chairs the Ways and Means Committee, says it is ironic that the United States' two partners in the North American Free Trade Agreement (NAFTA), Canada and Mexico, are "doing lucrative business with Cuba" while U.S. businesses are barred from such trade.

March 19 Following his testimony on March 17 in Washington against the embargo, Reverend Jesse Jackson meets with Jorge Mas Canosa of the Cuban American National Foundation in Representative Carrie Meek's (D-Florida) suite at the Airport Hilton in Miami. According to CANF's "Cuba in the News" newsletter — boasting a picture of Jackson with CANF leaders — they begin a "dialogue" and plan to hold further discussions about how they can cooperate for their "common goal to restore democracy in Haiti and Cuba." Jackson tells the *Miami Herald* (article March 27) that he hopes CANF "can begin to defend the rights of all opinions to be heard without fear" so that those whose "voices have been oppressed right here at home through intimidation and violence" can be heard.

March 19 Representative Charles Rangel holds a press conference in Miami with Eloy Gutiérrez Menoyo of *Cambio Cubano* to urge an end to the embargo.

March 21 The Academy Awards take place in Los Angeles without the performance of Cuban dancers Lienz Chang Oliva and María del Rosario Suárez because the State Department denied them visas. In solidarity with her dancers, Alicia Alonso, head of the troupe, does not attend.

March 24 At a hearing on Capitol Hill, Assistant Secretary of State for Inter-American Affairs Alexander Watson testifies in favor of the Free and Independent Cuban Assistance Act, reintroduced into the current Congress by Representative Menéndez.

March 31 An advisory panel set up by Congress advises conversion of TV Martí's transmissions from VHF, channels 1-13, to UHF, channels 14-69, because Cuba has no UHF channels and therefore the broadcasts would not break international regulations that prohibit interference with a country's domestic frequencies. As expected, the panel recommends continued operation of Radio Martí. Jorge Mas Canosa praises the panel's recommendations.

Representative David Skaggs (D-Colorado), member of the House Appropriations Committee that votes on funding the station, says, "TV Martí still is not being seen in Cuba" and it is "time to cut our losses and pull the plug on this failed experiment." Congress has agreed to fund Radio Martí for $19 million and TV Martí for $9.5 million in 1994 but had ordered part of the money withheld until this review. Chosen by USIA Director Joseph Duffey, the panel's executive director is Robert S. Leiken, who was a key Democratic adviser for the Reagan Administration's support of the Contras in Nicaragua.

April The U.S.-Cuba Business Council is established for the purpose of uniting U.S. businesses to support the embargo until Cuba establishes a "free-market" system. Otto Reich becomes president of the council, which takes the position of the Cuban American National Foundation that any companies with any connection to the present government of Cuba may be forced to move to the end of the line in a "post-Castro" Cuba.

April The Council of American Ambassadors, a group of more than 200 retired diplomats, sends a delegation to Havana to assess the impact of the embargo. They meet with President Castro.

April 4 Grenada announces it is reestablishing diplomatic relations with Cuba, severed at the time of the 1983 U.S. invasion.

April 6 Justice Department representative John Russell says Pastors for Peace will not be prosecuted for shipping millions of dollars worth of aid in three Friendshipment Caravans to Cuba. Moreover, the Justice Department is returning the 65 passports confiscated from people who participated in the Freedom to Travel campaign last October. Representative Torricelli announces that he is "furious" because the embargo is not being strictly enforced.

April 6 Cuba and Antigua and Barbuda establish diplomatic relations.

April 20 While fomenting rumors of some catastrophe having befallen Fidel Castro, Jorge Mas Canosa delivers a 15-minute broadcast on *La Voz de la Fundación*, the short-wave radio station of the Cuban American National Foundation, about how CANF plans to establish a transitional government of exiles and Cubans (*see* June 3, 1993).

April 22-24 More than 200 Cubans living in exile in 27 countries, mostly in the United States, accept Cuba's invitation to the Conference on the Nation and Emigration, announced on February 14 by Foreign Minister Roberto Robaina. On the closing day, President Castro meets with the participants, leading to an uproar in Miami when a video of that gathering (reportedly sold by the Cuban government-owned TV station INTERTV to a pool of Miami TV stations) appears repeatedly on Miami TV. During the conference, the first of its kind since *El Diálogo* in 1978, Cuban officials announce measures aimed at encouraging more visits and investments by the exile community of more than 1.5 million Cuban Americans: those who have emigrated legally will no longer have to wait five years before being allowed to return to visit and will no longer be required to spend money in government-owned hotels during visits; the Foreign Ministry will establish a special office for dealing with the needs of Cubans who have emigrated and a new magazine will deal specifically with their problems; a limited number of children of emigrants will be allowed to study in Cuban institutions, paying costs.

April 30 Congress approves the Foreign Relations Authorization Act for fiscal years 1994 and 1995 containing this nonbinding resolution in Section 525, titled "Free Trade in Ideas": "It is the sense of the Congress that the President should not restrict travel or exchanges for informational, educational, religious, cultural, or humanitarian purposes or for public performances or exhibitions, between the United States and any other country." Nevertheless, Section 526, titled "Embargo Against Cuba," states: "It is the sense of the Congress that the President should advocate and seek a mandatory international United Nations Security Council embargo against the dictatorship of Cuba."

April-May On the 25th anniversary of the Venceremos Brigade, 140 people travel from the United States to do agricultural work in Cuba.

May While in Bridgetown, Barbados, for a UN conference on Sustainable Development of Small Island Developing States, President Castro boards Greenpeace's *Rainbow Warrior*. From Barbados, he visits Ghana, where he meets with President Jerry John Rawlings before continuing to South Africa.

May 1 Cuba does not have the traditional May Day march. Instead the National Assembly meets in special session May 1-2 to deal with the economic crisis. The meeting is televised.

May 8 Piloting a Cuban passenger jet to the Bahamas, Basilio García Breto locks the other crew members out of the cockpit and hijacks the plane to Miami. Nobody else asks for asylum. The co-pilot flies the plane back to Cuba. The Cuban American National Foundation arranges a press conference for García on the following day. Later, FBI agent Paul Miller defines the seizure of the plane as a "diversion" rather than a hijacking because García "used no violence" and there were no injuries (*see* December 29, 1992). But U.S. authorities do question five American passengers about why they were in Cuba, checking to see if they were in violation of the U.S. embargo.

May 10 Rodolfo Frometa and Fausto Marimón announce that they and other members of Alpha 66 are forming a separate group, Comandos F4, to pursue a more militant strategy against Cuba. On June 2, they are arrested for trying to purchase a Stinger antiaircraft missile and other weapons. The Justice Department does not cite any violation of neutrality laws but is instead concerned that ownership of weapons like the Stinger must be strictly controlled and, for this reason, the two men are sentenced on December 20 to three and a half years and one year respectively. On February 6, while still in Alpha 66, Frometa and Marimón were detained along with several other Cuban Americans when the U.S. Coast Guard found them in a boat containing weapons, ammunition and thousands of dollars off Key Biscayne, but no charges were filed.

May 10 At the presidential inauguration in South Africa of Nelson Mandela, President Castro is the only foreign dignitary to receive a tumultuous welcome from the crowd. The two countries' foreign ministers, Roberto Robaina and Alfred Nzo, use the occasion to formally establish diplomatic relations.

May 18 The State Department releases a report that recognizes Cuba's efforts to keep drug traffickers from using Cuban territory. The report states that Cuba cooperated with U.S. drug enforcement "on an ad hoc basis" in 1993, including one episode in September when U.S. aircraft were allowed to enter Cuban airspace in hot pursuit of suspected traffickers aboard a boat. The

Cuban Border Patrol stopped the boat, found narcotics, and turned the suspects over to U.S. authorities. The report notes that a 1904 U.S.-Cuban extradition treaty is not currently in use.

May 29 In Mexico, a helicopter in which Representative Torricelli is a passenger makes an emergency landing because an oil line ruptures. Torricelli asks the Mexican government to investigate to see if it was sabotage because he has been greeted by demonstrators at the U.S. Embassy shouting "Gringo, go home" and newspaper headlines with the same message. Two of the three presidential candidates refuse to meet with him and Zapatista rebel leader, Commander Marcos of Chiapas, also shuns him. Torricelli tells reporters later that he encountered opposition to his position on Cuba during his Mexican visit.

May 31 The *Wall Street Journal* reports that two Canadian companies, Sherritt Inc. and Talisman Energy Inc., have announced an oil discovery in Cuba's Bay of Cárdenas.

June Cuba and Bahrain establish diplomatic relations.

June At the annual OAS meeting in Belem, Brazil, outgoing Secretary General João Baena Soares receives a standing ovation when he asks, "Hasn't the time come to readmit Cuba to the Latin American family?"

June 10 Dozens of sailboats race from St. Petersburg, Florida, toward Havana in resumption of the Florida-Havana regatta that was an annual event from 1930 until 1959 (except during World War II). Sponsored by the Sarasota Sailing Squadron of Florida and the International Nautical Club of Havana, the competition takes place despite threats and protests by some rightwing Cuban Americans. The sailors carry their own provisions to circumvent the embargo and their Cuban hosts are paying for docking and other fees. The sailors are also carrying food, medical supplies and clothing to donate to individual Cubans as allowed by law.

June 12 Three Cubans steal a crop-dusting plan to fly to Key West.

June 13 Mexican President Carlos Salinas de Gortari makes his first visit to Cuba on his way to the Ibero-American Summit, meeting for several hours with President Castro. This follows a donation in early June by the Mexican Congress of a day's work (approximately $75,000) to buy oil for Cuba. Criticizing the U.S. embargo, Salinas announces Cuba's first major privatization deal with a Mexican investment company, Grupo Domos International SA, to overhaul the telephone system. Representative Torricelli calls the deal "an almost shocking economic decision."

June 14 President Castro attends the Fourth Ibero-American Summit of Latin American countries, Spain and Portugal in Cartagena, Colombia. For the first time since the revolution, he wears a guayabera instead of a military uniform to an international event. The final communiqué by the 19 leaders in attendance calls for elimination "of unilateral coercive economic and trade measures."

June 14 Trying to stop a June 23 challenge of the travel ban, the Treasury Department freezes the $43,000 bank account of the Freedom to Travel Campaign. But individuals and organizations contribute money to replace the frozen funds, and the group subsequently files a lawsuit to challenge the ban, contending that U.S. citizens have a constitutional right to travel. In October, the Treasury Department releases the funds. The lawsuit is dismissed in December by the Federal District Court. The Freedom to Travel Campaign's appeal of that ruling is argued in September 1995 before the Ninth U.S. Circuit Court of Appeals in San Francisco by Michael Krinsky, general counsel for the National Emergency Civil Liberties Committee.

June 20-24 Mayor Michael Dow heads a delegation from Mobile, Alabama, to Havana, where they meet with Mayor Pedro Chávez González. Mobile and Havana have begun a Sister City relationship.

June 23 The *Wall Street Journal* reports that ING Bank of the Netherlands will become the first foreign bank to operate in Cuba since the 1959 revolution.

June 23-30 Almost 200 people from some 20 states participate in the second Freedom to Travel Campaign. When 115 of them return through Houston, U.S. Customs officials take possessions from nine people — everything that has "Cuba" on it, such as cigars, T-shirts and posters. But nobody is prosecuted for not requesting U.S. government permission to travel. The Campaign organizes six challenges with more than 600 travelers by September 1995.

June 25 The *New York Times* editorializes against the U.S. travel ban and the "Cuban Democracy Act."

June 25 During a meeting with Cuban bishops at the Vatican, the Pope endorses the statement they issued in September 1993, criticizing the Cuban government while calling for an end to the U.S. embargo.

June 28 President Clinton's advisers recommend reactivation of Guantánamo Naval Base as a processing center for Haitians. On the following day, the U.S. Coast Guard begins delivering hundreds of Haitians to the base, where a tent city will be built to handle a maximum of 12,500 refugees. Within a few days, the Clinton Administration announces plans to increase the capacity to 20,000.

July 1 So far this year 3,854 Cubans have arrived illegally in the United States. A total of 3,656 arrived in all of 1993.

July 4 *Trabajadores* [Workers], a Cuban newspaper, calls the processing center for Haitians at the U.S. naval base in Guantánamo a virtual concentration camp. The newspaper points out that under the terms of the agreements in 1903 and 1934 the base was to be used only for coal or for naval activities.

July 12 *El Diario* reports that the American Federation of State, County and Municipal Employees (AFSCME) with 1.3 million members in the United States and Puerto Rico passed a resolution at its international convention in favor of ending the embargo and normalizing diplomatic relations with Cuba.

July 12 Foreign Minister Roberto Robaina invites the UN's High Commissioner for Human Rights, José Ayala Lazo, to visit Cuba.

July 13 In Havana harbor, Fidencio Ramel Prieto Hernández, preparing to head for Florida, puts the night watchman to sleep with thorazine and then helps Raúl Muñoz García load about 63 Cubans aboard a leaky, wooden tugboat built in 1879 and fit only for use within the port, with life-saving equipment for only four people. When three tugboats give chase, there is a collision between one of them and the stolen vessel, which sinks. Cuba's Border Patrol rescues 31 people; the others, including Prieto, drown.

July 15 At a conference sponsored by former owners of sugar mills in Cuba, Representative Torricelli proposes that in a post-Castro Cuba the U.S. government would drop the quota system that decrees the amount of sugar imported by the United States from sugar-producing countries. This, he says, would give Cuba an edge because of its "natural advantages" for sugar production. Earlier, Dennis Hays, head of the State Department's Office of

Cuban Affairs, told this group, which is obviously looking forward to retaking their sugar mills, that a stabilized sugar industry could provide badly needed foreign exchange for a post-Castro government.

July 18 In Miami Beach, President Clinton addresses the annual convention of the National Council of La Raza, the largest U.S. Hispanic lobbying organization, primarily Mexican Americans and Puerto Ricans. On the dais with Clinton are several prominent rightwing Cuban Americans — banker Carlos Arboleya, a supporter of the Cuban American National Foundation, Representative Lincoln Díaz-Balart (R-Florida), and CANF official Agustín de Goytesolo.

July 22 In response to UN Secretary General Boutros Boutros-Ghali's request for information regarding fulfillment by the U.S. government of the General Assembly's vote in November 1993 (and in November 1992) calling for an end to the embargo against Cuba, Foreign Minister Roberto Robaina responds with a long letter describing how Washington is ignoring the General Assembly and reinforcing the embargo.

July 24 President Castro joins other heads of state in Cartagena, Colombia, to found the Association of Caribbean States (ACS) that includes 25 nations. Eleven dependent territories are associate members. The scheduled formal launch of the Association is later postponed from January to July 1995, reportedly because of U.S. pressure on would-be member states to avoid such trading links with Cuba.

July 26 In Havana harbor, a ferry with 80 to 100 people aboard is hijacked and several people are thrown overboard by armed hijackers. The ferry leaves the port and is eventually intercepted by the U.S. Coast Guard. More than half leave the ferry for Florida and the rest return to Havana aboard the ferry.

July 26 In a change of routine at Cuba's major July 26 celebration, Raúl Castro, Cuba's first deputy president and defense minister, makes the key speech that President Fidel Castro usually provides. The celebration takes place on the Isle of Youth at the site where both brothers were imprisoned by the Batista regime in 1953. The President is seated in the front row of the audience.

July 26 Writing from Havana, David Asman, editor of the Americas column in the *Wall Street Journal*, recommends ending the embargo against Cuba.

July 27 Following a 16-month review by the National Security Council, the Kennedy Library makes public two and a half more hours of White House tapes made during the Missile Crisis. The discussions, from October 18 and October 22, 1962, were recorded on secret equipment authorized by President Kennedy. The NSC ordered two minutes and 12 seconds deleted from these tapes.

July 31 The UN Security Council's 15 members vote 12-0 (Brazil and China abstain; Rwanda is absent) to authorize the U.S. government to invade and occupy Haiti if sanctions fail to force the military regime to fall. During the debate before the vote, Cuba, Brazil, China, Mexico and Uruguay express reservations about UN support of such an invasion. (Cuba, Mexico and Uruguay are not current members of the Security Council and therefore do not get to vote.)

August In Havana, about 1,000 delegates from 80 countries along with 400 Cuban librarians attend the International Federation of Library Associations and Institutions conference — the first time it has met in Latin America. More than 100 U.S. librarians form the largest foreign delegation.

August 3 A second ferry is seized in Havana harbor by armed hijackers. Some passengers jump overboard before it leaves the port, leaving 80 people aboard, including ten infants. The Border Patrol and two civilian vessels follow to pick up anyone in the water. When the U.S. Coast Guard intercepts the boat, some passengers go to Florida while the others return to Cuba.

August 4 A third ferry is seized by armed hijackers. A police officer, Gabriel Lamoth Caballero, is evidently pushed overboard and drowns and a second officer is missing. The Border Patrol takes over the boat when it runs out of fuel and returns all aboard to Cuba.

August 5 As rumors fly of another Mariel or at least another hijacked ferry, hundreds of people congregate at the port and along Havana's seafront drive, the Malecón. With no ferry departing, the crowd erupts into rock-throwing and looting. At first the police are outnumbered, but the ratio changes when authorities mobilize supporters who rush to the area. President Castro arrives on the scene and walks among the people, proving to be a reassuring figure for both groups of the citizenry. Of some 30 people arrested, most are released within 72 hours and all by the end of two weeks.

August 5 At 9 p.m. on both national television stations as well as CNN, President Castro says the U.S. strategy "is to create a situation, to promote as much discontent as possible" in order to cause "a bloodbath." He reiterates that Washington has not carried out its side of the migration agreement (*see* December 14, 1984, and November 19-20, 1987). As he had in the afternoon, Castro warns, "If the United States does not take rapid and efficient measures to stop the incidents of illegal exits from the country, we will feel obliged to tell the Border Patrol not to stop any vessel that wishes to leave Cuba." Nor will the Border Patrol intervene if boats arrive from the United States to pick up Cubans.

   While appearing on television, Castro is handed a note from the Foreign Ministry telling him that the chief of the U.S. Interests Section in Havana, Joseph Sullivan, has warned that the situation could become serious if President Castro speaks the same way he spoke in the afternoon. Castro proceeds to inform his audience about the note, concluding, "I not only speak that way, I confirm what I said."

August 6 Following the news of Cuba's new policy, Cubans in their own makeshift boats and rafts begin an unimpeded exodus, mostly from Havana and Cojímar west of Havana.

August 6-7 As Cuban and U.S. officials meet through the weekend at the U.S. Interests Section in Havana, Deputy National Security Adviser Sandy Berger chairs a White House meeting with Attorney General Janet Reno and other U.S. officials to review contingency plans for responding to an exodus. One option is a blockade by U.S. warships of the passage between Key West and Cuba.

August 6-7 President Castro is in Bogotá, Colombia, for the presidential inauguration of Ernesto Samper on August 7.

August 7 The body of Gabriel Lamoth Caballero, the police officer killed August 4, lies in state. More than half a million Cubans participate in a day of activities in homage to the dead officer and at a rally in support of the government. At the other end of the island on the following day, some 150,000 Cubans attend his funeral in Guantánamo.

August 7 The *San Francisco Chronicle* editorializes for ending the ban on travel to Cuba.

August 8 Another boat, a naval vessel, is hijacked and one of its officers, Roberto Aguilar Reyes, is shot. His body falls overboard and is not found until August 10. Three others are forced to jump overboard. The hijackers pick up other Cubans and head out to sea with 26 people aboard. The Border Patrol alerts the U.S. Coast Guard about the hijacking, giving the name of the man who committed the murder, Leonel Macías González, as well as the location and speed of the vessel. The Coast Guard delivers all those aboard to Florida on August 10. The INS detains Macías while releasing the other Cubans. State Department representative David Johnson says the "reported use of sometimes lethal violence by those taking over vessels to flee the island is a disturbing trend."

August 10 A crop-dusting plane is stolen and lands in the Florida Keys with 14 Cubans aboard, the seventh Cuban aircraft stolen since December 1992, according to U.S. media.

August 11 President Castro demands that Leonel Macías González (*see* August 8) be prosecuted for murder or returned to Cuba for prosecution. On February 2, 1995, a U.S. immigration judge grants asylum to Macías. The INS appeals but in April 1995 the INS appeals board rules in favor of Macías, who is released from detention April 17.

August 11 Attorney General Reno announces that U.S. authorities will seize vessels headed for Cuba to pick up emigrants and will prosecute U.S. citizens involved.

August 11 Representative José Serrano (D-New York) introduces a piece of legislation that contains one sentence: "The Cuban Democracy Act of 1992 is repealed."

August 12 The *Wall Street Journal* editorializes that it "had been inclined to the view that lifting the embargo would sensibly benefit Cuba's people" but now "'Do Not Resuscitate' seems the more human course," adding that "the better course at this volatile moment may be to redirect those departing back to support the courageous protesters in the streets." This is the position taken by the Cuban American National Foundation and its allies in Congress.

August 12 The Cuban government issues guidelines for the Border Patrol, making it clear that Cuba will not "continue to be the most ardent defenders of the United States' coasts, which leads them to pillory us for any incident, while they themselves constantly encourage the violation of their own immigration laws." The Border Patrol will not stop exiting boats unless they are hijacked or stolen, nor hinder incoming boats if they are picking up relatives and friends. A few days later, the Interior Ministry instructs the Border Patrol to do all it can to persuade emigrants not to take infants and young children on unsafe vessels, using force only when necessary.

August 13 In a four-hour struggle at the Guantánamo Naval Base, U.S. military police quell an uprising by some 750 Haitians. About 120 Haitians scale double rolls of concertina wire and try to swim across Guantánamo Bay, believing that they might reach Cuba on the other side and get jobs there. But the U.S. government controls both sides of the bay. Coast Guard and Navy ships pluck them from the water. For two days, the Defense Department does not release information about the rioting. Some 15,000 Haitians are being held at the naval base. Another brawl takes place August 17.

August 18 As he campaigns for re-election in November, Florida Governor Lawton Chiles declares an immigration emergency and asks for the federal government's help in coping with the influx of Cubans.

August 18 Following a top-level White House meeting, Attorney General Janet Reno goes on national television to announce that all Cubans arriving by boat will be detained, effective immediately. For years Washington has had a contingency plan, "Distant Shore," for dealing with an emergency migration problem, but U.S. officials say that current levels will not "trigger this kind of thing" (moving people from Florida to other states and sealing off coasts, for example). On the next day, Reno's announcement is broadcast on Cuba's state-run radio.

August 19 Ending the open-door policy for Cubans that has been in effect for more than 35 years, President Clinton orders the Coast

Guard, backed by the Navy, to intercept Cuban emigrants at sea and transport them to Guantánamo Naval Base.

August 19 Cuban American Representatives Menéndez, Díaz-Balart and Ros-Lehtinen, along with Representative Torricelli hold a news conference to call for a military blockade of Cuba to force the collapse of the Cuban government. They criticize Clinton for ending the policy of granting immediate asylum and demand that he stop all flights and cash transfers to and from Cuba.

August 19 In the evening, a group of Cuban Americans, including Jorge Mas Canosa, meet with President Clinton at the White House to tell him what they want him to do. Also present are Florida Governor Lawton Chiles; Cuban American María Elena Toraño, Democratic Party lobbyist; Cuban American César Odio, Democratic city manager of Miami; Luis Lauredo, Democratic businessman and coordinator of Florida's preparations for the upcoming Summit of the Americas; Vice-President Al Gore; National Security Council Deputy Adviser Sandy Berger; and Attorney General Janet Reno.

August 20 Following another meeting in the morning with Cuban Americans led by Jorge Mas Canosa, President Clinton announces new sanctions, tightening the embargo even further: cash may no longer be sent to Cubans by U.S. relatives except to help pay for lawful emigration or in case of demonstrable "extreme hardship"; Cuban Americans may no longer visit relatives on the island except on a case-by-case determination of "extreme hardship"; charter flights may carry only legal immigrants, U.S. and foreign government and international organization employees traveling on official business, journalists, and persons traveling "under specific license." Professional researchers will henceforth have to obtain individual licenses from the Treasury Department. Off the record, some Administration officials describe these measures as political payoff to the Cuban American National Foundation for its support of ending the policy of automatic asylum for Cubans. There will be increased and amplified broadcasts to the island by Radio and TV Martí, augmented by the use of EC130 surveillance planes to fly around providing electronic interference with Cuba's jamming efforts. And there will be efforts to focus the attention of the

United Nations and other international organizations on human rights in Cuba. (*See* August 26)

August 20 At a news conference in Miami, Jorge Mas Canosa praises President Clinton's new policy: "All Cubans should be grateful for what has happened last night and this morning." This leads to an outpouring of criticism by Cuban Americans against Mas Canosa for being in favor of putting Cubans in a concentration camp.

August 20 The New York *Daily News* editorializes for ending the embargo.

August 21 On ABC television, White House Chief of Staff Leon Panetta, asked about a possible naval blockade of Cuba, responds, "That's obviously one of the options that we would look at in the future as we see whether or not Castro begins to make some legitimate moves toward democracy." The Associated Press reports that Clinton Administration officials, speaking anonymously, say Panetta's remarks refer to blocking trade from other countries to Cuba and there is not any active effort to implement a naval blockade.

August 21 To those who have pointed out that the current U.S. policy of enforcing the "Cuban Democracy Act" hurts the Cuban people, Representative Torricelli declares, "It is impossible to bring fundamental political change to Cuba without doing damage to the people who live on the island."

August 22 At Guantánamo Naval Base, the Coast Guard deposits the first Cubans detained under the new rules: 2,338 in one day. There are 14,616 Haitians already there.

August 23 As a result of discussions at the Conference on the Nation and Emigration in April, Cuba announces changes in migration policy effective immediately. For example, Cubans who left the island legally will be allowed to repatriate permanently and to visit without having to apply to Havana for visas.

August 24 Following President Clinton's August 20 announcements, Radio Martí increases the power of its AM transmissions from 50,000 to 100,000 watts and its broadcasting to 71 hours a day on 17 short-wave frequencies. TV Martí boosts broadcasts by two hours — from 3:30 a.m. to 8 a.m.

August 24 *Granma* reports that since 1990 Cuba has treated more than 10,000 children and some 2,000 adults affected by the Chernobyl nuclear accident.

August 24 Speaking to reporters in Santiago, Chile, Cuban Foreign Minister Roberto Robaina describes Cuba's consistent position on negotiations: "the Cuban government is prepared to meet with U.S. representatives at any time, at any place and on any level." He states, "We are willing to talk with the United States with one condition, which is that there be no conditions."

August 24 Appearing on Cuban television as well as CNN, President Castro proposes direct talks with Washington on a broad range of issues, including the embargo. He recites the many memos sent by Cuba to U.S. officials about migration issues, including demands that hijackers be prosecuted.

August 25 President Clinton rejects President Castro's overture, telling reporters the policy of isolating Cuba will stand. Deputy Secretary of State for Political Affairs Peter Tarnoff, Clinton's coordinator on Cuba, tells reporters at the White House that U.S. and Cuban officials have been meeting once every six months for technical talks on migration matters and that the Clinton Administration has no interest "in having a higher-level political dialogue." Talks will deal only with migration.

August 25 In a closed session, Assistant Secretary of State for Inter-American Affairs Alexander Watson and senior National Security Council official Morton Halperin brief the Senate Foreign Relations Committee about developments regarding Cuba. Democratic senators criticize current policy and argue for broad discussion with President Castro. Afterward, the Committee's chair, Claiborne Pell, calls the policy of continuing the embargo contradictory: "We are enforcing an embargo that makes conditions worse and is driving people out." He criticizes President Clinton's failure to accept Castro's call for wide-ranging, high-level talks.

August 25 Because Krome detention center near Miami is full with 650 Cubans, an overflow group of 51 is transported to an INS holding center at Port Isabel, Texas, where they join some three dozen Cubans arrested for coming across the border from Mexico recently. For the first time, the Defense Department puts out a partial estimate of costs to U.S. taxpayers for holding Cubans at

Guantánamo: $100 million to expand facilities and at least $20 million a month for food and shelter.

August 25 The Inter-American Dialogue — founded in 1982 as a think tank for developing policy in the Western Hemisphere — issues a statement on U.S.-Cuban policy: "We urge the two governments to turn away from confrontation and begin to negotiate the issues that divide them." The organization is composed of prominent people from the United States, Latin America and the Caribbean. Its Task Force on Cuba, which prepared the study, is headed by former Attorney General Elliot Richardson and includes John C. Whitehead, Deputy Secretary of State under President Reagan; McGeorge Bundy, National Security Adviser to President Kennedy, and Raúl Alfonsín, former Argentine president. In 1992, the group called for gradual lifting of the embargo.

August 26 The Treasury Department issues new regulations, codifying the sanctions announced on August 20. These measures result in a booming industry of traveling to Cuba via "illegal" routes like the Bahamas, Canada and Mexico. Resistance to the increased violation of U.S. citizens' right to travel leads to growing challenges by people who openly refuse to obey such law. In addition, the amount of money sent by Cuban Americans to their relatives on the island reportedly is increasing rather than decreasing.

August 26 The *New York Times* editorializes for "broad negotiations with the Castro regime."

August 26 *El Diario* editorializes against the embargo while calling for a dialogue between President Castro and the Cuban people, including Cuban Americans.

August 26 Changing course, a *Wall Street Journal* editorial says that "we have slowly come to believe" ending the embargo is the best way to "help Cuba's people liberate themselves."

August 27 U.S. media report that Senators Patrick Leahy (D-Vermont) and Alan Simpson (R-Wyoming) have stated that President Clinton should talk to President Castro.

August 27 State Department representative Michael McCurry announces that the Clinton Administration will resume talks on migration with Cuba.

August 27 Representative Lincoln Díaz-Balart (R-Florida) suggests Washington allow exiles to launch attacks against Cuba from the United States, contrary to the Neutrality Act (which he wants to repeal).

August 28 Walter D. Cadman, Miami district director of the INS, says Cubans are covered by constitutional guarantees the minute they touch U.S. soil, so each case will be judged on individual merit.

August 28 On CBS television, Secretary of State Warren Christopher maintains that if President Castro "moves toward democracy in a tangible, significant way, we'll respond in a carefully calibrated way." The phrase, "carefully calibrated way," is taken from the "Cuban Democracy Act." Christopher presents Washington's policy as the moderate course weaving between the two extremes of imposing a military blockade and lifting the embargo.

August 28 Cuban Roman Catholic bishops urge "sincere and respectful dialogue" between Cuba and the United States.

August 29 At Guantánamo, 226 Cubans ask to return to their homes.

August 29 Cuba announces that it will sign the Tlatelolco Treaty for non-proliferation of nuclear weapons.

August 30 Attorney General Janet Reno, National Security Council Deputy Adviser Samuel Berger, and Deputy Secretary of State Peter Tarnoff meet at the White House to prepare formal negotiating instructions for migration talks to begin September 1. One task is figuring out how to raise the number of Cubans accepted each year to the ceiling of 27,845, the limit in one year for any country that went into effect in 1990. The INS list of foreigners waiting for visas at this time is almost 3,500,000. The number of Cubans is 19,700 of whom 18,100 are closely related to U.S. citizens and therefore supposed not to have difficulty getting U.S. visas.

August 30 During a protest by about 15 Cuban Americans outside the Cuban UN Mission, several place a chain across the front door of the Mission despite the presence of a police guard responsible for preventing such acts. In the resulting melee, police arrest seven people, four from the UN Mission. Two of them later return to Cuba as part of their routine assignment. The other two are expelled by the U.S. government in April 1995 because Cuba refuses to waive their diplomatic immunity in order for them to have a U.S. trial on charges of riot and obstructing government.

August 30 In a *Wall Street Journal* opinion piece, Elliott Abrams suggests creating at Guantánamo Naval Base "a West Berlin, a small free city within the communist nation," the "embryo of a Guantánamo Bay Free Trade Zone." Then, in an interview with editors and reporters at the *Record*, a newspaper in his New Jersey district, Representative Torricelli urges Cuban Americans to turn the base into the site of a government in exile. He urges Cuban Americans to send supplies and predicts the detainees will develop their own political leadership, newspaper and radio station aimed at the rest of Cuba. Later in the day he meets with a few dozen wealthy Cuban American businesspeople, including Remberto Pérez, director of the Cuban American National Foundation office in Union City, New Jersey. Torricelli claims that by the law of his "Cuban Democracy Act" the embargo cannot be lifted unless Cuba has elections deemed "free" by U.S. judgment. He opposes taking Cubans from Guantánamo to third countries, saying that if the exodus continues it would be "incumbent on the UN" to establish "safe areas" in Cuba, seizing more Cuban territory as necessary.

August 31 In Miami some Cuban Americans are staging a hunger strike, demanding a military blockade and the right to launch military attacks from U.S. soil. Among their supporters are Armando Valladares and Representative Lincoln Díaz-Balart.

August 31 Florida Democratic Senator Bob Graham visits Guantánamo. He is followed the next day by three Florida Republican Representatives — Díaz-Balart, Ros-Lehtinen and Porter Goss — and by two New Jersey Democratic Representatives — Menéndez and Torricelli.

September 1 A Cuban delegation led by Cuban National Assembly President and former UN Ambassador Ricardo Alarcón and a U.S. delegation led by Deputy Assistant Secretary of State for Latin America Michael Skol begin a round of talks in New York about migration. More than 19,000 Cubans left Cuba illegally in August.

September 1   U.S. Magistrate Thomas Wilson orders two Cuban exiles deported for smuggling 19 Cubans into the United States where they were detained August 31.

September 1   At a private banquet hosted with about 30 exile leaders in Coral Gables, Florida, Cuban American National Foundation members warn Congressional members (including Torricelli) and a Clinton Administration representative (Richard Nuccio) that Cuban areas of Miami will "explode" if negotiators make concessions to Cuba. CANF President Francisco J. Hernández threatens, "As much as we support the policies of the Clinton Administration, we certainly need a clearer message and a clear understanding of how far those negotiations are going to go, or you will see a different community."

September 3   The U.S. Coast Guard intercepts two boats and arrests five Cuban Americans for attempting to smuggle more than 60 Cubans into the United States. The Cubans are taken to Guantánamo.

September 4   In Miami's Little Havana, molotov cocktails are thrown at the office of *Replica* magazine, which has been bombed several times, starting in 1974. Editor Max Lesnick, who left Cuba in 1961, is a founding member of *Cambio Cubano* and attended the Conference on the Nation and Emigration in Havana in April.

September 6   U.S. troops begin moving Cubans to Panama. President Ernesto Pérez Balladares has agreed to accept 10,000 on two conditions: that they be confined to U.S. bases at U.S. expense and that they be moved to another country within six months.

September 6   Rock-throwing protests erupt in two incidents in two camps as hundreds of Cubans protest being kept at Guantánamo. These protests continue intermittently, with some injuries to Cuban detainees and U.S. soldiers.

September 7   U.S. authorities begin to release some Cubans — the elderly and children — from the Krome Detention Center in Miami.

September 7-8   At the urging of the Spanish government, Foreign Minister Roberto Robaina, while visiting Madrid, meets separately with three Cuban Americans: Ramón Cernuda, U.S. representative of the Cuban Committee for Human Rights and

National Reconciliation; Alfredo Durán, an official of the Cuban Committee for Democracy; and Eloy Gutiérrez Menoyo, head of *Cambio Cubano*. The Cuban American National Foundation condemns the meetings, which Cernuda says will continue in New York or Havana.

September 8 In a joint column in the *Washington Post*, the chairs of the Senate Foreign Relations Committee and the House Foreign Affairs Committee, Claiborne Pell (D-Rhode Island) and Lee Hamilton (D-Indiana), call for lifting the embargo in stages.

September 9 Ending talks that began September 1, Cuban and U.S. negotiators reach an agreement on migration policy, including these points: the INS will grant a minimum of 20,000 visas a year to Cubans, with an additional 4,500 to 6,500 to be admitted during the first year of the agreement; those already at Guantánamo, Krome and Port Isabel will be required to return to Cuba to get legal visas; the U.S. government agrees to "oppose and impede" hijackings of planes and boats; the Cuban government agrees to do what it can to stop the exodus and to repatriate those who are asking to be repatriated.

September 9 Cubans held at Guantánamo begin to stage various forms of protest against the new migration agreement. Over the next few days, thousands escape from their barbed-wire enclosures. Some are wounded by U.S. soldiers wearing riot gear and carrying fixed bayonets.

September 10 Carrying out its part of the new agreement, Cuba announces before noon that Cubans will have 72 hours to get their rafts off the beaches; after that, people will be prevented from leaving. The flow of Cubans leaving the island illegally slows to a trickle.

September 10 At the end of a Summit Meeting of the Río Group, the 14 Latin American and Caribbean presidents once again state their desire to increase contacts with Cuba and incorporate it fully into regional bodies. They urge the United States to end its embargo and call for "peaceful transition towards a democratic and pluralist system in Cuba."

September 15 Taking office as the new OAS Secretary General, César Gaviria, former president of Colombia, offers to define a new and ambitious agenda for the organization that would include readmission of Cuba.

September 21 Cuban and Mexican officials sign an oil and telephone deal that will virtually cancel Cuba's $340 million debt to Mexico.

September 22 The U.S. Coast Guard officially ends its rescue patrols in the Florida Straits, Operation Able Vigil, because of the sharp decrease in Cuban boat people. Some vessels will continue to patrol. There are 30,790 Cubans behind concertina wire at the U.S. naval base in Guantánamo and 1,500 on U.S. bases in Panama. There are 446 at the Krome Detention Center in Miami and 270 at Port Isabel, Texas.

September 22 At a meeting in Havana, the Cuban Conference of Catholic Bishops calls for further U.S.-Cuban negotiations about migration and other issues.

September 26 A wide-ranging interview with President Castro is published in *U.S. News and World Report*, part of the extensive coverage by U.S. media about Cuba during this period.

October 1 After studying the effect of a pilot program, Cuba allows the opening of some 130 farmers' markets that sell produce at whatever price the market will bear (after they fulfill quotas of produce for the state). The markets rapidly help alleviate food shortages. Because these products are purchased with pesos, the markets are one reason for a sharp reversal of the peso's fortunes. Previously down to 120 to 150 to the dollar, the peso rises to a value of 50 to 60 to the dollar in October and to 25 or fewer to the dollar by September 1995.

October 1-9 For the third time, the Freedom to Travel Campaign challenges the U.S. travel ban. The group includes Cuban Americans who visit relatives in Cuba in defiance of the August 20 sanctions.

October 3 At a breakfast hosted by the Board of Directors of the U.S.-Cuba Trade and Economic Council at Rockefeller Plaza in New York City, Foreign Minister Roberto Robaina and invited businesspeople discuss investment opportunities in Cuba. The Council, founded this year by John S. Kavulich, provides the U.S. business world with information and analysis on matters relevant to U.S.-Cuban commercial, economic and political relations.

October 4 Ten U.S. physicians and scientists together with the Center for Constitutional Rights file a petition against the U.S.

government with the Inter-American Commission on Human Rights of the OAS, charging that the embargo is causing misery and even deaths in Cuba. In February 1995, the OAS Commission holds a hearing on behalf of the civilian population of Cuba. Experts, including Dr Anthony Kirkpatrick who visited Cuba to study the situation, present evidence that the embargo has direct effects upon the current health crisis in Cuba. The OAS Commission consequently writes to the U.S. government to request that it "observe the traditional exemption under customary international law of medicine, medical supplies and basic food items" from any embargo.

October 4 In Florida, Hugh Rodham wins the Democratic primary and will run for the U.S. Senate in the November election (*see* September 6, 1992). His sister, Hillary Rodham Clinton, has campaigned for him. He has support from the Cuban American National Foundation, but so does the Republican, Senator Connie Mack, and the pattern has been that, where both parties' candidates favor its policies, CANF offers more support to the Republican.

October 5 The State Department announces that it has told the Federal Communications Commission it no longer has any objections to telecommunications links with Cuba because Cuba has agreed to drop its $4.85 surcharge to $1.00 per call. This means that six U.S. companies — AT&T, MCI, WilTel, LDDS, IDB and Sprint — could soon have direct phone service with Cuba, leading to an estimated jump from 100 calls a day to at least 25,000.

October 5 and 7 Senator Claiborne Pell, chair of the Senate Foreign Relations Committee, holds hearings on U.S. policy toward Cuba.

October 11 Visiting Harlem, Foreign Minister Roberto Robaina meets with 30 African American leaders, including Representative Charles Rangel (D-New York).

October 12 The Clinton Administration announces plans to use a lottery for choosing some of the Cubans who will be granted visas, with the aim of allowing legal migration for previously excluded people, an enticement to those at Guantánamo to return and try for the luck of the draw.

October 15 Cubans capture seven Cuban American infiltrators in camouflage uniforms after they landed near Caibarién and shot to death a Cuban fisherman, Arcelio Rodríguez García. The seven are members of the Democratic National Unity Party (PUND), founded in 1989. PUND representatives Sergio González Rosquete and Rodolfo Masferer tell U.S. media that this is only one of several planned attacks. Cuba charges the captives with murder and violation of Cuban territory.

October 15 After the September arrival of U.S. troops as UN "peacekeepers" in Haiti, President Jean Bertrand Aristide returns from exile to Haiti.

October 18 In a first for Cuban television, the chief of the U.S. Interests Section, Joseph Sullivan, appears for about a quarter of an hour on *"Hoy Mismo"* to discuss migration procedures. Sullivan contradicts official policy by saying that U.S. officials are "always ready" to discuss differences. Within 48 hours, State Department representative Christine Shelly states there is "no utility in discussing broader issues" until Cuba starts implementing reforms.

October 22 The executive board of the Organization of American Historians passes a resolution that "notes with alarm" the "menacing" restrictions on travel to Cuba and urges the Clinton Administration to "relax" the embargo.

October 24-26 Another round of migration talks takes place in Havana, with Ricardo Alarcón continuing to lead the Cuban delegation while Dennis Hays, chief of the State Department's Office of Cuban Affairs, heads the U.S. delegation. Neither delegation issues a final statement afterward. Cuba wants an end to the sanctions announced in August, arguing that there is no longer an exodus, the ostensible cause of the measures.

October 26 For the third year in a row, the UN General Assembly votes overwhelmingly for an end to the U.S. embargo against Cuba. UN Ambassador Fernando Remírez de Estenoz presents the resolution on behalf of Cuba. The vote is 101 to 2 (U.S. and Israel) with 48 abstentions.

October 28 At the *Wall Street Journal* Conference on the Americas meeting in New York, Assistant Secretary of State for Inter-American Affairs Alexander Watson maintains that the "Cuban Democracy Act" puts "pressure on the Cuban government for change (what we call Track One), while reaching out to the Cuban people through humanitarian donations and enhanced communications (Track Two)."

October 31 As a result of a lawsuit filed by some 25 lawyers, mainly Cuban Americans from Miami, Federal Judge C. Clyde Atkins issues a temporary restraining order to block repatriation of Cuban emigrants at Guantánamo and in Panama. This ruling is overturned November 4 by the Eleventh U.S. Circuit Court of Appeals in Atlanta. Noting that Cuban emigrants are risking their lives to escape detention, the Appeals Court rules that they can return to unoccupied Cuba and also have a right to speak to lawyers. On the following day, the flight that was supposed to have taken place on October 25 takes 22 Cubans from Guantánamo to Havana.

November General Mikhail Koleshnikov, chief of the Russian armed forces general staff, says Russia has agreed to pay Cuba $200 million a year in goods as rent for the use of Lourdes as a site for monitoring U.S. compliance with arms control agreements, as allowed by treaty between Russia and the United States. The agreement with Cuba runs through 1995 and is renewable. Senator Jesse Helms (R-North Carolina), who will head the Senate Foreign Relations Committee in the new 1995 Congress, and the three Cuban American members of the House suggest that Congress cut aid to Russia by the same amount.

November 1 Running as the Republican candidate for governor of Florida, Jeb Bush, son of the former president, says the current governor, Lawton Chiles, missed an opportunity to "tighten the noose" around Fidel Castro. Chiles wins the election a week later.

November 5-6 In a continuing series of escapes, dozens of Cubans flee from Guantánamo detention. Some reach unoccupied Cuba but others are captured and returned to camps.

November 7 At a news conference in Havana, former Tanzanian President Julius Nyerere, now president of the South Commission of developing countries, says Cuba's socialism must be defended because the island is an inspiration. If Cuba succeeds, "it's a battle won by all the struggling people of the world," and if Cuba loses, "it's not just Cuba but all the struggling people of the world."

November 8 In the U.S. elections, Republicans win majorities in both House and Senate.

November 12 Participants in the various routes of the fourth Friendshipment Caravan converge in Washington, joining supporters in a rally and march to protest the embargo. This Caravan proceeds to Cuba via Montreal, Canada.

November 15 Jorge Mas Canosa, head of the Cuban American National Foundation, sends a letter to the Washington embassy of a country that has relations with Cuba, warning that "your investments or commercial negotiations in Cuba are considered an act of collaboration with a totalitarian system" and will be considered "illegitimate" by the government of "a future democratic Cuba." The *Miami Herald* receives a copy and publishes it December 22, pointing out that CANF has sent the letter to several Latin American countries and has sent similar notices in the past to other nations, including Germany and Britain. This campaign comes amidst increasing investments by foreign countries and corporations in Cuban ventures, including a potential nickel-mining deal with Australia. Over the years, Cuba has negotiated compensation to property owners and to the governments of Britain, France, Canada, Italy, Sweden, Mexico and Spain. The U.S. government demands payment by Cuba to U.S. citizens and companies while imposing an embargo that makes it difficult if not impossible to conduct financial transactions. (*See* February 9, 1995)

November 15-18 Accepting Cuba's invitation, UN Human Rights High Commissioner José Ayala Lazo meets in Havana with dissidents and government officials. Before departing, he remarks that Cuba, like any other country in the world, could and should improve its human rights record but emphasizes that he is not in Cuba to acquit or condemn it.

November 18 National Assembly President Ricardo Alarcón, the most senior Cuban official to visit Washington since Fidel Castro's visit in 1959, tells the National Press Club, "Cuba is simply not a U.S. colony." The State Department dropped its usual practice of not granting visas to high-level Cubans (except to participate in the United Nations) to allow Alarcón to be part of a delegation to a Pan American Health Organization meeting.

November 20 In Miami, Representative Charles Rangel speaks at a rally attended by about 1,000 people who oppose the embargo and support national reconciliation.

November 21-25 In Havana, more than 2,700 participants from 109 nations, including many from the United States, attend a World Conference in Solidarity with Cuba. Among those present are Mexican opposition leader Cuauhtémoc Cárdenas, Nobel Peace Prize winners Rigoberta Menchú of Guatemala and Adolfo Pérez Esquivel of Argentina, and Pulitzer Prize winner Alice Walker of the United States. Delivering the closing speech, President Castro declares that the U.S. government is waging a continuing war against Cuba, still involving plots to assassinate leaders.

November 25 People in the United States can now make phone calls to Cuba by direct dialing.

November 26 At the Vatican, Pope John Paul II inaugurates 30 new cardinals, including Archbishop Jaime Lucas Ortega y Alamino of Havana. He is the first cardinal from Cuba to be invested since the revolution. (The only other cardinal from Cuba, Manuel Arteaga, was invested in 1946 and died in 1963.)

November 30 Wayne Smith, former head of the U.S. Interests Section in Havana and now a senior fellow at the Center for International Policy in Washington, launches a campaign to challenge U.S. restrictions on travel to Cuba, flying to the island with Professors Philip Brenner of American University and John Nichols of Pennsylvania State University. All travel without requesting permission from the U.S. government. Convinced that the current laws are unconstitutional, they are risking imprisonment and fines in the hope of taking the matter all the way to the Supreme Court if necessary. When the group returns, none of them is arrested. Smith proceeds to organize monthly challenges. The February 10, 1995, *Washington Post* quotes Smith: "We want to take this to court as an act of civil disobedience" but U.S. officials know that the "odds are against the government, so they simply hassle us and let it go."

November 30-December 3 In Mexico, President Castro attends the presidential inauguration of Ernesto Zedillo on December 1. He meets with several Latin American presidents and Spanish Prime Minister Felipe González and visits the home of opposition leader Cuauhtémoc Cárdenas.

December 2   The Clinton Administration agrees to admit some 7,500 Cubans — parents with minor children — from Guantánamo to avoid holding children in such inhumane conditions. In October the Administration decided to admit about 300 Cubans — children under age 13 not accompanied by adults, those over age 70 and the sick. Cubans in these categories are also admitted from camps at U.S. bases in Panama.

December 7   Cubans being held in Panama begin to rebel. On the following day more than 1,000 of about 8,500 Cuban detainees escape from the detention camps. In the ensuing rioting that continues off and on for a few days, Cubans and U.S. soldiers are wounded. At least two Cubans drown in the Panama Canal. The rebellion occurs as about 70 Cubans are being flown to Spain, which has agreed to accept that number, and almost 50 orphans and elderly people are being transferred to Miami. After the rioting dies down, U.S. troops stage two major raids on camps to arrest those who allegedly took part. Subsequently, two thousand additional U.S. troops arrive in Panama to guard the Cuban emigrants.

December 8   President Clinton signs the General Agreement on Tariffs and Trade (GATT) into law, authorizing the United States to join 123 other countries, including Cuba, in lowering trade barriers. This paves the way for establishing the World Trade Organization (WTO) on January 1, 1995.

December 9-11   The Summit of the Americas, including the leaders of 34 countries of the Western Hemisphere and excluding only Cuba, meets in Miami, the first such gathering since April 1967 in Uruguay. The only other Summit meeting was in Panama in 1956. The 34 countries agree to negotiate a Free Trade Area of the Americas (FTAA), the world's largest duty-free zone, by the year 2005. Clinton calls Mexico's economic policies a model for regional growth. On December 20, nine days after the Summit, Mexico plummets into financial crisis, shocking international markets with a major devaluation of the peso.

Before and during the Summit, Cuban Americans hold rallies both for and against the embargo. Hundreds of Latin Americans sign a statement published in the December 9 *New York Times* calling on the people of the United States to "reaffirm respect for the principles and norms of international coexistence, based on the sovereignty and self-determination of all peoples." Canadian Prime Minister Jean Chretien tells reporters in Miami that failure to invite President Castro was a missed opportunity.

December 10 A full-page ad in *El Nuevo Herald*, the Spanish arm of the *Miami Herald*, by eight travel agencies protests President Clinton's decision in August to increase restrictions on travel to Cuba.

December 11 At a news conference after formally ending the Summit meeting, President Clinton defends the Summit's failure to condemn President Castro by explaining that there was too much disagreement about the best way to promote democracy in Cuba. He admits that the U.S. embargo against Cuba was criticized by many of the heads of state during private meetings. In fact, of the 34 nations at the Summit, 26 voted against the embargo in the October UN General Assembly vote while only one, the United States itself, voted for it.

December 12 The *New York Times* front-pages an article about an interview of President Castro in Havana by *Times* reporters Tim Golden and Larry Rohter as the Summit conference in Miami was ending.

December 14 The *New York Times* editorializes once more against the embargo, noting that "the policy of isolating Havana, which has prevailed in one form or another for three decades, has not succeeded."

December 14 The UN General Assembly votes 62 to 22 with 54 abstentions that Cuba should cease violations of human rights.

December 18 Reported by the *Miami Herald*, results of a poll of 1,002 Cubans in 75 percent of the island include: 58 percent believe the Cuban revolution has brought more successes than failures and 77 percent think the United States is the "worst friend" of Cuba (Mexico is the best, followed by Spain). Designed by the *Herald* and CID-Gallup (the Costa Rican affiliate of the Gallup polling organization), the poll was conducted November 1-9.

December 23 *Wall Street Journal* reporter Mary Romano writes that Otto Reich, as president of the U.S.-Cuba Business Council, expects many companies to invest in Cuba "if Mr Castro somehow loses power and his government is replaced by one more friendly toward the U.S." Prospects include American

International Group, Anheuser-Busch, Chrysler, Coca-Cola, Colgate-Palmolive, Dow Chemical and Honeywell. The article notes that Peter Blyth, executive vice-president of Radisson Hotels International, is concerned that foreign competitors are "doing" while U.S. companies are only "planning." Radisson's parent company, Carlson of Minneapolis, hopes to build a hotel at Varadero Beach and to renovate one of Havana's downtown buildings into a hotel. Federal Express looks forward to shipping goods to Havana from Cuban Americans. This year 600,000 tourists have visited Cuba, up from about 300,000 in 1988.

December 29 The State Department informs Haitians held at Guantánamo (more than 4,000 remain) that they must return to Haiti. Meantime the Pentagon plans to spend at least $24 million during the next six months to improve camps for Cubans at Guantánamo.

December 31 Francisco Aruca announces that Radio Progreso is going off the air in Miami, but in September 1995 he resumes broadcasting.

1995

January Cuba and Panama upgrade relations to full diplomatic ties for the first time since the U.S. invasion of Panama.

January 4 The new Republican-led Congress convenes in Washington and several bills about Cuba are introduced in the House of Representatives on the very first day, including New York Democrat José Serrano's reintroduction of legislation that would repeal the "Cuban Democracy Act" and Florida Republican Lincoln Díaz-Balart's bills to "Oppose Cuba's Admission to International Financial Institutions" and to "Prohibit the Importation of Sugar from Countries That Import Sugar from Cuba." Later in the month, New Jersey Democrat Robert Menéndez reintroduces his "Free and Independent Cuba Assistance Act."

January 4 The New York City Council welcomes UN Ambassador Fernando Remírez de Estenoz to its meeting. Council member Jerome O'Donovan, a Democrat who heads the Economic Development Committee, invited the ambassador but Republican Mayor Frank Giuliani calls the invitation a "big mistake" that is "in contravention" of U.S. foreign policy.

January 5 On the Senate floor, Senator Claiborne Pell, ranking Democrat and former chair of the Foreign Relations Committee, calls for a "dramatic overhaul" of U.S. policy toward Cuba by expanding contact with the Cuban people and ending the embargo.

January 6 As U.S. authorities begin forced repatriation of Haitian refugees held at Guantánamo, Arthur Helton, professor of immigration law at New York University's Law School, tells the *New York Times* that although the U.S. lease of the base remains in force, the land is part of Cuba under international law. He says, "The United States is trying to compel foreign nationals to return to their home country from a third country, which is an unprecedented assertion of sovereign power."

January 11 *Granma* reports that Cuba has issued a new convertible peso (NCP) that will gradually displace various dollar certificates but will not proscribe the circulation of hard currency.

January 14 The Ninth U.S. Circuit Court of Appeals in San Francisco rules that the federal government can continue to imprison those who took part in the 1980 exodus from Cuba — Marielitos — if they are considered dangerous. The inmates have finished serving sentences for crimes committed in the United States but are incarcerated in federal prisons as "excludables." The decision appears to permit Cuban emigrants to be imprisoned for life but the Court contends that it is not ruling on the constitutionality of indefinite detention. Alexis Barrera Echeverría, the plaintiff in this case, has spent more than nine years in federal prisons since completing a state sentence in Florida. Mark Kemple, a lawyer for Echeverría, says there may be three to five thousand such inmates nationwide.

January 18 The three-judge Eleventh U.S. Circuit Court of Appeals in Atlanta unanimously rules that Cuban and Haitian refugees detained at Guantánamo may be repatriated because they do not have the same constitutional rights as U.S. citizens; those rights "bind the government only when the refugees are at or within the borders of the United States."

January 18 *Granma* reports that infant mortality in Cuba for 1994 was 9.9, up from 9.4 in 1993 (decreasing to 9.4 again in 1995).

January 18-19 As they did in October, Ricardo Alarcón and Dennis Hays head delegations to another round of talks about migration, this time in New York.

January 18-20 Havana hosts the annual meeting of the Caribbean Tourism Organization.

January 23 Representative Menéndez insists that Congress not approve a bailout loan of $40 billion to Mexico without getting Mexico's agreement not to invest in Cuba or allow its subsidiaries to do so.

January 26 At a workshop held by the law firm of Shaw, Pittman, Potts & Trowbridge in Washington, Pedro Monreal González of the Center for American Studies in Havana presents several formulas for possible resolution of compensation claims by individuals and corporations in the United States.

January 26 Inducting a Cuban orthopedic surgeon, Rodrigo Alvarez Cambras, into the Legion of Honor, French President François Mitterrand calls for an end to "this stupid embargo." The U.S. State Department later grants a visa to Dr Alvarez to attend a world conference of orthopedists in February in Miami.

February According to U.S. reports, including *Hispanic Business* magazine, Jorge Mas Canosa of the Cuban American National Foundation is one of the ten wealthiest Hispanics in the United States with a personal fortune of $155 million.

February 1 In his report on Cuba, special rapporteur Carl Johan Groth of the UN Human Rights Commission again condemns the U.S. embargo against Cuba while criticizing human rights violations on the island. Cuba refused to let him into the country (*see* April 21, 1992) although UN High Commissioner for Human Rights José Ayala Lazo was invited to Havana (*see* November 15, 1994).

February 1-18 U.S. troops force all Cubans held in Panama to board planes headed for camps at Guantánamo Naval Base.

February 9 Representative Charles Rangel reintroduces his Free Trade with Cuba bill that would end the embargo.

February 9 Senator Jesse Helms introduces the "Cuban Liberty and Democratic Solidarity (LIBERTAD) Act" that would tighten the embargo. Ignacio Sánchez, a trustee of the Cuban American National Foundation, helped draft this legislation, including the following measures: Cuban Americans would be empowered to make new claims on property expropriated decades ago; the International Claims Settlement Act of 1949, which currently applies only to U.S. citizens at the time of expropriation, would be amended to allow retroactive claims by any Cuban who has since become a U.S. citizen; U.S. citizens who formerly owned property in Cuba could pursue claims in U.S. courts against those who "traffic" in such properties; it would be unlawful for any U.S. "person" (citizen or corporation) to extend financing to any foreign person who "traffics" in Cuban property claimed by a U.S. person; within 90 days of enactment and each year thereafter, the President would have to submit a report to Congress on all foreign commerce with Cuba, including joint ventures merely "under consideration" along with names of the parties involved; no foreign "corporate officer, principal or shareholder of an entity" involved in deals concerning any property claimed by a U.S. person could enter the United States nor could such a person's husband or wife or child. The bill describes the kind of "transitional" government that would be acceptable to Washington, including an edict that neither Fidel Castro nor Raúl Castro could participate in "free and fair elections."

February 14 Representative Dan Burton (R-Indiana), chair of the House International Relations (formerly Foreign Affairs) Committee's Subcommittee on Western Hemisphere Affairs, introduces the House version of the Helms bill. Cuba begins nationwide teach-ins to inform the Cuban people that Cuban Americans could try, under the Helms-Burton law, to seize private homes, public schools, union halls, day-care centers, sugar mills and other property.

February 21 *El Diario* reports that Cuba has asked the UN Human Rights Commission to condemn the United States for racism, xenophobia and ethnic discrimination against minorities, citing as an example the passage in California of Proposition 187 (denying most government services to illegal immigrants).

February 23 Reacting to a February 20 *Time* magazine cover story about Cuba that mentions U.S. businesspeople visiting the island, Representative Burton announces that his subcommittee (*see* February 14) will investigate to see whether those visitors "are breaking the embargo."

March 1 The U.S. Interests Section in Havana opens a new building as headquarters for the Migration Processing Center responsible for issuing visas.

March 7 In Geneva for its annual session, the UN Human Rights Commission votes 22 to 8 with 23 abstentions for a U.S. resolution that "regrets profoundly the numerous unanswered reports of violations of basic human rights and fundamental freedoms" in Cuba.

March 8 Senator Helms attempts to attach his bill as an amendment to the Defense Supplemental Appropriations bill that reached the Senate floor on March 6 for debate, but withdraws it after

Democrats threaten to enforce the rules he would be violating by rushing the bill to the floor without debate.

March 8 Representative Jerrold Nadler (D-New York) sends a "Dear Colleague" letter to House members asking them to co-sponsor his bill to exempt medicines and medical supplies from the embargo.

March 12 In Copenhagen, Denmark, President Castro addresses the World Summit for Social Development, where world leaders sign a declaration urging richer nations to spend 0.7 percent of their gross national product on foreign aid and to cancel the debt of poorer countries.

March 13 Responding to a request from Senator Bob Dole (R-Kansas) and the three Cuban American members of the House, FBI Director Louis Freeh sends a letter assuring them of ongoing efforts to try to get Cuba to extradite 91 U.S. fugitives. The lawmakers had asked for the identities of the fugitives, and Freeh lists 77 individuals by name.

March 13-16 Traveling to France for the first time since the Cuban revolution, President Castro visits President François Mitterrand and his wife, Danielle Mitterrand, who was in Cuba in February to deliver $2.5 million to a hospital in the name of a human rights group to which she belongs (France-Libertés). Castro addresses the UN Educational, Scientific and Cultural Organization (UNESCO) and meets with 250 of France's top business leaders to urge investment on the island (telling them Cuba is studying projects where foreign companies may own more than 50 percent, possibly 60 to 75 percent and even 100 percent if the project is of sufficient benefit). He invites France-Libertés to visit Cuba to investigate accusations of political oppression and tells Danielle Mitterrand he will check a list of 43 prisoners that she gave to him. (After the group's visit, Cuba releases six prominent prisoners, including Sebastián Arcos Bergnés and Indamiro Restano Díaz, in May.)

March 14 Columnist William Buckley opposes the Helms-Burton legislation and the U.S. embargo.

March 19 Mentioning President Castro's visit to France as well as the UN General Assembly's vote against the U.S. embargo, the *New York Times* editorializes against the Helms-Burton bill and the embargo.

March 23 *El Diario* reports that the wife and three sons of Eloy Gutiérrez Menoyo, head of *Cambio Cubano*, arrived in Havana March 19 after flying to Cuba from a third country in defiance of the U.S. travel ban. Gladys Gutiérrez says she is on a private visit "without a message or a political agenda" but with a desire "to see my people, my country, reunited."

March 25 Foreign Minister Roberto Robaina signs the 1967 Treaty of Tlatelolco (*see* February 14, 1967) in the presence of President Fidel Castro and Mexican Foreign Minister José Angel Guerra. As a condition for Cuba's remaining within the treaty, Robaina maintains that the U.S. government should cease sending ships carrying nuclear weapons to Guantánamo Naval Base on Cuban territory. Cuba, says Robaina, favors destruction of all nuclear weapons as the only guarantee against their use. He argues that "the ones who should respect this principle first are the so-called nuclear powers."

March 26 Speaking on national television, President Castro says Cuba has proof that the CIA continues to try to overthrow the Cuban government and has protested to Washington.

March 27 The Cuban film, *Fresa y Chocolate* [Strawberry and Chocolate], is a finalist for best foreign film at the Academy Awards. Both directors, Tomás Gutiérrez Alea and Juan Carlos Tabío, and two of the actors, Jorge Perugorría and Mirta Ibarra, attend the ceremony in Los Angeles.

March 29 Considering that the U.S. Southern Command is scheduled to depart Panama by the end of the twentieth century, President Clinton announces that the new headquarters for U.S. military activities in Latin America, perhaps by late summer 1998, will be Miami.

April Because of the tighter restrictions on travel instituted last August, Marazul Charters is forced, for financial reasons, to suspend flights between Cuba and the United States.

April 7 Chile and Cuba reestablish full diplomatic relations for the first time since the military coup of 1973. Consular and commercial ties resumed in 1991. The State Department objects to the rapprochement and one official warns that this will make it more difficult for Chile to join NAFTA.

April 10 Bruno Eduardo Rodríguez Parilla formally presents his credentials as Cuba's ambassador to the United Nations.

April 13   During a trip to raise funds for his campaign to win the Republican nomination for president in 1996, Senate Majority Leader Robert Dole tells a joint session of the Florida legislature that it's time to "make the end of Fidel Castro's stay an explicit goal of American foreign policy."

April 13   Asked about the Helms-Burton legislation on CNN international television, President Clinton says new legislation regarding Cuba is not necessary because the "Cuban Democracy Act" is sufficient.

April 17   Appearing at a rally in Miami alongside Jorge Mas Canosa, Senator Jesse Helms endorses the Cuban American National Foundation's call for a naval blockade of Cuba. The *Baltimore Sun* reports that a fund-raiser adds $75,000 to Helms's re-election campaign during this visit.

April 17   Deputy Secretary of State Peter Tarnoff flies to New York City and meets secretly with National Assembly President Ricardo Alarcón.

April 18   Dennis Hays and Ricardo Alarcón once again head the U.S. and Cuban delegations to discuss migration, this time at the Cuban UN Mission. Hays is unaware of the secret meeting a day earlier.

April 19   After Dennis Hays finishes discussions about migration with Ricardo Alarcón, he speaks at a Cuban American rally in support of the embargo in Union City, New Jersey, and assures his audience that the Clinton Administration is not conducting secret talks or planning such talks with Cuban officials (*see* April 17).

April 27   Robert J. Nieves, chief of international operations for the Drug Enforcement Agency tells reporters at the 13th Annual International Drug Conference in Santo Domingo that Cuba has "always collaborated with us whenever we are trying to disrupt drug trafficking operations there."

April 28   A letter from the State Department (written by Assistant Secretary of State for Legislative Affairs Wendy Sherman) seeking some changes in the Helms-Burton legislation is sent to the House International Relations Committee. However, the letter supports "making the embargo more effective, accelerating planning for assistance to Cuba under a transition or democratic government and protecting the property interests of Americans abroad."

April 29-30 In Toronto, Canada, Ricardo Alarcón and Peter Tarnoff again meet secretly and reach the agreement announced May 2.

May The Paraguayan Senate votes in favor of renewing diplomatic relations with Cuba.

May A delegation from Madison, Wisconsin, visits Camagüey in east-central Cuba to establish a Sister City relationship. The head of the group, Ricardo González, left Cuba in November 1960 at age thirteen.

May 2 The Clinton Administration announces the new migration agreement. The U.S. government will allow all of the 20,916 Cubans held at Guantánamo to enter the United States at a rate of around 500 a month (some 6,000 were already scheduled for entry). About 5,000 will be eligible for entry on the same grounds as over 11,000 who have recently been admitted (children, the elderly, the medically ill, with their families); the remaining number, approximately 15,000, will be credited against the 20,000 annual Cuban migration figure at the rate of 5,000 per year for three years, beginning in September 1995 regardless of when they arrive in the United States. Cuba agrees to accept all Cubans who want to return or who are deemed ineligible for U.S. entry. To avoid another wave of *balseros* [rafters], the U.S. Coast Guard will return Cubans picked up at sea to Cuba once it is determined that they have no acceptable claim to asylum. Attorney General Janet Reno says Cubans who reach the U.S. mainland will be processed like immigrants from any other country.

May 2 At the press conference to announce the migration agreement, the commander in chief of the U.S. Atlantic Command, General John Sheehan, says, "We're going to move the fleet training center out of Guantánamo Bay, Cuba, because we can do the same thing in the continental limits of the United States at lower cost." But he says the base remains "essential for strategic reach reasons."

May 2 The migration agreement represents a White House break with the Cuban American National Foundation. CANF leaders complain that they were not consulted and CANF withdraws 15,000 sponsors who had agreed to handle resettlement expenses of Guantánamo immigrants. Jorge Mas Canosa vows to use his influence in Washington to cut funds for the Coast Guard. Dennis Hays, bypassed during the secret negotiations, immediately resigns as head of the State Department's Office of Cuban Affairs.

May 5 Senator Paul Simon (D-Illinois) introduces the Freedom to Travel Act that would limit the President's power to restrict travel to countries with which the United States is at war, where armed hostilities are in progress, or where there is imminent danger to the public health or safety of travelers.

May 6 Speaking on television in Bogotá, Colombian Foreign Minister Rodrigo Pardo suggests that U.S. Ambassador Myles Frechette should deal with U.S. issues rather than interfering in Colombia's right to conduct its own affairs. Frechette has criticized Colombian trade and diplomatic relations with Cuba.

May 7 In separate TV interviews, Senate Majority Leader Bob Dole (R-Kansas) and House Speaker Newt Gingrich (R-Georgia) oppose the new policy on migration.

May 9 CARICOM foreign ministers condemn the Helms-Burton bill.

May 10 Cuba establishes diplomatic relations with Saint Kitts and Nevis, leaving only three Caribbean nations without diplomatic relations with Cuba: Dominica, the Dominican Republic and Haiti.

May 11 On Radio Martí, Senator Jesse Helms delivers a six-minute "message to the Cuban people," informing them that the Helms-Burton bill is "to help you bring an end to Castro's tyranny."

May 12 The *New York Times* reports that U.S. intelligence officials, speaking anonymously, say Cuba has neither the money nor the will to support anti-American guerrillas and that of the seven countries labeled sponsors of terrorism by the State Department — Cuba, Iran, Iraq, Libya, North Korea, the Sudan and Syria — only Iran promotes "terrorism" aimed at the United States and its allies.

Mid-May In a classified cable to Washington, Joseph Sullivan, head of the U.S. Interests Section in Havana, criticizes Radio Martí's coverage of the May 2 agreement as "biased" in favor of opponents of the new policy.

May 15 Foreign Minister Roberto Robaina announces Havana will host another Conference on the Nation and Emigration November 3-6.

May 15-19 Visiting Cuba, Robert Pastor, who negotiated with Cuban officials during the Carter Administration and now heads the Carter Center's Latin American program in Atlanta, says the trip is "to get an assessment of the situation in Cuba and the prospects for political and economic change on the island." He meets with Cuban dissidents and Cuban officials, including President Castro.

May 22-23 Meeting in Ecuador, foreign ministers of the Río Group unanimously condemn the Helms-Burton bill.

May 23 Russia and Cuba plan to sign an agreement to exchange three million tons of oil for one million tons of sugar beginning in the second half of 1996 and continuing for three years.

May 25 President Clinton appoints Richard Nuccio, adviser to Assistant Secretary of State for Latin American Affairs Alexander Watson, to a new post as coordinator of policy toward Cuba.

June Meeting in Haiti, OAS foreign ministers call for reinstating Cuba as a member. Assistant Secretary of State for Latin American Affairs Alexander Watson and the U.S. representative to the OAS, Harriet Babbitt, oppose the move.

June 2 Cuban officials inform U.S. authorities that they have arrested Robert Vesco on suspicion of being a provocateur and foreign agent. U.S. officials again request his extradition, which they have sought for years. Cuban officials request more information about U.S. criminal charges against him. Donald Nixon Jr., nephew of the late president, with Vesco at the time of his arrest, is also detained, but his passport is returned on June 30 and he leaves Cuba July 2.

June 3 The Cuban American National Foundation hosts House Speaker Newt Gingrich (R-Georgia) in Coral Gables, honoring him for his support of Cuban causes.

June 8-July 6 Again defying the embargo, the fifth Friendshipment Caravan takes supplies to Cuba via Canada without permission from the U.S. government.

June 12 National Assembly President Ricardo Alarcón and Joseph Sullivan, chief of the U.S. Interests Section, meet so Sullivan can describe U.S. charges against Robert Vesco. On June 18,

President Castro tells CNN executives and correspondents in Havana that it would be immoral to extradite Vesco and turn him into a "pawn of U.S.-Cuban relations." On the following day, Sullivan meets with Cuban officials to try to persuade them, in vain, to extradite Vesco.

June 13 The *Wall Street Journal* reports the Treasury Department is expected to put four Canadian-Cuban companies formed by Sherritt Inc., a Canadian metals company, on its "blacklist" of "special designated nationals" considered Cuban agents and barred from trading with the United States. The article notes that Sherritt is exploiting a nickel mine and processing plant at Moa Bay which were expropriated from a New Orleans company soon after the Cuban revolution. Treasury does in fact blacklist the companies a few days later.

Mid-June On a tour of Cuban communities in Mexico, Puerto Rico and the United States, Cuban Cardinal Jaime L. Ortega attends the National Conference of Bishops meeting in Chicago.

June 14-25 Visiting Cuba, Eloy Gutiérrez Menoyo, head of *Cambio Cubano*, attends a three-day program on participatory democracy in Cienfuegos and later meets with President Castro.

June 23-30 On a trip organized by the Freedom to Travel Campaign, 34 U.S. students, ages 10 to 24 years, challenge the travel ban by going to Cuba on vacation. Prior to departure they received a letter from the Treasury Department's Office of Foreign Assets Control warning that they could receive sentences of ten years in jail and $250,000 each in fines.

June 26 The *Wall Street Journal* reports Cuba is seeking to restructure its estimated $6.4 billion in hard currency debt, owed to western countries and Japan.

June 30 The Cuban American National Foundation organizes a demonstration against President Clinton and the First Lady as they visit their three-week-old nephew Zachary, son of Tony and Nicole Rodham, in Miami.

June 30 Sandra M. Alfonso, head of a Louisiana trade commission established by Governor Edwin Edwards, testifies at a hearing on U.S.-Cuban relations before the House Ways and Means Committee that Cuba was Louisiana's primary trading partner before the imposition of the embargo that caused a loss of 6,000 jobs in the state.

July   At the home of Benjamino Stella, the Papal nuncio in Havana, President Castro meets with Cuban Catholic bishops and Cardinal Bernardin Gantin, a special envoy sent by Pope John Paul II. Despite differences, Cuba and the Vatican have never broken diplomatic relations.

July 9   Cuban municipal elections, which take place every two and a half years, bring 97.1 percent of registered voters to the polls; 4.35 percent of the ballots are blank; 7 percent are void because they break voting rules.

July 13   In Cuban waters, several boats organized by Brothers to the Rescue turn around and return to Florida after one of the boats collides with a Cuban Border Patrol vessel. *Granma* later reports that 11 boats, six small planes, and two helicopters penetrated water and air space of Cuba. One airplane flew over the coastal zone of Havana. Cuba officially protests and the U.S. government issues muted criticism of the incursions. When Brothers to the Rescue attempts another such voyage on September 2, they turn back after one boat sinks ten miles off Key West, dumping 47 people into rough seas, causing one death. The U.S. Coast Guard comes to their rescue.

July 16   Belize and Cuba establish full diplomatic relations.

July 17-18   In Havana, delegations headed by National Assembly President Ricardo Alarcón and Anne Patterson, who replaced Michael Skol as Deputy Assistant Secretary of State for Latin America in May, hold another round of migration talks to evaluate implementation of agreements reached in September 1994 and May 1995.

July 22   The *Washington Post* reports: "An investigation by the United States Information Agency into its Radio Martí broadcasts to Cuba documents pervasive influence by anti-Castro lobbyist Jorge Mas Canosa in management of the station and in news coverage that deliberately misrepresented U.S. policy toward the island." Four members of the President's Advisory Board for Cuba Broadcasting respond by demanding that USIA Inspector General Marion Bennett be fired. The head of the Advisory Board, Jorge Mas Canosa, says the Clinton Administration wants to turn Radio Martí into an instrument for its policy of negotiation.

July 22-August 6 The 26th Venceremos Brigade is in Cuba. More than 6,000 people have participated in these brigades during the past 25 years.

July 30 Ten years after the conference on Latin America's debt crisis hosted by Havana in 1985, Latin American debt has increased from $360 billion to around $600 billion.

August Cuba has 212 joint ventures with businesses from 53 countries.

August 1-7 *Cuba Vive!*, the International Youth Festival, attracts 1,300 people from 67 countries to Cuba, including 262 U.S. participants. On August 5, they march with President Castro and thousands of other Cubans past the U.S. Interests Section on the Malecón along the sea wall of Havana.

August 6 Foreign Minister Roberto Robaina calls the Clinton Administration's so-called "Track Two" policy — humanitarian aid and increased communication along with cultural and academic exchanges — an attempt to destroy socialism by using a razor and scalpel rather than the old dull knife. He says there are no discussions behind the scenes, aside from migration talks, to try to resolve differences.

August 17-18 President Castro attends the Summit Meeting of the Association of Caribbean States (ACS) in Port-of-Spain, Trinidad and Tobago. Because of Cuba's membership, the U.S. does not allow Puerto Rico or the U.S. Virgin Islands to participate as observers.

August 20 U.S. media report President Clinton may veto the Helms-Burton legislation, if passed by Congress, because it "would entangle the Castro government and its successors in new claims for property expropriated in 1959" and would "make it hard for a post-Castro Cuba to privatize property because of pending lawsuits."

August 27 The *New York Times* reports three views of U.S.-Cuban trade relations: during a recent pep talk to corporate executives at the State Department, Secretary of State for Inter-American Affairs Alexander Watson said his advocacy of free trade in the Western Hemisphere does not apply to Cuba, labeling Cuba "a special case"; John S. Kavulich, president of the U.S.-Cuba Trade and Economic Council, says even more U.S. executives are scouting Cuba in 1995 than in 1994 when more than 500 U.S.

businesspeople visited the island; and UN Ambassador Bruno Rodríguez Parilla says more than 100 of those U.S. businesspeople have signed "letters of intent" outlining areas of potential cooperation if trade relations are normalized.

September 4 Opposing the Helms-Burton bill and praising President Clinton for his threat to veto it, the *New York Times* editorializes for corporate pressure "to help the Administration find the courage to take on the conservative exile lobby."

September 5 Cuba passes a law allowing foreigners to own 100 percent of businesses, including the purchase of some real estate. Any business involving health, education or defense would not be up for sale.

September 10 The Associated Press reports Cuba is allowing Cubans, including those living abroad, to open bank accounts using dollars and other foreign currency.

September 20 Secretary of State Warren Christopher sends a letter to House Speaker Newt Gingrich, rejecting all the Helms-Burton bill's major provisions because they would "damage prospects for a peaceful transition in Cuba" and "jeopardize a number of key U.S. interests around the world." Christopher favors a veto if Congress approves the legislation. Since it was introduced in February, the bill has been repeatedly modified and has doubled in length.

September 20 The *Miami Herald* editorializes against the Helms-Burton bill.

September 21 With a vote of 294 to 130, the House passes the Burton companion bill to the Helms legislation, amounting to 80 pages about "strengthening" the embargo. Moreover, the House rejects by a vote of 283 to 138 an amendment, sponsored by Representative Jim McDermott (D-Washington), that would have exempted sales of medicine and food to Cuba from the embargo.

September 22 The *Washington Post* editorializes against the Helms-Burton legislation.

September 22 Cuba establishes diplomatic relations with Swaziland. Cuba has diplomatic relations with more than 150 countries.

October 2 Meeting in Luxembourg, the foreign ministers of the European Union agree to begin talks with Cuba about EU-Cuban relations, discussions that could lead to a trade accord. The EU opposes the Helms-Burton legislation.

October 6 Speaking at Freedom House in Washington, President Clinton announces a few changes in travel regulations. Echoing the "Cuban Democracy Act" of 1992, Clinton states, "We will tighten the enforcement of our embargo to keep the pressure for reform on, but we will promote democracy and the free flow of ideas more actively." Undergraduates may now study in Cuba if the course is sponsored by a U.S. college or university, and more academic exchanges will be authorized. According to the new regulations as published in the Federal Register, people traveling for "religious activities" or "investigating human rights violations" will be eligible for specific licenses. News organizations and Western Union will be allowed to open offices in Cuba. However, Cuba will not be permitted to open news bureaus in the United States until U.S. officials are satisfied with Cuba's responses to U.S. media. The fundamental embargo against trade, including food and medicine, remains in effect and will be strengthened. Penalties for visiting Cuba can still lead to ten years in prison and $250,000 in fines. U.S. tourists continue to be barred from the island. Even citizens who obtain permission from the Treasury Department must adhere to certain rules. Freelance journalists, for instance, must present "a record of publications" and submit for approval a "detailed itinerary and a detailed description of the proposed research" that demonstrates the research "could not be accomplished in a shorter period of time." Groups approved by the U.S. government may provide direct aid to Cuban dissidents. To that end, Clinton announces to his hosts that Freedom House will receive a government grant of half a million dollars for publishing and distributing pamphlets and books in Cuba. (*See* November 3-6 for the change regarding travel by Cuban Americans.)

October 6 Organized by Time Inc. Tours, about 47 executives from U.S. corporations dine with President Castro in Havana. Before leaving for Cuba, the group met with Clinton Administration officials. U.S. businesspeople are increasingly restive about the U.S. policy of being the only country in the world that refuses to trade with Cuba.

October 9 For the first time since 1979, President Castro applies for a visa to enter the United States, this time for the UN's 50th anniversary celebration October 22-24. Senator Robert Dole and other legislators, including the three Cuban Americans in the House, call for not allowing Castro into the country even though, as host to the United Nations, the U.S. government is obligated to allow foreign leaders to participate in UN proceedings.

Mid-October Cuba opens offices where Cubans may buy and sell U.S. dollars and convertible pesos for Cuban pesos.

October 13 President Castro makes a state visit to Uruguay, meeting with President Julio María Sanguinetti and other officials; he is cheered by tens of thousands of supporters in the streets of Montevideo.

October 15 President Castro arrives in Argentina for the Fifth Ibero-American Summit in San Carlos de Bariloche October 16-17. The Summit's final declaration calls for an end to "unilateral coercive measures" that affect the welfare of Ibero-American nations, preventing free trade and violating "principles governing regional coexistence and the sovereignty of states." The statement specifically expresses concern about legislation being debated in the U.S. Congress contrary to those principles.

October 16 In an article in *U.S. News and World Report*, Linda Robinson reports that Amstar, formerly American Sugar, would like to negotiate with Cuba about its property claim of $81 million, the seventh-largest of the 5,911 claims certified by the Foreign Claims Settlement Commission. Amstar, no longer in the sugar business, claims an area on the Cuban mainland "larger than that inside Washington, D.C.'s beltway" plus two islands, Cayo Romano and Cayo Cruz. Roger Chesley, Amstar vice-president and chief counsel, proposes that development of those islands "could generate revenues for paying compensation." But the U.S. trade embargo forbids any such arrangement even if Cuba were to agree. Amanecio Boitel and Rafael Cuesta, workers since childhood at a huge sugar mill once owned by American Sugar, told Robinson that pay increased fourfold after 1959. Before the revolution, Cuesta says, "We worked like animals." Scoffing at the idea of compensating American Sugar, Boitel says that by 1959 the company "had already taken out 10 times more than [the mill] was worth."

October 18 In Cartagena, Colombia, President Castro addresses the 11th Summit Meeting of the Nonaligned Movement, which now numbers 114 nations. A primary issue is reform of the UN Security Council where a veto by one of the five permanent members outweighs the vote of the entire 185 members of the General Assembly. Castro maintains that the United States aims at using the Security Council to dominate the world. The Final Declaration opposes the U.S. trade embargo against Cuba, U.S. legislation aimed at intensifying the embargo, U.S. occupation of Cuban territory at Guantánamo, and U.S. radio and television broadcasts designed to interfere with Cuba's internal affairs. The Declaration calls for negotiations between Cuba and the United States and enforcement of the resolutions against the embargo approved by the General Assembly for the past three years.

October 18 State Department representative Nicholas Burns announces that a visa will be issued to President Castro for his visit to New York, but he must remain within 25 miles of Columbus Circle in New York City and leave on October 25.

October 18 In order to end a filibuster being led by Senator Christopher Dodd (D-Connecticut), Senate Majority Leader Robert Dole and Senator Jesse Helms agree to drop Title III of the Helms-Burton bill — the section that would empower Cuban Americans to make new claims on Cuban property they lost before they became U.S. citizens (*see* February 9). The Senate then votes for cloture, clearing the way for a vote on the bill itself. Two previous cloture votes on October 12 and October 17 failed.

October 19 The Senate passes the Helms-Burton legislation, minus Title III, with a vote of 74 to 24. Before this bill can be sent to President Clinton for signature or veto, it must go to a House-Senate conference to resolve differences between Senate and House versions. On March 12, 1996, President Clinton signs this bill, including Title III, into law.

October 19 At the Nonaligned Summit, Cuba and Kenya establish diplomatic relations.

October 21 President Castro arrives at New York's Kennedy International Airport as more than 2,000 people march through torrential rain from the United Nations to Columbus Circle in New York City to protest against the embargo. Castro begins to accept as many as possible of more than 200 invitations by various groups and individuals. The Cuban Mission to the United

Nations and John Kavulich of the U.S.-Cuba Trade and Economic Council have been flooded with requests to arrange meetings with Castro. While Mayor Rudolph Giuliani hosts a dinner for heads of state to which he is not invited, President Castro dines with business executives and other guests at a dinner hosted by Peggy Dulany, daughter of David Rockefeller. He meets at the Cuban UN Mission with members of Casa de las Américas, most of whom came to the United States during Batista's dictatorship and have remained supporters of the revolution.

October 22 With representatives from its 185 members, including more than 140 heads of state and government — the largest summit meeting in history — the United Nations begins the celebration of its 50th anniversary. President Clinton, as head of the host country, leads off and then leaves, with his secretary of state and UN ambassador in tow, before President Castro's turn at the podium. Castro receives the most tumultuous applause of any speaker, especially when he mentions the need to reform the Security Council. While in New York, Castro confers with several heads of state, including Chinese President Jiang Zemin; establishes diplomatic relations with Andorra; and meets privately with at least two members of Congress, Democratic Representatives Joe Moakley of Massachusetts and Bill Richardson of New Mexico.

October 22 President Castro is interviewed by Bernard Shaw of the Cable News Network (CNN). During his visit, Castro also grants interviews to cable television's Spanish-language TV network, Telemundo, and to CBS's Dan Rather. On CBS, he says communism remains a viable future project while capitalism has not resolved any of the world's social ills. Castro also visits the *New York Times*, the *Wall Street Journal*, *Time* and *Newsweek*.

October 22 While President Clinton hosts a party for heads of state excluding the Cuban leader, President Castro returns to Harlem for the first time in 35 years. Invited by a coalition called Africans in the Americas Committee to Welcome Fidel Castro, he addresses more than 1,300 people in Reverend Calvin Butts's Abyssinian Baptist Church, filled to overflowing with invited guests, including Representatives Charles Rangel, José Serrano and Nydia Velazquez, all Democrats of New York. He elicits one of several standing ovations with an offer to send Cuban doctors to help look after people in Harlem or any place in the United States in need of medical care.

October 23 President Castro addresses the Council on Foreign Relations, including Mario Baeza, Tom Brokaw, Robert McNamara, David Rockefeller, Arthur Schlesinger, Ted Sorenson, Laurence Tisch and Mortimer Zuckerman. He visits Jimmy's Bronx Cafe, where he is welcomed by Representative José Serrano to a meeting of Puerto Rican community and business leaders, including Representative Nydia Velazquez. At the UN Mission, he confers with Spanish-speaking members of Congress and other political leaders.

October 24 Mortimer B. Zuckerman, publisher of the New York *Daily News* and editor-in-chief of *U.S. News and World Report*, hosts a luncheon for President Castro with media guests including Mike Wallace and producer Don Hewitt of CBS; *New York Times* columnist William Safire; Peter Jennings, Diane Sawyer and Barbara Walters of ABC; and talk show host John McLaughlin. At the UN Mission, President Castro hosts a reception for a varied group from the worlds of business and entertainment, Congress, and people who have worked to improve U.S.-Cuban relations.

October 25 Before departing for Cuba, President Castro meets at the UN Mission with about 100 religious leaders, an event organized by the Interreligious Foundation for Community Organization (IFCO).

October 25 Specialists from the United States, the Cuban government, the Pan American Health Organization, the World Health Organization and Nicaragua's Ministry of Health are working together in Nicaragua to investigate a dengue-like disease which has killed 12 people and infected 869 others. On November 6, it is identified tentatively by the Center for Disease Control and Prevention in Atlanta, Georgia, as leptospirosis.

October 25 The Newark *Star-Ledger* reports that Merck & Co., the transnational pharmaceutical company, has paid a $127,500 fine for violating the trade embargo. According to the article, the Treasury Department says Merck contracted with a Cuban laboratory to perform testing and also engaged in unlicensed business, but Merck spokesperson Sharyn Bearse maintains no testing ever took place. Other corporations have been fined lesser amounts recently.

October 25   Organized by the British weekly, *The Economist*, the Third Round Table on the Cuban economy is meeting in Havana with the participation of more than 200 economists and business-people from 24 countries, the largest yet.

October 31   Radio Havana reports that, despite Cuba's economic crunch, more than 2,000 foreign students are currently studying in Cuban universities as part of the scholarship program initiated November 7, 1960.

November 2   For the fourth year in a row, the United Nations General Assembly votes overwhelmingly for a Cuban resolution calling for an end to the U.S. trade embargo against Cuba. The vote is 117 to 3 (the United States, Israel and Uzbekistan) with 38 abstentions and 27 not voting. Since the first vote in 1992, the number of nations opposing the embargo has almost doubled.

November 3-6   Cuba hosts the second Nation and Emigration Conference attended by some 350 invited members of the Cuban emigré community, of whom more than 200 are from the United States and Puerto Rico. The Treasury Department has not authorized the special license that would exempt U.S. participants from the restrictions of the embargo. Current U.S. rules, announced in October, limit Cuban Americans to one visit a year for emergency humanitarian reasons (for example, family illness or death); any additional visits "must be specifically licensed" by the Treasury Department. On Cuba's part, Foreign Minister Roberto Robaina announces on November 6 that Cuban emigrés may apply for travel documents, renewable every two years, that will allow them to enter and leave Cuba whenever they choose.

November 8   A group of U.S. veterans — from World War II, Korea and Vietnam — arrive in Havana from Cancún, Mexico, on the seventh Freedom to Travel Campaign, challenging the travel ban by not requesting permission for going to Cuba.

November 27-December 15   After a stopover in Denmark, President Castro makes state visits to China and Vietnam, followed by an unofficial visit (his first) to Japan and a stopover in Canada on his way home.

December 1   President Castro arrives in China for his first visit, staying for nine days, touring the country and meeting with

President Jiang Zemin and Premier Li Peng. He then travels to Vietnam for the first time since 1973.

December 13 By a vote of 62 to 23 with 73 abstentions, the UN General Assembly's Third Commission, which includes all UN members, approves a U.S.-sponsored resolution criticizing Cuba for human rights violations.

December 13 *Granma* reports that the Italian liner *Costa Playa* has docked in Havana, ending a long period when Caribbean cruises bypassed Cuba. The first visit brings more than 400 tourists from Europe, Latin America, and "even the United States" for a 16-hour stop. The cruise ship also visits Santiago de Cuba and Nipe, on Cuba's northeastern coast.

December 26 Cuba's National Assembly approves a one-year economic plan for 1996 aiming at a Gross Domestic Product growth from 2.5 percent to five percent. The 1996 budget, also approved by the Assembly, projects a decrease in the deficit from 775 million pesos to 580 million pesos and an increase in funding for health and education.

Glossary

ANC: African National Congress (South Africa).

Arias plan: *See* Esquipulus II.

Association of Caribbean States (ACS): Established at a convention in July 1994 to facilitate trade and cooperation among states with Caribbean coastlines. Full members at the time of founding: Antigua and Barbuda, Bahamas, Barbados, Belize, Colombia, Costa Rica, Cuba, Dominica, the Dominican Republic, El Salvador, Grenada, Guatemala, Guyana, Haiti, Honduras, Jamaica, Mexico, Nicaragua, Panama, St. Kitts and Nevis, St. Lucia, St. Vincent and the Grenadines, Suriname, Trinidad and Tobago and Venezuela. Eleven dependent territories are associate members.

CANF: Cuban American National Foundation.

CARICOM: The Caribbean Community and Common Market nations. Founded July 4, 1973 in Chaguaramas, Trinidad and Tobago. Members include Antigua and Barbuda, Bahamas, Barbados, Belize, Dominica, Grenada, Guyana, Jamaica, Montserrat, Saint Kitts and Nevis, Saint Lucia, Saint Vincent and the Grenadines, Suriname and Trinidad and Tobago.

CDA: Cuban Democracy Act also known as the Torricelli bill.

CIS: Commonwealth of Independent States.

CMEA: Council for Mutual Economic Assistance, a trade alliance of socialist countries from 1949 until disbanded in February 1991. Also known as Comecon. Members were Cuba, Bulgaria, Czechoslovakia, East Germany, Hungary, Mongolia, Poland, Rumania, the Soviet Union and Vietnam. Albania was a member until 1961. Yugoslavia attended as an associate member. East Germany merged with West Germany in 1990. At the January 9, 1990, meeting the Soviet Union proposed to begin trading on January 1, 1991, on a hard-currency basis at real market prices. After that change was instituted, the CMEA formally disbanded.

Comecon: *See* CMEA.

CORU: Commanders of the United Revolutionary Organizations.

CREEP: Committee for the Re-election of the President (Nixon, U.S.).

DEA: Drug Enforcement Agency (U.S.).

DGI: Dirección General de Inteligencia (intelligence service of Cuba).

Esquipulas II: Plan of August 7, 1987, for a negotiated settlement in Central America; also known as the Arias plan and the Guatemala plan.

FAO: Food and Agricultural Organization (UN).

FMLN: Farabundo Martí National Liberation Front, El Salvador.

FNLA: National Front for the Liberation of Angola, Holden Roberto's group.

FSLN: Sandinista National Liberation Front, Nicaragua.

F.Y.: Fiscal year.

GATT: General Agreement on Tariffs and Trade, an international compact that regulates world trade. In 1993, after years of negotiations, members agreed on a new world trade agreement aimed at lowering trade barriers among the member nations. In April 1994, 124 member nations, including Cuba and the United States, signed the agreement. The U.S. Congress approved it and President Clinton signed it into U.S. law on December 8, 1994. (*See* WTO)

Granma: Official newspaper of Cuba's Communist Party, named after the yacht used by Fidel Castro and other revolutionaries to travel from Mexico to Cuba in 1956.

Group of Eight: *See* Río Group.

Group of 77: *See* UNCTAD.

Guatemala Plan: *See* Esquipulus II.

ICAP: Instituto Cubano de Amistad con los Pueblos (Cuban Institute of Friendship with the Peoples).

IMF: International Monetary Fund based in Washington, D.C.

INS: Immigration and Naturalization Service (U.S.).

LASO: Latin American Solidarity Organization, founded in 1966 and based in Havana.

MPLA: Popular Movement for the Liberation of Angola, the governing party of Angola.

NAFTA: North American Free Trade Agreement that went into effect January 1, 1994, with three members: the United States, Mexico and Canada.

NATO: North Atlantic Treaty Organization founded in 1949.

NLF: National Liberation Front of South Vietnam.

NSAM: National Security Action Memorandum (U.S.).

NSC: National Security Council (U.S.).

OAS: Organization of American States. Established in 1948 under the United Nations Charter for nations of the Western Hemisphere. Its headquarters are in Washington, D.C. Canada did not join until 1989.

OAU: Organization of African Unity formed in 1963.

OPLAN: Operation plan of the U.S. military.

PLO: Palestine Liberation Organization.

Prensa Latina: Cuban news agency established June 1959.

Río Group: Formed in 1986 to develop common positions on regional problems by Argentina, Brazil, Colombia, Mexico, Panama, Peru, Uruguay, Venezuela. It has expanded by 1995 to 14 members.

SGA: Special Group (Augmented) set up in 1961 by President John F. Kennedy to oversee Operation Mongoose.

SR-71: U.S. surveillance plane.

SWAPO: Southwest Africa People's Organization of Namibia.

UNCTAD: United Nations Conference on Trade and Development, which met first in 1964. Participants from developing nations are known as the Group of 77 (though the number has increased).

UNITA: National Union for the Total Independence of Angola led by Jonas Savimbi and supported by South Africa and the U.S.

USIA: United States Information Agency.

USSR: Union of Soviet Socialist Republics (Soviet Union).

U-2: U.S. surveillance plane.

WTO: The World Trade Organization, successor to GATT, set up January 1, 1995, to oversee the new world trade agreement (*see* GATT). Its ruling body is called the General Council.

ZAPU: Zimbabwe African People's Union.

INDEX

CIA TARGETS FIDEL
The secret assassination report

Only recently declassified and published for the first time, this secret report was prepared for the CIA on its own plots to assassinate Cuba's Fidel Castro. Under pressure in 1967 when the press were probing the alliance with the Mafia in these murderous schemes, the CIA produced this remarkably frank, single-copy report stamped "secret — eyes only." Included is an exclusive commentary by Division General Fabián Escalante, the former head of Cuba's counterintelligence body.
ISBN 1-875284-90-7

FACE TO FACE WITH FIDEL CASTRO
A conversation with Tomás Borge

The issues confronting a changing world are frankly discussed in this lively dialogue between two of Latin America's most controversial political figures.
ISBN 1-875284-15-X

CHE — A MEMOIR BY FIDEL CASTRO
Preface by Jesús Montané
Edited by David Deutschmann

For the first time Fidel Castro writes with candor and affection of his relationship with Ernesto Che Guevara, documenting his extraordinary bond with Cuba from the revolution's early days to the final guerrilla expeditions to Africa and Bolivia. Castro vividly portrays Che — the man, the revolutionary and the thinker — and describes in detail his last days with Che in Cuba.
ISBN 1-875284-15-X

CHE GUEVARA AND THE FBI
The U.S. political police dossier on the Latin American revolutionary
Edited by Michael Ratner and Michael Steven Smith

This book publishes for the first time the U.S. secret police dossiers on legendary revolutionary Ernesto Che Guevara and shows how the FBI and CIA monitored his movements and activity in the United States, Mexico, Cuba and Latin America. Details also emerge in the documents of U.S.-sponsored plots to assassinate Guevara.
ISBN 1-875284-76-1

AFROCUBA
An anthology of Cuban writing on race, politics and culture
Edited by Pedro Pérez Sarduy and Jean Stubbs

What is it like to be Black in Cuba? Does racism exist in a revolutionary society that claims to have abolished it? How does the legacy of slavery and segregation live on in today's Cuba? *AfroCuba* looks at the Black experience in Cuba through the eyes of the island's writers, scholars and artists. The collection mixes poetry, fiction, political analysis and anthropology, producing a multi-faceted insight into Cuba's rich ethnic and cultural reality.

ISBN 1-875284-41-9

HAVANA–MIAMI
The U.S.–Cuba migration conflict
by Jesús Arboleya

This book examines the origins of the migration conflict and why it remains one of the most difficult issues in U.S.-Cuba relations.

ISBN 1-875284-91-5

GUANTANAMO
Bay of Discord: The story of the U.S. military base in Cuba
by Roger Ricardo

This book provides a detailed history of the U.S. base on Cuban soil that has remained from the beginning of the century to the present day. It documents how the base has been used for continued violations of Cuban territory and why it remains a sticking point in U.S.–Cuba relations.

ISBN 1-875284-56-7

ISLAND UNDER SIEGE
The U.S. blockade of Cuba
by Pedro Prada

Cuban journalist Pedro Prada presents a compelling case against this "last wall" of the Cold War, showing how the 35-year blockade has affected life in the tiny island nation.

ISBN 1-875284-88-5

CUBA AT THE CROSSROADS
by Fidel Castro

What future lies ahead for Cuba as it faces the new millennium? Must it now turn its back on the past four decades since the 1959 revolution? In a series of speeches over recent years, including his address to the United Nations in October 1995, President Fidel Castro of Cuba discusses the main issues confronting the small Caribbean nation as it tries to adjust to a changing world.

In a rare personal mood, Castro reflects on his university days, the influences on him and what drew him into student politics and then national political life.

ISBN 1-875284-94-X

CUBA: TALKING ABOUT REVOLUTION
New, expanded edition
Conversations with Juan Antonio Blanco by Medea Benjamin

A frank discussion on the current situation in Cuba, this book presents an all-too-rare opportunity to hear the voice of one of the island's leading intellectuals. Juan Antonio Blanco considers new political and ethical issues that have arisen in Cuba in recent years.

ISBN 1-875284-97-7

OCEAN PRESS DISTRIBUTORS:

Australia and New Zealand:
    Astam Books, 57 John St, Leichhardt, NSW 2040, Australia
Britain and Europe:
    Central Books, 99 Wallis Road, London E9 5LN, Britain
Canada:
    Marginal Distribution, 277 George St. N., Unit 102, Peterborough, Ontario K9J 3G9, Canada
Cuba and Latin America:
    Ocean Press, Apartado 686, C.P. 11300, Havana, Cuba
South Africa:
    Phambili Agencies, PO Box 28680, Kensington Gardens, 2101
United States:
    LPC Group/InBook, 1436 West Randolph St, Chicago, Il 60607

Ocean Press, GPO Box 3279, Melbourne, Vic 3001, Australia ● Fax: 61-3-9372 1765
Ocean Press, PO Box 020692, Brooklyn, NY 11202, USA ● Fax: 1-201-864 6434